ADVENTURE
CAMBODIA

AN EXPLORER'S TRAVEL GUIDE

MATT JACOBSON
FRANK VISAKAY

Mrs S Oconnor
10 James Jackson Road
Dersingham
Kings Lynn
Norfolk
PE31 6UX

SILKWORM BOOKS

Text & photographs © 2001 by Matt Jacobson & Frank Visakay
Maps & line drawings © 2001 by Silkworm Books
All rights reserved. No part of this publication may be reproduced in any form and by any means, without permission in writing from the publisher.

ISBN 974-7551-48-9

First published by Silkworm Books in 2001

Silkworm Books
104/5 Chiang Mai-Hot Road, M7, T. Suthep, Muang, Chiang Mai 50100, Thailand
E-mail address: silkworm@loxinfo.co.th
Website: http://www.silkwormbooks.com

Typeset by Silk Type in Garamond 9 pt./Helvetica 8 pt.
Maps by Pundit Wattanakasiwit
Line drawings by Umaphon Seotphannuk
Printed in Thailand by O.S. Printing House, Bangkok

TO THE TRAVELER

Maps and map records of practically every town in Cambodia were destroyed during the fanatical campaign of the Khmer Rouge in which they tried to dispose of all records and institutions of the existing Cambodian society. Amazingly, even today most town government centers do not have an official map of the town. We found this to be true even in Battambang, the second largest city in Cambodia! Although we had no official map of streets for each town, we have done the best we could to make maps that will help you find your way around. Many of the maps in this book are not to scale since we had no official maps to refer to or aerial equipment to get up in the sky and photograph layouts. The government is just now involved in a project to map out the entire country, which they say will take some time yet to accomplish. The maps we include here are, however, useable and should do the job of helping to get you around quite well. We tried to be as accurate as possible and are fairly proud to be able to bring you maps that nobody else has.

Also, please note that no fees or advertisements were accepted from any business or service listed in this book. All information included is meant to assist our readers in their travels.

ACKNOWLEDGMENTS

Many thanks are in order for my partner in adventure, Mark Abatangelo. Mark jumped at the chance to ride along on most of the original research trips and was an invaluable help and took the responsibility of creating a good number of the maps in the book. Big thanks to a close friend, Um Sopheap, for help and assistance as our Khmer interpreter and knowledge seeker on a number of the original research trips. Tough as nails and never complaining, she thought nothing of helping to push the motorcycles through the muddy quagmires of a very wet rainy season—usually becoming caked with mud from head to toe in the process. Thanks to Morris Gregory for riding along on the interesting Anlong Veng, O'Smach and Samraong journey. Thanks to Dave Manson for riding along on the trip to conquer the old and abandoned route from Sre Amble to Koh Kong and the new route through the Cardamom Mountains, from Koh Kong to Pailin. Special thanks to my fellow fireman sidekick and Vietnam war veteran Randolph Jacobson for pointing me in the direction of Southeast Asia way back when. A big thanks to Silkworm Books for their efforts in making the book look good. Lastly, thanks to Steppenwolf for providing the theme song for Adventure Cambodia, "Born to Be Wild."

Matt Jacobson

Many thanks to Susan Zurndorfer for your support, friendship and those marvelous martini hours.

Frank Visakay

CONTENTS

INTRODUCTION

Cambodia is an exotic, mystical, enchanting land with an amazing history, the spectacular ancient ruins of the Angkor Empire, beautiful beaches, remote hill tribe villages and more.

For a small country, Cambodia has excellent name recognition around the world. Unfortunately, only a small part of this is due to the ancient empire of Angkor, which ruled over vast stretches of Southeast Asia for about 500 years and was responsible for leaving the world an amazing legacy of its genius and glory: the magnificent temples and monuments of Angkor. Neither has this been due to Cambodia's status as the Number One tourist destination in Southeast Asia during the relatively tranquil heydays of the late 1950s and the '60s, a time when French-style villas dotted the beautiful coastline and mountaintop casino retreats brought in the international jet-set crowd. It was also a time when Phnom Penh's colonial architecture, wide tree-lined boulevards and idyllic setting at the confluence of three rivers (Mekong, Sap, Bassac) captivated many a visitor.

No, instead of these images, the name Cambodia conjures up the "Killing Fields" and the murderous Khmer Rouge of the late 1970s. This was a terribly tragic period from which no Cambodian escaped without the loss of family and friends, if they were fortunate enough to live through it themselves. The country's infrastructure, cultural heritage and identity were all but destroyed.

But the Cambodians are an amazingly strong and resilient people. While not forgetting the past, they took the little that they had and forged ahead, slowly but surely putting back together the pieces of their society, culture and lives. It hasn't been easy and there has been a lot of slipping and tripping along the way.

Today, Cambodia appears to have finally settled into a mode of fairly peaceful coexistence. The Khmer Rouge has been eradicated as a threat to the government and countryside. Amid a huge sigh of relief from the international community, it appears that the government is finally on somewhat of an even keel and its leaders are rolling up their shirt sleeves to get down to the serious business of governing and rebuilding the country.

The security situation has improved markedly for tourists wanting to visit and move about the country. There are no guarantees of safety in any country, but during extensive adventure and research travel to every part of Cambodia, we have always come across genuinely friendly people— Cambodians who seem happy and relieved to see foreigners and the improved situation for the country that their presence implies.

Is it safe to travel around Cambodia now? The answer is a resounding yes! Are there fantastic sites to see and adventures to be had? You bet there are. Take us with you and we'll help you get there!

A BRIEF HISTORY OF TIME, CRIME & POLITICS

People were living in Cambodia as early as 4000 B.C. There is evidence of civilization from 1500 to 1000 B.C., showing that Cambodians hunted, fished, grew crops and built houses. The first century brought Indian and Chinese traders to Cambodia. Indian influence seems to have steered Cambodians toward the worship of Shiva and Vishnu as in India, with Buddhism following later. Jayavarman II united the country in the 800s and was worshiped as a god-king. His reign was followed by a succession of kings and rulers in and around Angkor in the northwest area of the country. War with Siam (now Thailand) continued for centuries, with both sides fighting for control over the region.

Suryavarman II ruled from 1112 to 1152 and invaded the area that is now Malaysia, Burma, Thailand and Vietnam. He is remembered for building one of the grandest temples of all time, Angkor Wat, which he dedicated to the Hindu god Vishnu. The Angkor Empire and King Suryavarman's rule eventually declined a bit, for more than one reason. Some say that Angkor was overbuilt and its reservoirs and irrigation canal systems could not support agriculture and the population. Another theory is that as Buddhism became more popular, the people were less willing to work for and worship a god-king. It is known that Suryavarman led an ill-fated attack against Vietnam late in his reign. About twenty-five years later, Southern Vietnam, under the domination of the Khmers, revolted and attacked Angkor, destroying and pillaging the city. Four years later, the city was returned to Khmer rule by Jayavarman VII, who added the Bayon to the city of Angkor

and also built the temples of Preah Khan, Banteay Kdei and Ta Prohm.

Siam invaded Angkor in the year 1351 and things see-sawed back and forth between the two powers for a while, with Siam invading again in 1431. The Khmers finally decided to move the seat of their government to a safer location, not quite so close to Siam, and with a couple of stops along the way, finally ended up in Phnom Penh, where it remains today.

War with Siam continued for hundreds of years and in 1594 Phnom Penh fell to the Siamese. The Cambodian king, Satha, asked for the help of Spain in the fight with Siam. Help arrived from the Philippines in the form of Spanish adventurers who helped defeat the Siamese, and Satha's son was crowned king. Resentment of the Spanish grew until the Spanish garrison was overrun by the Khmers and Satha's brother was made ruler with the help of Siam.

By the late 18th century, Siam dominated Cambodia and controlled Battambang and Siem Reap. The French arrived in 1864 and signed a treaty of protectorate with King Norodom as the start of their bid to take control of the country. In 1884 King Norodom was forced by the French to sign another treaty and Cambodia became a French colony.

The French virtually ruled Cambodia for eighty years. In 1941 France installed young Prince Norodom Sihanouk on the throne in the hope that he would be easy to control. When the Japanese occupied the country during World War II, the French left, only to return after the war to declare the country an autonomous state under French rule.

In 1953 King Norodom Sihanouk declared martial law and asked for international recognition as an independent country. Independence was granted in the same year and recognized by the Geneva Conference in the following year. Sihanouk dominated politics for the next fifteen years.

Sihanouk feared South Vietnam and Thailand (formerly Siam) during the 1960s, along with the United States. At the start of the Vietnam conflict, Sihanouk declared Cambodia to be neutral in international affairs and in 1965 broke diplomatic relations with the United States.

In 1969 the United States began an illegal and secret bombing campaign of communist forces in northeastern Cambodia. This was approved by President Nixon, Secretary of Defense Melvin Laird and National Security Advisor Henry Kissinger, but was conducted without the knowledge of the American people.

Playing both sides against the middle, and maneuvering to keep his country out of the Vietnam conflict, Sihanouk did not protest the bombings at that time and even furnished the U.S. government with intelligence on the Vietnamese Communist bases, while giving in to the Viet Cong and North Vietnamese Army in their use of Cambodian territory.

The bombing was stopped in 1970 by the American people, with the help of Congress, although it was resumed in 1973. By this time huge areas of the northeastern part of the country had been destroyed and thousands of innocent civilians killed. The bomb crater-filled roads of today, in the east and the north of Cambodia are a living legacy of the carpet bombing campaign.

Sihanouk was deposed in March 1970 by General Lon Nol and subsequently fled to Beijing, China, to set up a government in exile. In April of 1970, the United States and South Vietnam invaded Cambodia and drove the communist forces deep into the jungles. These forces joined a revolutionary group and became known as the Red Khmers, or the Khmer Rouge, and they fought against the Cambodian government as a guerilla force for the next few years.

The Khmer Rouge overthrew the government and took control of Phnom Penh in April 1975. Thus began one of the most terrible events in the history of the world. Headed by Pol Pot, the Khmer Rouge proceeded to destroy every part of past and present Khmer society. They attempted to transform the country into a peasant-dominated agricultural society. The entire population of the capital was force-marched into the countryside to do farming. Currency and postal services were stopped. Industries and electrical plants were destroyed in an effort to return to the past. Anyone with an education was murdered. People wearing eyeglasses were considered educated and thus dangerous, so they were executed. People able to speak a foreign language were considered enemies of the state and executed, after torture. It is estimated that in the years of turmoil 1.7 million Cambodians died from execution, starvation, or disease. At the time, these events were largely unknown to the rest of the world, as the country was effectively cut off from the outside world.

The Khmer Rouge brought about their own downfall by conducting frequent border raids on Vietnam. On 25 December 1978, Vietnam invaded Cambodia and overthrew the Khmer Rouge in two weeks. Vietnam installed leaders of the ex–Khmer Rouge, who had previously defected to Vietnam, as the heads of the new government. The Khmer Rouge fled into the countryside and eventually joined up with the Royalist-backed forces and a couple of other groups near the Thai border. They waged war on the new government from the safety of the jungles, with the help of Thailand, China, and the United States, among a few others. In the following years, thousands were killed in the civil war.

In 1982, Sihanouk, still in China, started the political party FUNCINPEC (National United Front for an Independent, Neutral, Peaceful and Cooperative Cambodia), and fighting from the jungles against the communist Vietnam-backed government continued.

In 1989, Vietnam, under international pressure, withdrew all of its troops, and the Khmer Rouge continued to fight the government. In 1990, two thousand Cambodians were killed in the civil war.

In September of 1990, the UN Security Council produced a plan to end the fighting and hold free elections, with the resulting Paris Peace Accords signed in 1991. A United Nations Transitional Administration (UNTAC) basically ran the country until elections were held in 1993.

The FUNCINPEC Party led by Prince Norodom won fifty-eight seats in the National Assembly, as opposed to fifty-one seats won by the Cambodian People's Party. Hun Sen refused to step down and Cambodia ended up with two prime ministers, with Norodom Ranariddh as first prime minister and Hun Sen as second prime minister. Both sides struggled for power in the next few years and the Khmer Rouge continued to control the northwest and other assorted pockets, engaging in illegal logging, and drug and gem smuggling. The Cambodian government outlawed the Khmer Rouge in 1994 and the Thai government stopped supporting the rebels. The Khmer Rouge was still a force to be reckoned with and both government prime ministers tried to line up their support.

In 1995, Sam Rainsy, a government minister thrown out by Prince Ranariddh for being an outspoken critic of the govern-

ment, tried to start his own political party, the Khmer Nation Party. It was declared illegal by the government.

In 1996 Khmer Rouge number 3 leader Ieng Sary worked out a surrender for autonomy deal and aligned with the Phnom Penh government. This took a lot of the wind out of the Khmer Rouge's sails, as the defecting force was about twenty thousand strong and covered a big chunk of turf. The government at this time also tightened its grip on the country by jailing journalists critical of the government. Things were looking better, although plenty remained bothersome.

The beginning of 1997 saw several worrisome incidents, such as a grenade attack on a political meeting led by Sam Rainsy. Rumors of an imminent coup flooded the capital. It had been expected for some time by both parties, as Hun Sen's gunships stopped boats with supplies meant for Prince Ranariddh from docking at Sihanoukville. Prince Ranariddh and key officers were shuttling back and forth between Anlong Veng and Phnom Penh, trying to work out a surrender deal with the remaining hard-line Khmer Rouge faction. This was interpreted by Hun Sen as collusion between the two groups, an attempt to form a force capable of defeating forces loyal to him. Paranoia on both sides of the dual government kept growing. In July of the same year Hun Sen seized control of the government in a bloody two-day fight. Prince Ranariddh and Sam Rainsy both fled the country, and over a hundred of their supporters disappeared or turned up dead while Hun Sen solidified his power base.

ASEAN, the Association of South East Asian Nations, stalled in accepting Cambodia as a member, denying the country important trade options. Foreign aid slowed to a stand-still. Foreign investors held back cash much needed for development and employment in a country that looked unstable and unpredictable.

The year 1998 brought a brokered deal to bring the prince and Sam Rainsy back to Cambodia to compete in the elections scheduled for July of that year and also to end the fighting with the prince's resistance forces along the Thai border—the area that they fled to after the coup. The internationally monitored elections saw Hun Sen's ruling party win and hold their lock on power. Sam Rainsy and FUNCINPEC protested the election results. A deal was worked out after massive demonstrations and protests by the forces and sympathizers of the two combined parties. Sam Rainsy's party was to be the opposition party, while Prince Ranariddh became the head of the National Assembly. It seems that the formula has been acceptable to all parties, at least for now. ASEAN accepted Cambodia as a member in 1999—a diplomatic coup for Hun Sen, who has finally brought a measure of peace and stability to the country.

The past few years have seen the Khmer Rouge disintegrate into a small band of rebels. In an effort to weaken the Khmer Rouge and secure the northwest, the government accepted the surrender of three Khmer Rouge leaders, Ieng Sary, Nuon Chea and Khieu Samphan over a period of a couple of years. They were granted amnesty and not brought to trial for their crimes against humanity. The notorious Pol Pot died in 1997. Pol Pot's military chief of operations, Ta Mok, was arrested by the government in 1999. Also known as "The Butcher," he had led his troops in sweeping purges of suspected disloyal members and was responsible for the murder of thousands of innocent civilians. He is awaiting trial in Phnom Penh but, interestingly enough, at first had only been charged with violating the 1994 legislation that outlawed the

Khmer Rouge. He has not been charged with murder or genocide, even though he was also responsible for several massacres of ethnic Vietnamese people in the 1990s, along with his involvement in Khmer executions.

Also found in 1999 was Kaing Khek Iev, known as Duch. He headed the Santebal or internal security organization and directed Tuol Sleng, a former Phnom Penh high school where almost twenty thousand people were imprisoned, tortured and murdered, including a few Thai, Indian, Chinese, American, English, and Vietnamese. Victims were chained to their bed frames and tortured in gruesome ways to force false confessions, often of spying for the United States and Vietnam and other baloney. The victims were then executed in a field outside the capital. Experts say that prosecution would be easy. Duch's signature and detailed comments appear on hundreds of documents, some ordering electric shock, pulling out of toe nails, submersion in water and other gruesome torture methods.

Duch was finally arrested on 10 May 1999, and charged with the same three statutes that Ta Mok has been charged with. The charges are: belonging to the Democratic Kampuchea Party, crimes related to Khmer Rouge activities, and actions taken against the government (coercing citizens to take up arms against public authority). A government source has said that Duch would eventually be tried in connection with his activities in Tuol Sleng Prison. It is believed that Duch could also be a key witness and implicate many people who were above and below him.

Arrested in 1999, awaiting trial and charged with the murder of three backpackers in 1994, was a Khmer Rouge guerrilla commander, Nuon Paet. He led a band of rebels who kidnapped three male tourists from a train on its way to the seaside resort town of Sihanoukville. The three men were from France, Australia, and England. Many Cambodians were also killed. Under Cambodian law, Paet, if convicted, could have received as little as three years in jail or as much as life imprisonment. In fact, former General Nuon Paet has been found guilty and sentenced to life imprisonment. There is talk of bringing ten more of his men to trial on the same charges.

It will be interesting to watch all of these events unfold and see where they lead. Some say that it's all cosmetic surgery to help Hun Sen gain international recognition and acceptance. Cambodia has hired a public relations firm, the David Morey Group in Washington, D.C., to rebuild its image and it seems to be working as far as the U.S. government is concerned. In a burst of public relations, the Cambodian government has banned porno films from being shown on television and has ordered all of the shooting ranges closed. At one time you could fire an AK47, a rocket launcher, or a heavy machine gun, or throw hand grenades in these establishments. Hun Sen also closed all of the gambling casinos in Phnom Penh, but closure was short-lived, as probably some well-placed money reopened a couple of them.

The UN, foreign governments, and aid organizations have pumped billions of dollars into this small country since the Paris Peace Agreement was signed. Where has all the money gone?

Most of the population still lives in extreme poverty without even the basics to live a fairly healthy life. After all the money and studies and programs, many people don't even possess the knowledge of how to collect rainwater or boil water from streams to make it fit for human consumption. The relatively inexpensive task of traveling around and teaching people such basic things to improve the lives of rural families has never been fully taken on despite the piles of money thrown into the country.

The infrastructure, especially the rural highways, is in a shambles, making it difficult, time-consuming, and costly for the rural peasants to move their crops to market and go about daily life.

Rampant corruption in the Cambodian government is one reason that all the money poured into this country has not made a noticeable difference. There certainly needs to be more transparency and accountability for all projects. Greedy government officials at all levels have lined their personal pockets instead of helping the people who need it the most. Multiple fancy homes and vehicles, servants and mobile phones owned by people who make modest government salaries are common in Cambodia. It's particularly grotesque in a country as poor as this one is.

Along these lines, the pillage of Cambodian temples is accelerating at an alarming rate. On 5 January 1999, Thai police in Sa Kaew Province near the Cambodian border were checking for drug shipments and intercepted a ten-wheeled truck with eighty-five bags of antique sandstone carvings destined for Bangkok. The 117 heavy pieces had been stolen from the Banteay Chmar temple just north of Sisophon, Cambodia (see Banteay Meanchey and Sisophan chapter), where pneumatic drills had been used to remove a forty-foot-long carved wall. The Cambodian Ministry of Culture states that the very people who are supposed to protect the monuments are the ones who are selling it off in pieces, that is, the Cambodian military. Haing Tin, the representative of the Culture Ministry said that the army had looted the temple in 1998 and removed almost half of the walls with heavy equipment. RCAF Army Division 7 removed more than thirty tons of the temple and brought it to the Thai border at San Ro

Chang and sold it to Bangkok antique dealers. Very few of the missing pieces from temples have been discovered and returned, and this is an on-going problem.

In July 1999, customs officials in Thailand seized an eight-ton shipment of Cambodian antiques. The forty-three priceless sculptures were smuggled by ship from Cambodia to Singapore and then on to Thailand for certification and were destined for markets in Thailand, Europe and the United States. The haul included large, sandstone heads measuring at least thirty centimeters wide, which appeared to have been stripped from ancient Khmer temples or monuments. Three shipping business owners in Samut Prakan, Thailand, are being questioned. The antiques were shipped by the Singapore-based Shanghai Fine Arts Gallery Co.

Running in tandem with corruption is inefficiency. Paper projects by non-government organizations (NGOs) in which a need and remedy are defined, studied, developed, and pushed around some more

—only to go through the same process all over again—constitute another reason why more hasn't been accomplished.

It seems to many observers within Cambodia's expatriate foreign community that a fair number of NGOs are on a self-perpetuating mission. Just keep the office, staff, salaries, and comfortable benefits going, by making it appear on paper that they have or will accomplish something worthwhile—while not getting too wrapped up in making actual improvements for poor people. Far too many NGO staffers, it seems, are leading cushy lives—even the life of a jet-setter—in Phnom Penh and rarely if ever get out to the rural areas and get their hands dirty doing a project. Fat salaries, hefty per diems and fancy new vehicles are the norm…yes the money has gone somewhere.

To be fair, some good has been done. But a look around Cambodia today, after all the money that has come into this country, can only make one grieve at where it has gone.

FACTS ABOUT THE COUNTRY

CLIMATE & GEOGRAPHY

Cambodia has a mild tropical climate similar to that of Thailand. It has two main seasons. The rainy season extends from May to October, and even then it does not rain constantly, usually only in the afternoon. The dry season is from November to April. The weather is coolest from October to January. It is hottest in April with temperatures about thirty-five degrees centigrade and coolest in January with temperatures in the high twenties. It is hottest in the northwest. The temperature in Battambang reaches forty degrees.

Cambodia has the same rip-roaring thunder and lightning storms as other areas of Southeast Asia during the rainy season. But you will be surprised at just how much nice weather there is in between. The rainy season can be a very pleasant time to visit.

One thing you are bound to notice in Cambodia, especially during the dry season, are the huge towering clouds. The size, shape and colors are the most beautiful I've ever seen. Whether you are in Phnom Penh or near the border in Banteay Meanchey Province, they are there. Oddly enough, they seem to stop at the border; the clouds on the other side don't look nearly as spectacular.

I'm not sure if it's weather patterns, topography or a gift from the gods, but the clouds seem to go all the way up to the heavens, sometimes in intriguing shapes. I've seen huge clouds over Angkor Wat that match the five towers of the structure—and I was completely sober at the time.

Cambodia covers an area of 181,000 square km. The country has three small mountain ranges. In the north are the Dangrek Mountains near Thailand, the Cardamoms near the Thai border in the southwest and the Damrei Mountains to the southwest of Phnom Penh. The mountain areas are densely wooded and have huge teak trees in the north.

There's always a treat in store when you ride around rural Cambodia. Beautiful natural scenery, rice fields dotted with the ever-present sugar palm trees and glimpses of the simple and decades-back-in-time lifestyle of the peasant farmers await you. The sugar palm trees are a beautiful part of the rural landscape as they dot the countryside throughout Cambodia. Besides providing beauty and a bit of shade, they provide an important source of income for the owners who extract the sugar juice from the fruit near the top.

If you look closely, you can see narrow handmade bamboo ladders attached to the trunk of each tree allowing an easier climbing alternative than the old hand and foot shimmy-climb. Use caution if you decide to try a climb for yourself, although I found the bamboo ladder that I climbed to be surprisingly sturdy.

Late afternoons and early evenings are especially enjoyable as the sun works its way down and the locals are gearing down for the evening. You will see families walking to a nearby pond, river or roadside ditch for an evening bath, the ladies with sarongs wrapped around them. Children are out and about playing games in the cool of the setting sun and everyone seems to be in a friendly and festive mood.

The Tonle Sap or Great Lake in the northwest flows southward, joins with the Mekong River and empties into the Gulf of Thailand. That is, sometimes it does. Other times it moves northward. Cambodians say that this is why things are always so crazy in their country: the water in the Tonle Sap seems to flow both ways. During the rainy season, the Mekong fills up and overflows into the Tonle Sap, pushing the water up into the Great Lake. The Tonle Sap reverses its course in the dry season and the water flows out of the lake, southward and into the Mekong.

The central areas of the country contain rice paddies and fields of corn and tobacco.

The country has many wild animals including bears, leopards, elephants, rhinoceroses and tigers. Birds include cranes, egrets, herons, pelicans, pheasants and ducks. Cambodia also has four of the world's deadliest snakes, cobra, king cobra, banded krait and Russell's viper. As in Vietnam, wildlife is in danger from poachers who kill for profit. Parts of the animals are valuable and used for herbal medicine. Examples are tigers teeth and penis, bear claws and liver. Illegal loggers also kill all kinds of animals for food.

Lower Vietnam was at one time a part of Cambodia. During the French colonial period the border was changed by the French, who deemed that its interests were best served by making the change. Cambodians will never forget this or give up the hope that some day this wrong will be righted and the land will come back under Cambodian control. The Vietnamese are hated for holding on to it.

The saddest part of the whole situation is the people who live in this area. They are historically Cambodians and share the same language and customs as the Cambodian people, even though the Vietnamese tried for years to change them to their liking. The Vietnamese look down on them as being inferior. The sad irony is that the other Cambodians also look down on the people from this area, believing that they are too much like the hated Vietnamese. It's as if they can't win, and their predicament is not their own doing.

PEOPLE

Ethnic Khmers or Cambodians account for over 90% of the population, according to official statistics. The majority of Cambodians are Buddhist. This does not take into account the many illegal immigrant Vietnamese. The Vietnamese are by far the largest non-Khmer ethnic group in Cambodia.

It was the Vietnamese who ended the brutal reign of Pol Pot, and it would seem that the country should be grateful, but the hatred from centuries of fighting wars with Vietnam is so ingrained in Cambodians that there is much anti-Vietnamese feeling in the country.

To this day anger and hatred can be stirred up among the Cambodians very easily when an opposition member claims that the government regime (some of whom are former communists aligned with the Hanoi government) is letting Vietnam encroach and take over border territories and freely take valuable resources such as timber.

Vietnamese have been settling in Cambodia since the 17th century. Many families have lived there for generations. Vietnamese inhabitants were killed by the Lon Nol regime in 1970 and by the Khmer Rouge later. There are pockets of Vietnamese now in much of Cambodia and they are occasionally the subjects of violent attacks, as in the turbulent days of the 1998 elections.

Ethnic Chinese are estimated to number over 100,000—mostly merchants and businessmen. Thousands of Chinese were killed during Pol Pot's reign of terror but the Chinese have again begun to be an economic force in Cambodia, due to overseas Chinese investments.

The Cham Muslims live in villages along the banks of the great rivers, mostly in Kompong Cham and Kompong Chhnang provinces. Chams were also murdered by Pol Pot and their temples were destroyed. Many of the temples have been rebuilt and a few of the older ones are still intact. Chams number about 200,000 in Cambodia.

Hill tribe people live in the northeast. They remain separate from the rest of Cambodian society, having their own customs and culture. They are animist, as opposed to the main population, which is Buddhist. The hill tribes practice the ancient methods of swidden agriculture. Because they lived in the country and were not educated, they were mostly spared by the Khmer Rouge experiment of returning to ground zero.

As with the Vietnamese, ancient battles between the Khmers and Thais account for the ancient dislike and distrust between the two peoples. Much of it may be well founded, as the Thais controlled much of Battambang, Banteay Meanchey and Siem Reap Provinces in earlier centuries. In 1907 Cambodia (more specifically the French) regained control, only to have the Thais grab the area again in 1941, with Japanese assistance. After World War II, the Allied forces helped to persuade the Thais that the region was originally a part of ancient Cambodia and the world community would not take kindly to the Thais holding onto it further.

As for the Thai provinces of Buriram, Surin and Si Saket, the Cambodians were not so fortunate. This region has Khmer roots: many of the people living there have distinctly Khmer facial features, speak the Khmer language and follow Khmer customs. Khmer ruins are also in abundance in this area.

To this day Khmers are terrified at the thought of their country being swallowed up by their big neighbors. There is anger and resentment in the belief that the Thais have taken many ancient Khmer temple artifacts and natural resources and brought them back to Thailand. Many Khmer people have asked me, usually during times of government disturbances, if I thought the world community would give Cambodia to Vietnam and Thailand.

CULTURE

The music of Cambodia started as an accompaniment to religious rituals. The stone murals of Angkor Wat show musicians and apsaras, or heavenly nymphs, dancing. Many of the instruments in the murals are still used today. They include single-and three-string fiddles, drums, flutes, cymbals and xylophones. Today, apsara-like dancers often reenact scenes from the Hindu Ramayana as they did centuries ago. In this respect Cambodian dance is similar to the dance and culture of Thailand, Indonesia, and India. Most of the dancers, musicians and teachers were murdered in the Pol Pot years. The School of Fine Arts opened in 1981 and rebuilt much of what was lost during the Khmer Rouge regime. They often give recitals of both modern and ancient music and dance and have taught a new generation of Khmer classical and ancient style dancers.

In Cambodia one may still find the Lkaon Khaol or masked theatre. In years past, groups would travel the country presenting performances of the Ramayana. Men usually play all of the roles and wear masks. A narrator tells the story, accompanied by a small group of musicians.

Cambodia is famous for its sculpture and architecture. Sculpted statues of the Indian god Vishnu exist from the 6th century. The National Museum in Phnom Penh has fine examples of pre-Angkor art including not only Hindu but also Buddhist sculptures. The museum has Banteay Srei-style statues from the 10th and 11th centuries. These are said to be some of the best pieces in existence. Angkor sculpture from the Bayon period in the 12th and 13th centuries is also famous; many pieces are displayed in the museum.

The best examples of ancient Khmer architecture are Angkor Wat, Angkor Thom and Preah Vihear temple.

Today, as in centuries past, most Cambodians in rural areas live in wooden houses built on stilts. The raised housing structure provides shelter for animals, shade from the sun and an outside living area during the rainy season. It also keeps out unwanted animals, such as snakes. The houses near the Tonle Sap Lake certainly need to be raised, as the lake overflows every year. The rural houses have straw roofs, and the walls and floors are made from woven palm or bamboo. In Phnom Penh you can also see examples of French colonial architecture in the grand old villas that escaped the mass destruction of Pol Pot.

The illiteracy rate in Cambodia is said to be just under 40%. The Khmer Rouge started the terrible trend after they came to power by closing down schools and killing teachers as a part of their campaign to destroy everything and start from scratch with their plans of an agrarian utopia—in reality, a bleak slave-labor commune.

An entire generation was affected, being denied an education, among other things. The continued instability after the Khmer Rouge downfall has seen the continuance of extreme poverty for most and has meant that going to school is a luxury that few have been able to afford or bother with as all hands are needed to try to scratch out a living.

Teachers must be paid extra money by students and on a regular basis in order to stay in class. Additional costs for books and uniforms means that many folks can't afford to send their children to school. It's a shameful situation that must be dealt with before the cycle of poverty will be broken.

The affected people are ashamed and embarrassed by their illiteracy. Remember to be tactful when seeking help in translating Khmer, as many of the people you ask will not be able to read.

ECONOMY

Rubber at one time was Cambodia's largest export. Today, foreign aid is the biggest money supply. Over twenty foreign companies hold permits to cut down trees for timber. In 1965, Cambodia had about 75% forest area and now it is down to less than 49%. It is feared that many of Cambodia's natural resources will be removed and not replaced. A great deal of the money brought in comes from timber exports and logging —much of it illegal and carried out by ex– Khmer Rouge guerillas with the blessing of the government. All too little of the timber money ends up in government coffers, which is a frequent complaint of donor nations. It's an issue that obviously needs to be resolved as the national budget could certainly use a boost from legal logging.

The Cambodian government earns money by allowing the shipping of gold and cigarettes through its country from Singapore and China to Vietnam, which has higher import duties.

Cambodia is badly in need of foreign investors who have been holding back for a more stable environment. Hun Sen, ruling the country with an iron fist and restrictive rules, has helped to make the country a bit more stable, if less free, and foreign investment is eagerly awaited. Korean businessmen opened large garment factories and sewing factories a few years ago, but these were more on the order of taking advantage of cheap labor than investing in the country. The Cambodians were paid approximately US$0.75 per day to work long hours under unpleasant conditions.

Tourists are also needed to help the economy but with the violence of the 1998 elections, tourism dropped 14.8% to 186,000 visitors, compared to 218,843 in 1997. The largest number of tourists came from France, followed by Taiwan, China, and the United States. Thankfully, things today appear to have turned for the better. It looks like the government may have finally learned to peacefully coexist, and tourism has been climbing steadily.

Some kinds of shrimp farming have been legislated against in Thailand, and as a result, the shrimp farmers have moved into Cambodia near the seaport in Koh Kong Province, for a handy exporting location. The problem is that fertilizer and chemicals are used in the water on the shrimp farms and then the water is drained, polluting the surrounding areas. In a few years, the farmers move on, leaving unusable land behind. The Cambodian people do not profit from this as they are only considered cheap labor and the profits go to big business. Most of the shrimp are exported to Thailand.

Commerce of all kinds seems to be unhampered by environmental restrictions or law enforcement. The Ministry of Agriculture reports that farmers spray huge amounts of pesticides on crops. Pesticide applications occur from eight to thirty times per crop. These include DDT and Folidol, which have been banned in most countries. DDT is an accumulative poison which does not break down easily, is stored in animals' bodies, and is suspected of causing cancer. Folidol can be absorbed through the skin, is hazardous to eyesight and to the reproductive and central nervous systems. Viet-

nam and Thailand have banned these chemicals and the companies have been selling them here. The Agriculture Ministry estimates that ten tons of DDT and Folidol have ended up in the Tonle Sap as runoff and have killed fish and wildlife and damaged residents' health.

The big foreign-owned tobacco companies are also having a field day in Cambodia, where the industry is completely unregulated. One would think that they might have learned some lessons from the lawsuits and regulations that have been slapped on them in their home countries and take a moderate and thoughtful approach when they vie for market share in the emerging market countries.

Great examples for Cambodia's youth are saturating the local TV: cigarette commercials show smiling, laughing and beautiful people being cool and smoking cigarettes. The commercials' voice dub-ins tell the audience that it's fun and relaxing to smoke, with your troubles and cares just drifting away. Billboards and magazines are fair game for the nonsense as well. It's a shining example of capitalism at its best.

RELIGION

Buddhism

Most Cambodians are Theravada Buddhists. This school of Buddhism was introduced into Cambodia between the 13th and 14th centuries from India. It follows the original doctrines of Buddha more closely and with less interpretation than other types of Buddhism. These thoughts came to Siddhartha Gautama in the 6th century, B.C. Siddhartha was an Indian prince who disavowed his wealth and searched for enlightenment. He believed that life is mostly suffering and to be happy one must cast out reasons to be unhappy. Gautama declared that there are four noble truths and an eight-fold path to Nirvana. The Four Noble Truths are:

1. The truth of suffering—existence is suffering.

2. The truth of the cause of suffering—suffering is caused by desire.

3. The truth of the cessation of suffering—eliminate the cause of suffering or desire and suffering will cease to arise.

4. The truth of the right path—the Eightfold Path is the way to eliminate desire and to extinguish suffering.

The Eight-Fold Path is:

1. right understanding
2. right mindedness
3. right speech
4. right bodily conduct
5. right effort
6. right attentiveness
7. right concentration
8. right livelihood.

Buddhists believe in reincarnation and that a person living a good life and making merit will have either fewer or better rebirths and reach Nirvana sooner. Eventually after many births and deaths and rebirths, a state of enlightenment may be achieved, the cycle is broken.

In Cambodia, you will see orange-robed Buddhist monks making their rounds early in the morning with their round black alms bowls, usually attended by a young novice. Westerners believe that they are begging but in actuality they are giving you the opportunity to make merit by donating rice, food or money to them. Other ways of making merit are giving to the temples and performing regular worship. Every Buddhist male is expected to become a monk, and a look at temples all over Cambodia confirms that ordinations are again on the rise. Ordination usually occurs after a boy finishes school and before he is married, and is usually between his late teens and mid twenties. Monkhood can be for as short a period as two weeks but usually lasts for three months. During this time the young man must follow 227 vows or precepts as part of the monastic discipline, including not being touched by a female.

The Khmer Rouge murdered many monks and almost all of their three thousand temples were damaged or destroyed. Thankfully, the Cambodians dug in after the Khmer Rouge were run out of power, and temples have been restored or rebuilt. There seems to be a real surge of new temples being built these days and you will notice it in your travels.

Other Religions

Muslims in Cambodia originally came from Vietnam in the 15th century. There are many mosques just northeast of Phnom Penh, most of which have been rebuilt after the destruction of the Khmer Rouge. The faithful are called to prayer by the banging of drums rather than the muezzin as in other countries. Many Muslims in Phnom Penh are of Afghanistan or Pakistan origin and are known as Cham.

Christianity was brought to Cambodia by the French. Today there is a Catholic minority in Cambodia, many of whom are Vietnamese.

SOCIETY & CUSTOMS

Cambodians traditionally greet each other with a *wai* or *sompiah* as in Thailand. This is a pressing of the palms together as in prayer and bowing the head slightly. Younger people or people of less status usually initiate the greeting and the lower the bow and the higher the hands are held, the more respect is shown. Hand shaking has also been largely accepted in Cambodia. If you are visiting a friend in Cambodia, you might bring a small gift. Always remove your shoes before entering some-one's home.

When visiting a *wat* or temple, men should wear long pants, and women should wear long skirts. Shirts with sleeves are more acceptable than tank tops. Remove your hat when entering the temple grounds and your shoes before entering the temple. If you sit on a chair or squat on the floor, be careful not to have your feet pointing at the Buddha or a person. It is very offensive to directly point your foot at someone.

Like the Thais, the Cambodians are a quiet and gentle people and it is imperative to keep your voice low and to be calm. Never show anger or speak loudly to a Cambodian. It is impolite behavior. Never pat anyone on the head. It is a sacred part of the body.

While traveling around rural Cambodia, you will see many temple donation drives set up next to the roadside. There are usually beautiful Khmer girls dressed in traditional attire and holding donation bowls for the passing traffic to drop a donation in for the construction or renovation of a temple or school. Additionally, there is always a loudspeaker set up with a donations MC talking a mile a minute at full volume, trying to talk passersby into anteing up some money and thanking those who do. It's always a fun roadside diversion and a good chance to make a donation and mingle.

The sex scene in Cambodia, as in other Asian countries, did not spring up for the foreigners; it was built by the Cambodians, for the Cambodians. The percentage of foreign customers using these establishments (brothels, karaoke bars, etc.) is quite small compared to the numbers of Cambodian customers. The world's oldest profession has always been enmeshed in Asian culture.

You will see some wild sexual awareness billboards as you travel about provincial towns. Rocket ship condoms with people riding away on them to remind people to guard against the spread of HIV and unwanted pregnancies will put a smile on your face. I'm not sure if the intended message is being absorbed, but the Cambodians sure seem to enjoy the crazy cartoons.

The country seems to be caught in a time warp—that is, simple and far behind the times—maybe the 1960s, before the turmoil of the recent decades. The simple, corny quality of Cambodia TV entertainment shows and commercials and the way they do the old-style dancing at all the Khmer nightclubs always makes one chuckle and think that these people may not be real hip or cool. In reality, it's all a way to just have some fun. The young have, of course, taken in many of the global trends in fashion, TV and music. But the whole society, from the young to the elderly, seems to share a genuine liking of the older and simpler life.

The outlying provinces certainly don't have to worry about being taken over by new trends. They seem to be at least a hundred years back in time.

Most towns around Cambodia have loudspeakers mounted near the markets and other strategic locations. In the early morning and early evening the government blares out daily news, propaganda and Khmer music for the pleasure of the people, I assume. The Khmer music is okay, but you are going to hear everything, whether you like it or not.

PUBLIC HOLIDAYS & EVENTS

Some Asian holidays are celebrated according to phases of the moon. For this reason some of the dates listed below will be approximate.

January 7. Commemoration of the 1979 defeat of the Khmer Rouge by the Vietnamese government and a ragtag group of disgruntled and disenchanted ex–Khmer Rouge officers.

Late January/early February. Chinese Lunar New Year and Vietnamese Tet. This is a big celebration with many restaurants offering special dishes. Full Chinese dragon dances are also seen in the streets. Many businesses close for the holidays.

Mid April. Khmer New Year. A three-day celebration. Cambodians visit the Wat and exchange presents. This is probably the most festive of all the holidays in Cambodia. It's a time to start anew and make merit to improve one's fortune for the coming year. It's also important to remember and try to please deceased relatives so that they will be happy and not make problems for the family in the coming year. Even the poorest of families saves up throughout the year so they can buy New Year decorations for their home and put up shrines with lavish offerings of fruit, alcohol, rice dishes and joss sticks to please deceased relatives and bring the best luck money can buy. Supposedly, after the spirits have had their fill in spirit, everyone gets to pig out and eat the offerings.

The temples are usually the center of activity as people also present the monks with blessings of food and money as they try to cover all the bases in their quest for good luck in the upcoming year. Different types of celebration events take place during the holidays at the temples, as well.

The markets are frantic and packed leading up to the New Year celebrations as people make many trips to buy everything that they need. It's a fun atmosphere as all are getting into the holiday spirit.

One of the many traditions of the holiday has been the blessing of the elders with a small amount of clean, pure water. This tradition has evolved over the years to the modern-day full-scale water fights that target everybody, including any foreigners who are out and about. The toy sections of the markets are doing a robust business selling water squirt guns and rifles as people arm themselves for at least three days of water fights. As New Year occurs during the hottest time of the year, the water throwing can be a welcome relief from the heat as everybody interacts in the name of fun.

Extremes that are not much fun have also developed as part of the water fights. Some people fill up small, thick plastic bags and hurl them at pedestrians or motorcyclists. The bags really hurt if you get hit in the head and I've seen plenty of hyperactive teenage boys throwing these bags as hard as they can at girls they are obviously trying to impress. It borders on assault, as the girls who get hit are clearly in a good deal of pain. This part of the festivities was never a part of the traditional celebrations. If it happens to you, try to remember the simple rule of the day—don't get mad, get even.

White talcum powder is also rubbed on faces as a blessing for good luck. This part can also be fun as the participants of the opposite sex have an opportunity to forget their shy nature and rub powder on the face of somebody they like. A water bottle or clean handkerchief is good to have on hand as the powder really stings if it gets in your eyes.

It's fun to buy a water gun and join in the festivities, but if you do, put everything you want kept dry in a water-tight baggie or it will be as soaked as you—and you will be soaked, from head to toe. If you tire of it and don't want to smile and be a part of the Cambodians' fun, it's best to stay holed up in your hotel during this time.

May 1. International Workers Day.

May 9. Genocide Day. To pay respect and pray for the victims of the Khmer Rouge.

Mid May. Chat Preah Nengal or Holy Furrow Ploughing Ceremony. An agricultural ceremony led by members of the Royal Family. Celebration and prayers for the start of the rice planting season.

Late May. Visakha Puja. This is considered to be the date of Buddha's birth, enlightenment and death. It falls on the 15th day of the 6th lunar month. Many activities, processions and ceremonies will take place in the temples. All public business offices will be closed for three days.

June 19. Anniversary of the founding of the Armed Forces.

July. Buddhist Lent or Chol Vassa. A two-day Buddhist holiday with activities at the temples for people keeping the faith.

September. Pchum Ben, a two-day celebration to end Buddhist Lent. Cambodians visit *wats* and cemeteries to pray for departed relatives and ancestors. In some parts of Cambodia this holiday is celebrated for two weeks. It is also called the Festival for the Dead. Buddhist monks chant prayers and accept ceremonial offerings of food from the relatives of the dead. People dedicate food and good wishes to their deceased relatives, whose spirits, according to the Buddhism practiced by most Cambodians, come back once a year.

October 31. King Sihanouk's birthday. A three-day celebration that serves as a wind-up to the Water Festival.

Late October/early November. Water Festival. Held on the day of the full moon, this celebrates the reversal of the flow of the water in the Tonle Sap River. There will be boat races on the Tonle Sap opposite the Royal Palace. Up to a million people flood into Phnom Penh from the provinces to be a part of the festivities and either race or watch the boat races, especially the racesinvolving their home province and commune. About 300 boats, each with teams of forty-five to sixty crew members, run heats and races over the three-day festival. Very festive and fun, with the activities concentrated along the river road, near the Royal Palace and beyond. Activities and a festival are centered in Angkor as well.

November 9. Independence Day. French control of Cambodia was officially declared to be over.

December 10. International Human Rights Day.

PRACTICAL INFORMATION

PLANNING AHEAD

Before you visit Cambodia, find out as much as you can about the country in order to decide what kind of trip you want. Do you prefer air-conditioned luxury hotels or are you all right staying in budget accommodations? Will you go hiking and camping in the country or will you stay in the urban areas? Cambodia has all of this to offer but your plans will determine what you will need to bring. Buy some guidebooks and check the Internet—there is a wealth of information to be found.

Cambodia is great to visit any time of year but if you plan to visit upcountry you might prefer not to travel in the rainy season, from April to October. The cities and the south are fine all year round.

MONEY MATTERS

Credit Cards

You can leave home without your American Express card. It will be accepted only in the most expensive of hotels. Visa is the card most widely accepted. Most of the less expensive hotels will not accept credit cards. Use your credit card as little as possible in the hotels, stores and restaurants so that there will be less chance of credit card fraud. You may obtain cash advances with your Visa card at the local banks; the standard charge begins at 2%. Cambodia Commercial Bank in Phnom Penh, Battambang, Siem Reap and Sihanoukville is currently the best place for Visa Card cash advances at 2%, with larger withdrawals available than most other places. Most stores and travel agencies will add on a 4–4.5% credit card charge to your bill. Large hotels and airline offices will not do this. There are no credit card cash machines anywhere in Cambodia, but hopefully there will be soon.

Traveler's Checks

Banks and large hotels will accept traveler's checks. It is best to have American Express traveler's checks in U.S. dollars. Other brands may not be recognized in Cambodia. Cambodian banks will charge you from 1–2% to cash your checks. This plus the 1% charge to purchase them can add up.

Cash

There's nothing like it. By all means bring some, in U.S. dollars. Bring an assortment of singles, fives and twenties. U.S. dollars are accepted and preferred everywhere in Cambodia. Restaurants, stores and hotels all quote prices in U.S. dollars. When obtaining dollars, check them carefully; a slight tear can mean that nobody in Cambodia will accept the note. Check the Safety section for suggestions on keeping your cash yours.

Riel

This is the official currency of Cambodia but it is less used than the dollar in hotels and for major transactions, and more used than the dollar in the far-out provinces and for small transactions in Phnom Penh. The riel comes in amounts of 100, 200, 500, 1,000, 10,000, 20,000, 50,000 and 100,000. The most popular is the 500 riel note. You should have some of these to pay the moto-taxi drivers and to leave for tips. Riel can be obtained at the bank or at any market, with the exchange rate better at the markets or moneychanger stands than at banks. You will see packs of it in glass cases at the markets. The exchange rates are pretty uniform but it's always a good idea to check the rates at a couple of different places, which is easier these days, as the money changers have begun posting the daily exchange rate. Use the ones that do. A lot of the other money changers like to try pulling one over on you with the rate they quote you. Your best bet is to use the changers that post the daily buy-sell rate.

You will notice packets of old and new riel. You will get a slightly better rate of exchange if you take the older bills. We're not sure why, as even the old torn riel notes are accepted everywhere.

The rate in June of 2000 was hovering around 3,900 riel to one U.S. dollar.

The Thai baht is accepted in most places, especially in the northwest and southwest of Cambodia.

It can be confusing at times walking around the country with three different currencies in your pocket: U.S. dollars, Thai baht and of course the Cambodian riel. It's always a good idea to have some riel on hand both in the boondocks and in the city. When you pay for small purchases at the market in dollars, for example, the vendors will usually slight you when they give you change in riel. All this can make for a very money-crammed wallet.

An easy conversion rule for Thai baht and Cambodian riel: take two zeros from the Cambodian riel and you have the amount in Thai baht. For example: 5,000 riel is 50 baht. Reverse the process for finding the amount of riel to the baht. For example: 1 baht is 100 riel and 100 baht is 10,000 riel.

Tipping

Certainly not required, a tip for good service provided by the friendly Khmer staff you usually encounter can have a very positive effect in a country as poor as Cambo-

dia. We westerners usually leave a tip at a restaurant in our home country, even when service is not too friendly or is a bit lacking. Yet we think nothing of coming to a country like Cambodia, where service is usually very friendly and attentive, and leaving nothing. In a country where the average salary is US$10–30 a month, tourists and visitors moving about the country and leaving a minimal tip at restaurants could increase the incomes of some Cambodians.

A 500-riel tip in a small, informal Khmer restaurant (whether in Phnom Penh or out in the provinces) is much appreciated, while 1,000–1,500 riel is a nice tip in the nicer restaurants. This of course does not apply to the hotels that tack on a service charge to the bill. If you want to make sure that a certain waiter/waitress personally gets the tip, put it directly in their hand, not on the table or in the bill folder, as is common practice in the West. Doing the former means the person gets to pocket the tip, where the latter means the tip is either shared by all (which is fine) or kept by the owners (which is not).

Along similar lines, remember as you travel about that it doesn't take much to have a positive effect on the lives of ordinary Cambodians. Buying a drink, snack or fuel from one of the small stands set up along the roadway wherever you go, is a good opportunity to give a boost to the regular working stiffs.

COMMUNICATIONS

Post

It's easy to find the large main post office just north of Wat Phnom, off of Sisowath Quay. They do have a poste restante. Postal rates are 1,800 riel or about US$0.75 for an airmail letter. Registered mail is available. Use this if you must send something important. Try not to have anything valuable sent to you in Cambodia, as things have a way of getting lost in the mail. The post office is open Monday through Saturday from 7 am to 7 pm. It's best to stick to Phnom Penh when mailing letters, as the provincial mail service is very unreliable. Even Phnom Penh can be a crapshoot with mail ending up missing frequently. But it's your best bet.

Telephone

There are about sixty public telephone booths in Phnom Penh. You will need a phone card, which can be purchased at the post office or in some hotels or stores. They come in denominations of 2, 5, 20, and 100 dollars. Local calls are inexpensive but international calls can be quite dear. You might wait until the weekend when there is a 20% discount, or call home collect. For the United States, use a Telstra phone booth and dial 1 (800) 881-001, or for Australia call 1(800) 881-061. Collect calls to Europe cannot be made at this time. For more information in Cambodia call Telstra at (023) 426-022. If you are staying in a large hotel and call from your room phone, the hotel will tack a service charge onto your bill.

Fax

You can send or receive faxes at most hotels and the Foreign Correspondents' Club of Cambodia (FCCC). This will be a bit expensive at approximately US$6–8 a page. The main post office has a fax desk and is cheaper.

Internet

Good news! It's here and it's the cheapest way to communicate. All shops are now US$3–4 per hour. There are shops springing up everywhere, but the most user friendly seem to be:

CAMBODIA COUNTRY CODE: 855

Café Asia. First floor of the FCCC on Sosowath Quay. Knowledgeable staff with full range of services available.

Kids. Located across from the National Museum on Street 178. Friendly staff, and a few other services are available as well.

Khmer Web. This is brand new and is located just four houses east of Lucky Market on Sihanouk Blvd. Full range of services.

Riverside Web. Located underneath the Wagon Wheel Restaurant on the river road, they have free candy and soft drinks. Full service.

Phnom Penh Web. Located on the river road between Garden Bar and Rendezvous Restaurant. Free candy and soft drinks. Full service.

Outside of Phnom Penh, forget the Internet. It's either not available or its cost is prohibitive in the provinces. Your best bet is to take care of your business in Phnom Penh before you set off on a journey, or upon returning.

Newspapers

The Cambodian Daily is a small paper published Monday to Friday, with a special weekend edition on Saturdays. It is sold at newsstands and in many restaurants. It has good local news and reprints from international papers. The Friday "Calendar" section of the paper lists local events such as dances, movies and plays and is worth checking out. There is a Khmer and Japanese language section in the back.

The Phnom Post is an excellent paper published every two weeks. It has good local news and the inside scoop on most stories. Its reporting and editorials do not spare anyone and they are quite outspoken for a paper in Cambodia. It also has a map of Phnom Penh with restaurants and businesses listed.

The Bayon Pearnick is a free monthly information magazine found at the airport, restaurants and Western bars and clubs. It mostly contains stories on tourism and the adventures and escapades of the expatriate community, along with local gossip, and is quite interesting and cleverly written. Some useful info is always included.

The Bangkok Post, a wonderful daily paper published in Thailand, has local and international news. It can be found a day later on some newsstands and boys sell it in front of Lucky Supermarket, along the river and at stationery and book stores for about US$1 a copy.

The International Herald Tribune, *USA Today*, *Time* and *Newsweek* magazines and also other French, American and English magazines may be purchased in the bookshop of the Sofitel Cambodiana Hotel and a few of the Phnom Penh supermarkets.

If you are neatly dressed and quiet, it's possible to sit in the lobby of most big hotels and read the house papers for free. You can also visit the FCCC, buy a drink, relax in an easy chair overlooking the river, and read the daily papers.

Monument Books is at 46 Norodom Blvd. Tel: (023) 218-948. They have many books on Cambodia and Asia, magazines and newspapers.

PHOTOGRAPHY, FILM & PROCESSING

You don't have to bring a lot of film to Cambodia, as film and processing are very cheap in Phnom Penh, Siem Reap and Sihanoukville. It's interesting to have your film developed as you go along to see how your pictures are turning out and if your camera is working properly. Most Cambodians do not mind having their photos taken. It's best to ask first. Smile and point to your camera. Never take photos of police, soldiers, army vehicles or roadblocks.

You never know if they will disapprove and you could then be in for an unpleasant experience, like losing your film. It's just not worth it. Agfa, Konika and Kodak shops will process your film the same day for approximately US$4 for a 35-mm roll of thirty-six exposures. To buy the same film costs US$2.50–3.00 for 36/100 ASA . Black and white, slide film and videotapes are also available.

ELECTRICITY

The electricity in Cambodia is 220 volts. The power sockets are usually the round hole variety. If you are staying in a reasonably priced hotel, you can expect the power to fail on occasion, although the problem has improved quite a bit recently. Keep a flashlight on the table near your bed. The top and mid-priced hotels and restaurants have their own power supply backup.

BUSINESS HOURS

Khmers as a whole are early risers with the business day starting at 7 am. There is a long afternoon break, typically between 12 and 2 pm when people eat and rest before continuing the workday, which then usually stops at 5 pm. Banks, as in many other countries are a bit different. The term "banker's hours" has always meant an easy workday schedule and in Cambodia it's no different. Banking hours are usually Monday through Friday, 8 am to 3:30 pm.

WHAT TO BRING

There is no need to bring too much or worry that you forgot something as one can buy almost anything in Phnom Penh. Here are some things that you may want to have before you go.

Guidebook

This one, we hope, is the one you'll bring. You need to have in mind where you will go in Cambodia and how much time you will spend in each place. A guidebook will help you to do this. You should have an idea of the accommodations you would like to have before you step off the plane and you should locate your hotel on the map. The more information you have ahead of time, the safer you will be. Check the airport when you land for those free giveaway maps and advertisements.

Luggage

I like a soft shoulder bag with a strap and handles. It is easy to carry and I prefer not to look like a tourist with a suitcase. A small daypack-style backpack is the most manageable for zipping about on a motorcycle. In any event, the large bag you decide on should have a good lock.

Travel in Cambodia can be very dusty during the dry season and wet during the rainy season. It's a good idea to line your bags with plastic garbage bags (without the garbage) to keep your things clean and dry. Ziplock baggies are good for small things and spaces.

Clothes & Necessities

Jeans can be a bit warm, but they offer good leg protection on a motorcycle. Or bring cotton pants in short and long lengths. T-shirts, short-sleeved shirts and one long-sleeved shirt. Bathing suit, socks, hat or baseball cap and underwear. Take a pair of sandals and wear a pair of comfortable shoes. Thongs or flip-flops for the shower. You can buy umbrellas or ponchos at the market cheaper than at home. It is too warm for a sleeping bag, but if you plan to go upcountry you should bring a bed sheet and certainly a mosquito net. Sunglasses, sunscreen, Nivea or Aloe Vera moisturizing cream, alarm clock, shampoo, toothbrush, toothpaste, anti-bacterial soap, flashlight, and mosquito repellent.

First Aid Kit

Items are listed in the Health section.

Money Belt

The ones that go around the waist and under the shirt are quite common and are fine if they are not too bulky and obvious. There are some new money holders on the market. One attaches to your belt and hangs down inside your pants. This is easy to access and is my favorite. There is also an ankle holder that attaches with velcro.

You could also sew a hundred dollars into your belt or put it inside of your shoe lining, so that if you do lose everything else, you will not be penniless.

You might want to take advantage of the Khmer Buddhist culture. The feet are the lowest part of the body, physically and spiritually, and are to be avoided. Most robbers don't want anything to do with your feet. Inside your shoe or sock (securely fastened) may be a good hiding place.

I always carry money and valuables in three places on my person: I carry a small amount of bills and change in my pocket for food and drinks and other small purchases; I carry a wallet or billfold with a little more money for larger purchases; And I always have a money belt or stash in my sock or hanging from my waist with a larger amount. If I need to access this, I go into a rest room and lock myself inside a stall for safety. Don't flash money anywhere. As in the Old West, play your cards close to your vest. You never know who is watching you.

Be careful and alert when handling cash or your wallet, wherever you are. A friend of mine took out his wallet on Khao San Road in Bangkok and it was immediately snatched up by two boys speeding by on a motor scooter.

There are also money holders that hang inside of your shirt from around your neck. These are not great, especially if someone tries to rip one from your neck on the run… ouch. Many travelers wear fanny packs— in the front, of course; this is OK as long as you do not have anything valuable in there. They are so obvious that if you are robbed, it will be the first thing taken.

Safety Deposit Bag

You may be using a safety deposit box in a hotel. Some of these are no more than gym lockers with padlocks. In any event, you do not want everyone to see your valuables. You should have an envelope for your valuables and passport. An ideal one is an overnight bank safety deposit bag. These are made of cloth and have a zipper and lock. They may be purchased in any large stationery or office supply store. Another friend of mine traveled to Manila and plunked five thousand dollars in cash and travelers checks into a hotel box and by the next day it had turned into five hundred dollars. He was too obvious and showy in his behavior. He did not get any of his missing money back…

Locks

Take a few padlocks of different sizes. Certainly, you should be able to securely lock your backpack or luggage. I take a chain and further lock my suitcase to my bed frame. This is especially useful if you are traveling by train.

Locksmith or security stores sell a type of lock that slips into a dresser drawer or a hotel door. I often use one of these to lock my hotel door from the inside.

Cash, Traveler's Checks, Credit Card

Yes, you will need to carry some cash with you. You will need it for the cab ride into

town or to the bank. American dollars are readily accepted in Cambodia. I always take a mixture of singles, fives, twenties and hundreds.

For traveler's checks, bring your initial purchase slip, as some banks may want to see this. Of course, make a copy or a few copies of this and record the serial numbers on the slip provided by American Express.

A major credit card is good in case of emergency and you can carry less cash with you. Record the credit card number, expiration date and home office phone number in case of loss and carry this in a separate place.

Documents

Passport. Make sure that it is valid for more than six months after your trip ends. Many countries will not let you depart if you have less than six months left before expiration.

Visa. You can now obtain a visa on arrival, whether entering by land or air. You should have your own pen for filling out the form and one passport photo. A 30-day tourist visa costs US$20; a business visa costs US$25 for those wanting to stay beyond 90 days. See the Coming and Going chapter for a list of embassies if you want to obtain a visa beforehand.

Visa extensions. The visa extension office (Department of Foreigners, Immigration) is located directly opposite Pochentong Airport on Pochentong Blvd. Visas can be extended for 1 month (US$25 tourist visa, US$30 business visa), 3 months, 6 months, or 1 year, although the 6-month and 1-year visas are only for business. The fees for extended period visas are reasonable but have been inching up, so check at the office for current fees. Express, 1-day turn-around service is available at a slightly higher fee.

Document Copies & Photographs

Make and carry copies of all of your documents, passports, visas and credit cards. The copy of your passport will help you obtain another one from your embassy in case of loss. It is also useful to have an extra copy if you rent a motorcyle and need to leave your passport as collateral. Have a numbered list of your traveler's checks, and the telephone numbers of your credit card and traveler's check companies. Keep these in a separate place from your wallet or money belt.

I also always carry at least four passport-sized photographs wherever I travel. You will need a small photo to enter the temples of Angkor.

Driver's License

If you have an International Driver's License bring that also. When you rent a motorbike, no one will ask you for a license but it's still good to have one. Phnom Penh has its own traffic police who will occasionally ask you to stop and produce your license and they will hold on to it while they tell you that you are in some violation and that you will have to accompany them to the police station. Now is a good time to have a few dollar bills in your pocket. No matter how ridiculous you believe the charge to be, remain calm, smile and hand over a few dollars. This is all they want and there is no sense in making a fuss over it. In the country, you will see a few military or police roadblocks (lots at night at in the rural areas of upcountry provinces, so don't travel the countryside at night). Drive through slowly; they are just checking the papers of the locals or asking for a few riels.

If you are waved over, by all means stop.

Inexpensive Accessories

Do not carry anything that you would not want to hand right over to a robber. Leave your Rolex at home. Even with all the fake ones around, I believe that the bad guys or girls can spot one on your wrist from the far end of a dark bar. There is no sense in taking chances and making yourself stand out.

Black Electrician's Tape

I always carry a small roll for instant repairs. If I do go somewhere with my Nikon, I tape over the word Nikon on my camera and case, as this is another brand name recognized all over the world. I had taken my Rolex on one trip and after having it admired by several people, I wrapped the band and most of the case with black tape. It looked like hell but it was an effective cover.

Motorcycle Helmet

If you have the room and inclination, and have a motorcycle helmet already, bring it with you. During the day, you will be traveling mostly by moto. These are local men who hire out to drive you around on their motorcycles. The bikes and the guys may be small, but boy, are they fast. There is a great deal of traffic and it just seems to merge into a free-flowing stream like your unconscious mind on amphetamines. It takes a few days to become accustomed to this. Before I get on the back of a scooter, I always say "Go slow" and I put my hand out, palm down, and say SLOW. I am not afraid to be a pain and ask the kid to drive slowly if they get too crazy. I don't do this at night, as there is less traffic and you are less of a target if you are moving fast. You might buy a helmet in the market and then discard it when you leave town.

Velcro

I always take a sewing kit and strips of velcro. I sew one of my front pockets with velco. It is very difficult to pick a pocket that is entirely closed with velcro.

Less

Yes, take less with you. The less you have, the easier it will be to travel and the less rich you will look. The old story about putting all of your traveling items on the bed and dividing it into two piles and then taking only one pile is still not a bad idea. When moving about, it's also nice to have your hands as free as possible.

HEALTH

Your health will not be at risk any more in Cambodia than in any other place in Asia if you take the proper precautions while you are traveling, and as in life and checkers, planning ahead is important.

Before you leave, visit your doctor and dentist to make sure you are in good health. If you need to take any medicine with you, write down the brand name and generic name and keep it in a separate place. Bring the prescription and the packaging with you. There are many pharmacies in Phnom Penh and the rest of Cambodia and you will be able to buy most drugs without a prescription. Check the dates as some may be out of date or worse yet, counterfeit. Anti-malarial medicines, Mefloquine and Artesunate sold in Phnom Penh were found to be fakes, packaged in bottles indistinguishable from those used for the real medicine.

Check your medical insurance and health plan to see if you are covered outside of your home country. You may want to look into health insurance for travelers but I have found the comprehensive plans to be very expensive.

Vaccinations

You should have a tetanus shot in case you step on a nail or cut yourself. These are good for ten years, so you may be protected already.

Typhoid protection comes in oral capsules or in an injectable vaccine.

You should be sure that you have had the following immunizations: polio, measles, and influenza.

You can take a vaccine for Hepatitis A. Havrix provides long-term protection, but you will need to have two shots about a month apart and it will take three more weeks for them to provide proper protection, so you will need to plan ahead. If you do not have the time, consider gamma globulin, which is an antibody to build up your resistance. This should be taken as close to your departure time as possible as it is most effective in the first two weeks and the effectiveness slowly wears off in about six months.

Malaria tablets can be taken once a week starting from a week before your trip until a week after. These should be considered if you are traveling upcountry. I've personally never taken anti-malarial drugs and have just relied on insect repellent and proper clothing. Anti-malarial drugs do not prevent you from getting the disease but kill the parasite during a development stage. Chloroquine and Mefloquine are often recommended but if you are going into high-risk areas up north you should take doxycycline. Please check with your doctor first. These are not foolproof and precautions while you are there may be a better safety option. Long pants and shirtsleeves, socks and mosquito repellent or coils are advisable, especially in the evening. Mosquito netting for sleeping is not a bad idea, especially in malarial areas.

First Aid Kit

You should include the following items: Aspirin for headaches or pain. Antihistamine or decongestant cough medicine. Bandages of different sizes and band-aids. Adhesive tape and two-inch gauze for wrapping wounds. Antifungal cream for athlete's foot. Jock itch spray or powder. Antibiotic ointment for cuts, burns and scrapes. A thermometer; if you think you may have a fever, at least you can find out. Sunscreen, don't fool around; get an SPF number 20 or more. Insect repellent; check the label for 30% DEET; this is a must. Pepto-Bismol is a good mild anti-diarrhea medicine. If you take Imodium or Lomotil, follow directions carefully and use only if you must travel, as these do not cure the problem; they just stop the symptoms. Water purifying pills or liquid such as Halazone tablets or tincture of iodine. Hydrocortisone cream for insect bites. Tweezers to remove splinters or ticks. Anti-bacterial hand gel; use this to clean your hands wherever you cannot wash them with soap and water.

Condoms. The most popular national brand is Number One. If a Cambodian says you are Number One while wearing a smile, you know what you are being called. There are also other brands now available as well.

Food & Drink

What to eat and drink while you are in Cambodia will be two of the most important decisions that you will make. Try the local food but be careful and follow these guidelines.

Don't drink the water. There, I've said it. Let me say it again. Don't drink the water. Brush your teeth with bottled water. Do not drink from any bottle that is not opened in front of you, it may have been re-filled. While you are at it, avoid most of the ice. The round pieces with holes in them or ice at the decent restaurants should be okay. Other ice may be contaminated, as it is moved from the ice truck in blocks and is handled by staff who cut it up into small pieces. Have a nice cold beer or Coke and

wipe the bottle top before you put your mouth to it.

It is best to avoid eating protein as in meat or fish while you are traveling, unless you are in a decent restaurant. If you are going to get food poisoning it is most likely to come from these two sources. Eat items that require cooking on the spot and that require little handling. If you have been to Thailand and have tried the great street food stands there, you will be in for a bit of a disappointment here. The Cambodian food stands are lacking in hygienic standards. Be careful before you eat from a street stand, especially if the food is just sitting there and not under refrigeration. Do not eat salads, lettuce or any vegetable that has not been cooked. It is OK to eat things like oranges and bananas that you can peel yourself. Do not drink milk or have any local ice cream. Do not eat shellfish, as it is one of the main sources of hepatitis. Do not drink juice that has not been squeezed in front of you; unclean water may have been added.

The cleanliness of so many small Cambodian restaurants, especially out in the provinces, leaves much to be desired. Used tissues and such are simply wiped off the tables between customers and onto the floor where the stuff piles up, because once the table is clean, that's good enough. Even if the restaurant is not busy and has plenty of staff sitting or milling around they do not think to take the time to sweep up the garbage lying on the floor attracting flies. The health department needs to start a countrywide health information campaign.

Look for restaurants that have people in them and are busy. The restaurant should look clean and well run. Busy places mean that there is less chance of the food sitting around or being old. The good news is that there are many fine restaurants in Phnom Penh and other provinces and they are listed in this book.

Do not pet dogs, cats or other animals, no matter how cute or friendly they look. They may have rabies but show no signs of it yet.

Never walk barefoot, indoors or outside. You will avoid cuts, infections and contagious diseases.

Avoid direct sun, wear sunscreen, a hat and sunglasses.

Drink plenty of water to avoid dehydration. If you are traveling, take plenty of bottled water with you. Don't worry about taking too much—you will always use it.

Mosquitoes spread dengue fever and malaria. There is no prophylactic for dengue and if you get it you will probably wish you had malaria. Symptoms include severe pain in the joints and muscles, fever, headaches and a rash that starts on the body and spreads to the arms and legs. Full recovery can take up to a month but the first two weeks will be the worst. Mosquitoes are prevalent during the rainy season from July to October. This does not mean that you will be safe any other time. Malaria mosquitoes come out from dusk till dawn but dengue- and encephalitis-carrying mosquitoes are out during the day. One must put on a good defense. Wear long pants and long-sleeved shirts. Wear mosquito repellent and sleep under a mosquito net.

General Health Concerns

Prickly Heat. A skin rash caused by excessive perspiration. This will usually appear between your legs on either side of your crotch. You can try to avoid this by wearing loose clothing, but this rash is difficult to avoid. You can use St. Luke's Prickly Heat Powder for some relief. This is sold all over Asia. Yoki Powder comes in a small yellow plastic container and is mixed with water to make a paste which is spread on the rash area or on athlete's foot. It provides excellent relief and will make the rash go away after a week.

Fungal Infections. To help avoid fungal infections, wear loose cotton clothing. Wear shower thongs in the bathroom. Dry your skin carefully. Use the strongest medicated soap that you can find. If you are infected, use anti-fungal powder or ointment or jock itch spray for relief.

Diarrhea. There are many different degrees of food poisoning and diarrhea, which are caused by eating or drinking contaminated food or water. A light case will have you running to the toilet a half dozen times with loose stools. Drink plenty of liquids. If you have a severe case of diarrhea that lasts for days and includes vomiting and/or fever, see a doctor. Taking Lomotil or Imodium may help with milder symptoms.

Giardiasis. This is caused by a parasite present in contaminated water. The symptoms may be diarrhea, swollen stomach and frequent gas. These can last for several weeks and disappear and come back. If you suspect that you may be infected, see a doctor.

Dysentery. Like diarrhea, this is caused by contaminated food or water but is much more serious. Symptoms may include severe diarrhea, blood in the stool, vomiting, stomach pains and headaches. You will surely need to see a doctor.

Cholera. This is usually caused by drinking water contaminated with human waste. Symptoms are severe diarrhea, muscular aches and pains, vomiting and a feeling of weakness. Drink plenty of liquids and see a doctor as soon as possible.

Typhoid. Again, contaminated food or water is responsible for this. You should have had a vaccination against typhoid but they are sometimes not totally effective. Symptoms may include headaches, fever, sore throat, vomiting, diarrhea, and in the second week, pink spots on the body, trembling, dehydration and weight loss. See a doctor immediately.

Hepatitis. Hepatitis A is caused by contaminated food or water. Symptoms may include, fever, headache, fatigue, aches and pains, vomiting, stomach pains, dark urine and yellow skin color. Hepatitis B is caused by exposure to contaminated blood, body fluids, sexual contact and unsterile needles. Avoid having a tattoo or shave or haircut in a barbershop. If you suspect that you may have hepatitis, see a doctor immediately.

Worms. Worms can be picked up by walking barefooted or by eating unwashed vegetables. They may also be present in undercooked fish or meat. A stool test is needed to diagnose this disease. You can buy a treatment for common worms called Zentel. It comes in tablet form. Buy six tablets and take two a day for three days at the end of your trip as a precaution. It's not harmful if you do not have worms and will kill the worms if you do have them. The technical name for Zentel is (albendazole SK&F).

Opisthorchaiasis. These are tiny worms that are present in infected freshwater fish. You may contract this disease by eating under-cooked fish or by swimming in infected lakes or rivers. These worms can go right into your skin. There may be no symptoms at all as in bilharzia, or you may have a fever, swollen or tender liver, abdominal pain and worms in your stool. If you suspect that you have this you will need to have a stool sample tested by a doctor or laboratory.

Tetanus. Tetanus occurs when a cut or wound becomes infected and it can be fatal. Clean all cuts immediately with antiseptic. Obtain a tetanus shot before you leave your home country. These are good for ten years and are a good investment.

Sexually Transmitted Diseases include AIDS, gonorrhea, and syphilis. Buy good condoms at home and always use them.

HIV/AIDS. Human Immunodeficiency Virus develops into AIDS. Both exist in Cambodia. Use condoms. HIV and AIDS can also spread through infected blood. The blood supply in Cambodia may not be adequately screened and single-use, disposable syringes may not be available. If you need serious treatment try to fly to Bangkok or Singa-pore. Ta-Cheng Hospital at 160 Mao Tse Toung is a fairly modern and clean facility and may be the best choice in Phnom Penh for a problem needing immediate attention.

Medical Facilities

Ta-Cheng Hospital. Previously mentioned. Located on Mao Tse Toung Blvd. The doctors here seem to be pretty good.

SOS International Medical Center 83 Mao Tse Toung Blvd., ☎ (015) 962-914.

Hours are from 9 am to 5 pm Monday to Friday, 9 am to noon Saturday. This is another good bet. They have a trauma room and can do lab tests. They have a 24-hour emergency service and can arrange for evacuation in a medical crisis.

Access Medical Services, corner of Street 63 and 310, ☎ (015) 913-358. Hours are 8 am to noon and 2 to 5 pm, Monday to Friday. 9 am to noon on Saturday. This is another good facility that's run by westerners.

The Camette Hospital, 3 Monivong Blvd., near Boeng Lake, ☎ 725-373, 423-173. They have a 24-hour emergency service. Ta Cheng Hospital is probably a better bet, as Camette does not always have staff to meet you and many just don't seem very interested in the problems of patients. There have also been complaints about the quality of care here. It is hoped they will improve. as Phnom Penh sure needs more good facilities.

The Cambodiana Hotel on Sisowath Quay has Raffles Medical Center. ☎ 426-288 or (017) 814-088.

European Dental Clinic, 195A Norodom Blvd., near Street 380. It is run by a French dentist who can also be reached after regular hours in an emergency. ☎ (023) 362-656, (018) 812-055.

Total Dental Care. This is a fairly modern facility located at 193 Street 208, Phnom Penh. ☎ (023) 212-909 or (015) 836-609.

SAFETY

Cambodia is no more dangerous than any other country, and in fact it is a good deal safer than most countries. Places in the Middle East, Eastern Europe, and Africa can be much more hazardous.

Guidebooks that warn against the foolhardy risks of venturing to the outer provinces in Cambodia are outdated and have been for some time. There has been a lack of current information and updated reports from the provinces. This is a disservice to the long-awaited recovery effort underway in Cambodia, as tourism can give a much-needed boost to the economy. The Khmer people are very friendly and hospitable and are happy to see some travelers finally coming back. When we traveled to the countryside on our motorcycles, adults and families would smile and wave, and as we turned down small dirt paths, dozens of children would follow us, laughing and talking with us.

You should take care in traveling, just as in any other country. We list some precautions here for you. Included are many tips for safety in general. Just choose the ideas that may be best for you.

If you have the use of a computer you might visit www.cnn.com/travelnow or www.fieldingtravel.com for current information sent in by travelers.

In the United States, travel advisories are freely provided by the government. For a list of countries or for travel advisories you may contact:

U.S. Dept. of State
Bureau of Consular Affairs
Washington, DC 20520
Tel: (202) 647-5225
Internet address: www.travel.state.gov
Fax: (202) 647-3000

The British government has a website, updated every day, with a great deal of information on different countries: www.fco.gov.uk/.

Arrivals

Arriving at an airport or town or traveling to your hotel is always a time for concern and a time to be especially alert. Why? Because when you are traveling with luggage the bad guys know that you also are carrying all of your cash and valuables. Try to arrive during the day. It's always safer. The same rules apply for leaving. This will be easier, as you will be more familiar with your surroundings and the prices for transportation and can possibly book your travel arrangements at your hotel or with someone who is known and recommended by your hotel. If I have good advance information or am visiting a country a second time, I often prefer to take a bus from the airport. There are fewer hassles than with the cab drivers; they seem to be a pain all over the world. However in Cambodia there are no buses from the airport and there are also no taxicabs, as we know them. Not to worry—there will be plenty of drivers with cars and some who have parked their cars outside the gate to avoid the parking cost. They should charge you five dollars for a ride to your hotel. Pick up one of those free maps that all airports hand out, or if you have one ahead of time, all the better. Possibly you can point to your hotel location on the map. Try to learn where your hotel is ahead of time. The driver will never say he does not know where to go, as he will not want to lose the fare. I have never had a serious problem with a cab driver at the Cambodian airport on any of my visits. Always set the price ahead of time and make sure that it is clear to both sides. Never put your luggage in the trunk if you can possibly help it. Once your luggage is secured in the trunk, the driver has the advantage over you. He has your luggage under lock and key. If you have your luggage in your possession and for some reason you have an argument with the driver, you can always get out and walk.

Once, in Bangkok, the driver sped past my hotel, which was on the other side of the street and said he would just turn around. Fifteen minutes later he was still speeding away from my destination trying to build up the meter. I jumped out with my suitcase at the next traffic light and took a bus back. Just be sure of the price BEFORE you enter the cab. Once you enter the car some of your bargaining power has dwindled.

On the trip into town, every single cab driver in every country will strike up a conversation with you and eventually ask "Have you been here before?" This is for two reasons. One is that they are trying to gauge how much you know about the town and customs and how much they can charge or overcharge you. Always say, "Yes, many times," even if you have never been there. Another reason is that they want to arrange to show you the town and/or hire out for the night or next day. Never agree to this without checking around for the prices first. And you may want to take a driver from in front of your hotel. Do not make any prom-

ises to your driver, or he will surely show up and wait for you in front of your hotel.

The driver will suggest that you try a hotel of his choosing. This of course is so he can obtain a commission on your room rate. Stick to your guns and go where you have planned to go. You will always end up paying more for the driver's suggestion. I try not to let the cab driver come into the hotel with me, either. If he insists (and you can't really stop him) I always tell the desk clerk that the driver did not recommend the hotel to me. But just by having shown up with you, the driver will sometimes come back to the hotel to ask for a commission.

Accommodations

Never leave valuables in plain sight in your hotel. Lock them in your luggage. Don't think that you can find a hiding place in your room. Believe me, the cleaning ladies and bellboys know more than you do. Items like air and travel tickets, cash, and traveler's checks should be kept in your hotel safety deposit box. Larger items like cameras should be locked in your luggage —not left on the dresser if you go out.

In Cambodia, you may have the occasion to bring a guest to your room for an overnight stay. In this case, on arrival in your room, lock your door from the inside with the key. Place the key in your pocket with your wallet. If the hotel door is one of those with only a bolt, use the sliding door lock that you have brought from home. When your guest goes to take a shower, place your valuables deep underneath your mattress. They will be difficult for your friend to reach while you are sleeping on the bed. This may seem like an old and corny trick, but it works. Also, if the door is securely locked from the inside, no one will walk out with your luggage. If you take a shower first, take your wallet and key into the bathroom with you.

Hotels are the perfect place to meet other travelers. Say hello and ask how long they have been in the country and if they have been to any places that you are planning to visit. Fellow travelers are the perfect people to ask for current information. Restaurants and other hotels are good places for information. In Phnom Penh, good places to visit for information and to meet other travelers are: Capital Guesthouse, Sharkey's Bar, and the Foreign Correspondents Club of Cambodia, along with a few other spots. While we are talking about obtaining local information, call or visit your local embassy for a safety update. They will have information available for you.

Check to make sure that your windows are locked. Avoid staying on the first floor, if possible. Access is too easy there. Do not leave your windows open and do not put anything on the balcony that you can't afford to lose. Do not open the door right away if someone knocks. It could be the wrong kind of somebody. Call the desk to check if it really is a hotel employee. This is especially true in the evening.

The following part is one that we unfortunately don't see in other guidebooks. This is a safety issue we should consider while away from home—it just makes good sense.

Fire Safety

Unfortunately, this is not something that most people think about, either guests or management. We recommend that you purchase and bring your own small battery-operated smoke detector. It may sound overzealous, but small ones can be purchased and it's a personal safety item that can help insure your good health on your holiday. Just pop in a battery, test it and put it in the open part of your sleeping room—on top of a high dresser or wardrobe cabinet. Put it on the nightstand next to the bed, if nothing else. The whole point is to wake

you up if there is smoke from a fire present and give you a little time and a fighting chance to get yourself out alive.

A few other suggestions to increase your chances of surviving a fire:

• Don't stay in a high rise hotel above the third floor. If the hotel doesn't have a room on lower floors, change hotels. You just might be forced to jump from a burning building.

• Check to see if the hotel has a working smoke detector.

• Don't stay in a room without a window that you can use as an alternative exit. You may otherwise be staying in a room that traps you like a closet.

• Make sure you can fully open the window. Some are sealed or not maintained well, so they won't open.

• Check out your fire exit route of escape. Search out the stairways and exit doors for your floor, become familiar with them and make sure they are not blocked. If they are, tell the management to remove the obstruction. If they do not, change hotels. Your safety is not an issue to take lightly.

Remember the simple rule if your clothing catches fire: **stop** (don't run or walk), **drop** (lie flat on the floor or ground), and **roll** (to extinguish the fire). If you remain standing, your body acts like a chimney and all the heat and fire proceed upward to burn your face and put smoke and heat into your lungs, which is a killer. Lying flat and rolling does not allow this to happen and can put the fire out.

Going Out & About

If you would like to travel around town and need to hire a moto-taxi or car you will have no trouble finding them outside your hotel. This is especially true of the moto-taxi guys. It is good to use the people in front of your hotel as they are more likely to take care of you. Of course a car is much safer. It just depends on how much money you want to spend. A moto-taxi may hire out for US$7 a day while a car will cost you US$20–25. Another means of transportation is to hire your own motorbike. You will need some experience to do this, as driving can be frightening during the day because of the traffic and during the night because of the darkness. Most of the streetlights and traffic lights have not worked since Pol Pot put them out of commission. If I go out to Martini's at night on my motorcycle, I usually blast over and blast back. If the bad guys can catch me, more power to them. At night, the bigger bikes are safer than the small, slow ones. If you would like to be taken there, a moto-taxi or car are your options. A moto will cost about US$1 and a car will cost US$3, but it is good insurance. Take a city map with you. You need to learn where you are and where you are going in case your driver veers off course. Half of the moto drivers only know where the tourist stops are and the other half don't know anything at all but will take a guess.

Do not make yourself accessible to a criminal. Don't walk around Cambodia late at night. Do not walk on dark streets, in parks or empty areas at night. Hire a moto to take you from place to place or hire one for the evening for about US$5.

There are many interesting markets in Cambodia and you will be able to buy colorful checked cotton scarves, silver items and woodcarvings. You will also see marijuana sold in brick-sized bundles or loose in large burlap bags (although recently there has been a crackdown on this at the Russian Market). This does not mean that selling marijuana is legal, and unless you want to take the chance that the police will always continue the practice of loosely applied rules, it's best not to buy or smoke it in public. If you feel that you must smoke

it, do it in the privacy of your hotel room with the window open. For safety reasons, legal drugs like alcohol should be taken in moderation when you are out at night. It reduces your senses and impairs your judgement—a fact we all know too well, but some real dumb situations can arise when we ignore it.

Avoid crowds and demonstrations. They may seem interesting or seem like good photo opportunities but they can be unsafe. I attended a peaceful demonstration by garment workers led by Sam Rainsy at the Independence Monument. There were more soldiers with automatic weapons than demonstrators and they eventually opened up the water cannons which were mounted on large trucks. I moved away quickly. The following week, I did not attend another demonstration in the same place. It turned out that when a few motorcycles drove past, the pillion riders lobbed hand grenades into the crowd of demonstrators. Many people were killed and wounded. Though it was never proved, the word is that they were Hun Sen's men. Demonstrations are magnets for trouble in Cambodia. Stay away.

Never, ever, point your camera at or take pictures of police or military personnel, vehicles or buildings. In 1997 Hun Sen seized power in a bloody takeover of the government. It was an opportune time to get rid of political opposition and many members of opposing parties were taken and later found dead. There were soldiers and tanks in the streets. Citizens and soldiers alike looted and pillaged stores and homes. A Canadian citizen on vacation thought he might get some good photographs. It should not have been too difficult, as he was using a telephoto lens and was also of Cambodian heritage. He was wrong! He was shot dead by soldiers from a block away.

Do I have to suggest that you not walk around with your Walkman and earphones? You know better.

You do not want to attract attention to yourself. Do not wear fancy clothes or white pants and shoes. You want to look like a traveler and not a tourist. OK, chances are that you can't blend in with the locals. You just don't look like them, but you don't have to look rich or like a mark either. A friend of mine always wore his shirt or jacket inside out (not a bad idea, as then your pockets will be on the inside) and mussed up his hair. He was not outrageous enough to stand out but he did not look wealthy, either.

Robbery—Surreptitious or Up Front & Personal

Cambodia does not have anywhere near as many pickpockets or muggers as there are in Europe and South America. The best defense against pickpockets or muggers is to be alert. If you notice or feel anyone watching you or following you, change directions. While you are walking around, keep alert when turning corners, around cars or building obstructions, doorways or places where you might bump into someone unexpectedly. Walk on the sidewalk closer to the street side and keep your camera or bag on the inside shoulder. Don't be flattered by the attention of a stranger. Pay no attention to offers of being taken to a really good sale, great money exchange, or any other "special offers."

If you are faced with a threat or challenge, leaving is the best response. WALK AWAY. Move out of the situation. Don't wait. It does not matter if you are in a nightclub or on the street, if you feel that an uncomfortable situation may arise, it is your duty to yourself and family to move to safety.

Don't let a stranger distract you from attending to your belongings. Don't be afraid to appear rude if you do not want to talk to someone. Of course, do not be rude unnecessarily. I like to talk to the locals but I usually initiate the conversation at a stopping point, not while on the move. Don't think that you cannot be robbed or conned by fellow travelers. The usual tale is that they lost all of their money, or they will try to sell you a camera or something else that they have stolen, or they may steal from you.

Unfortunately, you must beware if someone offers you help after an unexpected accident or assault. They may not quite be the Good Samaritan they seem to be. A good rule of thumb is not to accept unsolicited help. Do not be afraid to say, "I do not want your help" or "I have just called the police, they will be here any minute." If you do need help, seek it out first. No need to wait until someone comes along to offer help. You are safer choosing your own help.

Never accept offers of drinks, candy, cookies, fruit or food of any kind from strangers. Do not accept complimentary drinks or candy on a tourist bus—there have been cases of passenger druggings and theft in Southeast Asia.

If you are held up at gun or knifepoint or are mugged, cooperate; do not resist. Avoid eye contact. Keep calm and do not show fear. Some people feed like sharks on this emotion. Move slowly if you are asked to hand over your wallet, watch or money. Point to your pocket first, preferably with your left hand, the reason being that most people defend or strike out with their right hand. I would not, however, volunteer the money hidden in my shoe. The bad guys in Cambodia, and there are not that many, don't want to kill you, they just want your cash.

The idea of carrying a weapon may occur to you. My advice is, do not. Avoiding confrontation is generally safer. The bad guys are more accustomed to violence than you are and the fact that you have a weapon will put you at risk. You already have, however, the most powerful weapon in the world at your disposal already. More about this in the following section.

Using Your Sixth Sense

You have at your disposal the most powerful safety device in the world. Your mind is the best weapon you have. It is aided and abetted by your eyes and ears to make up your instinct. Trust your instincts. They have been with humans and animals for a very long time and they are always right. Learn to listen to your inner self. If you have a gut feeling, hunch, suspicion, an anxiety, doubt, or just a funny feeling of unease that something is not quite right, LISTEN TO IT.

Human violence, robbery and murder rarely happen at random. They are usually planned. They do not happen "all at once" or "all of a sudden." If you are alert and have your mind open to your intuition, you will receive a warning first. Something will usually happen. A stranger will step out of the shadows in front of you, someone will be walking a little too close behind you. You will feel that there is something odd about a situation or person. You will probably be right.

It is possible that you may be the victim of violence or a robbery. Don't think "That couldn't happen to me." It is your responsibility to come home safe. You have to depend on yourself, not the police or your friends. Don't feel macho and think "I can take care of myself." Just listening to one small survival signal or taking one safety step or one precaution may save your life or at the least your vacation. A little bit of fear is a powerful ally. A bit of fear can be your friend sending you a signal.

I landed in Hanoi Airport late one night (mistake 1), tired from a 24-hour flight and not listening to my senses. I did hear the signals but I just didn't listen. There were no buses at that late hour, just local cars and drivers. Everyone wanted US$18 except one kid who wanted only US$9. I said OK (mistake 2) and he went to get his car at the edge of the lot. Everyone else had their cars right there (3). I got in the car and a local lady-traveler also entered with me but sensed something and exited the vehicle (4). Leaving the parking lot, the driver stopped to pick up his friend at the gate (5). I should have exited the car right then and there, but reasoned that I was bigger than both of them and hey, I can take care of myself (6). A few miles away, they stopped on a dark road and asked me for an additional US$20. Luckily I had refused to put my luggage in the trunk. I left them and the car and was stuck at 2 am in the dark in the middle of nowhere. I started waving down passing headlights and was lucky again when I was picked up by the second passing vehicle and arrived safely in Hanoi. I have always "listened" since that time.

Having said all of this, I assure you that you are unlikely to encounter problems on your travels. A couple of words of precaution are in order, though. It's best to avoid places such as restaurants and nightclubs where soldiers, police and even civilians are drinking heavily. The problems usually occur (the same as in our home countries) during or following these bouts of heavy social drinking. Cambodians are usually very friendly to foreign strangers, but a group drinking and sending surly looks in your direction means it's time to get the bill.

Tourist Police

Good news coming for Cambodia! The Tourism Ministry wants to assemble its own police force to improve security for travelers. The plan would place hundreds of police officers who speak English and other major foreign languages at airports and major tourist destinations. They would provide safety information and assist foreigners with any unforeseen troubles and accidents. The Tourism Ministry will invite experts from Thailand to train them on how to become "best friends to our visitors." Thailand's tourist police have been successful in their operations and we are looking forward to the implementation of this plan, scheduled to begin early in the year 2000.

Landmines

Actually, you are in minimal danger from the estimated six million mines still buried in Cambodia if you follow some simple rules. You can go out in the country all you want and walk around as long as you stick to well-worn and well-used paths. Stay out of signed landmine areas, of course. But the most important thing to remember is to NEVER STEP OFF THE PATH OR ROAD. If you have to go to the bathroom in the country, I suggest you do it right there on the path or side of the road. Do not take even one step into the bushes. Never pick up or handle anything that looks like a mine or shell or any type of ordnance.

Unfortunately many landmine fields sit undiscovered until a farmer or child strays through the area for work or play. If you must bring your children into these areas outside of the towns or tourist attractions, keep very close watch and control of them. You can have a safe, fun and pleasurable adventure in Cambodia as long as you keep yourself aware of the possibility of landmines.

Here's a recent example of why the landmine problem has been so hard to tackle in Cambodia: after the factional fighting of July 1997 broke out in Phnom Penh and Second Prime Minister Hun Sen's forces got the upper hand on First Prime Minister Prince Ranariddh's forces, the prince's top

military people fled and eventually ended up at O'Smach to set up a resistance force. O'Smach is a small town near the Thai border in Northwest Cambodia, a typically strong area for the prince's party. The resistance went north of town and took over a hill next to the Thai border, with their backs facing Thailand. Prime Minister Hun Sen then ordered the government's forces to capture the hill and destroy the resistance.

I spoke with a mid-level officer of the resistance who was on the hill until the end, when the government finally was so frustrated with its losses and inability to take the hill from so small a force, that they finally worked out a deal with the prince. The officer said there were only about five hundred soldiers in the resistance on that hill.

The only way that they could survive and keep the government forces from over-running them and killing them all was to lay and keep laying landmines. The officer was trained in explosives and landmines in Malaysia and knew the craft very well. He said he could make and lay five hundred landmines a day. When the war was finally over, people went back to their home provinces, but the landmines stayed buried and hidden. They were very effective at stopping the advancing forces, but now they maim or kill those who unknowingly happen upon them.

Similar scenarios have been played out time and again in the past few decades in Cambodia, so it will be a long time before the countryside is finally cleared of this silent killer.

Prime Minister Hun Sen is planning to slash the size of the country's large army, now that the civil war has ended, and send demobilized soldiers to help in de-mining operations. The massive demobilization plan has yet to start so stay tuned to see if this really happens.

One Last Tip

We have loaded you up with a good deal of advice in this chapter, but here is one final tip. Relax! All of these things are good to know and think about, but do not walk around in a state of tension or anxiety. It's nerve-wracking and not good for your health or holiday. The fact is that strangers commit only 20% of all murders. This means you have a much better chance of getting killed by your spouse or friend. Relax and have a good time while you are traveling, and enjoy your vacation. You will be safer just for having read this chapter.

HAPPY TRAILS!

KHMER LANGUAGE

Your trip to Cambodia will be a great deal more interesting and fun if you learn some of the language. You don't need to know much to have the local people responding to you in a favorable manner. It is not a difficult language to learn. Khmer, unlike Thai or Vietnamese, is non-tonal, so you do not have to worry about changing the meaning of a word by saying it in the wrong tone. That is partly offset, however, by the seemingly strange and difficult to duplicate (for the Western tongue) sounds used in the words. Cambodians realize, though, that not many westerners speak their language and are very helpful in trying to figure out what it is that you are attempting to say. So the good news is that with a little bit of effort and a smile, you will do just fine.

Khmer grammar is very simple. There are no verb conjugations as in past, present or future. Just adding a word or two will take care of that for you. There are no endings for single or plural or for masculine and feminine. So throw your shyness and reservations to the wind and just go for it—try to speak a bit of Khmer every day. You will find the Cambodians will be very supportive of your efforts to learn their language. You will also find your adventure in Cambodia to be more fun and enjoyable as you try to interact with the locals in their own language.

GUIDE TO PRONUNCIATION

The system of pronunciation used here is an attempt to make things as simple as possible for the traveler with no prior knowledge of the Khmer language. It is by no means completely accurate, but should be close enough to enable you to communicate. Each English-speaking country has it's own style of pronunciation, so it is appropriate to mention that the romanized pronunciation in this section has an American slant to it.

Vowels

a	as in *bat*
ah	as in *father*
ai	as in *Thai*
ao	as in *Laos*
aw	as in *jaw*
ay	as in *play*
ee	as in *bee*
eh	as in *net*
eu	as in **eh** + **uh**
ew	as in *new*
i	as in *it*
ia	as in **ee** + **ah**
oo	as in *zoo*
oa	as in **oh** + **ah**
oh	as in *Ohio*
oy	as in *toy*
uh	as in *rum*

Consonants

bp	in between **b** and **p** sounds, but more like **p**
ch	as in *ch*est
dt	in between **d** and **t** sounds, but more like **t**
ng	as in si*ng* (will appear at the beginning of a word also, so practice isolating the sound)
ny	as in ca*ny*on (will also appear the at beginning of a word, so practice isolating it)
r	rolled with the tongue at the top of the mouth

Note: Many Khmer words begin with more than one consonant sound, e.g. *p'sah,* market, and *t'lai,* expensive. In these cases an apostrophe is used to show a slight break of the different consonant sounds. It's important not to add a vowel sound in between, as there is not one.

Also note that the dash used in the romanized transliteration of the Khmer words below are for your convenience in pronouncing the word. It does not indicate a pause between the sounds.

There is no v sound, so if you see a *v* in a transliteration somewhere (e.g. on a map), it is pronounced as a w.

WORDS & PHRASES

Basics

I or me	*K'nyohm*
You	*Nee-uhk* (an all purpose choice—*k* at end usually silent)
You (male)	*Lohk*
You (female)	*Lohk s'ray* (older), *Nee-ung s'ray* (younger)
He, she, they	*Goh-aht*
We, us	*Yehng*
Yes (men)	*Baht*
Yes (women)	*Jah*
No	*Dtay* or *awt dtay*
Please	*Sohm*
Excuse me	*Sohm dtoh*
Thank you	*Aw koon*
You're welcome	*Awt ay dtay*
Good luck	*Sahm-nahng lah-aw*
Hi	*Soo-ah-s'dai*
Goodbye	*Juhm ree-uhp lee-ah*
Good morning	*Ah-roon soo-ah-s'dai*
Good afternoon	*Ti-weh soo-ah-s'dai*
Good evening	*Sah-yohn soo-ah-s'dai*
Good night	*Reh-tray soo-ah-s'dai*
How are you?	*Sohk sah-bai jee-ah dtay?*

I am fine	*Sohk sah-bai jee-ah dtay* (same as the above, oddly enough).
See you later	*Jew-ahp k'nee-ah t'ngai grao-ee*
Money	*Loo-ay*
Help	*Joo-ai*

Travel

North	*Kahng jewng*
South	*Kahng d'bohng*
East	*Kahng kaot*
West	*Kahng lait*
Map	*Pan-tee*
Compass	*Dtray-vih-sai*
Airplane	*G'bahl haw*
Bus	*Lahn ch'noo-uhl*
Car	*Lahn*
Motorcycle	*Moto*
Rent (a motorcycle)	*Joo-uhl*
Taxi	*Tahk-see*
Motorcycle taxi	*Moto-dahp*
Train	*Roht plewng*
Boat	*Dtook*
Fast boat	*Dtook loo-uhn*
Cyclo	*See-kloh*
Bicycle	*Gohng*
Airport	*Wee-uhl yohn haw*
Bus station	*Sah-tah-nee lahn ch'noo-uhl*
Train station	*Sah-tah-nee roht plewng*
Share taxi stand	*Sah-tah-nee tahk-see*

Places

Hotel	*Oh-tel*
Guesthouse	*P'tay-ah suhm-nah*
Bank	*Toh-nee-ah-kia*
Embassy	*Sah-than-toot*
Hospital	*Mohn-tee-peht*
Market	*P'sah*
Museum	*Sah-rah-mohn-tee*
Post office	*Prai-sah-nee*
Temple	*Waht*
Police station	*Sah-tah-nee poh-lee*

Telephone	*Too-rah-sahp*
Bathroom	*Bahn-tohp dtuhk*

Food

Small restaurant	*Hahng bai*
Fancy restaurant	*Poh-jah-nee-yah-than*
Beef	*Sai-koh*
Pork	*Ch'rook*
Chicken	*Moan*
Fish	*Dtrai*
Crab	*K'dahm*
Shrimp	*Bahng-gia*
Egg	*Bohng moan*
Vegetables	*Bun-lai*
Fruit	*Plai-cheu*
Oranges	*Groh-ih*
Bananas	*Jayk*
Water/bottle	*Dtuhk soht/dahp*
Coke	*Koh-kah-koh-lah*
Beer	*Bee-ah*
Ice	*Dtuhk kohk*
Coffee	*Kah-fay*
Ice coffee/with milk	*Kah-fay dtuhk kohk/*
	dtuhk dah-koh
Fried rice	*Bai chah*
Spicy	*Huhl*
Sweet	*P'aim*
Salty	*Prai*
Sour	*Jew*

Medical

Hospital	*Mohn-tee peht*
Doctor	*Peht*
Pharmacy	*Kon-laing looahk t'nahm*
Medicine	*T'nahm*
Condoms	*S'raom ahn-ah-mai*
Mosquito repellent	*T'nahm kah-pia-moo*
Sunblock	*Krehm kah-pia pohn-*
	lew t'ngai
I'm allergic to	*K'nyohm awt dtroh*
penicillin.	*tiat pehn-ee-cil-in*
I am sick.	*K'nyohm choo*
I have diarrhea.	*K'nyohm mee-uhn*
	rohk joh ree-ahk.
I have a fever.	*K'nyohm mee-uhn kroon.*

I have a headache.	*K'nyohm mee-uhn*
	choo g'bahl.

Numbers

Zero	*Sohn*
1	*Moo-ay*
2	*Bpee*
3	*Bai*
4	*Boo-uhn*
5	*Bprahm*
6	*Bprahm moo-ay*
7	*Bprahm bpee*
8	*Bprahm bai*
9	*Bprahm boo-uhn*
10	*Dahp*
11	*Dahp moo-ay*
12	*Dahp bpee*
20	*M'pai*
21	*M'pai moo-ay*
22	*M'pai bpee*
30	*Sahm suhp*
40	*Sai suhp*
50	*Hah suhp*
60	*Hohk suhp*
70	*Jeht suhp*
80	*Pah-eht suhp*
90	*Kao suhp*
100	*Moo-ay roy*
101	*Moo-ay roy moo-ay*
102	*Moo-ay roy bpee*
1,000	*Moo-ay poan*
10,000	*Moo-ay muhn*
100,000	*Moo-ay sain*
1,000,000	*Moo-ay lee-uhn*

Time Talk

What time is it?	*Maong pahn-mahn*
	hao-ee.
Hour	*Maong*
Minute	*Nia-tee*
12:00 am	*Ah-tree-uht/ maong*
	dahp bpee yoop
1:00 am	*Maong moo-ay yoop*
2:00 am	*Maong bpee yoop*
5:00 am	*Maong bprahm pruhk*

6:00 am	*Maong Bprahm-moo-ay pruhk*
12:00 pm	*T'ngai trahng/ maong dahp bpee rah-sial*
1:00 pm	*Maong moo-ay rah-sial*
2:00 pm	*Maong bpee rah-sial*
5:00 pm	*Maong bprahm l'ngia*
6:00 pm	*Maong bprahm moo-ay l'ngia*
7:00 pm	*Maong bprahm bpee yoop*
8:00 pm	*Maong bprahm bai yoop*

Add minutes by using the counting system (sixty minutes per hour) and the Khmer equivalent of "and" (*hao-ee nuhng*) followed by the Khmer period of the day marker (e.g. afternoon/*rah-sial*). Examples:

2:23 pm = *maong bpee hao-ee nuhng m'pai bai nia-tee, rah-sial.*

10:15 pm = *maong dahp hao-ee nuhng dahp bprahm nia-tee, yoop.*

Note: In everyday conversation, Cambodians usually omit the period of the day word (e.g. *rahsial, yoop*) as they figure everyone present already knows what is meant.

Days, Weeks, Months, Years

Today	*T'ngai nee*
Tomorrow	*Sah-aik*
Yesterday	*M'sehl mehn*
Everyday	*Rahl t'ngai*
Night	*Yoop*
Last night	*Yoop mehn*
Morning	*Pruhk*
Noon	*T'ngai trahng*
Early afternoon	*Rah-sial*
Late afternoon	*L'ngia*
Day	*T'ngai*
Week	*Ah-tuht*
Monday	*T'ngai chahn*
Tuesday	*T'ngai ahng-kia*
Wednesday	*T'ngai puht*
Thursday	*T'ngai prah-hoa*

Friday	*T'ngai sohk*
Saturday	*T'ngai sao*
Sunday	*T'ngai ah-tuht*
Month	*Kai*
January	*Kai mah-gah-rah*
February	*Kai Gohm-piak*
March	*Kai mee-nah*
April	*Kai may-sah*
May	*Kai oh-sah-pia*
June	*Kai mi-tohk-nah*
July	*Kai kah-kah-dah*
August	*Kai say-hah*
September	*Kai gahn-yah*
October	*Kai dtoh-lah*
November	*Kai wech-ah-gah*
December	*Kai t'noo*
Year	*Ch'nahm*
Next year	*Ch'nahm groa-ee*
Last year	*Ch'nahm moon*
New year	*Ch'nahm t'mai*

Sightseeing

Temple	*Waht* (usually *wat*)
Lake	*Buhng*
River, small/big	*Stuhng/ tuhn-lay*
Waterfall	*Dtuhk cheu* or *dtuhk t'liak*
Reservoir	*Ahng dtuhk tuhng*
Ocean	*Dtuhk srah-moht*
Wave	*Roh-lahp*
Island	*Kaw*
Mountain/hill	*P'nohm*
Mountain temple	*Waht p'nohm*
Very beautiful	*Sah-aht nah*
Cave	*Ruhng p'nohm*
Highway/road	*Plao*
Village	*Poom*
Town	*Dtee krohng*
City	*Krohng*
Border	*Bpruhm*
Palace	*Wee-ehng*
Monument	*Wee-mee-ehn*
Monarchy	*Ree-eh jee-eh tee p'dtai*

Useful Phrases

Have/I already have
Mee-uhn/ K'nyohm-mee-uhn hao-ee.
Don't have
K'mee-un.
Where are you going?
Nee-uhk doh nah?
Where did he/she go?
Goh-aht doh nah?
He/she already left.
Goh-aht doh hao-ee
What time is it?
Maong pahn-mahn hao-ee?
What time does it open?
Wia-baok maong pahn-mahn?
What time does it close?
Wia boot maong pahn-mahn?
Sorry but I don't speak Khmer.
Sohm dtoh, k'nyohm awt jeh pee-sah k'meh.
I only speak a little bit of Khmer.
K'nyohm jeh pee-sah k'meh tik-tik.
Do you speak English?
Jeh pee-sah ahnglay dtay?
I don't understand.
K'nyohm awt yuhl dtay.
Do you understand?
Nee-uhk yuhl dtay?
I understand.
K'nyohm yuhl hao-ee.
I don't know.
K'nyohm awt duhng dtay.
I know that already.
K'nyohm duhng hao-ee.
I cannot.
Awt bahn dtay.
Please say that again.
Sohm tah m'dawng tee-uht.
Please speak slowly.
Sohm nee-yay yoot yoot.
What's this?
S'ai nee?
What's this called?
Nee hao tah ai?
I like this.
K'nyohm joal jeht.

What are you doing?
Tweh ai?
No problem.
Awt mee-uhn bahn-yah hah
Never mind/don't worry about it.
Awt ay dtay
Difficult
bpee-bahk
Easy
S'roo-uhl
Good
Lah-aw
Beautiful
Sah-aht

Conversational Phrases

What's your name?
Nee-uhk ch'moo-ah ai?
My name is…
K'nyohm ch'moo-ah…
I'm pleased to meet you.
K'nyohm dtrai-aw dail bahn s'koh-uhl nee-uhk
Where do you come from?
Nee-uhk mao bpee nah?
What country do you come from?
Nee-uhk mao bpee proh-teh nah?
I come from…
K'nyohm mao bee proh-teh (say your country slowly)
Are you married?
Gah hao-ee roo now?
Do you have any children?
Mee-uhn gohn hao-ee roo now?
Are you free today/tonight?
T'ngai nee/yoopnee, nee-uhk dtoom-nay roo dtay?
Do you want to go anywhere today/tonight?
T'ngai nee/yoop nee, nee-uhk jawng doh nah-layng dtay?
Where do you want to go?
Nee-uhk jawng dtoh nah?
Is it fun?
Suhb-ai-rig-ree-ay dtay?

It's very hot.
K'dao nah.
It's very cold.
Dtray-jee-uhk nah.

Coming & Going

Where is...?
...now ai nah?
Where is the Central Market?
P'sah T'mai now ai nah?
I want to go to...
K'nyohm jawng dtoh...
Do you know (place)
...s'koal dtay?
Do you know the Cambodiana Hotel?
Oh-tel Cambodiana s'koal dtay?
How much is it to go there?
Doh t'lai pahn-mahn?
That's very expensive.
Oh, t'lai nah.
That's very expensive, how about 2 dollars?
Oh, t'lai nah, joh bpee dah-lah bahn dtay?
How many Cambodian riel to the U.S. dollar?
Moo-ay dah-lah pahn-mahn ree-uhl?
I want to change U.S. dollars into riel.
K'nyohm jawng doh dah-lah, jee-ah loo-ay ree-uhl.
Where is it?
Now ai nah?
Is it far away?
Ch'ngai dtay?
Is it nearby?
K'bai dtay?
How far is it?
Ch'ngai pahn-mahn?
Turn left.
Baht doh kahng ch'wayng
Turn right.
Baht doh kahng s'duhm
Go straight.
Doh trawng
Stop here.
Chohp trawng nuhng hao-ee

Getting Accommodations

Do you have a room available?
Mee-uhn bahn-tohp toom-nay dtay?
Does it have a fan or A/C?
Me-uhn Duhng-huhl roo mah-seen dtray-jeh-uhk?
How much is it per night?
Moo-ay yoop t'lai pahn-mahn?
Can I see the room?
Sohm mehl bahn-teh bahn dtay?
It's expensive, can you lower the price a bit?
Joh t'lai, bahn teh bahn dtay?
I'll stay in this room
K'nyohm yohk bahn-tohp nee.

Eating

I'm a vegetarian.
K'nyohm tohm sai.
It's delicious.
Ch'nguhn.
No MSG, please.
Sohm kohm dahk bee jehng.
I'm hungry.
K'nyohm klee-uhn.
I'm thirsty.
K'nyohm klee-uhn dtuhk.
I'm full.
K'nyohm ch'ait hao-ee.
I've already eaten.
K'nyohm nyuhm hao-ee.
What would you like to drink?
Bpee-sah dtuhk ai?
I can't eat spicy food.
K'nyohm nyuhm m' hohp huhl muhn bahn dtay.
Please bring me the menu.
Sohm yohk tah-rahng-m'hohp Mao mehl.
Check, please.
Sohm geht loo-ay.

A few simple orders:

I'd like a bottle of Coke and a beer.
K'nyohm jawng bahn koh-kah-koh-lah Moo-ay dahp hao-ee nuhng bee-ah Moo-ay dahp dai.

I'd like a plate of chicken fried rice and a 7-Up.
K'nyohm jawng bahn bai chah sai Moan, moo-ay chahn, hao-ee nuhng Seh-wehnuhp moo-ay dahp.

I'd like a plate of mixed fruit.
K'nyohm jawng bahn plai cheu moo-ay chahn.

Shopping

How much is this?
Nee t'lai pahn-mahn?

That's expensive, can you lower the price?
Joh t'lai, bahn the bahn dtay?

Can you sell it for this much? (start at half the quoted amount)
Bprahm pahn ree-uhl bahn dtay?
(Is 5,000 riel okay?)

How much is it per kilogram (fruit or what ever)?
Moo-ay kee-loh t'lai pahn-mahn?

I would like 1 kilogram of oranges.
K'nyohm jawng bahn groh-ih moo-ay kee-loh dtay.

Motorcycle Touring

Is there a guesthouse in the village?
Poom mee-uhn p'tay-ah suhm-nah roo dtay?

Could I/we sleep in your home tonight?
K'nyohm/yehng sohm suhm-rah p'dtay-ah nee-uhk yoop nee?

Do you have clean water and food we can eat?
Nee-uhk mee-uhn dtuhk s'aht hao-ee nuhng m'hohp s'aht dtay?

Is the road good or bad?
Plao lah-aw roo awt lah-aw?

Is there a bridge going over the river?
Stuhng mee-uhn spee-uhn roo dtay?

Does this highway have any problem with robbers?
Plao nee mee-uhn jao plawn roo dtay?

I've been robbed.
K'nyohm dtrao jao plawn.

How many kilometers to… (destination)?
(destination) *bpee-mahn kee-loh?*

Where is a good mechanic (motorcycle)?
Jee-uhng tweh moto l'aw now ai nah?

I want to change the oil.
K'nyohm jawng doh prayng mah-sehn.

Please oil the chain.
Liap prayng jah-wah.

Please adjust the chain.
Tweh jah-wah ao-ee dtuhng.

Please adjust the clutch.
Tweh ahngia ao-ee dtuhng.

Please adjust the brake.
Tweh prahng ao-ee dtuhng.

Gasoline
Suhng

Full (as a full tank)
Bping

Note: It's always polite to say the Khmer equivalent of "excuse me" (*sohm dtoh*) first.

COMING & GOING

There are a number of options for you to choose from when deciding how to enter or exist the country. We'll begin with the most obvious and easiest.

AIR

Royal Air Cambodge has two to three flights per day to Bangkok and on the other side of the border, four flights per week to Ho Chi Minh City. Other international destinations include Hong Kong, Singapore, Kuala Lumpur and Guangzhou.

Bangkok Airways has three daily flights from Bangkok to Siem Reap, along with one daily flight from Bangkok to Phnom Penh. ☎ (023) 426-624 in Phnom Penh.

Thai Airways serves Phnom Penh from Bangkok. ☎ (023) 722-335 in Phnom Penh.

Vietnam Airlines serves Phnom Penh from Ho Chi Minh City and Hanoi. ☎ (023) 363-396 in Phnom Penh.

Laos Aviation serves Phnom Penh from Vientiane. ☎ (023) 216-563 in Phnom Penh.

Malaysian Airlines serves Phnom Penh from Kuala Lumpur. ☎ (023) 426-688 in Phnom Penh.

Dragonair serves Phnom Penh from Hong Kong. ☎ (023) 217-665 in Phnom Penh.

Silk Air serves Phnom Penh from Singapore. ☎ (023) 364-545 in Phnom Penh.

Travel Agencies

A few travel agencies for international and domestic travel are:

Hanuman Tourism near the National Museum at 223, Street 13, ☎ (023) 724-022, fax (023) 427-865, e-mail <hanuman@bigpond.com.kh>.

Diethelm Travel at the FCCC on the river road, ☎ (023) 219-151.

There are scores of others on all the main drags around town.

WATER

Laos

The trip from Laos to Cambodia by boat makes for an enjoyable adventure and is chock full of opportunities for viewing the rural river life of Cambodians up close, as well as seeing the spectacular scenery along the stretch of river between Kratie and the border. To do so you will need to pick up a Cambodian visa beforehand.

You can also go the other way, from Cambodia into Laos, provided you have a Lao visa already. You will need to get a letter of permission from the police in Stung Treng telling the Cambodian border officials that it's okay for you to cross from here. See the Stung Treng chapter for the map location of the police station as well as the details of making the trip in the What's Up section.

LAND

Thailand

Much cheaper than air fares, land crossings have gained in popularity with tourists as well as expat residents of both countries making visa, supply, and R&R holiday runs. Many stretches of the journey afford great sightseeing of the countryside as well as beautiful coastal regions. So the upside is that you can kill two birds with one stone by seeing the sights while getting to your destination, instead of seeing just the airports of the two countries.

EMBASSIES

CAMBODIAN EMBASSIES
Australia 5 Canterbury Court. Deakin, Canbera, ACT 2600 ☎ 273-1259

China 9 Dong Zhi Men Wai Dajie, 100600 Beijing ☎ 86 10 532-2101

France 4 Rue Adolphe Yvon, 75016 Paris ☎ 4503-4720

Germany Gruner Weg 8, 53343 / Wachberg Pech, Bonn ☎ 49 2 28332 8572

Indonesia Panin Bank Plaza, 4th Floor, Jalan, 52 Palmerah Utara, Jakarta ☎ 548-3716

Japan 8-6-9 Akasaka, Minato-ku, 107 Tokyo ☎ 3478-0861

Korea, North. Rue de l'Universite Commune, Monsou Arrondissement, Daedongang, Pyong Yang ☎ 850-2-817283

Laos Bane Saphanthong Nua, A.B.P. 34, Vientiane ☎ 856-21-341951

Thailand 185 Rajadamri Road, Bangkok, 10330 ☎ 254-6630

USA 4500 North West 16th Street, 20011 Washington D.C. ☎ (202) 726-7742

Vietnam 71 Tran Hung Dao Street, Hanoi ☎ 253-789 Consulate: 41 Phung Khae Khoan Street, Ho Chi Minh City ☎ 292-751

FOREIGN EMBASSIES IN PHNOM PENH
Australia 11, Street 254 ☎ 426-000

Canada 11, Street 254 ☎ 426-000 (same facilities as Australia)

China 256 Mao Tse Tung Blvd. ☎ 427-428

France 1 Monivong Blvd. ☎ 430-020

Germany 76-78 Street 214 ☎ 426-381

India 782 Monivong Blvd. ☎ 735981

Indonesia 179 Street 51 ☎ 426148

Japan 75 Norodom Blvd. ☎ 427161

Korea, South. 64 Street 214 ☎ 721901

Korea, North. 39 Street 268 ☎ (015) 912-567

Laos 15–17 Mao Tse Toung Blvd. ☎ 426-441

Philippines 33 Street 278 ☎ 280-048

Thailand 4 Monivong Blvd. ☎ 426-182

U.K. 27–29 Street 75 ☎ 427-124

USA 27 Street 240 ☎ 426-438

Vietnam 436 Monivong Blvd. ☎ 752-482

The downside is that both routes—the Aranyaprathet-Poipet crossing and the Trat-Koh Kong crossing—are real marathon affairs that take about thirteen to sixteen hours if you go straight through without any overnight stops along the way. The roads into the Cambodian interior from Poipet are atrocious, mostly bomb-cratered dirt roads that still have not been repaired from the decades of war. The Trat-Koh Kong alternative involves a long boat ride, in addition to the six hours it takes between Bangkok and the Thai border.

But if an adventure is what you are looking for, one of these routes would be the choice. My recommendation here is to take a look at these two regions of the country (northwest and the coastal southwest) on the Cambodia map and work in some of the sights and adventures that we take you to in this book. One could also custom-make a "circle tour" of Cambodia by coming in at one of the land crossings, seeing the sights on the way to Phnom Penh, then heading for the other land crossing, working in the sights and adventures along that route. This could be expanded quite easily to include any or all of the rest of the country.

Visas
The Cambodian immigration authorities at the border in Koh Kong are now issuing visas, both tourist and business, the same as their counterparts at the Poipet border crossing. This is another big development toward easing the way for tourists to come in and explore Cambodia. It's US$20 for a tourist visa and US$25 for a business visa—period!

You can apply for a visa at the Cambodian embassy in Bangkok or wherever else you may be coming from. Droves of travel agencies around Bangkok, as well the infamous Khao San Road backpackers' area, will get your visa lined up for you at a cost.

Guesthouses in the Khao San Road area also offer mini-bus transportation directly to the border.

Aranyaprathet-Poipet Crossing

Air-con buses leave Bangkok's northern bus terminal starting at 5:30 am and almost hourly after that. The fare to Aranyaprathet is about 150 baht.

Upon arrival at the Aran bus station, you will find tuk-tuk drivers asking you if you are going to Cambodia. The fare for the six-kilometer trip to the border is 40 baht.

If you are looking for a last chance to communicate cheaply with the outside world before you cross over, an Internet center is conveniently located next to the bus terminal in Aran with the rock bottom rate of 50 baht per hour. You won't see rates anywhere near that cheap again until you leave Cambodia. If you are not in a big hurry to try to make a transportation connection on the Cambodian side, there's a big bustling market on the Thai side of the border selling a wide range of goods and every type of cheap food that one might want. It's also quite entertaining to watch the parade coming and going across the border. Droves of Khmers make the crossing throughout the day to bring their goods to market and to shop on the Thai side. You will see all manner of pushcarts the Khmers use to get their goods to the Thai market. The time warp between Thailand and Cambodia becomes very apparent as you watch the shabbily dressed Khmer peasants try to negotiate the fully laden carts across the border. It's also the first place you will see amputee ex-soldiers (most are landmine victims), children, and the elderly begging for money. You will also see smartly dressed Khmer ladies coming and going to do some marketing across the border.

The difference between Cambodia and Thailand here is like night and day, with great roads, markets and every possible convenience on the Thai side and really none of the above on the Cambodian side. The Cambodians know all too well the state of their poor country and that it will be a long time before they come close to catching up with their affluent neighbor. But give them a smile or try to say a word in Khmer and you will always be rewarded with a day-brightening response.

The border crossing itself is a fairly quick and easy process. Thai immigration will stamp you out and you simply walk with your possessions across to their Cambodian counterparts who will stamp you in after you complete the arrival card and present your passport and US$20 for a visa.

Just beyond immigration wait motorcycle taxis that will take you to a hotel or guesthouse, if you are staying in town, or to the share taxi stand to catch a ride to either Siem Reap or toward Phnom Penh. It's 5 baht for either. See the Poipet section for share taxi rates to the destination you are headed for.

Don't worry about changing your money over to Cambodian currency at this point as the Thai baht is preferred in northwest Cambodia. U.S. dollars are also gladly taken, but it's nice to have baht or Cambodian riel for the small transactions.

Note: to figure out how many riel there are to the Thai baht and vice-versa, simply add or take away two zeros to the currency. Example: to 50 baht add two zeros and you have 5,000 riel. From 2,000 riel, take away two zeros, and you have 20 baht. Nothing could be easier.

For those travelers who feel they are carrying too much money with them, the two official Thai-Cambodian border crossings give them the opportunity to part with some of their hard-earned cash. There are casinos on the Cambodian side of the border just beyond the immigration checkpoints. Most of the clientele are Thai, as it is not legal for them to gamble in their home country and it's relatively easy for them to cross the border for a day or two on the gaming tables or the one-arm bandits. Most of the staff speak Thai but they are very indiscriminate about whose money they try to take. All with money are welcome.

If you are leaving Cambodia via this same crossing, simply look at the Coming and Going section of wherever it is you are departing from and make your way to Poipet, then the 5-baht moto-taxi to the border crossing. After you are stamped out of Cambodia and into Thailand, you can just reverse the process with the tuk-tuk ride to the bus station or catch a ride to Khao San Road on the mini-bus that waits at the border to see who shows up from the Siem Reap share taxis. The driver waits in the afternoon next to the Thai immigration checkpoint and approaches foreign travelers to see if they want to head to the Khao San Road area. It's 200 baht and it will leave between 4:30 and 5 pm. It gets you into Bangkok faster than taking the bus, as they don't make all the stops that the buses do. One can always go this way and then take a bus or taxi once in Bangkok if you won't be staying in the backpacker's haven.

Trat-Koh Kong Crossing

If you want to cross into Cambodia at the Trat-Koh Kong border crossing instead, the preliminaries with the visa are of course the same.

To get to the Cambodian border, take the Bangkok-Trat a/c bus from the eastern bus terminal for about 150 baht, then take one of the mini-buses that now ply the road between Trat town and the border for 100 baht a head. Or you could take one of the pickup truck taxis that follow the same route. Either way you stop once in the border trade town of Klong Yai to load and

unload a few passengers, then continue down this narrow panhandle of Thailand to the border market area of Hat Lek. There are a couple of good Thai food restaurants with reasonable prices and great ocean views just west of the Thai checkpoint, so you can replenish yourself with some great Thai food before the next leg of your journey.

Once you've checked out of Thailand and into Cambodia you will find drivers of beat-up old taxis waiting to take you to the river across from Koh Kong town for 50 baht a person. The taxis line up close to—you guessed it—the big border-crossing casino. This one features a nice resort (details in the Koh Kong chapter), complete with a great pool-restaurant area overlooking the ocean. Again, the place caters almost exclusively to Thai gamblers and merry-makers over for a holiday.

Once the taxi gets you over the bumpy road to the river, it's 20 baht a head to have a small boat taxi take you to the other side and Koh Kong town. There you can find a room, if staying, or arrange for your bullet boat ride to Sihanoukville or Sre Amble (600 and 500 baht, respectively) and on to Phnom Penh.

The problem with using this border crossing instead of the Aran-Poipet border crossing to enter Cambodia is timing. The border crossing opens at 7 am and you have to do the paperwork, take the taxi to the river and then get across in the boat taxi to buy your ticket for the Sihanoukville boat that leaves around 8 am. Should be enough time to do it, with the only problem being if the boat is already full by the time you arrive. The boat to Sre Amble leaves at 7:30 am so Sihanoukville's later departure is the best bet. See the Koh Kong chapter if you must or want to stay the night. Unlike Poipet town at the other border crossing, Koh Kong is a beautiful province that offers a few adventures that may entice you into spending some time there.

Also see the Koh Kong Coming and Going section for more transport information on getting you the rest of the way to your destination.

If you are leaving Cambodia via the Koh Kong crossing, and are coming from Phnom Penh, you have the option of taking a share taxi to Sre Amble for 7,000 riel per person (see Transportation section for share taxi stand location), which is a shorter ride from Phnom Penh than is Sihanoukville.

If going via the Sihanoukville bullet boat you can either take a share taxi or the a/c Hoh Wah Genting bus.

Either way, once you arrive in Sihanoukville you will have to hire a moto-taxi to take you to the bullet boat (2,000 riel). Just tell the moto driver you are going to Koh Kong and he will get you there—probably.

The trip from either Sihanoukville or Sre Amble to Koh Kong is 500 baht and takes about the same length of time.

During the dry season Sihanoukville has two boats a day making the trip, with one leaving at 10:30 am and the other at noon. During the rainy season there is only the noon boat and it becomes the "Barf Boat Express" as the waves can get fairly big and most of the passengers work at filling the complimentary baggies that are handed out upon departure.

The Sre Amble boat leaves at 11 am all year around with the same fun-filled entertainment during the rainy season.

Both boats also feature TVs that play very loud Khmer karaoke videos to add to your boating experience. A much nicer option during the dry season is riding outside and enjoying the beautiful coastal scenery. You'll see some of the lush blanketed mountains and endless barren beaches and islands that Koh Kong is blessed with.

New Service: There is now a fast boat from Sre Amble to Koh Kong that cuts the travel time in half and is only 300 baht! It leaves at 10:30 am from Sre Amble, and at 7:30 am from Koh Kong on its return trip. This saves both time and money.

By taking the Sihanoukville boat, you have the option of taking the air-con Hoh Wah Genting bus which is usually more pleasant than the hair-raising share taxis. This way you can also work in a stay at Sihanoukville, which is Cambodia's top beach resort area.

If you choose this option and just want to head to the Koh Kong-bound boat once you arrive in Sihanoukville, tell a moto-taxi guy at the bus station that you are going to Koh Kong. The usual fare is 2,000 riel or 20 baht.

The boats from either town make one stop at the island of Koh Sadat, about half-way into the trip. Just a quick loading and unloading of people and goods here, then you're off again. Just off the mainland is a scenic area where fishing and logging are the mainstays of the people.

Once you arrive at the river immigration police checkpoint just before Koh Kong town, boat taxi guys will come over to ask you if you want to go to Thailand. This isn't the border, just an extra check by the Cambodians to try to keep better track of who is coming and going.

When leaving Cambodia it saves a step if you take one of these boat taxis instead of going the last little bit to Koh Kong town on the bullet boat, then crossing the river to the road taxi. For 100 baht a head you are loaded in a small boat at the checkpoint and when there are enough people to fill the boat, they take off for the water canals heading to the ocean beach near the border. It's about a fifteen-minute trip and it is quite scenic, going through mangrove areas, although depending on the weather, it can be a bumpy ride on the last little ocean stretch as the boat guys rarely think of cutting the throttle back a bit.

Once you are stamped out of Cambodia and into Thailand you will see a sign in English next to the road offering the mini-bus to Trat town and the bus station for the hook-up to Bangkok.

Vietnam

This section will be very brief because there just are not as many options in dealing with the communist government in Vietnam. They are hammering tourists traveling to Vietnam with hefty visa fees and making you pay even more for each increased level of service (or the lack of it). You can only cross at the Moc Bai border crossing in Svay Rieng Province, provided you already have a visa for Vietnam and provided you specifically stated on the visa application that you would be crossing by land here and not flying into the country. You cannot change your mind once you have the specific visa, or all manner of trouble will break out with the Vietnam immigration officials: you will either have to pay a hefty sum, or more likely, you will be sent back to where you came from. Going in the other direction, you will need a current Cambodian visa to cross here.

Visas

This is quite a racket for the profiteer communists. While Thailand can issue an instant one-month visa at a border crossing or a two-month visa the same day from their embassy in Phnom Penh (the one-month visa is free, two months is US$15), Vietnam has made tourists pay through the nose if they want decent service on a sliding scale, depending on how many working days you are willing to wait for your visa to be processed. Lucky! Lucky! Motorcycle Rental on Monivong Blvd. and the Capital Guest-house have information on the sliding scale, but we will not encourage the Vietnamese government scam by printing it here. The charges quoted at the Vietnamese embassy in Phnom Penh are as follows: a single entry 30-day visa costs US$50 and takes four working days to get; a double-entry visa costs US$80 and takes two working days to get. Check for current information as the rates do change.

Getting to the Border Crossing

Check out the chapter on Svay Rieng and Prey Veng for all kinds of travel info about the route heading to the border.

The share taxi stand near the Olympic Market in Phnom Penh is where you depart from. The cost per spot is 5,000 riel —for either the border crossing or Svay Rieng town.

The Capital Guesthouse and another outfit in Ho Chi Minh City have joined together to offer air-con bus service to the border, from where the other guesthouse will take you the rest of the way to Ho Chi Minh City. It's reasonably priced at US$6 and leaves at 6:45 am.

Crossing by Motorcycle

To take a motorcycle across the border to Thailand or Vietnam for any period of time you must get permission from the Customs Department in Phnom Penh (SE corner of Norodom Blvd. and Street 118). A form letter requesting permission for a temporary exit for your motorcycle is needed to satisfy officials that you do not intend to sell the bike once you cross the border and that the bike is not stolen. Stop into the office that handles this (ground floor, NE corner) and they will show you a copy of the form letter that you must submit. You will need the registration card for the motorcycle and a copy of your passport and Cambodian visa to submit with the application. Officials say there is no fee and it takes two days to get the approval back to you. Cambodian immigration officials will not let you cross with your motorcycle without this letter.

Thailand

It is possible to take your motorcycle into Thailand for a journey (Poipet land crossing only, at this time) if you want to make your adventure an international one.

The Thais will require you to present your passport, identification and title paper (or card) for the motorcycle and do some paperwork informing them exactly how many days you want to have the bike in Thailand. It is then important to keep your stay in Thailand with the bike to just that many days as the paperwork procedure at the border becomes a nightmare, upon your return, if you deviate from your stated schedule. There can also be penalty fines involved in overstaying.

To turn this procedure around and bring your bike into Cambodia from Thailand, either go to or telephone the Cambodian embassy in Bangkok, (02) 254-6630, for information. The paperwork required by the Thais can all be accomplished when you get to the border crossing at Aranyaprathet, according to Thai officials.

Vietnam

It is also possible to cross with your motorcycle into Vietnam from Svay Rieng Province (Highway 1). As for what the Vietnamese authorities will require from you, check with the Vietnamese embassy in Phnom Penh at 752-482 for the current information on crossing the border with a motorcyle from Cambodia. The Vietnamese immigration officials at the border crossing have been known to change the rules or make up their own for the crossing procedure from time to time, usually because they decided they should benefit financially from your wanting to cross by bike. Vietnamese authorities have also said that no motorcycle with an engine larger than 125 cc can be brought into the country, but this also is not necessarily etched in stone, so again, check with the embassy in Phnom Penh.

For reversing the procedure and bringing a motorcycle into Cambodia from Vietnam, check with the Cambodian embassy in Hanoi (253-789) or Cambodian consulate in Ho Chi Minh City (292-751) and with Vietnamese immigration in Ho Chi Minh City for their requirements.

Laos

The Lao embassy says that it is still not possible for a foreigner to cross into Laos with a motorcycle from Cambodia as of April 2000, at least not officially . . .

GETTING AROUND

Traveling in Cambodia is easy and safe these days, with many choices of transportation to choose from, especially to the tourist sites. Yes, most of the roads are still terrible, but if you like off-track riding, you will love Cambodia. If you want to go by motorcycle but don't like bad roads, there are alternatives. And as you will see in different chapters throughout the book, a fair number of roads are in pretty good shape, giving you a lot of easy-to-reach destinations to choose from. Other options include going by air or by fast boat along Cambodia's well-developed network of rivers. There are also air-con buses and share taxis and car rentals for those who want to go by road, but in an enclosed vehicle. The train is also an option as a pleasant way to see the country and interact with the locals, though it takes more time.

Road travel will be safest if you travel only during the day out in the rural countryside; the towns and cities are safe enough in the early evening hours. Plan to try to wrap up your daily journey and be back in town by, or shortly after, sunset and you will not have to worry about things like police and military checkpoints out in the countryside. The checkpoints are illegal these days around most of the country, but the police and soldiers feel they are safe operating them by night, so they set up with surly looks to ask for donations (read: whiskey money) from passersby.

Distances: There are specific distances listed throughout the book describing how to get to different sites, attractions and towns. These were obtained mostly by motorcycle odometer readings between various points. Because odometer readings for distance always seem to vary from vehicle to vehicle, please keep in mind that they may not match what you are reading on your own odometer whether or not you are renting a motorcycle or driving your own. Nevertheless, the mileage listings will help you find your way.

Negotiating fares: With all hired modes of transportation in Cambodia, you will almost always be quoted a high fare, so you should try to negotiate it down—with a smile, of course. Try one half of the quoted fare, and go from there.

AIR

There are now a few choices for domestic air travel within Cambodia. Check the appropriate town map for locations of offices in the provinces. Domestic flight schedules are constantly changing, so it's best to check with the airlines for updates.

Royal Air Cambodge. ☎ (023) 428-891. The office is at 206a Norodom Blvd, Phnom Penh—just past Wat Than on the left side of the street going away from the Independence Monument. Office hours, Monday to Saturday, 7 to 11 am and 2 to 5:30 pm. You can purchase tickets here or at the airport or through your hotel or travel agent.

The airline also flies from Phnom Penh to:

Siem Reap—every day, at least twice a day, usually a morning flight and one or two afternoon flights. The cost is US$55 one way.

Battambang—daily service with flights at 7 am, except Mondays when the flight departs at 2:20 pm. The fare is US$45 one way.

Koh Kong—service has been suspended for quite some time. Check for current status.

Rattanakiri—daily flights at 10:55 am, except Friday, when there is no flight. The fare is US$55 one way.

Stung Treng—flights are scheduled for Monday, Thursday & Sunday at 3 pm. The fare is US$45 one way.

Mondulkiri—two flights a week with Monday's flight departing at 6:50 am and Friday's at 10:50 am. The fare is US$45 one way.

Inter-provincial flights are also available from Siem Reap to Battambang and from Rattanakiri to Stung Treng and Mondulkiri.

President Airlines. ☎ (023) 212-887, (023) 210-338. This is one of the new additions on the flight scene. The head office in Phnom Penh is at 50 Norodom Blvd.

Flight schedule, Phnom Penh to:

Siem Reap—Sundays only, thus far, at 7 am and 3 pm. The fare is US$55 one way.

Battambang—Flights are Tuesday through Saturday at 7 am. The fare is US$45 one way.

Rattanakiri—Flights are Tuesday, Thursday & Saturday at 10 am. The fare is US$55.

Stung Treng—Wednesday & Friday flights depart at 10 am. The fare is US$45 one way.

Phnom Penh Airways. ☎ (023) 217-419. Another new addition offering a few more choices. The office is located at 209 Street 19, Phnom Penh.

Flights from Phnom Penh to:

Siem Reap—daily at 7:30 am and 3:10 pm

Battambang—Tuesday, Thursday & Saturday at 7:20 am

Rattanakiri—Monday, Wednesday, Friday & Sunday at 10:00 am

Stung Treng—Monday, Wednesday & Friday at 10:00 am

Koh Kong—Thursday & Saturday at 10 am

Sihanoukville—Friday & Sunday at 12:05 pm

Mondukiri—Sunday at 10:00 am

FAST BOAT-BULLET BOAT

The mighty Mekong River offers splendid scenery and easy travel by bullet boat to Kampong Cham, Kratie, Siem Reap, and Stung Treng (only when the water level along the Mekong is very high). The boats stop along the way to pick up and let off passengers and it's a pleasant and fairly quick trip with great river scenery. Local vendors along the way sell food and drinks.

Bullet boats also ply the sea route to and from Koh Kong (and thus, the Thai border as well). Check the Koh Kong and Coming and Going chapters for more details.

There are some additional routes along a few of the other rivers around the country. These options are also discussed in the provinces' Coming and Going sections.

BUS

Air-con bus service is now available heading out from Phnom Penh to a number of different provinces and you also have the option of using these buses for destinations between Phnom Penh and the final provincial destination. There are a few different companies available on the Phnom Penh-Sihanoukville route, but we are not going to list them because they run old buses that don't seem to be maintained on a regular basis. It's a crapshoot to see if the brakes are going to work, or if the bus can make its appointed destination.

Hoh Wah Genting Bus Company has fairly new buses and does seem to maintain

BUS FARES & SCHEDULES

Phnom Penh to Sihanoukville

7:30 & 8:30 am	10,000 riel
12:15 pm	8,000 riel
1:30 pm	10,000 riel

For interim destinations such as Kirirom National Park, see 2,000 riel knocked off the fare.

Sihanoukville to Phnom Penh

7 am, 8 am, 12:15 pm, 2 pm.

The fare is 8,000 riel for each.

Phnom Penh to Kampong Chhnang

6:40 am, 8 am, 9 am, 10 am, 11:30 am, 1 pm, 2 pm, 3:30 pm, 4:30 pm.

Kampong Chhnang to Phnom Penh

6:30 am, 7:30 am, 9:30 am and 11 am, 12 pm, 1 pm, 2 pm, 3:30 pm, 4:30 pm.

Cost is 4,500 riel and if you get off at Udong it's 2,000 riel.

Phnom Penh to Takeo

6:50 am, 8 am, 9 am, 10 am, 11:30 am,1 pm, 2 pm, 3 pm, 4 pm.

Takeo to Phnom Penh

6:30, 7:30, 9:30, 10:30, 11:30 am,12:45 pm, 2 pm, 3 pm, 4 pm.

Cost is 4,500 riel and if you get off at Tonle Bati, the Zoo or Phnom Chissor it's between 3,000 and 4,000 riel.

Phnom Penh to Kampong Spue

The bus service begins each day at 6 am and runs every 45 minutes throughout the day, going both ways. The cost is 3,000 riel, with in-between destinations costing 2,000–2,500 riel.

them. The buses have air-con and are pleasant to travel in. This outfit offers the most extensive network of routes. In the various province chapters we do mention the bus as an option and where you can jump off to get to a day-trip destination. This is not a paid advertisement, just a personal recommendation. Anyway, here is their schedule. The Phnom Penh terminal is located off the southwest corner of the Central Market on Charles de Gaulle Blvd.

Phnom Penh along National Highway 1 serves the many day-trip destinations enroute to Nat Luang town, near the ferry crossing for the Mekong River (where service now stops). Buses start at 5:45 am and go hourly throughout the day with the final bus leaving at 4 pm. The same schedule applies for the return trip, with the last bus leaving Nat Luang at 5:30 pm. Cost is 2,000–4,500 riel.

Phnom Penh to Kampong Cham

6:45 am, 7:45am, 9:30 am, 11:30 am, 1:45 pm, 3:45 pm.

Kampong Cham to Phnom Penh

6:45 am, 7:45 am, 9:30 am, 12:30 pm, 1:30 pm, 3:30 pm.

SHARE TAXI

Share taxis get started from 5:30 am on. These are cars and vans and sometimes open-back trucks that load up with passengers for longer trips. In Cambodia, due to lack of choices in most places, it's the most popular mode of transportation between the different provinces. Instead of paying for an entire taxi, which is not affordable for most, you "buy" a spot either in the cab area or the bed area of a pick-up truck or sedan share taxi. The ride is usually a social occasion for the fun-loving Khmers, with the driver playing a Khmer music tape at a loud volume and the different passengers exchanging everyday conversation. You may find that as a foreigner you are the center of attention. It's a good place to practice your Khmer language if the road surface and your sanity level allow.

Be it the pickup truck or car variety, they are almost always grossly overloaded with people and goods. Combine this with the bomb-cratered and chewed-up highways throughout the country and you have a good chance of a breakdown en route. It's best to be prepared for the possibility. You can save money riding in the back end of a share taxi pickup truck, but I don't recommend it. The area is crowded with people and goods and the passengers riding here are left to hold onto the sides for dear life as the driver gives them no consideration, driving like a madman around and through chuckholes and other road hazards. Pay the extra money and grab an inside seat.

It gets cramped there as well, as the driver's idea of a seating area is about half of what you would consider a seating spot. It's a good idea to pay extra and buy two spots to give yourself an acceptable level of comfort. Just remember that on the bad roads the ride inside isn't that great either.

Here are some rates for share taxis departing from Phnom Penh. The Coming and Going sections of each provincial chapter have rates and info listed for those particular destinations.

SHARE TAXIS	
Phnom Penh to:	
Udong	5,000 riel
Kampong Chhnang	5,000 riel
Battambang	18,000 riel
Sisophan	23,000 riel
Poipet & the Thai border	28,000 riel
Kampong Thom	4,000 riel
Siem Reap	20,000 riel
Kampong Cham	4,000 riel
Sre Amble	7,000 riel
(for a bullet boat alternative to Koh Kong)	

TRAIN

Some Cambodians are too poor to travel on anything but the train. But many say that they are very happy to take the train because they can see the beautiful scenery of rural Cambodia at a slow pace. Train travel in Cambodia is definitely a community experience . . . The Cambodians get into an almost festive mood on the longer routes and turn the trip into a social event, with plenty of eating and interacting amongst each other going on. You will not be isolated from their socializing, either —you can count on that. Cambodians wanting to practice their English language skills will come over to strike up a conversation, while others try to figure out if you understand Khmer language or simply the human language of smiles, curiousity, and flirting.

The scenery is spectacular at times, much more so on the Phnom Penh to Kampot and Sihanoukville runs, with views of the Dangrei Mountains, rivers and coastal scenery to go along with the endless rice fields and sugar palm trees.

Passenger cars are old and crusty with hard wooden seats and provide the ultimate of luxury to be found on the daily runs. Most people sit in or on the roofs of the boxcars and passenger cars, with the lucky ones finding a place to lay out a hammock to catch some sleep while being rocked by the swaying cars of the train. Riding on the roof of a car is a great way to take in the scenery, but remember that there are some bad sections of track en route so it's a good idea to keep an eye on the cars to the front of you and grab onto a vent pipe or brace yourself for the jolts. Don't try this one at home folks, but since the train moves so slowly and since I've always been a fan of the old Wild West films, I had to try the bit where the character runs across the top of the moving train cars. As you can see, the trip is so long that passengers have loads of time to think up all kinds of stupid situations to get themselves into. It's just another example of the fact that there are very few rules and regulations in Cambodia and like the locals, we foreigners can get ourselves into all kinds of trouble and hurt when left to our own devices. Be careful out there.

There are plenty of vendors at the railway stations along the way so you don't have to bring food and drinks yourself. It's not a bad idea to bring along a flashlight, however, because it will be dark on the train before you get to Sihanoukville or Battambang (and Phnom Penh in the reverse) if you are going to the end of those routes. The continuation of the Phnom Penh to Battambang-Sisophan route commences the following morning after a much needed sleep in Battambang.

A word of warning: Don't stray too far from the train at the stops along the way—even when the locals tell you that the train will be stopped at a station for awhile. I was five minutes into a supposedly one-hour stop in Kampot and walking around the station when the engineer blew the train whistle and took off. I tried the other old Wild West movie stunt of running alongside the train and jumping into the doorway of a passing passenger car, but found that there was a missing door handlebar when I jumped up to pull myself into the train. The Cambodians were cheering me on and having a good bit of fun watching my stunt—a bit too much fun to be able to reach out and help pull me in. I was a flop in that Hollywood stunt, so I was left scrambling at the station in Kampot—looking for and grabbing a moto-taxi and setting off on a 18-km train chase scene—first through Kampot town and then along the coastal road between Kampot and Sihanoukville. After much chasing and maneuvering, the moto-taxi and I were finally able to cut the train off at a pass. The Cambodians on the train were having a real hoot watching this entire event and I think they appreciated the entertainment value that I was giving them—all that fun for the price of one cheap

ticket. They did finally give me a much appreciated round of applause, after I again had run alongside of the moving train and found a couple of guys that yanked me up by my outstretched hand. Who said the train ride has to be boring?

Phnom Penh to Battambang & Sisophan: Departs between 6:20 and 7 am and arrives in Battambang 12 ½ to 14 hours later. The Battambang to Sisophan segment continues from Battambang at 6:45–7:15 the next day and takes about 3 ½ hours (if you are lucky).

Sisophan to Battambang: Departs at around 2:00 pm and the Battambang to Phnom Penh run goes the next day at 6:40–7 am.

Phnom Penh to Kampot & Sihanoukville: Departs at 6:40–7:30 am and arrives in Kampot between 2:30 and 4:30 pm. The train eventually arrives in Sihanoukville 11 ½ to 13 ½ hours after departing from Phnom Penh.

Sihanoukville to Kampot & Phnom Penh: Departs between 6:45 and 7:15 am and gets to Kampot between 10:30 and 11:30 am. It eventually arrives in Phnom Penh probably 11 ½ to 13 ½ hours after departing from Sihanoukville.

All of the above routes are daily.

In direct contrast to everything that travelers in Southeast Asia have become accustomed to, the foreigner is not charged more than the locals for the ticket . . . we are in fact charged nothing! The train service is still so unorganized and unaccustomed to dealing with foreigners wanting to ride on the slow trains that the authorities still have not quite figured out how to handle them. This surely won't and actually should not last forever. It is of course better for the Railway of Cambodia if everyone pays their own way. But get in on one of the few freebees while you can.

CAR RENTAL & TAXI SERVICE

There are no major car rental agencies in Cambodia. Renting a car and driver is cheap enough and you don't have to worry about the traffic. You will find ordinary cars and drivers waiting outside of most hotels. The average charge is US$20–25 a day for car and driver (June of 1999 saw prices quoted at US$20 per day). Hourly rates are about US$5 per hour and that's negotiable, depending upon how many hours you are talking about. Always make sure that the hours and the price are clear to you and the driver before you set out. Don't be afraid to bargain and then to walk away, as there are always more drivers than customers.

CYCLO

A cyclo is a three-wheeled bicycle with a seat for two passengers in the front. Most of the drivers do not speak much English but you can motion with your hands if you know where you want to go. The fare is generally 1,000 to 1,500 riel for a trip, more for a longer distance or time. Showing the driver the amount of money you want to pay is not a bad way to avoid confusion. They are a pleasant and leisurely way to travel. Because they are slow you will have time to view the scenery and people and maybe take a few snapshots. You will see cyclos loaded with entire families. It is definitely a reminder that you are in Indochina as you see them slowly plying the scenic river road in Phnom Penh.

MOTO-TAXI

Motorbike taxis (moto-taxis, motos)—motorcycles with a driver ready to take you around on the back—are the most popular way to get around town. An average trip in town will be about 1,500 riel in Phnom

Penh and 500 riel in the provincial towns. If you are going to make a few stops, rent a moto for about US$5–7 per day (extra added on for the nighttime). The drivers don't always know where they are going, so try to find your destination on a map and follow along as you go or pick out a famous temple or hotel near to where you want to go and give that as the destination. Sometimes even that doesn't work. The motos do not carry helmets for the passenger and I sometimes bring my own. It always takes me a few days or a few drinks to be able to relax riding behind one of these guys. Some drivers speak English well and some do not. If you take one for more than a short trip it's worth it to look a bit to find one who does speak English. If you hire a moto to take you to a bar or restaurant, your driver will want to wait for you. They do want extra for that, so make sure you both understand the final figure if he says he wants to wait for you.

MOTORCYCLE

Riding a motorcycle is the best way to see the country and have an adventure. With the majority of the roads in Cambodia in pretty tough shape, it's easier to get to many areas on a motorcycle which can edge around big craters in the road, whereas a four-wheeled vehicle has to go through them. Small dirt roads to many destinations also favor a motorcycle. It's your best choice if you like independent travel and setting your own agenda.

Motorcycle rental is a wonderful way to see the countryside for day trips. We rented a bike for a week and drove out of Phnom Penh in every direction for a few hours. The roads are good on the way out of town and the traffic is not too bad once you get out. The great advantage to this is that you can stop where and when you want. It is inter-

BIKER CHECKLIST

❏ Spare inner tube
❏ Patch kit
❏ Portable tire pump
❏ Three small tire iron bars
❏ A couple of chain links
❏ Spare clutch cable
❏ Rain gear. Plastic ponchos are inexpensive and available at any market
❏ Plastic bags, large and small, to keep your belongings relatively safe from dust and rain.
❏ Long-sleeved shirt and long pants
❏ Sun screen and mosquito repellent
❏ Helmet
❏ Compass, can opener, instant soup packets, fruit. You can never be sure when you will find the next food stand.
❏ Iodine or water purification tablets
❏ Swiss army knife
❏ Solex padlock. This is the best brand available and better than any lock supplied by the bike rental store. An ounce of prevention… you know the rest.
❏ Clear safety glasses—$3 at the markets
❏ Sunglasses—$3 at the market
❏ Small tool kit to use on a motorcycle trip: key metric wrenches for the simple repairs, screwdrivers, long nose pliers. The rental shop can probably help in this department.

Look in the container attached to your motorcycle for a tool kit. They all originally come with tools. Better find out now what you have.

Spares and parts for big dirt bikes can be difficult to find in many outlying provinces. It's also good preventive maintenance to stop at a motorbike shop and check chain adjustment and have it oiled at least every 200 kilometers.

TWO KEY WORDS TO LIVE BY: SLOW AND CAREFUL.

esting to go down some dirt roads off the main highways and see where they lead. We found old temples and little villages not far from Phnom Penh and every single person we met was friendly and nice. Check out the list of day trips and overnight trips following the Phnom Penh chapter for a number of fun trips on decent roads.

Part of the adventure of road touring around Cambodia, especially by motorcycle, is that the road is almost always somewhat of a challenge. Bomb craters scattered along shredded tarmac highways or rain-soaked slippery clay roads (with the same potholes), are either like a fantasy come true for dirt bike enthusiasts, or a real tiring experience as you travel from one outlying province to the next. You will probably find that you are somewhere in between, enjoying yourself some of the time and just wanting to get your road-weary tail end off of the motorcycle at others. Some roads are so full of craters and potholes that you will find yourself unable to look away from the road to get a glimpse of the scenery. That's why it's best to take your time and stop to enjoy the view now and then.

During the dry season you only have road dust and potholes on the dirt roads to contend with, while during the rainy season the craters along the roads can become big lakes with no way around them. It's impossible not to end up covered in mud. The fighting of the recent decades took a heavy toll on the bridges around the countryside, especially in the north and northwest parts of the country. During the dry season you can usually find an alternative pathway around a missing bridge, but during the rainy season you could find yourself checking the depth of a stream as you try to walk or float your bike across.

The adventure motorcycle trips to the regions with particularly bad roads are best done during the dry season. It's just too much extra work in the rainy season. You will have your hands full enough without having to contend with lakes in the road and slick mud and clay that fill up your motorcycle's drive train. This does not mean that you can't head to interesting destinations by motorcycle during the rainy season. Check out the Motorcycle Touring Info section of each province destination throughout the book for detailed road reports. It's all part of the adventure in Cambodia.

Motorcycle Rental

As for renting a motorcycle, don't do it if you are not an experienced rider with good defensive driving skills and a lot of patience. Traffic in Cambodia (especially in Phnom Penh) is crazy and unpredictable, with vehicles and motorcycles coming at you from all directions, including what is supposed to be your lane of traffic. People turn into your lane at full speed without looking for traffic and don't give a second thought to cutting right out in front of you if they want to drive across the street. There are lanes within lanes, as it's common practice for people to drive down the street the wrong way. It's like a wild video game that you are a part of and the faster you go, the faster the rest of the video game goes.

Check to see if the odometer is working before you go too far. Many shops disconnect them to keep the mileage down. It is easy for the shop to reconnect if you ask them and you will need to see how far you have traveled to accurately use the directions in this guidebook.

There are basically three types of rental bikes to choose from:

1. Small 100-cc motor scooters that do not have a clutch and may be easier for a first-time driver. However Phnom Penh is no place to start driving; save it for the beach.

2. Street motorcycles that have comfortable seats and soft suspension. These are fine for around town or traveling if you are sure that the roads will be well paved.

3. Off-trail bikes, also called dirt bikes or moto-cross bikes. You will recognize these by the knobby tires and exhaust pipes that go over the rear axle. This is so water does not get into your exhaust pipes when you ride across a stream. The suspension is stiff and the ride is a bit hard but it's the only kind of motorcycle that you want to have for country travel, and it's probably the best choice for Phnom Penh as well. We recommend a 250-cc size. It has all the power you need and will be easier to pick up or push if you have to do it. Make sure you rent one that has an electric starter. It's easier if the bike dies in traffic or on a muddy hill in the boondocks.

With rentals, you are required to deposit your passport. I've never heard of anyone having problems with their passport as a result of this. If you need to use the passport to go to the bank, just head to the rental outfit and they will bring you to the bank with your passport, free of charge. It's a good idea to make copies of the passport front page and Cambodian visa section in case you need to have it for something.

It's also a good idea to buy your own Solex padlock at any market. They take about an hour to cut through, as opposed to about two minutes for the ones that you get from the motorcycle rental shops.

To get an idea of what to bring on a long distance bike trip in Cambodia, check the Biker Checklist.

For motorcycle rentals, try:

Lucky! Lucky! Located at 413 Monivong Blvd., three doors down from the Hong Kong Hotel in Phnom Penh, this rental shop is personally recommended for honesty and service. Mr. Lucky and his side kick Kid Lucky are a couple of nice guys who offer good service and are flexible in helping you equip the bike for trips. They can help throw together a tool kit and have ideas if you want to "trick a bike out" for a trip.

The small bikes are US$4 a day, or US$3 a day for a week or more. Dirt bikes, street bikes or 250-cc bikes are US$7 a day, US$6 a day for a week or more, or US$160 per month. Just ask for the "Mr. Lucky Special."

For motorcycle sales and repairs, check out this shop:

Flying Bikes Shop. They have many different varieties of new and used dirt bikes for sale for those who will be in Cambodia for a while. Ask for the owner, Chove, a very helpful gentleman. ☎ (012) 841-567, (023) 210-765. Located on Street 114 (Pochentong Blvd.) between Norodom and Monivong Blvds.

For group touring, try this:

Angkor Dirt Bike Tours. This outfit has done a couple of annual adventure trips taking in some of the beautiful scenery that Cambodia has to offer. The trips are completely organized by a friendly, long-time motorcycle enthusiast and resident in Cambodia, who rides along with the group. Previous rides have gone to Rattanikiri and Mondulkiri provinces, among other places. The proposed ride for December of 2000 will take in the Preah Vihear mountain temple next to the Thai border, stopping at other spots en route. Those interested in more information can contact Ben by e-mail at:<angkordirtbiketours@hotmail.com>.

PHNOM PENH

Sitting on the western edge of the confluence of the Mekong, Sap and Basak Rivers in Kandal Province, Phnom Penh is a beautiful city in the heart of Indochina. Attractive French colonial architecture and wide tree-lined boulevards blend beautifully with the Asian features of the city, such as its lovely Buddhist temples featuring Khmer-style architecture that dot the entire skyline of the city. And unlike other Asian capitals, in Phnom Penh the skyline is free of the cluttered mess of high-rise buildings that detract from the original beauty of other, more modern, cities in Southeast Asia.

Also blending in smoothly with this Indochina potpourri of culture and style are the Royal Palace compound and the royal boat landing facing the Sap and Mekong Rivers directly in front of the palace in the old district of the city. Cyclos gliding slowly along the coconut tree-lined River Parkway complete the scene. It is almost as if Phnom Penh traveled through a time warp and landed squarely back in its idyllic years of the 1960s. The simple lifestyle of the people, the pace of the city and the unabashedly cheesy style of Cambodian entertainment and television shows only add to the feeling that this place really does not belong to the modern-day world. And it's this feeling that captivates and brings back many a visitor.

To be sure, Phnom Penh's recent past was anything but idyllic and much of the city gives testament to the seemingly endless years of turmoil that it endured. Just a quick turn off the charming River Boulevard can often land you right in the middle of an area that is a scene from the war years of the past, with crumbling pot-holed roads and filthy-looking dilapidated buildings surrounding you. The horror and terror that gripped Phnom Penh and its residents is a bit easier to imagine when one comes upon these yet-to-be-renovated areas of the city, of which there are many.

Buildings, roadways and infrastructure have been slowly but surely given a facelift, bit by bit and piece by piece. For returning visitors there always seems to be some new surprise in the form of an improvement, addition, or renovation project. This is just another exciting feature of visiting Phnom Penh and Cambodia in general—one is able to witness a city and country on the rebound and on the move.

There are plenty of sights and activities to keep you busy during the daytime in Phnom Penh, and the night scene is very fun indeed. And don't forget to check the next chapter on day trips from Phnom Penh when you are looking for something a bit more adventurous. The trips give you the opportunity to sample the flavor of rural Cambodia and its people.

A LOOK AT PHNOM PENH'S HISTORY

The Angkor empire had already been on the decline for some time before it was finally abandoned in the first half of the 15th century in favor of Phnom Penh (and Udong at various times). The Thais (Siamese at that time) turned the tables on the Khmers and became a dominant force constantly giving the kings of Angkor much more than they could contend with. Ditto for the Vietnamese. Northwest Cambodia turned out not only to be a difficult place to defend, but strategically speaking, not well connected to regional trading routes. Phnom Penh's

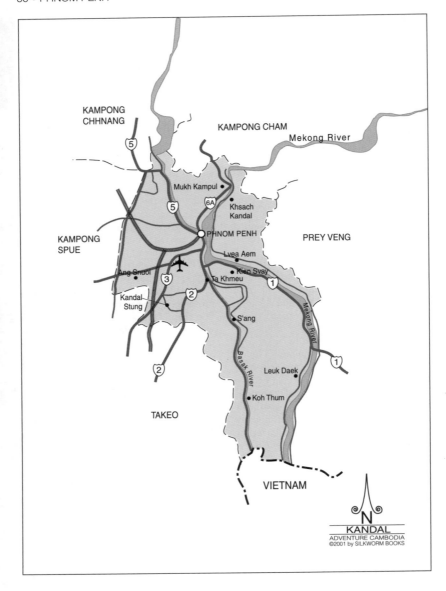

location at the confluence of three rivers provided much better access all the way around, with Vietnam and the South China Sea to the southeast via the Mekong and Basak Rivers, Laos and China to the north on the Mekong River, and The Great Lake Tonle Sap and Thailand (Siam) just beyond. By the 16th century, Phnom Penh had become a major trading hub in Southeast Asia.

Problems with the now more powerful Siamese and Vietnamese continued. However, as history has since shown, they were merely a precursor of what was to come, as Cambodia was caught in the middle of these opposing regional powers, not only then, but all the way up to modern-day history.

The French became the administrative and actual power in Cambodia in 1863 and the ensuing colonial period was positive in one respect, as the country was then fairly well protected from problems with its neighbors. Phnom Penh again thrived, but there were, of course, troubles arising from the colonial arrangement. Cambodia finally gained independence in 1953 and King Sihanouk played the key role in steering the country through a time of turmoil in the region.

Unfolding regional problems in the form of the Vietnam War and a radical communist guerilla movement finally caught up with Phnom Penh (and the whole of Cambodia) and after many bloody years of battle against the Khmer Rouge, Phnom Penh finally fell to them on 17 April 1975. Phnom Penh was virtually stripped of population and ceased to exist as a city from 1975 to 1979, as the Khmer Rouge sacked the city and force-marched all of its residents into the countryside to begin an ill-conceived experiment to form the country into a communist-inspired agrarian Utopia. Some Utopia.

Following Vietnam's unceremonious ousting of the Khmer Rouge regime in 1979, Cambodians began pouring back into the ghost town and began the mammoth job of making Phnom Penh livable once again. Phnom Penh has struggled long and hard, but it's looking pretty good these days and the future appears bright.

WHAT'S UP

The capital of Cambodia certainly has no shortage of sights to see and things to do. Take a peek at the following and see what strikes your fancy.

Royal Palace

The Royal Palace is a large walled compound with its entrance on Sothearos Blvd. between Streets 184 and 240. The palace is open every day except Monday from 8 to 11 am and from 2 to 5 pm. Visitors are not allowed into some portions of the grounds, as the palace is the official residence of King Sihanouk, but lately the palace guards have allowed visitors to walk through vast areas of the palace grounds which were closed to the public before. Admission is US$3 and another US$2 to bring in a camera. If you do not want to pay the US$2 for your camera, they will want to hold it at the ticket office (unless you just put it in your pocket beforehand). The charge for the use of a video camera is US$5.

Inside the Royal Palace compound are the Chan Chaya Pavillion once used for classical dances and the Throne Hall which is still used for coronations, state anniversaries, and other official ceremonies. The walls of the Throne Hall are painted with scenes from the Ramayana story.

The Napoleon III Pavilion was built and presented as a gift to King Norodom in the 1870s by the wife of Napoleon III.

Silver Pagoda

The Silver Pagoda has a floor covered with over five thousand decorated silver tiles, each one weighing over one kilogram, for a total of more than five tons. It was built by King Norodom in 1892 and rebuilt by King Sihanouk in 1962. Lining the walls in glass cases are dozens of expensive gifts given to Cambodia's kings and heads of state. There is also an extraordinary collection of valuable Khmer artwork, including colorful jeweled masks and gold Buddhas. The Silver Pagoda holds a life-sized gold Buddha covered with 9,584 diamonds, some as large as twenty-four carats.

The beautifully landscaped grounds hold many other interesting statues and buildings, such as a library, an image of what is supposed to be a huge footprint of Buddha, a bell tower and a statue of King Norodom on horseback that makes him look remarkably French. The compound walls are painted with a large mural, over one hundred years old, telling the story of the Ramayana. It's in a bit of disrepair but is still beautiful.

National Museum

The National Museum is also on Sothearos Blvd a few blocks to the north. It's open every day except Monday from 8 to 11:30 am and then from 2 to 5:30 pm. Admission is US$2. Photographs are not permitted. Many fine postcards and books about the art on exhibit are for sale in the lobby. Open rooms that branch off from a large open courtyard in the middle of the building house many fine artifacts, carved stonework and statues. French- and English-speaking guides are available, as is a pamphlet for US$3 with stories and illustrations about the art on display. The collection available for viewing is quite impressive and the place is definitely worth a visit.

There has been quite a bit of concern about the large population of bats living in the roof of the museum. It is estimated that this is the largest bat population living in a building (maybe in the world) and is thought to be almost 2 million. They drop a tremendous amount of guano every day, with some of it falling on the art work. It takes many man-hours to pick up the bat guano (I wonder how much this job pays?), but the guano is very valuable fertilizer and is sold to help care for the museum!

Tuol Sleng Museum

Street 113 just north of Street 350. Open every day from 7 to 11:30 am and then from 2 to 5 pm. Admission is US$2. Guides are available to take you through for a charge of a few dollars. They are well worth hiring for the full story of this infamous place of torture. In 1975 the Khmer Rouge turned Toul Svay Prey High School into a prison. Over twenty thousand men, women and children were held and tortured here and then taken to the Choeung Ek fields to be killed. An average of a hundred people a day were murdered in this fashion. This figure includes several westerners from Australia, France and America. Their photographs and "confessions" are on display. Everyone was photographed and then tortured. The more important prisoners had their own rooms; others were chained together on the second and third floors. The outside hallways were fenced with barbed wire to prevent the prisoners from throwing themselves off. The prison held teachers, educators, artists, doctors and any other educated persons. When close members of Pol Pot's regime objected to the horrors, they themselves were put in there. There were only seven people left alive when the Vietnamese Army liberated the prison and these prisoners were artists sculpting busts of Pol Pot and drawing pictures. Instruments of torture are on display along with walls and walls of photographs of the prisoners. You can expect to be very disturbed by the experience of seeing this museum.

The "Killing Fields" of Choeung Ek

A visit to Choeung Ek, like Toul Sleng, is an interesting and anything but uplifting experience. Almost twenty thousand people were killed here with a shovel or ax blow to the back of the neck and were buried in over a hundred and twenty mass graves. Today you can see the burial depressions in the earth, with bits of clothing sticking up. A glass case displays over eight thousand skulls. Displays feature photos of some of the victims and plaques telling a bit of the gruesome history of the Khmer Rouge holocaust. Although this is the spot everyone usually thinks about when they hear the phrase "the killing fields," the entire country was virtually one big "killing field" and every town and village throughout the country had its own area where locals were executed and buried.

Admission is US$2. To get there, head southwest from Mao Tse Toung Blvd. on Samdech Monireth Blvd., cross the bridge and continue on. At 1 km past the bridge you come to a fork in the road (with a Sokimex fuel station in the middle of it). Go left. At 7 km past the bridge is a metal arch gate on the left that reads "Choeung Ek Genocidal Center." Turn left for the center.

Landmarks from the "Killing Fields"

Le Royal Hotel. Phnom Penh's contingent of international journalists and photographers covering the civil war in Cambodia became virtual prisoners inside the hotel's compound during that fateful April of 1975, when the Khmer Rouge were pounding Phnom Penh with every type of artillery at their disposal during their final push into the city. Many terrified residents of Phnom Penh sought refuge from the battles at Le Royal, and the swimming pool area was overflowing with these people, along with journalists and other hotel guests. Closed for a number of years, the place was given a massive facelift by The Raffles Group a few years ago. The hotel has since been open for business and is a fine example of Phnom Penh's colonial architecture. It is located along Monivong Boulevard, just west of Wat Phnom.

The French Embassy. The French Embassy is on Monivong Blvd. just up the street from Le Royal Hotel. When the Khmer Rouge marched into Phnom Penh in 1975, about 800 foreigners and 600 Cambodians sought shelter here. The Khmer Rouge demanded the surrender of the Cambodians in exchange for the safety of the foreigners. The Cambodians were turned over to the KR and never heard from again. This story is graphically told in the movie "The Killing Fields."

Independence Monument (Victory Monument)

At the intersection of Norodom Blvd. and Preah Sihanouk Blvd., this was built in 1958 as a memorial to Cambodia's war dead. Various ceremonies are held here, including the celebration of Cambodia's independence from France. It's in the middle of a huge traffic circle, which is shut down during state ceremonies.

Cambodia-Vietnam Soldiers Monument & "Democracy Square"

Smaller-scale monuments were erected in many cities across the country during the ten-year Vietnamese occupation (or Vietnamese-puppet Cambodian government), following the defeat of the Khmer Rouge regime. These monuments are a constant reminder of the resentment that most Cambodians have for the Vietnamese for overstaying their welcome by ten years—that's on top of the ancient hostilities.

Later, demonstrators protesting the results of the election of July 1998 took over the park and dubbed it "Democracy Square," while they camped out there for weeks. Opposition figures gave speeches to the thousands that massed at the park on a daily basis, until finally, later that fall, the demonstration was crushed and swept aside by the ruling party (who won the suspect elections) that was the subject of the demonstrations. Bulldozers were then quickly moved in and the makeshift buildings that the demonstrators had put up were razed and a major project to give the park a facelift got underway. Admittedly, the results of the park project look nice, soldier's monument and all.

The park was also near the scene of a deadly grenade attack at the National Assembly building just across the street. The attack, directed at opposition figure Sam Rainsy on 30 March 1997, killed 19 people and wounded scores of others. Lifeless bodies and moaning victims lay along the boulevard and in the park. Almost all political demonstrations in Phnom Penh take place at or pass by this area.

Olympic Stadium

The Olympic Stadium is near the intersection of Monireth Blvd. and Prea Sihanouk Blvd. It was actually built for the 1966 Asian Games, which Cambodia hosted. The grounds are not locked and you can run to the top of the stairs, taking the same path as the torchbearers. It helps the atmosphere immensely if you play the theme from the movie "Rocky" on your Walkman. During the Sihanouk regime, sports flourished in Cambodia and the teams were very competitive with the rest of Asia. The national soccer team won a silver medal at those games in 1966.

The Olympic-size swimming pool and diving platforms are open to the public. The cost is US$2. Pool hours are 6 am to 6 pm daily, except Monday and Friday mornings.

There are tennis courts on the grounds and the hourly court fee is US$2. Racquets are rented at US$3 an hour. Hours are 5:30 am to 6:30 pm. Stop by the tennis office or phone: (018) 810-040.

Jogging on the Olympic-size track is also okay.

Naga Dive gives scuba-diving lessons at the pool. ☎ (023) 365-102 or (012) 807-922.

Boat Rentals

Take a tour around Phnom Penh and beyond on the Sap, Mekong and Basak Rivers. The cost is a negotiable US$8–10 per hour for the boat and they are flexible as to where you can go. You will see a couple of small English-lettered signs reading "Boat For Rent" on the north end of the river parkway, near the boulevard that cuts west to the train station.

Chaktomuk Theater

Located on the river road, north of the Cambodiana Hotel, this theater occasionally features performances of the National Classical Dance Troupe. Check the big board outside for details. Admission is US$3.

River Scene & the Phnom Penh Promenade

The River Parkway on the Phnom Penh side of the Sap River is a picturesque, pleasant stretch of road and you would be hard pressed to find anything as nice in any other city of Southeast Asia. It's a great place for a stroll or jog, with interesting things to view on and next to the river. Fishermen and women are out on the river all day long, working their nets and hand-rowing their small wooden fishing boats, trying to catch fish for the family and to sell at the market. The river scene is very placid and undeveloped and gives this part of Phnom Penh a small-town feel. But the scene changes each day as the late afternoon merges with the early evening hours and the area becomes the scene of the "Phnom Penh Promenade." Loads of drink and food stands, offering everything from corn-on-the-cob to beer, set up at this time along an almost horseshoe-looking stretch that starts at and takes in Sihanouk Blvd. to the south and goes eastward to the side and rear area of the Cambodiana Hotel, then follows the River Parkway (Preah Sisovath) north and finally cuts west to the Wat Phnom park area.

It's a festive and fairly cool part of the day when Cambodians love to *"Doh Dah-layng"* (Go for Fun!) and head over to this part of town on cyclos, motorcycles, in cars, or just walking to see and be seen by everyone. It's in full swing seven days a week, but becomes particularly frenzied on weekends. The Royal Palace Park and Royal Boat Landing are main focal points and kids tear around the place playing games and having fun with their families. As in small towns of the Old West and the "Traveling Medicine Shows" that took their shady act and products to them, Cambodian touts set up at a couple of spots along the river, complete with loudspeakers, and jabber their pitch at mile-a-minute speed, trying to

River Boulevard in Phnom Penh

arouse interest among the spectators who circle around them. It's all great entertainment and it's free. Some visitors and foreign residents of Phnom Penh join in the fun, others just find a watering hole or restaurant along the parkway, kick back and get a real fill of people-watching.

The Peninsula (Chruoy Chang War)

This is the landmass that you see from the Phnom Penh side of the river. It's entertaining to ride around and explore and gives one a bit of a feel for life out in the provinces. The view of Phnom Penh is nice from here as well. Fishermen live in the villages over there and the Cham people, who are Muslims, live in harmony with the Buddhist Khmers who share the area. There is a mosque at the south end of the peninsula and also a strange-looking newer temple nearby.

The Boat Temple, Wat Araik-saht, was opened for business, amid much celebration and fanfare, a couple of years ago. The temple was built so that it appears to sit on a boat, which is complete with painted eyes on each side of the bow—something Khmers do with many of their boats as it's supposed to keep watch over those water spirits that are always lurking about. There is a picture of the king and queen on the ship's deck and images of water, water spirits and crocodiles to complete the scene.

To get there, cross the Japanese Bridge and take the first left that you can after you pass over the bridge. This comes back sharply to the river road, where you take a left and follow this all the way down, past the villages and to the temple on the right. On the south side of the temple is a small dirt road that you can take out to the confluence of the Mekong and Sap Rivers, almost directly across the river from the Royal Palace and Boat Landing. There's a nice view and it's a great place to watch the finish line action during the boat races of the "Water Festival."

There are plenty of cold drink stands around the peninsula.

Kin S'vay

Just outside of Phnom Penh on National Highway 1 is the picnic area of Kin S'vay. Located on a small tributary of the Mekong River, this is a popular spot with the locals, who rent bamboo stands and shacks built alongside and out over the river. Lots of Khmer food, BBQ fish and chicken, and plenty of cold drinks is the order of the day. Most people just while the day away talking and playing cards, but there are small rowboats to take those interested on a tour of the river area. The cost is 4,000 riel, which includes the person doing the rowing. It's easy to be a real sloth here. Some people swim here, but it looks a bit too skunky for me. There are also jet-skis for rent. For those interested in scouting around, the small bridge that you see from the picnic area takes you down to a huge meadow overlooking the Mekong River. There are also some brothels along the river banks to entertain picnic merry-makers. In a strange little story that appeared in the *Cambodia Daily* newspaper, a picnicker got more than he bargained for while lazing the day away, sitting on a small river hut and eating a BBQ fish. Like many Asians, he liked to eat the stomach of the fish, and he noticed that he had a particularly chewy piece in his mouth that just would not break apart. Finally growing weary of the tasty but unmanageable morsel, he pulled it out of his mouth and was shocked to find that it wasn't a part of the fish's stomach, but rather a condom! The fish apparently lived in the surrounding waters and had been caught fresh that day. And the moral of our little story for the day: Stay away from those fish stomachs!

To get to Kin Svay, set your odometer at the Monivong Bridge traffic circle and head out on Highway 1. At just over 11 km from the circle, you come to a sign on the left announcing the "Japanese BBQ Restaurant Tagoshi," where you turn left and go on to the T in the road. Turn right and after 200 meters you see the Japanese restaurant, but continue on and there will be locals on the road touting for their river huts next to the road. If you continue on you will eventually see on the left the small bridge mentioned earlier and just beyond that, on the left, are some decent picnic spots. Check on all prices before you rent, or you may be handed an outrageous bill at the end. The area is fairly quiet during the week, but fills up on weekends.

Takhmau River Area

Going south 4 km from the same traffic circle we just mentioned (near the Monivong Bridge), you come to a fork in the road, where you veer to the right. You then come into the town of Takhmau and following the same road you come to a traffic circle (just under 6 km from the Monivong Bridge traffic circle). Take a left turn here (a sharp left takes you back to the town market) and you end up at the Basak River and River Parkway. There are drink and snack stands lining this quiet and scenic stretch and there is a small ferry you can take across, with your motorcycle, to explore around the Cham villages. It's just a few hundred riel for you and your motorcycle.

Once again, flip to the following chapter, Day Trips from Phnom Penh, for some pretty cool and easy trips, complete with all the details.

Wats (Temples)

Wat Phnom. Wat Phnom is on top of a small hill north of the city that the city was named after, along with, according to popular Khmer legend, a lady named Penh. Penh, as the legend goes, was bathing and washing her clothing along the banks of the Sap River (near its confluence with the Mekong) when she spotted four Buddha images that had floated downstream and landed against the river bank. She took them to this nearby hill, where the wat was eventually built to house them. Phnom means hill or mountain in Khmer, hence the name Wat Phnom or literally, Temple Hill. The city was also supposedly named after this temple and this lady, hence the name Phnom Penh. The hill and its temple are at the far north end of Norodom Boulevard.

The wat and surrounding park recently received a massive facelift. The results were quite good and the structures and beautifully landscaped area on and around the temple hill are once again a landmark that Cambodians can be proud of.

A long staircase leads up to the temple with cement snakes and lions on the banister. There is much to see here: a stupa containing the ashes of King Ponhea Yat, a statue of Madame Penh, a statue of Vishnu and other small shrines and statues. There are many food and cold drink stands, souvenir stalls and even elephant rides in the surrounding park, which is centered in the middle of a huge traffic circle. It's a favorite spot for locals on weekends and holidays and one of the spots passed by on the Phnom Penh Promenade.

The park and traffic circle used to be dark at night and were once prime places for armed robbery. At one time you didn't even have to walk in the park—just drive by and someone would step out of the shadows with a gun and wave you over, or two armed riders teamed on a motorcycle would park in the dark area and go after passersby. There seemed to be a contest between the bad guys and the off-duty police and military (most think they are one and the same) as to who

could perpetrate the most crimes. There were so many complaints by the embassies and tourists that the city government finally put in a large number of streetlights and at times, uniformed police, with the favorable result that robberies around the circle went way down.

Wat Ounalom. This temple is the headquarters of the Cambodian Buddhist Society. The large compound is on Sisowath Quay. Visitors are welcome. It was founded in 1443 and holds forty-four buildings. Set along the banks of the Sap River, it's a beautiful place, and more so during Buddhist holidays when it's one of the main centers of festivities in Phnom Penh.

Wat Langka. This temple is on Preah Sihanouk Blvd. by the Independence Monument. The building and adjoining stupas were repaired along with most wats after the demise of the Khmer Rouge. You may visit the grounds and buildings that house the school for new monks.

Wat Than. Wat Than is on Norodom Blvd. south of the Victory Monument on the left side of the street. King Sihanouk has visited and prayed here many times, and his son, Prince Ranariddh, took a respite from his job as first prime minister of Cambodia at one time, shaved his head and spent a week in the monkhood. On the rear of the grounds is a rehab center for mine victims who make and sell the handicrafts on sale in a small shop near the entrance gate to the temple. It's well worth a visit and you will make merit by purchasing an item.

Wat Koh. Wat Koh is on Monivong Blvd. between Streets 174 and 178. It's one of the oldest wats in the city and has a small lake on its grounds.

Wat Prayuvong. This temple is down a small road off of Norodom Blvd. on the left-hand side going south from the Independence Monument. It is before you arrive at Wat Than and you will recognize it by the large number of Buddhas and statues lined up alongside the sidewalk. There is a whole little industry on the nearby side road and many workshops making all kinds and sizes of statues. You can walk along the dirt road and possibly purchase a Buddha image directly from the source.

MARKETS AND SHOPPING

Markets in Cambodia are not what you might expect to find, coming from a modern country or even next-door Bangkok, which is turning into one enormous modern shopping plaza. Markets are still very old-style in Cambodia, another of those throwbacks in time that we spoke of earlier. Until just recently, there was not one real indoor shopping plaza or mall in all of Cambodia (and the new one hardly qualifies by Western or Thai standards). The markets here are big sprawling outdoor affairs with some kind of enclosure or partial enclosure for walls and ceiling, whether it's corrugated metal, wood or cement. They are usually fairly tacky looking, but having said all of that, I like them and they are a lot of fun for visiting westerners not used to taking a step back into time in Indochina. And if you are a fan of garage sales or flea markets, you may think that you have died and gone to heaven.

Cyclo driver

Central Market. This place goes by three names: P'sah T'mai to the Khmers, New Market (same name, but in English) and of course, Central Market. It's in the center of town and the big yellow art deco building is hard to miss. It has a domed center hall and four large extensions filled with small booths. Everything from gold and jewelry to electronics shops and Khmer checkered scarves to souvenirs and T-shirts, it's all here and on a large scale. And as in all markets in Cambodia, bargaining is expected. Don't buy anything without shopping around and trying your negotiating skills first. Start at a price that is much lower than you want to pay. Then both parties work their way to a middle ground. Don't be afraid to walk away; you can always come back, and many times they call out for you to come back and settle for your price when they see you leaving. Of course speak softly and be polite. I bought a pocket calculator here three years ago for US$2.50 and it's still working fine. On the outside of the market are stands selling fresh fruit, meat, vegetables, flowers, fish and cooked foods. Many stands sell used clothing. It is rumored that this clothing was sent to the Cambodian people by charitable organizations in the United States but somehow got diverted and sold instead. I picked up a tie from Gimbels—a store in New York City that has been closed for over thirty years—so yes, some of the stuff really does come from donations. This is also the all-time favorite place for beggars, most of them amputees who can be a bit aggressive. It's a good place to pick up a moto-taxi. The market is on an island in the center of a traffic circle. The stores on the opposite sides of the street are interesting and sell a variety of items, mainly electronics and jewelry.

Russian Market—P'sah Tuol Tom Pong. This is a huge covered market a block square, located south of Mao Tse Toung

Blvd., at Streets 440 and 163. It may actually have some genuine antiques, but for sure it has many very good reproductions. You will see gems and silver jewelry, foot-high old cast-iron soldiers painted or coated in silver/pewter for about US$30. Serving spoons and forks with large decorated handles made from silver/pewter. Many carved wood Buddhas and stone statues. Bolts of woven silk and other fabrics. Electronics, tapes and CDs. I did buy a Madonna CD that looked great but turned out to be an Asian woman who did not even know all of the lyrics. Some stands will let you try the tapes first. The market also has food stands and soup stalls.

This market is loosely divided into sections: hardware, fabrics, antiques and so on. The Russian Market has always been famous for selling marijuana at rock-bottom prices, but police have recently cracked down on the activity. It used to be that one would see the stuff being sold by the brick and in pre-rolled cigarettes, out in the open and usually stacked on top of the tourist T-shirts. Now the vendors say the police have told them to knock off on the grass sales. It's still very easy to find in Phnom Penh for those looking for it.

Old Market. *P'sah cha*, the old market, is at Streets 108 and 13, just a block in from the river. This is a large outdoor market that has stationery stalls, new, used and name-brand knock off clothes, sunglasses, bread, fruits and vegetables. Many food stands branch out from here and the dirt paths become a bit cluttered with debris.

Orussey Market. This one is on the corner of Streets 182 and 111. It's very popular with the Cambodians because they claim prices are a bit cheaper. It's a big sprawling Cambodian affair selling electronics, stereos, imported canned foods, and luxury toiletries. This market and almost all

of the markets have food stands branching out in all directions.

Olympic Market. This market is near the Olympic stadium between Streets 193 and 199 and it sells motorcycle helmets and parts, bicycle parts, clothes, electronics, along with everything else you can think of.

Parkway Square. This is the only "new-style" shopping mall in Cambodia, but it probably wouldn't get too far in another country. Anyway, it's a welcome addition. A Lucky Supermarket and Lucky Burger are in the mall, along with a fitness center and swimming pool. There is also the "Hollywood Nightclub" and a decent Chinese food restaurant on the third floor.

At a golf driving range on the roof you can hit a bucket of 80 balls for US$4.

A bowling alley and a cheap-food court are also inside.

Prayuvong Buddha Factories. These were mentioned earlier and are near Street 308 on the eastern side of Norodom Blvd., about a kilometer south of the Independence Monument. Turn down the street and you will come upon a whole village of craftsmen.

Custom T-shirts. On the other side of Norodom are two stores that print signs and T-shirts. You can buy plain T-shirts there or bring your own and have some clever wording, design or phrase put on a shirt for a dollar or two, depending on the quantity you want to have. Be sure to price both stores.

Souvenirs, Paintings and Silver Shops. There are many small silver and souvenir shops all over Phnom Penh. You will find them across the street from the Cambodiana Hotel, on and around Street 178 near the National Museum, near the Lucky Supermarket on Sihanouk Blvd. and all along Monivong Blvd. Bargaining is a must at all of the shops.

Western Food

To satisfy those cravings for familiar foods and products, try one of these markets:

Lucky Market, on Sihanouk Blvd. between Norodom and Monivong Blvds. has a large selection of fresh and frozen foods, ice cream, cakes, and breads and a large selection of wines and cheeses, magazines and newspapers, and canned goods. There is a clothing store upstairs and a hamburger stand right next door.

Bayon Market at 133 Monivong Blvd, across the street from the City Central hotel is smaller but has a nice selection of canned delicacies and wines, among other items.

Thai Huot Market, just north of Bayon Market, on the same side of the street. This one is a bit smaller yet and features a similar line of foods and products.

You Nam Supermarket, on the south side of Kampuchea Krom Blvd., about four blocks west of Monivong Blvd.

Star Mart Mini-Marts, at Caltex Gas Stations, popping up all over town. They feature a small range of Western food products and the junk food that we all love to hate.

KEEPING FIT & KNOCKING AROUND

Swimming Pools, Health Clubs & More

Phnom Penh can get pretty toasty during the dry season. Fortunately there are several places to cool off. Several of these pool sites also offer fitness facilities.

The International Youth Club. Located on the Parkway, just west of Wat Phnom, on Street 96, it has a large swimming pool, fitness facilities and tennis courts. They have daily rates and rates for longer periods.

Olympic Stadium. Already mentioned in the What's Up section. It's US$2 to use the Olympic-size pool and diving platforms.

The Intercontinental Hotel. Located on Mao Tse Toung Blvd. near Monireth Blvd., it has a swimming pool and fitness facilities.

The Cambodiana Hotel. Located on Sisovath Parkway (the river road), it features a swimming pool overlooking the confluence of the Mekong and Sap Rivers.

Le Royal Hotel. Located just off of Monivong Blvd., on the parkway to Wat Phnom (Street 92), they have a swimming pool and fitness center.

Parkway Square. This new mall also has a swimming pool and fitness center. It's located on Mao Tse Toung Blvd. near Street 173. There's also a golf driving range on the roof and bowling lanes inside.

Taillal Fitness Center. Located at 53 Street 178, they offer a complete workout facility, but no swimming pool.

L'Imprevue. This is a small French resort located about 7 km from the Monivong Bridge, on Highway 1. They have a swimming pool, tennis courts, mini-golf course, pool table and more. There are also bungalows to rent and a poolside restaurant.

Phnom Penh Bowling

This place has bowling lanes and snooker tables and is located 50 meters in from Monivong Blvd., on Street 294.

Pool Tables

Free pool tables (with a drink or something to eat) are available at:

Sharky Bar. 126 Street 130 (just east of Norodom Blvd.)

Sunway Hotel. On the Wat Phnom Parkway (Street 92), near Wat Phnom

Elephant Bar. Le Royal Hotel, on the Wat Phnom Parkway (Street 92), near Monivong

Pink Elephant Bar. The River Parkway, just north of Street 178

Heart of Darkness Bar. 26 Street 51 (Pasteur St.)

Walkabout Hotel. The corner of Streets 51 and 174

Cathouse. The corner of Streets 63 and 118.

Jet Skiing

Alligator Ski-Club. Just over the Japanese Bridge, 1.7 km, and turn right after the Caltex gas station, near Wat Klean Klang and the sign. ☎ (012) 835-850.

Go-Cart Race Track

Ta Prohm. Head out over the Monivong Bridge just over 7 km from the Monivong Bridge traffic circle and turn right at the corner Shell gas station. The racetrack is 100 meters down on the left. A ten-minute race is US$3, and if you go alone, the staff is happy to jump in another car and give you someone to race with. They also have fishing ponds there and rent out rods and reels for US$5 an hour. There is a restaurant as well.

Kambol F1. Located 8 km past Pochentong Airport on Highway 4 (towards Sihanoukville) and turn right where you see their sign.

Shooting Ranges

With the stated intention of cutting down on violent crime, the government announced that they were closing down all shooting ranges in Phnom Penh. There still seems to be a clandestine range operating (with government knowledge, of course) and the guesthouse and hotel moto-taxi guys know right where it is.

Golf Courses

Golfing is fairly pricey in Cambodia, but if you want to golf, you have only two places to tee up at. Both are located off of Highway 4, heading towards Sihanoukville. Here are directions using the front gate at Pochentong Airport for an odometer reading.

The Royal Cambodia Phnom Penh Golf Club. This new club and course has a billboard marking where you turn right off of Highway 4 (4 km from the airport gate). Follow the dirt road down another 4 km to the clubhouse. They rent out shoes and clubs and have a restaurant on the premises.

Cambodia Golf & Country Club. Keep heading towards Sihanoukville on Highway 4 and turn left where you see the big golf ball (22 km from the airport gate). They also have clubs and shoes for rent and have a restaurant on the premises.

Moto-Cross Track

Just across the Japanese Bridge (on the south side of the road) is a moto-cross track for city-bound dirt-bikers. If you're not city-bound, head out on a trip to the faraway provinces. The entire countryside is like one non-stop moto-cross track out there.

Casinos

If you get the urge to give others your money, there are two casinos in town.

Naga Floating Casino sets its anchor behind the Cambodiana Hotel.

Holiday Casino is located in the Holiday Hotel complex on Street 84, just east of Monivong.

Cinema Halls

Another sign of Cambodia's place back in time is the lack of English-language movie theaters. A couple of places have tried to open, but they just haven't been able to survive. These small places show video movies. If it is not already scheduled, you can request your choice.

Mittaheap Hotel. Located on the first floor of the hotel (Monivong Blvd. and Street 174), they have regularly scheduled movies that change daily.

Parkway Square. The fitness center also has a selection of video movies that you can request be played just for you. The cost is included in your workout pass fee. Some workout! Located on Mao Tse Toung Blvd. and Street 173.

International Youth Club. Movies are shown here every day at 8 pm, with a different movie shown each day. They are located on the parkway (Street 96), just west of Wat Phnom.

FCCC. They feature a film on occasion. Check in at the restaurant's bulletin board for details. Located along the river road at Street 178.

Each Friday *The Cambodia Daily* newspaper has a back page feature called "Calendar." Check it out for current featured events, as well as on-going happenings around Phnom Penh.

GETTING AROUND

Information on motorcycle rentals and other forms of transportation within Phnom Penh is listed in the general Getting Around chapter.

COMMUNICATIONS & INFORMATION

Post Office

The main post office is located on Street 13, a block in from the river and near Wat Phnom. This is probably the only fairly reliable place in the country to mail letters from. Curiosity among postal workers makes it a real crapshoot to see if the letters get through. If you have something coming or going and need to be sure about it, use EMS.

Postal Servie EMS. Located in the same complex as the main post office, this service offers the cheapest guaranteed mail service.

Overseas Calls

The main post office is also your best bet in Phnom Penh for international telephone calls and faxes. It's a bit cheaper here. The card phone booths around town are also fairly reasonable.

Internet

Outside Phnom Penh, they are almost non-existent in Cambodia. These places are probably the most user-friendly out of ever-increasing choices in Phnom Penh. All charge US$3–4 per hour for Internet service:

Café Asia. Located in the FCCC building on the river road. Full range of other services as well.

Kids. Across from the National Museum on Street 178. "Happy Hour" from 8 to 10 am.

Khmer Web. Just east of Lucky Supermarket, this is the newest addition on the scene and offers a full range of other services as well.

Riverside Web. 351 Sisovath Quay on the first floor of the Wagon Wheel Restaurant. It is owned and operated by Khmers who provide full services. The charge includes a free soft drink. Discounts for longer usage.

The Internet Bar. Street 278, just south of Sihanouk Blvd. and west of Pasteur St.

Phnom Penh Web. Located on the river road between Garden Bar and Rendezvous Restaurant. Now the cheapest place in town. Free candy and soft drinks. Full service.

National Library (Bibliotheque)

The place has an interesting old collection of works. It's open 7 to 11:30 am and 2 to 5:30 pm each day except Monday. Located on Street 92, just east of Le Royal Hotel.

Language Classes

Khmer Language Learning Center offers a ninety-hour course and guarantees that you will be able to communicate in the language at the end of the program, which includes books and cassette tapes. ☎ (012) 867-117. Other language courses are advertised on the bulletin board of the FCCC.

Newspapers

English newspapers including *The Cambodia Daily, Phnom Penh Post, Bangkok Post, The Nation* and the *Herald* are available from newspaper sellers along the river, in front of Lucky Supermarket, at the newsstands along Sihanouk Blvd., and at Monument Books on Monivong, to name a few places.

The Bayon Pearnik. This tourism and information magazine is available at Western food restaurants, bars and nightclubs.

Book Stores

Monument Books, 46 Norodom Blvd. and Street 154, located at the southeast corner of this intersection. ☎ (023) 218-948. They have a collection of new books, maps, magazines and newspapers.

London Book Center, 65 Street 240. They feature a large collection of used books.

Central Market. The eastern side of the central market has stationery shops that also sell maps and books.

Photo Shops

Developing film is a bargain in Phnom Penh. Good quality photo shops are all over, but are especially concentrated along Monivong Blvd. and Sihanouk Blvd. Kodak, Konica, Fuji and Agfa are all well represented. Always a good bet is the Fuji shop, City Color Photo, on Monivong Blvd. just north of the Bayon supermarket.

CURRENCY EXCHANGE

The best place to change money, including US dollars, Cambodian riel and Thai baht, is at the money changer booths in and around a number of markets in Phnom Penh. Just look for the glass case out front with wads of currency bundled up inside. The southeast corner and north side of the Central Market have stands set up with the daily exchange rate of the dollar/riel posted outside. The rate is usually the best where it is posted like this. Many of the businesses that change money are jewelry shops.

Banks

Cambodian Commercial Bank. Located on the corner of Monivong and Pochentong Blvds., this place has the best rate for a cash advance on a Visa card, at 2%.

Foreign Trade Bank of Cambodia. Located on the corner of Norodom Blvd. and Street 118.

Canadia Bank. Located on the north side of Pochentong Blvd. (Confederation de la Russie), between Norodom and Monivong Blvds.

Thai Farmers Bank. Located on the east side of Monivong Blvd., near Street 174.

Banker's hours in Cambodia are 8 am to 3:30 pm, with only a couple banks open for a half day on Saturday, so get your dough on Friday.

MEDICAL FACILITIES

Probably the two best spots in Phnom Penh for a medical emergency are:

Ta Cheng Hospital. 160 Mao Tse Toung Blvd. ☎ (023) 219-248 to 9.

AEA International SOS Clinic. 161 Street 51. ☎ (023) 216-911.

For minor problems try:

Access Medical. 4 Street 432. ☎ (023) 364-877, 813-358.

RESTAURANTS

Phnom Penh has a wonderful variety of restaurants with prices to fit every wallet.

There are so many that it's difficult to list them all and one always comes across more delightful surprises from soup stands to fancy international restaurants. Here is a list of some of the popular ones by location —Sisovath Quay (the river road), Wat Phnom area, Center of Town, Sihanouk Blvd. and over the Japanese Bridge. Not entirely listed but equally interesting are the many Chinese and Khmer restaurants located on every street and surrounding the Central Market. Also there are the good but pricey restaurants found in all of the larger hotels.

Khmer-Thai Restaurant. New Thai restaurant at Wat Phnom traffic circle. This is a new spot, on the north side of the circle. They have good Thai dishes to work on while watching the traffic circle.

Café Freedom Restaurant & Bar. 15B Street 93 near Boeng Lake. ☎ (012) 807-345. This is at the guesthouse of the same name. Thai, Khmer and Western food, open-air seating with a view of the lake. Inexpensive good food. A nice place to meet fellow budget travelers. Owners can arrange tours and rentals.

Le Bistro. 76 Street 108. ☎ (015) 830-796. South of Wat Phnom. French and Italian foods, specializing in pasta. A friendly staff serves lunch and dinner.

Le Deauville Restaurant & Bar. North side of Wat Phnom. ☎ (012) 843-204. International and French menu. Western breakfast, lunch, dinner. Billiards table. Indoor and outdoor seating with a nice view of the wat.

Tell Restaurant & Beer Garden. 13 Street 90 behind Le Royal Hotel. Swiss and German cuisine. Draft beer. Open Monday to Friday, 5 pm to 10:30 pm. Sat and Sun 11 am to 10:30 pm.

The Indian Restaurant. Monivong Blvd. near the railway station. Good breads, vegetarian dishes and tandoori.

La Casa. Street 261 just off Kampuchea Krom Blvd. in a large old house behind the Pediatric Hospital. Khmer and French foods and pizzas. A bit of a trip from the center of town but for a good cause. The restaurant was established by an NGO and trains Khmer orphans in the food service industry.

Center of Town

Capitol Guesthouse & Restaurant. 14A Street 182. ☎ (023) 724-107. Open 6:30 am to 9:30 pm. Very busy and reasonably priced. A good place to meet travelers and view the passing scene if you can take the noise and traffic. The Capitol also books reasonably-priced tours and has lots of travel information.

Thai-Vietnamese Restaurant. Huge picture windows in this second-floor restaurant allow you to look down on others —those on Charles De Gaulle and Monivong Blvds. The food is good and the service is even better.

Soriya Restaurant. This new place is located just off the southwest corner of the Central Market. It's a huge building that's hard to miss. They have good Khmer and Chinese food at reasonable prices and the service is very good.

La Paillote Restaurant. Corner of Streets 130 and 53, opposite the Central Market. ☎ (023) 722-151. Interesting French menu and serves good food. Open 7 am to 11 pm.

Peking Canteen. 93 Street 136 close to the Central Market. ☎ (012) 840-158. Inexpensive Chinese restaurant. Open 8 am to 9 pm. You will see a few more Chinese restaurants in this area. They are all OK.

Athena Greek Bar and Restaurant. 140 Norodom Blvd. Entrees US$7–10. Air conditioned. Open 11 am to 11 pm. Brunch served on Saturday and Sunday.

Soup Restaurant. Corner of Street 214 and Monivong Blvd. A busy restaurant with an all-you-can-eat soup specialty theme, with plates of vegetables and meats brought to your table, where you stir them into the table-top pot cooking on your table. Cheap.

Ly Lay restaurant. 321 Kampuchea Krom Street. Near Sivutha Blvd. ☎ 428-516. One of the better Chinese restaurants in town with different sized portions and prices.

The River Road-Sisovath Quay

The river road is lined pretty solidly with restaurants. Just take a walk along the parkway and see what looks good. Here's a sampling.

River 2. This is one of four gazebo-style places built near the river bank of the Sap River. They have good English and Khmer food. Hard-to-beat view of the river from the sidewalk tables.

The Globe Restaurant. 389 Sisovath Quay. ☎ (023) 215-923. Chinese and Western cuisine in a French colonial townhouse on the river. Upstairs bar and outdoor patio. Open 10 am to midnight. Open from 8 am on weekends.

Chiang Mai Restuarant. 227 Sisovath. Good Thai food on the river road.

EID Restaurant. 327 Sisovath Quay on the river. ☎ (023) 367-614. Inexpensive Thai food. 6:30 am to midnight.

Foreign Correspondents Club of Cambodia (FCCC). 363 Sisowath Quay. ☎ (023) 724-014. Located in a beautiful French colonial building with the bar and tables on the second floor overlooking the river. Intimate dining in the rear with a view of the Royal Palace. There are piles of free newspapers to peruse or you can sit on a ledge and watch the river scene. Open 7 am to midnight.

Happy PP Pizza. 157 Sisovath Quay. ☎ (023) 300-157. Inexpensive. Serves spaghetti, steak, salads and beer. Delivery available from 9 am to 11 pm.

La Croisette. Street 144 and Sisovath Quay. ☎ (012) 876-032. French and Khmer food, specializing in charcoal grilling. Nice river view with indoor and outdoor dining. Open 7 am to 11 pm.

La Taverne. 373 Sisovath Quay. ☎ (023) 725-258. French/Khmer/Brazilian food. Sidewalk café. Open 8 am to 11 pm.

Pon Lok Restaurant. 319 Sisovath Quay. ☎ 428-051. Look for the lights and banner extending over the street. Khmer and Chinese cuisine. Three stories with fish tanks, fish pools and catering rooms. The second floor terrace overlooking the river fills up first. A very pleasant and helpful owner and some of the cutest waitresses in Phnom Penh. A large menu with different sized portions so you can choose and order many dishes if you wish. Excellent food and ambiance. A personal favorite.

California Restaurant. Located next to Pon Lok Restaurant, this place features good Mexican and American food.

Le Rendezvous Restaurant. Sisovath Quay and Street 144 on the corner. ☎ 723-835. Great breakfasts and imaginative French food with good fish dishes. A very pleasant place and another one of my favorites. If the Rendezvous is full go to the Khmer restaurant right next door.

Saigon House Restaurant. 121 Sisovath Quay near the Hong Kong Center. ☎ (023) 300-152. Good and inexpensive Vietnamese food. Open 8:30 am to 10:30 pm.

Happy Herb Pizza. Close by the FCCC on Sisovath Quay. The original Happy Herbs. Good pizza, salads and Italian food. You will see a few happy pizzas and extra happy pizzas on the menu. If you are not sure what this means, ask before ordering.

Wagon Wheel Restaurant. Just north of the FCCC. ☎ 363-601. A German restaurant with an American Old West and covered wagon train theme? Go figure. Great view of the river and the food is good, if a bit pricey.

Sihanouk Boulevard

Le Siam. 11 Street 78, just south of Sihanouk Blvd. next to the Golden Gate Hotel. ☎ (023) 213-228. Excellent Thai food.

Lucky Burger. 160 Sihanouk Blvd. next to Lucky Super Market. Inexpensive fast food, burgers and french fries, hot dogs, ice cream. Open 7:30 am to 7 pm.

Mex Restaurant. 115 Norodom Blvd. close to the Independence Monument. Tacos, burritos, burgers, fries and Western food. Reasonably priced. Air conditioned. Open 7 am to 9:30 pm.

Phnom Khieu Restaurant. 138 Sihanouk Blvd. ☎ (023) 720-765. Reasonably priced and popular Khmer food. Open 7 am to midnight.

Royal India Restaurant. 310 Monivong Blvd. just north of Sihanouk Blvd. ☎ (023) 300-080. Reasonable prices and good food, especially the breads. Clean. Delivery available. Open 9 am to 10 pm.

Royal Kitchen. 97 Sihanouk Blvd. across from Lucky Market. ☎ (023) 363-342. Inexpensive Thai food. Delivery available. Open 10 am to 10 pm.

Chao Praya Restaurant. 177 Mao Tse Toung Street, corner of Street 163. ☎ (023) 426-695. Open for dinner only, 6 to 10 pm. Named after the famous Bangkok river, serves Thai food buffet style. Fine indoor and outdoor dining, set dinners from US$12. Visa cards accepted.

Ban Thai Restaurant. 306 Street off Norodom Blvd., south of the Independence Monument. Good Thai food in an intimate atmosphere. Entrees from US$3–6. Air conditioned.

Baggio's Restaurant. Street 51 near Sihanouk Blvd. Italian dishes. Some say they have the best pizza in town.

Over the Japanese Bridge—"Restaurant Row"

There are many fascinating restaurants on the other side of the Japanese Bridge, starting about 2 km out of town on the right side of the road and facing the river. Most are large affairs with extensive menus, air-conditioned rooms and open-air terrace dining on the river. There are dozens of restaurants, hence the nickname "Restaurant Row." Some are small and simple and some are huge, grand affairs along the bank of the Mekong River, such as **Heng Ly Restaurant**, to name just one. These places have plenty of parking space. There are painted statues of all sizes, fish ponds, water fountains, landscaped grounds and colored lights. Take some time to stroll through the area which sometimes reminds one of a small Disneyland gone haywire. Once inside the spacious restaurants the fun begins. Your table will be surrounded by beautiful beer girls all in different uniforms requesting that you order "their" beer. They make a semi-circle around you and are so pleasant you can't be annoyed. The larger restaurants also have Remy Martin, Johnny Walker and cognac girls. The menus are extensive with very good food and are reasonably priced for the experience that you will have here. These restaurants and many of the others have a stage and feature entertainment throughout the evening as singers, dancers and comedians keep the pace going.

This is your chance to see some Cambodian comedy in action (especially at the Heng Ly Restaurant). In yet another display of the country's weird time warp, you may notice that every male comedian must don a small "Charlie Chaplin" moustache before performing—whether live or on TV. He is simply not recognized as a funny man unless he does. The nation is caught up in a Charlie Chaplin craze and has been for decades. Cambodian national TV stations feature Charlie Chaplin films each Sunday, in another of Cambodia's strange and surreal features.

The large staff provide good service, and it's a pleasant evening at these restaurants. It does get busy at night so if you want a quiet meal, lunch is also served and one can spend a peaceful afternoon here. **Hang Neak Restaurant**, located near the end of the line on your right (going away from Phnom Penh), has a huge deck overlooking a wide and gorgeous stretch of the Mekong River.

Some of the other restaurants on the strip worth checking out are **Kompong Cham**, **Continental**, **Som Tam**, **Neak Samot** and the **Ta Ta Restaurant**. If you don't have wheels just hire a car for the evening; it's worth the trip. A car and driver should cost about US$8 for the trip out and back, and the driver will wait for you. A moto-taxi will charge about half that price.

The left side of the road going away from Phnom Penh also provides quite a few nice eating places. **The Gold Fish Restaurant**, about the second restaurant on the strip (from the bridge) is especially good.

Hammock Row. A few kilometers down from the last of Restaurant Row is a big line-up of simple wood shacks built next to the road, with hammocks laid out in all directions. This is where the locals go to chill-out—what they refer to as "sit down for smile." They serve corn-on-the-cob that is grown in the fields behind and also have coconuts and every cold drink you can imagine. It's very cheap and there is a view of the temple hills of Udong.

NIGHT SCENE

Khmer Nightclubs

It's a real trip going to Cambodia's brand of nightclubs in Phnom Penh, as well as in the rest of the country. They almost always feature a live band and in most places the music volume is cranked up way too loud. During a good portion of the music sets, the lights in the entire place are shut off, with the exception of a bit of light on the dance floor area. If you can handle all of that, the people-watching in the nightclubs can be quite entertaining. There are loads of taxi-girls (girls to dance and sit with) to look at; some are real stunning. There are gangs of beer girls who accost a customer as he approaches a table, circling the wary victim, each calling out the name of her brand repeatedly until the dazed customer calls out his choice. These nightclubs also feature Khmer music medleys where most of the house head to the dance floor, form a circle and dance around doing some kind of corny take-off of classical dancing. There are generally a few sets of Western songs thrown in at intervals throughout the night and this provides a nice break from the Khmer vocals, which sound a lot like Minnie Mouse singing.

Most of the clubs are thoughtful enough to put a sign at the entrance telling customers to leave all of their hand grenades, AK47's, rocket launchers and handguns at the desk check, where they can pick them up on their way out.

Bophar Toep 1 & 2. These two clubs are fairly popular with the locals and can get quite rowdy at times. Bophar Toep 1 has a hotel next door to the club and is located across from the Cambodiana Hotel on Sisovath Street. Nightclub 2 is located on the north side of Mao Tse Toung Blvd., just east of Monivong Blvd.

Phkar Chhouk Tep Nightclub. This lively place is located on a small strip that has a few hotels. From the circle near the Olympic Stadium torch (Sihanouk Blvd. and Monireth Blvd.) go north one block on Jawaharlal Blvd. and turn left. The nightclub is down just a bit on the right.

Li Lay Nightclub. A bit smaller, but fairly lively most nights. It's located on the north side of Kampuchea Krom Blvd., halfway between Monivong Blvd. and Mao Tse Toung Blvd.

Floating Khmer Nightclubs. These sit right on the river, just south of the Japanese Bridge. It's hard to miss at night because it's lit up like a Christmas tree.

Western (more or less) Nightclubs

Martini's. Might just as well put the most famous spot first. Some say that this place has gone downhill a bit over the last few years, but it's still rocking and loaded with ladies, depending upon the time and day. It seems to be at its best between 11 pm and 1 am in the latter part of the week.

There is an outdoor courtyard area where you can pig out on good, cheap Khmer and Viet Cong food, while you drink beer, watch a big-screen movie and gaze at the female talent as it walks by. Let's not forget the loud and dark disco on the inside, next to the courtyard. It's still fun. Located at 402 Mao Tse Toung Blvd., across from the back of the Intercontinental Hotel.

Khmer Nightclub. Next door to Martinis is a Khmer nightclub. It's not one of the better clubs, but gives you a place nearby to stumble over to and check out.

Sharky Bar. This place is a bit of a mix between a nightclub and a large watering hole. There are free pool tables, good tunes, an outdoor balcony area and loads of ladies everywhere. The guys who run the place, Bob, Dave and Jay, are affable sorts and can be a good source of info on Phnom Penh (especially it's seedy side). The bar is located on Street 130, two blocks east of Norodom Blvd. They also feature what may very well be Cambodia's biggest indoor running track, in the form of a huge endless bar counter. American, Thai and Russian food is also available.

Manhattan's. This frenetic place is usually jam-packed with "wanna-bees," but also some very nice-looking local talent that start streaming in at about 1 am and keep the place hopping until 6 to 7 am some days. Pricey drinks: beer is US$5–6 a pop. The club is located in the Holiday Hotel complex, at Street 84, a couple of blocks east of Monivong Blvd.

Casa Nightclub. Generally a bit more on the boring side, this place does seem real popular with the local NGO (non-government organization) crowd—is there a connection here? They usually have a live Thai band until midnight, when the techno-music kicks in. Located in the Sharaton Hotel, just north of Wat Phnom.

Watering Holes

Tuekei Bar. Meaning "gecko" in Khmer, this is a friendly place to hang out, much as a gecko might. French bar with an international crowd, great food, cheap drinks. Street 111, just north of Street 214.

Cat house. This is an old standby from the United Nations administration days, with new ownership. It has a laid-back atmosphere with a pool table. Corner of Streets 63 and 118.

Duck Tub Bar. This is another small place with live music and food. Located at 22 Street 51.

Heart of Darkness. Colonel Kurtz (Marlon Brando) never made it this far south, but this bar has been a popular hangout in Phnom Penh for a number of years, regardless. They also have a pool table and are located at 26 Street 51.

Pink Elephant Pub. This is a great location for watching the show going by along the River Parkway, especially early evenings. Outdoor sidewalk tables, free pool, and cheap drinks are what's on tap. They also have a number of food choices.

Walk about. This place is up and running 24 hours and has a nice pool table, which can sometimes be used as a bed by the occasional customer who can't quite keep up with the bar's long hours. Corner of Streets 174 and 51.

River 2. This is a restaurant/pub on the river side of the parkway that features a nice view of the Sap River, good English and Khmer food and drinks. There are a few of these in a row. The new owner, a European, is none too friendly, however. During the crowded Water Festival holiday he put up a barbed wire perimeter around his stores. Just a bit over the top, we think.

Check the *Bayon Pearnik* (free magazine) for more info on nightspots, as well as entertaining info and articles on Cambodia. Available at westerner-oriented spots in Phnom Penh.

ACCOMMODATIONS

There are plenty of places to stay in Phnom Penh, from budget guesthouses to five star hotels and a great variety in between. Here's a list with prices and locations.

Wat Phnom Area

Freedom Guesthouse & Restaurant. Near Boeng Lake south of a large mosque, ☎ (012) 807-345. Fan rooms US$5.

9 Guesthouse. Overlooking the lake, restaurant on premises. A word of warning: many motorcycles have been stolen from here after the place was secured for the evening. Inside jobs? Seems fairly obvious.

Lake Side Guesthouse. (10 Guesthouse) 10 Street 93. ☎ (012) 851-652.

Located on Boeng Kak. Singles US$2–4. Restaurant, pool table, and TV on premises.

Cathay Hotel. 123–125 Street 110 (Ang Doung St.). ☎ (023) 722-471, fax (023) 426-303. All rooms are US$15 and have TV, a/c, h/w, phone and mini-bar in rooms, fridge, free laundry service and free local calls. Safety deposit boxes. A friendly place and it's a good location near the river and train station parkway.

Tai Seng Hotel. 56 Monivong Blvd., just north of Le Royal Hotel. Good location and a fairly lively place. Prices descend as you ascend the stairway: US$30 at the bottom and US$15 on the fifth floor. View of the lake in front and of the neighborhood in back. I've stayed here at times, but they seem to be getting a bit too money-oriented, charging high prices for laundry and local calls.

The Sharaton Hotel (spelled this way). Street 47, north of Wat Phnom. ☎ (023) 360-395, fax (023) 361-199. Rooms start at US$40 and include breakfast. In-room safe. TV, a/c, restaurant and room service twenty-four hours. Business center includes photocopying, language translation, personal computers, meeting rooms. Swimming pool, night club, karaoke, coffee shop, airport pick-up service, tour arrangements, hair salon, laundry and dry cleaning services. Car parking. Quite a lively place, day and night.

Holiday International Hotel. 84 Monivong Blvd. and Street 84. North of Wat Phnom. ☎ (023) 427-402, fax (023) 427-401, e-mail <holiday@cambodia-web.net>

Singles US$60, Doubles US$70. Laundry and valet service, mini-bar, safety deposit boxes, 24-hour room service, business center open 24 hours, Thai and Chinese restaurants, beauty salon, fitness center and massage, tour desk and guide services, car parking and rentals, two swimming pools, outdoor cafeteria, 24 -hour restaurant, gambling casino, karaoke rooms and the famous Manhattan Dance Club.

Sunway Hotel. This newer place is located on the parkway close to Wat Phnom. It's a nice upscale operation that's very well run. There is a buffet-oriented restaurant and a lounge area with a pool table on the premises as well. Prices start at US$100 per night.

Hotel Le Royal. 92 Rukhak Vithei Daun Penh, off Monivong Blvd, northwest of Wat Phnom. ☎ (023) 981-888, fax (023) 981-168, e-mail: <raffles.hir.ghda@bigpond.com.kh> Singles, US$260, US$280 (pool view), US$300, US$400. Doubles, US$290, US$300, US$320, US$370. Suites can run from US$1,300 to US$2,000.

Renovated by the Raffles Group in 1998 in the spirit of a tropical palatial residence, the hotel occupies an entire city block and is set amidst fragrant tropical gardens. Art deco-style furnishings blend with traditional Cambodian folk art. The property has nine distinctive restaurants and bars. The business center offers secretarial support, computer stations, CD Rom, Internet and translation services. The Spa at Le Royal has exercise equipment, sauna, aerobics room, jacuzzi, steam, massage and a hair salon. The swimming pool area includes a 25-meter lap pool and a family pool with light meals and barbecue at hand. Three hotel shops offer gifts, souvenirs, books, newspapers, and clothing. Catering and banquet facilities are available. Between 1970 and 1975 most of the international journalists stayed here, and sought shelter here again when the Khmer Rouge invaded Phnom Penh. (Part of the movie "The Killing Fields" was supposedly set in this hotel. However, it was actually filmed in the Hotel Sofitel Central Hua Hin in Thailand.)

Center of Town

Capitol Guesthouse. 14 Street 182, corner of Street 107. ☎ (023) 364 104. One of the oldest guesthouses for tourists in the city, it's in a dirty, noisy section of town but always seems to be busy. Single rooms with shared bath are from US$2–4. Doubles are US$4–5. Singles with bath are US$4 and doubles US$7. Many of the rooms are dark with no windows. There is an inexpensive, open-air restaurant on the first floor that is always filled with young tourists and backpackers, as well as expat residents. The hotel arranges city and country tours and these are also reasonably priced.

Hello Guesthouse. 242 Street 107, corner of Street 198. One block from the Capitol Guesthouse. Single rooms with fan are US$4. Doubles US$5, singles a/c US$8. Clean but small rooms, Western bath.

Happy Guesthouse. 197 treet 107, ☎ (018) 815-370. Next door to the Capitol Guesthouse. Singles, US$2–3. Doubles with Asian bath are US$5.

Lux Orissey Guesthouse. 22 Street 115, ☎ (023) 210 508. Near the Capitol. Fan rooms US$5. Rooms with a/c US$10.

Singapore II Hotel. 21 Street 136, between Street 49 and Norodom Blvd. ☎ (023) 213-836. Singles with fan US$5. Singles with a/c US$10. Clean rooms with TV and fridge. Good location near Central Market. No h/w. Massage available on premises.

Lucky Ro Hotel. 122 Street 110. Two blocks east of Norodom Blvd. ☎ (023) 212-963. Fan rooms are US$7 for a single and US$8 for a double. Rooms with a/c US$10. TV and fridge in rooms for US$15. Safety deposit boxes available.

Mittapheap Hotel. 262 Monivong Blvd, corner of Street 174. ☎ (023) 213-331, e-mail <mittapheap@cambodia-web.net> Central location near Wat Koh.

Singles US$10. Doubles US$15. Includes a/c and TV. Small restaurant with good food, snooker hall upstairs and video movie house on premises.

Hong Kong Hotel. Monivong Blvd. and Street 214. ☎ (023) 427-108. Located at a very busy part of town, this place has been renovated and has rooms with a/c, TV, h/w and fridge for US$15–$20.

Asia Town Hotel. 406 Monivong Blvd. ☎ (023) 721-539. Singles US$15. Doubles US$15. Includes h/w, TV, a/c, fridge in room. Free local calls. No safety deposit boxes. Khmer-Chinese Restaurant reasonably priced.

Neak Pean Hotel. 299 Monivong Blvd. ☎ (023) 216-543. Nea Street 168 and east of the Orussey Market and bus station. Singles/doubles US$15, with a/c, fridge, TV. The famous and busy KTV Nightclub is on the first floor. Live entertainment.

Hawaii Hotel. 18 Street 130. Good location one block east of the Central Market. ☎ (023) 362-679, ☎/fax (023) 426-652. Standard rooms US$20, deluxe US$30, suites US$40. A/c, TV, fridge. Excellent and very clean restaurant serving good breakfast and Chinese, Thai, Khmer and Western food.

Pailin Hotel. 219BC Monivong Blvd. near corner of Charles de Gaulle Blvd. ☎ (023) 26698, fax (023) 26375. Singles $20, doubles US$28, deluxe rooms US$45, suites US$55. A/c, TV, fridge, mini-bar, safety deposit boxes, parking facilities, mini-bus service to and from airport, flight confirmations and travel services. Two restaurants on the premises. Large clean lobby and helpful staff. Accepts cash only.

Dusit Hotel. 2 Street 120, just east of Monivong Blvd and north of the Central Market. ☎ (023) 427-483, fax (023) 427-609. Singles US$20, doubles US$30. 10% tax added. A/c, TV, fridge, parking on premises, gem and jewelry store, photocopy service, business meeting rooms, airline and travel office. Just a bit the worse for wear these days.

Asie Hotel. 113–119 Monivong Blvd, corner of Kampuchea Krom Blvd. ☎ (023) 427-037, fax (023) 426-334. Rooms from windowless US$16 rooms to spacious US$27 rooms. A/c, TV, fridge. Chinese restaurant, shops, and travel office on premises. Free shuttle-bus to and from airport.

Ho Wah Genting Hotel. 132 Monivong Blvd. ☎ (023) 725-531, fax (023) 723-296. Just one block northwest of the Central Market. Standard rooms US$40. Superior US$45. Suites US$90. A/c, TV, Western bath, safe deposit box, mini-bar and fridge. Restaurant and room service. Business center, tour guides and other facilities.

Princess Hotel. 302 Monivong Blvd. Just south of the Central Market and close to the American embassy. ☎ (023) 801-089, fax (023) 801-217. Single $40. Double US$50. Deluxe US$60. Suite US$80. Queen and king-size beds, Safety deposit boxes, a/c, TV, fridge, mini-bar, room service, airport pick-up and sending service, casino on premises. Jewelry and gift store, restaurant and bar. Credit cards accepted. 10% tax and 10% service added to bill.

Diamond Hotel. 172–184 Monivong Blvd, corner of Charles de Gaulle Blvd. near the bus station, in the center of town. ☎ (012) 217-325, fax (023) 426-635. Singles US$40. Doubles US$50. A/c, TV, mini-bar, bathtub and shower, in-room safe. Very clean rooms and public areas. Restaurant on premises. All credit cards accepted.

City Central Hotel. Street 128 and Monivong Blvd. just west of the Central Market. ☎ (023) 722-022, fax (023) 722-021. Standard rooms: single US$50, double US$60. Superior rooms: single US$60, double US$70. Executive rooms: single US$70, double US$80. Includes breakfast, free laundry service and local calls. Restaurant and bar on premises.

Room service is available from 6:30 am to 11:30 pm. A/c, TV, fridge. 10% service charge and 10% government tax. All credit cards accepted.

Juliana Hotel. 16 Juliana Road at Street 152. Near the Batook School and just north of Charles de Gaulle Ave. ☎ (023) 366-070, fax (023) 366-072. Singles US$66. Doubles US$77. These rates may go higher; be sure to ask for the "best price." A stunningly beautiful hotel in a garden setting, but in a very poor location. The swimming pool is surrounded by tropical plants, plush lounge and a bar. The Vanda Restaurant features Western and Asian cuisine. The Shark's Fin Restaurant specializes in Chinese and shark's fin dishes. Fitness center, sauna, and massage available, hair salon, business center with computer, Internet and e-mail access. This hotel is Thai-managed and is favored by wealthy Cambodians. Not in the nicest neighborhood, just north of the Olympic Stadium and down a side street, but once you are there, it's worthwhile. Excellent and reasonably—priced lunch and dinner buffet.

Near the River

The Last Home Guesthouse. 47 Street 108. Just in from the river, this place has a good location and offers basic accommodations at US$4–5 a night for a fan room.

Chi Cha Hotel. 27 Street 110, near Wat Sangkat. ☎ (023) 366-065. Singles with bath US$4. Doubles US$5. Guests may use lobby refrigerator. A bit funky, with mostly Indian and Pakistani customers. Hala, Chinese, Bangladesh and Indian food served in restaurant.

Bophar Toep Hotel. 463 Sangkat Chak. ☎ 724-251 or (018) 813-591. Good location directly across the street from the Cambodiana Hotel. A/c, TV, h/w and

fridge. Request a front room with river view for the same price. Nightclub next door with live music and taxi girls. Great panoramic view of the river, parkway and temples from the roof. Food stands and good restaurants nearby. Can get a bit noisy. US$10–15.

California Restaurant & Guesthouse. 317 Sisovath, located across the street from the Sap River. This is another spot with a great location. They have nice rooms and 3 have a great view of the river area. The rooms go from US$14–17 for a river view room and have TV, h/w, a/c, fridge. There is also a restaurant on the premises that has Mexican food, pizza and other Western food, along with Khmer food. E-mail for reservations at <cambodia_hotel_california@hotmail.com>.

Mekong Thmey Hotel. 30 Street 108. On the boulevard heading to the railway station, just in from the river. ☎ 724-556. Singles/doubles are US$15 with a/c, TV and fridge. Close to P'sah Cha Market.

Hotel Indochine. 251 Sisowath Quay, corner of Street 144 on the Tonle Sap River. ☎/fax (023) 427-292. Singles US$10. Doubles US$15 and US$20. Large clean rooms with TV, fridge, a/c. Good location, but can be a bit unfriendly.

Sunshine Hotel. Sisowath Quay, next door to and a step up from the Hotel Indochine. Five floors with a rooftop restaurant, which provides a super view of the river area. A/c, h/w, fridge. Inside windowless rooms are US$15 (not good in case of fire). Rear rooms with a window, US$20. Front rooms with a river view are US$25. Friendly staff.

Thai San Hotel. 19 Street 148. Not far from the river. ☎ (023) 723-956, fax (023) 216-878. Singles US$15 and US$20. Doubles US$20 and US$25. A/c, TV, fridge. Safety deposit box available. Restaurant on premises.

Renaske Hotel. Opposite the main entrance for the Royal Palace and Silver Pagoda. ☎ (023) 722-457. With nice, but aging colonial architecture, the place has finally undergone some renovation work. Rooms with a/c, TV, h/w, and fridge go for US$20–25. They also feature a nicely landscaped outdoor restaurant area.

Riverside Hotel. On the river road, near Wat Phnom. ☎/fax (023) 725-050. Singles US$30. Doubles US$35. River view, a/c, TV, fridge, mini-bar, in-room safe, indoor car park, large pleasant rooms. Restaurant and bar open 24 hours.

Hotel Sofitel Cambodiana. 313 Sisovath Quay, near the confluence of the Mekong and Sap Rivers. ☎ (023) 426 288, fax (023) 426-392, e-mail: <sofitel.cambodia@ worldmail.com.kh>. Singles US$120–170. Doubles US$150–200. Suites US$280 –400. The first international class hotel in Cambodia. Started in 1967 and used as a military base by the Lon Nol government. Cambodians took refuge from the fighting here from 1970 to 1975. Work on the huge complex resumed in 1987 with an investment of 20 million dollars by two Singaporeans. Foreigners took shelter here during the violence of the factional fighting between the two prime ministers in 1998.

The property has a swimming pool with a river view and food and beverage service, tennis courts, business center with audiovisual equipment, computers, secretarial services and multi-lingual staff. They also have a beauty salon, gift, book, newspaper and clothing stores, souvenir shops and a travel bureau. There's a lounge and bar area, three first class restaurants, including The Mekong Restaurant, French cuisine at L' Amboise Restaurant and Cantonese cuisine at the Dragon Court Restaurant. Also a bakery in the lobby area.

Royal Phnom Penh. Samdech Sothearos Blvd., south of the Cambodiana Hotel and next to the Basak River. Deluxe Rooms US$180. Suites US$240–540. This is where Khmer Rouge big-boys (plenty of blood on those hands) Nuan Chea and Khieu Samphan, stayed when they were given a red-carpet welcome to Phnom Penh after working out a deal with the government. Go figure.

It's a lovely hotel with first-class amenities and facilities, but the location is not very good. Sothearos Blvd. along this stretch is dark and one of the worst nighttime robbery spots in Phnom Penh.

Sihanouk Boulevard & Olympic Stadium Area

Vimean Suor Hotel. 31 Monireth Street opposite Olympic Stadium. ☎ (023) 720-277, fax (023) 722-697. Singles US$10. Doubles US$15. Large clean bathrooms and large beds. A/c, fridge, TV, and h/w.

Sangker Hotel. 5 Street 217, corner of Charles de Gaulle Blvd. near the Olympic Stadium. ☎/fax (023) 427-144. Singles/doubles US$15. Five-day rate is US$10 per day. A/c, fridge, TV, h/w. No safe box facilities.

Phkar Chhouk Tep 1, 2 & 3. Three different buildings, all sharing the same fun-to-say name. They have TV, a/c, h/w and are kept up well. Fun nightclub of the same name located here. US$10.

Lucky Star Hotel. This is located next to and a step up from 1, 2 and 3, listed above. All the amenities, with rooms going for US$20–25 per night.

Borei Thmei Hotel. 13 Monireth Blvd. (Charles de Gaulle Blvd.) ☎ (023) 880-239, fax (023) 427-476. Near the Olympic Stadium and open-air street markets. Singles US$15. Doubles US$20. Suites US$25. All of the rooms are spacious and very clean and have a/c, TV, h/w, fridge. Pleasant and helpful staff. Restaurant on premises.

Golden Gate Hotel. 6CD Street 278, corner of Street 57. ☎ (023) 721-161, fax (023) 721-005. Singles US$15. Doubles US$20. A/c, TV, fridge, free laundry service. Restaurant veranda and sitting area with newspapers and magazines. Very clean and often full. Phone ahead.

Golden Bridge Hotel. 6D Street 278. near the Golden Gate. ☎ (023) 721-396, fax (023) 721-395. It's been a spillover from the Golden Gate Hotel next door, but the rooms are actually a better value. New and very clean. Singles or doubles US$15. A/c, TV, fridge, free local calls, free laundry service.

Tokyo Hotel. 15 Street 278, Near Monivong St., behind Lucky Market. ☎ (023) 721-050, fax (023) 721 051. Not far from the Golden Gate and Golden Bridge.

Singles US$15. Doubles US$18. A/c, TV, fridge, free local calls and free laundry service. Safe for valuables is available.

Scandic Hotel. 4 Street 282. Singles US$15. Doubles US$20. A/c, TV, h/w. Bar and restaurant on premises.

Beauty Inn Hotel. 100 Sihanouk Blvd. Between Monivong and Norodom Blvds. ☎ (023) 211-515, 722-676, fax (023) 212-929. Singles US$18. Doubles US$25.

A/c, fridge, TV, h/w, mini-bar, clean and pleasantly decorated rooms. A restaurant inside is open 24 hours and there is a tour service on the premises.

Royal Palace Hotel. 93 Monireth Road. Near Olympic Stadium. ☎ (023) 720-875, fax (023) 720-874. Singles US$30. Doubles US$35. Suites US$60. A/c, TV, fridge, large rooms with choice of double, queen and king-size beds. Swimming pool with food and beverage service. First-class Chinese restaurant. Conference room, gift shop. The Crystal Night Club has live entertainment and also private karaoke rooms.

Rama Inn West. 8–10 Street 282 and Voie Nine Street just behind the Green Hotel near the Independence Monument. ☎/fax (023) 218 898. Singles US$35. Doubles US$45. Deluxe rooms US$55. A/c, TV, fridge. Great open-air restaurant and bar. Quiet and pleasant setting. Breakfast is included in the price. The nearby Rama Inn East is the sister hotel.

Hotel Intercontinental. This new addition to the luxury hotel scene in Phnom Penh was actually the city's first true five-star hotel. Very nicely done and loaded with style, it combines bits of Cambodia's cultural heritage with the more modern amenities that one would expect in a pampered environment. They have complete business facilities, a modern fitness center, fine restaurants, a bakery and deli, souvenir shops and conference facilities. It's also right around the corner from Martini's for those who want convenience in their nightlife. Priced from US$120 to the sky.

COMING & GOING

Flip to the general Coming and Going and Getting Around chapters for all the options and details of getting to and leaving Phnom Penh, including bus, train, and motorcycle. Below is information on transportation that is particular to Phnom Penh.

Fast Boat-Bullet Boat

There is a popular boat service from Phnom Penh to Siem Reap at a cost of US$25 each way, very expensive by Cambodian bullet boat travel standards because it's a tourist route so the price is higher. (I guess they figure, why not stick it to those tourists?) The trip takes about four hours and there are a number of outfits that ply the routes and have ticket booths along the river road, north of the Japanese Bridge. The boats leave Phnom Penh at 7 am every day.

Your hotel or guesthouse can also arrange tickets for you. The fast boats are long, enclosed and look like large floating cigar tubes. They hold about eighty people. I feel less trapped if I sit on the roof. The inside of most of these boats is like a floating karaoke hall, where the video screens loudly scream out all the Khmer favorites. Topside you can see some river life along the way; just bring your bag of valuables up with you and lock up bag zippers down below in the storage area up front. The scenery is most interesting once you get to the Great Lake Tonle Sap.

Bus

Refer to the general Coming and Going chapter for schedules, destinations, and fares.

Share Taxi

Refer to the general Getting Around chapter for rates. Below are the taxi stand locations.

Most share taxi stands are located between the northwest corner of the Central Market and Monivong Blvd. in Phnom Penh. See each chapter listed below for a complete road report as well.

Prey Veng. Easiest choice is to use the taxi stand at Olympic Market. 4,000 riel

Svay Rieng. Easiest choice is to use the taxi stand at Olympic Market. 5,000 riel.

Vietnamese border. Easiest choice is to use the taxi stand at Olympic Market. 7,000 riel.

Takeo. The share taxi stand is at Deum Kor Market, catty-cornered from the Hotel Continental.

Kampot and Kep. The taxi stand is at Deum Kor Market, catty-cornered from the Hotel Intercontinental.10,000 riel.

Sihanoukville. The taxi stand is located just south of the southwest corner of the Central Market. 10,000 riel.

Car Rentals & Taxi Service

First refer to the general Getting Around chapter. Here are a couple of outfits offering cars and English-speaking drivers for US$20 a day:

Ronakse Tourist Service. Call Mr. Nik at (012) 878-625.

Lim Bun Hok. ☎ (015) 839-413 or (023) 982-933.

A couple of taxi outfits available for short trips or longer service are:

Taxi Vantha. ☎ (023) 982-542 or (012) 855-000.

Baileys Taxi. ☎ (023) 300-808 or (012) 853-179, (012) 871-103.

Motorcycle Touring Info

See specific chapters for touring information to and from Phnom Penh.

Sex education

DAY TRIPS FROM PHNOM PENH

Are you getting itchy feet in Phnom Penh and feeling the urge to break outside to explore the countryside? One of the nice things about the urban area of Phnom Penh is that it doesn't take much time, traveling in any direction, to get to rural Cambodia. There are plenty of interesting sights, activities and great rural scenery to be enjoyed within an easily accessible distance and believe it or not, on decent roads. Even the areas fairly close to Phnom Penh don't see many tourists or foreigners and on some of these trips you will notice that some people look surprised to see you passing through. This only adds to the fun and you will find rural Cambodians to be genuinely friendly people.

There are several day-trip transportation options, including renting your own motorcycle, having a moto-taxi take you out, or renting a car with a driver. (Avis has not yet come to Cambodia). Another good option is to use the extensive route network of Hoh Wah Genting Bus Company. Just check the Getting Around chapter for full details on how to do it and bus schedules and fares. The chapter also has rental and moto-taxi information as well.

TAKEO

Heading South from Phnom Penh on Highway 2 leads to day trips, day trips, and more day trips in Takeo.

- Tonle Bati and Ta Prohm temple ruins
- Takhmao Zoo and Phnom Tamao hill top temple area
- Phnom Chissor
- The ancient capital of Angkor Borei, Phnom Da and the ancient water canals of Takeo.

Takeo Province is chock full of interesting sights and it's just a quick shot down there on Highway 2, making all of these trips easy to do as a day trip, even if you combine a few of the sites. Just flip to the Takeo chapter for all the day-trip info on these sights.

KAMPONG SPUE & SOUTHWEST

Heading southwest on Highway 4 you can take in Kirirom National Park and Ompe Phnom Resort.

Ompe Phnom Resort (Bohpay Phnom), Wat Ompe & Khmer Rouge Victims Memorial

Located in Kampong Spue, this area is popular for weekend picnics with residents of Phnom Penh and Kampong Spue alike. Weekdays are quiet, so that's a good time to go.

There is a picnic area consisting of bamboo huts and shacks built along both sides of the Kampong Spue River, with an old suspension walking bridge connecting the two sides. The charge is 500 riel to walk across the bouncy bridge, from which you get a nice view of the river area. Besides a pretty fair selection of Khmer foods and barbecued meats, vendors also offer your favorite Khmer snacks in the form of fried beetles, cockroaches, grasshoppers, and snake eggs.

Wat Ompe is on the far side of the river. It's a fairly simple temple with colorful murals inside. Monkeys seem to control the woods surrounding the temple and there are elephant rides at 5,000 riel for a half-hour jaunt in the area.

Going west from the temple and across the courtyard area, continue down the path to a small wooden shack. There are signs in English describing the place as a memorial to the victims of the Pol Pot regime. The place is filled with skulls, bones and clothes. It's not a pleasant addition to your picnic.

To get there, start at the front gate of Pochentong Airport for an odometer check. Head southwest on Highway 4, veering to the right when you reach the big traffic circle just beyond the airport. Kampong Spue town is about 35 km from the gate and at 36 km you will see a school gate on the right and a big white Stella-Artois Beer billboard on the left; turn left here. At the first fork you come to, stay left, then go right at the second fork you come upon. The parking area is just another 100 meters. The Hoh Wah Genting bus bound for Kampong Spue can get you to the turn-off on Highway 4 as well.

Kirirom National Park

Located in the Damrei Mountains and straddling the border area of Kampong Spue and Koh Kong Provinces, Kirirom National Park is a gorgeous area, and it is landmine free, so it offers great hiking potential. The thickly forested mountain area contains mountain lakes, rivers, and waterfalls and is a former summer palace and home of King Sihanouk.

Like Bokor Mountain and Kep Resort in Kampot, the villas and palace of Kirirom were almost all destroyed during the Khmer Rouge years. The Summer Palace is still standing and furnished, giving visitors a feel for how the area used to be. A helicopter pad from the period sits unused and collecting weeds on a nearby hilltop. There is also a park dedication ceremony display area showing photos of the king and queen dedicating the park at its official opening.

Backing up to Highway 4, here's a rundown of directions to additional sites in the park. Heading southwest on Highway 4 from Phnom Penh (using the entrance gate at the airport for an odometer check), continue well beyond Kampong Spue town for

Rickety toll bridge at Phnom Ombe Resort, Kampong Spue

a total of 80 km. On the right side of the highway is a large sign that reads "Preah Suramarit Kossomak National Park," the name the area used to go by (use this sign for an odometer checkpoint for the national park). Turn right on the asphalt road here. There are sandwich, fruit, drink and fuel stands just beyond the turn if you need a refresher. Follow the paved road about 10 km and you come to another welcome sign and a park ranger shack. The current staff do not speak English, but that's not a problem, so just continue on. There is no admission fee at this time.

Most of the roads that weave around the main park area are paved, so it's easy to enjoy the pretty mountain scenery that they cut through. The road also passes by stands of fragrant pine trees that complete the picture. Twenty-two kilometers from the park sign on Highway 4 you come to the gate for the peaceful forest temple of Wat Kirirom. A shrine near the gate has a sign in English script: "Grandmother Mao." Could it be that the late communist leader was a closet cross-dresser?

One and a half kilometers from the temple gate is a sign for the old Kirirom Tea Company, that used the pleasant mountain climate and soil to grow tea leaves. Only a couple of building shells remain, but the trails do lead to a very scenic valley area with a mountain lake off in the distance—great for hiking.

Continuing along the main paved road, you come to a Johnny Walker sign that reads "Welcome to Kirirom" (25 km from Hwy 4 sign). This is where you will find the Kirirom Restaurant and Guesthouse. Perched on a hill, the restaurant offers a great view of the mountains from an outside deck eating area. The menu and food are good and English is spoken here. The small guesthouse has five rooms for rent, each with a Western bath, for US$15 per night. They usually fill up on weekends but sit empty on weekdays. The manager of the place is a friendly sort and can give additional info on hiking around the area. ☎ (018) 815-403. The restaurant is only a 1 ½-hour ride from Phnom Penh, confirming the park as an easy day trip.

One kilometer from the restaurant welcome sign is a cobra head statue in the middle of a traffic circle. To get to the small waterfall and the surrounding picnic area, go right. Follow this to a fork and go left. Go left at the following T in the road and left again at the next fork in the road. Follow this until you come to a stone building and follow the road that goes to the left here. Take a right at the next T and you will come upon the shell of a 1958 T-Bird in the road (in Cambodia, of all places!). Follow the road to the right to the picnic and waterfall area.

There are scores of roads and trails winding around the entire mountaintop area, so pick another direction from that cobra traffic circle and have fun exploring.

Kirirom National Park would also make a nice side trip if you are coming or going from Phnom Penh to Sihanoukville. Also, for alternative travel if you don't have your own set of wheels, you could use the Hoh Wah Genting bus between these two cities and then time your return for a later bus heading back. There are moto-taxis near the food stands by Highway 4.

UDONG & NORTH

Several interesting day trips lead north of Phnom Penh, and with Highway 5 straddling the Sap River for a good portion of the way, it's a scenic journey. There are also a number of temples and mosques along the way.

Udong

Udong town is a sleepy little place these days that does not suggest, as you pass through on Highway 5, that it once served as the capital of Cambodia. Phnom Udong has a smattering of temples and monuments on the top and has recently had a great deal of activity going on there. Tremendous changes have taken place, in the form of smart, new hilltop temples and shrines and landscaped terraces to relax on while admiring the nice views. Udong is definitely worth a visit these days.

The new temple archway at the base of a new stairway leading to the top is the best place to head up from. The next level is partly a Buddhist theme park with statues of wise men and animals roaming about. From here a newly built and landscaped stairway, complete with viewing terraces, leads to the new temple structure at the top.

The structure is huge and a spiral stairway on the inside leads to the top where there is a magnificent panoramic view of the mountains to the west and the glistening rice fields of the countryside. The Sap River, with its surrounding marshlands and irrigation channels, is also visible here.

A path connects this area with the other shrines and temples on the hill and the twin-sister hill beyond. Much damage from the war years is evident; one readily notices that bullet holes cover most of the old structures. The other hilltop and a working temple compound area are accessible from a road that winds around the hills as well. It's a nice hike and there are plenty of interesting temple structures to look over on the way. A number of girls walk around the hilltop area carrying cold drinks and wet towelettes in coolers. Their cute faces are usually dripping with sweat as they follow the normal handful of visitors around, lugging their coolers with them.

To get to Udong, set your odometer at the Japanese Bridge and head north on Highway 5. At 38 km from the bridge the road has already circled around the hills of Udong and this is where a large picture sign on the left announces the site. Turn left here and follow it all the way to a fork in the road near the base. Going to the right takes you to the new archway and stairs to the top. Near the base is a friendly Khmer family's drink and fuel stand. They will look after your motorcycle if you buy a drink from them. Secure it with your padlock just to be sure.

You could also jump on a Hoh Wah Genting bus bound for Kampong Chhnang and get off at the Udong billboard, where moto-taxi guys can take you for the round trip and will wait for you while you explore about. Check for details in the Getting Around chapter.

Kampong Chhnang

Just another 60 km beyond Udong is Kampong Chhnang town. The road is in good condition, making it an easy addition to a day trip. Check the Kampong Chhnang chapter for more details.

Prek Kohk Ferry & "Triangle Trip"

The Prek Kohk ferry is just over 29 km from the Japanese Bridge along Highway 5 and on the way to Udong. Crossing on it gives you the option of making a circle route of sorts to connect with the day-trip sights along Highway 6 to the northeast of Phnom Penh. The fare is 200 riel per person and 300 riel for a motorcycle, and the big ferry makes the trip every twenty minutes throughout the day. There are restaurants and drink stands on both sides of the river. The paved road on the other side heads through a nice quiet stretch of countryside for 16 km before hooking up with Highway 6. Going to the right would take you back to Phnom Penh; going left leads you to either Kampong Cham or Kampong Thom and the day-trip sights along the way. It would be easy to connect day trip sights on Highway 5 and Highway 6 by using this ferry and custom-making your own "Triangle Day Trip."

NORTH & NORTHEAST

Kampong Cham & Kampong Thom

Heading over the Japanese Bridge from Phnom Penh, Highway 6 is a very smooth road that allows for a fairly short ride to the town of Skon, a junction for Highway 6 continuing to Kampong Thom (and Siem Reap) and Highway 7 continuing to Kampong Cham. Either town and a couple of their sights could be done as a day trip by the gung-ho traveler, but both towns actually warrant an overnight trip. Check both chapters for the full scoop.

The following is a list of day trips along Highway 6 that are easily done together, if you like, or you could also combine them with sites along Highway 5 by using the Prek Kohk ferry on the "Triangle Trip" we suggested.

Wat Ahkahkow

This temple sits on the banks of a very scenic stretch of the Mekong River, which in itself is reason enough for making the journey. The river temple has very tall temple spires, each guarded by tigers, standing out in front of the temple. This place is a landmark for boat travelers heading to or from Kampong Cham, as it really stands out on the Mekong River. There are drink stands near the temple gates.

To get here head out across the Japanese Bridge, set your odometer at the bridge, and enjoy the scenery. About 29 km from the Japanese Bridge there is a huge Mild Seven billboard with a picture of a guy in a kayak —it appears that you are going to run right into it as you approach it. Highway 6 then curves to the left and you go straight ahead on the dirt road 2 km to the temple and the Mekong River.

River Crossing: There are several small ferry boats crossing the Mekong River off of Highway 6 along this stretch from the Japanese Bridge. The boats are announced by small blue signs along the road and to get to them, just take a right at the sign and go a block or two to the Mekong. The area on the other side is definitely rural Cambodia and exploring it is kind of fun. Just remember that the ferry boats stop crossing over at 5 pm.

Back at Highway 6 and continuing on towards Kampong Cham, the road comes to another huge fork. Going to the left takes you 16 km to the Sap River and the Prek Kohk ferry crossing to Highway 5 (here's the other access to the "Triangle Trip" described earlier).

Following to the right is Highway 6 and the way that you get to the following.

Wat Neeuhk Hilltop Temple

This hilltop temple and its radio tower are visible from a distance, not far after you passed by that last fork. The temple gate is on the right, about 42 km from the Japanese Bridge. There is a stairway straight ahead, but if you veer around to the right you can actually drive up and around to the top. The first level on the hill has the monks' quarters and some shrines. Continuing up, the first structure you come to at the top is a small outdoor temple with a sitting Buddha and a small Chinese-style temple garden, with statues surrounding a landscaped pool area. Just beyond is the main temple, which has some colorful murals on the inside walls.

And, you guessed it, there is a commanding view of the surrounding rural countryside from the top—it's a worthwhile stop.

Dam Site

At 113 km from the Japanese Bridge (on Highway 6, towards Kampong Thom town) is a large picture billboard with English writing that reads "Dam Site." The picture shows what people normally do there—swimming, tubing and picnicking. There are vendors there on weekends. Turn right at the sign, which also lets you know just how far down the road it is.

SOUTH

This is a nice quiet stretch of road that cuts through the rice-field landscape that dominates the region. The road is paved and the ride pleasant. Both sites straddle the border of Kampong Spue and Takeo Provinces.

Irrigation Canal Area & Boulder Spillway

A bridge, boulder spillway, and irrigation canals were built around this small river and marshland area recently to supply the area's agriculture. It's fairly impressive during the rainy season when the water is rushing over the boulders and through the spillway. Locals use the surrounding body of water for fishing, swimming, and riding inner tubes on the fast water. Enterprising Khmer ladies have set up drink stands next to the bridge and spillway area to serve people passing by on their way to Kampot to the south or Phnom Penh to the north.

Setting your odometer at the main entrance gate at Pochentong Airport, head southwest to the big traffic circle. Go straight through it and you are on Highway 3. At 13 km you go over a small dam and spillway. Go another kilometer beyond that to the boulder spillway area.

Wat Rahnong Joyhop Hilltop Temple

Continuing south from the spillway area, after about 27 km (from the airport gate), you will see a hilltop temple off in the distance on the right. Continue on and at just over 29 km you turn right toward the temple. (The turnoff is in a small village and you don't see the temple right away when you turn.) Follow the road through the countryside and stay on it as it goes to and then around the backside of the hill. There is another small road at the backside that can be followed to the top.

Wat Rahnong has been doing well these past few years, and they have a few new structures to show for it. The monks' quarters are at the top of the road and next to them is a beautiful outdoor temple built on the edge of the hill and facing a great view of the Damrei Mountains of Kampong Spue Province. Colorful wall murals and a large sitting Buddha image complete the setting.

Walking over to the simple main temple structure and around its back side, you will find a small stairway going up to the highest point of the hill and the gazebo built on it. It's a nice spot to catch a breeze and the view of the rice fields and sugar palm trees that stretch out as far as you can see.

On the way here you pass by barbecued chicken and sticky rice stands on Highway 3. One could pick up some chicken and drinks and have a nice quiet picnic while enjoying the view.

SOUTHEAST

Neak Loeung Ferry & Phnom Chi-gaht Hilltop Temple

Heading out over the Monivong Bridge on Highway 1 toward Vietnam takes you out to these day-trip destinations. The road straddles the Mekong River, making the journey out an interesting and scenic one. For all the info on these day trips, just flip over to the Svay Rieng and Prey Veng chapter.

OVERNIGHT TRIPS FROM PHNOM PENH

These are suggested overnight trips that will give you the opportunity to break out of Phnom Penh and get a taste of rural Cambodia. Each trip takes you along a manageable asphalt highway and is easy to do the year around. There are plenty of sights to see along the way, as well as when you arrive at your destination. We are calling them overnight trips because it's easy to get to these spots, take in some of the local fun, get off to a late start on the following day, and still make it back to Phnom Penh before evening settles in. However, most of these trips could easily warrant spending at least a couple of nights as they do offer a number of recreational opportunities along with some interesting sites.

Below is a quick reference list. Simply turn to the applicable chapter on the destination listed below and you will find all the information about that area, along with transportation information and options. A motorcycle is a great year-round form of transport on all of these routes.

1. Kampong Cham
2. Kampong Thom
3. Kampong Chhnang
4. Svay Rieng and Prey Veng
5. Takeo
6. Kampot
7. Sihanoukville

Apsara dance style

National Museum at Phnom Penh

Governor's House at Phnom Penh

GPO at Phnom Penh

Silver Pagoda at Phnom Penh

The King's Throne Hall at Phnom Penh

New exhibition hall at Phnom Penh

The Royal Palace at Phnom Penh

Napoleon Pavilion in the Royal Palace at Phnom Penh

Independence Monument at Phnom Penh

Cambodia-Vietnam Friendship
Park

Central market (or New
market) of
Phnom Penh

Watching the dragon boat
races at Phnom Penh

Water festival in Phnom Penh

*A view of the National
Museum from the
FCCC cafe*

*Beer girls in action on
"Restaurant Row"*

◀
*Pondering
death at the
Killing Fields of
Choeung Ek*

▶
*Khmer New Year
water fights in
Phnom Penh*

◀
*Typical gallery on St.178,
Phnom Penh*

▶
*Buried behind colorful
stock at Russian Market*

▲ *Statues for sale at the Russian Market*

Dirt cheap CDs and cassettes ▲
at the Russian Market, Phnom Penh

Panoramic view from
Phnom O'Dong, Kampong
Spue

Rapids at Kirirom National
Park at Kampong Spue

▲
Who needs an eighteen-wheeler?

(top left)
The ancient temples and king's tombs of O'Dong, Kampong Spue

Children at Kampong Spue—the kid in front apparently thought it was a hold-up

Killing Fields monument at Phnom Ombe Resort, Kampong Spue

KAMPONG CHAM

With its Mekong River location and relatively close proximity to Phnom Penh and Vietnam, Kampong Cham has always been an important trade and transportation hub. The highway from Phnom Penh is in excellent condition—you can get here in just under two hours by road or by the bullet boats that are a main mode of transportation between towns on the Mekong River. Either way it's a nice ride, with views of the rural countryside or river area, depending on which way you go.

The town itself is quaint and charming with its bustling morning river scene and wide boulevard streets in from the river. There are a few worthwhile attractions nearby and with its location on the way by boat or road to Kratie, Mondulkiri, Rattanakiri and Stung Treng Provinces, it's a nice jump-off point.

Kampong Cham is a mix of the old and the new, with a new temple being built in and around old ruins and the big ferry boats taking people and goods to the other side of the Mekong, right next to the construction of the first bridge ever built here.

WHAT'S UP

River Scene

With a scenic Mekong River location and a nice river boulevard, the town is a pleasant place to enjoy a stroll, jog, or just to kick back with a cold drink and watch the people swarming the area late afternoons and early evenings.

The area near the Mekong Hotel and the boat station is where the action is centered and it's full of food and drink vendors late in the day.

Wat Nokor (Angkor Bahjay)

Definitely an interesting mix of the old and the newer Buddhist styles of temples and worth a look. The walls and grounds around the old temple still have some nice sculptures intact from its 11th-century origin. Newer temple structures (mostly sixty to seventy years old) have been built in and around the old structure and it's actually a fascinating blend. There is also a reclining Buddha in one of the temple outbuildings, just west of the main complex.

Located on the west end of town, right off from the multi-headed cobra circle.

Phnom Bproh & Phnom Sray

These two hilltop temples are on the north side of Highway 7, about 5 km back toward Phnom Penh. Phnom Sray (Woman or Sister Hill) is the higher of the two and has a long stairway leading to the top. The top of Phnom Bproh (Man or Brother Hill) can be reached by road.

There are varying legends as to how they were built and named. Believers in the different theories are sure their version is accurate. Anyway, one legend has it that a guy and girl wanted to marry. Khmer custom says that the man must go to the woman's parents and then to his own to seek permission and blessings. The guy did not want to bother with all of this, which did not please his girlfriend, a traditional girl who decided that she must then be the one to visit both sets of parents to get their blessings.

In Khmer society, the husband is supposed to be in the elevated position of the relationship. But when it was decided to build these two sites in the couple's honor, the guy got the lower hill and the girl was honored with the higher peak, closest to the

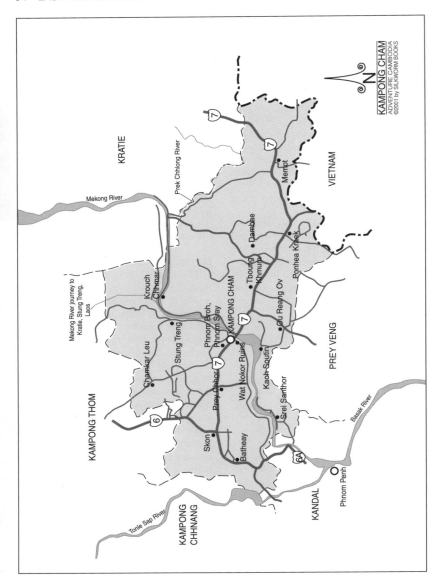

heavens since she was the one who did things properly while he shirked his duties.

These temples are very popular pilgrimage places for locals on holiday. There are good views of the countryside and the Mekong River to the east.

Wat Prah Tohm Nah Day Doh

A real mouthful for a real fine-looking place. Situated on a river bend on the far south end of town are a couple of temple buildings set amid nicely landscaped grounds. The main temple is about seventy years old and has a hundred-year-old sitting Buddha image and some interesting wall murals. Stupas and monuments, including a four-faced Bayon-style one, are not in short supply.

Wat Joy T'maw

This temple is on the opposite end (north) of the river road, overlooking the Mekong.

King's Residence

It's been unused for over three years, and the local government has let the outside building and grounds go in a way that does not show much respect for the monarchy.

MARKETS

Kampong Cham market has a gaudy look similar to that of the Central Market in Phnom Penh, and it has a complete supply of just about anything that you may need. A night market springs up on the western side in the evening. There are plenty of photo shops and pharmacies on the perimeter roads.

GETTING AROUND

There isn't a rental shop in Kampong Cham and the moto drivers for hire are not keen on renting out their bikes. They charge 4,000 riel an hour for taking you around.

COMMUNICATIONS & INFORMATION

The international phone rates are similar to those in Phnom Penh—pricey.

CURRENCY EXCHANGE

There is a branch office of Pacific Commercial Bank across from the north side of Kampong Cham Market (the main market). You can exchange traveler's checks here. You will see the familiar glass cases of the money changers along the perimeter of the market.

MEDICAL FACILITIES

The Kampong Cham Provincial Hospital has Khmer and foreign doctors on staff.

RESTAURANTS

Apsara Restaurant. Near the Kampong Cham Market. They serve a good breakfast and continue throughout the day. They have some western food and an English menu.

Kimsrun Guesthouse & Restaurant. The guesthouse has a small rice dish and noodle soup restaurant.

Haoan Restaurant. This place is popular with locals and the Kampong Cham NGO crowd. It looks like a two-story hotel and has some a/c rooms for private dinners, in addition to the main eating area. Good Chinese and Khmer food along with the usual beer girls.

Phnom Prosh Hotel & Restaurant. This newer hotel also has a restaurant. Good Chinese, Khmer and a bit of western food.

There are also small food and drink stands along the River Parkway.

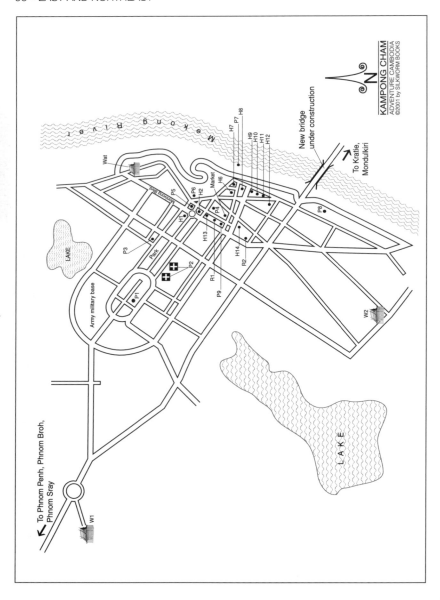

EAST & NORTHEAST

KAMPONG CHAM

H=Hotels

H1   Phnom Prosh Hotel
H2   Hotel Mittapheap
H3   7 January, Angkor Thom, Chann Chhaya Guesthouse
H4   Nava Guesthouse
H5   Kampong Cham International Resort
H6   Monorom Guesthouse
H7   Mekong Hotel
H8   Bopear Guesthouse
H9   Pounleurasemei 2 Guesthouse
H10 Kimsrun Guesthouse
H11 Chamnortunle Guesthouse
H12 Sengly Guesthouse
H13 Bopharik Guesthouse
H14 Hotel Ponleurasmei

R=Restaurants

R1   Apsara Restaurant
R2   Haoan Restaurant

See hotel list for:
- Kimsrun Restaurant & Guesthouse
- Phnom Prosh Hotel & Restaurant

P=Places

P1   King's residence, no longer used
P2   Hospital
P3   Post & Telecommunications
P4   Share taxi stand
P5   CPP Party headquarters
P6   Royal Fine Art Department
P7   Bullet boat landing
P8   Ferry crossing
P9   Konica photo

W=Wats

W1 Wat Nokor Angkor Bahjay
W2 Wat Prah Tohm Nah Day Doh

NIGHT SCENE

The top spot in town is the nightclub in the Phnom Prosh Hotel, with a live Cambodian band and all the extras you have come to expect in a Khmer nightclub.

ACCOMMODATIONS

There is no shortage of choices in Kampong Cham.

Cheaper Places

These two places are next to the river:

Pounleurasemei 2 Guesthouse. Names this long should be illegal. It's good value at US$5 for a fan room and US$10 a/c. The rooms have a Western bath and some have a view of the river.

Chamnortunle Guesthouse. A shorter name than the neighbor, but not by much. There is a nice second-floor terrace overlooking the Mekong River. There are US$3 fan rooms on the third floor. The other rooms have a Western bath and TV added. US$5 for a fan room and US$10 for adding a/c.

These next four places are close to the market and river:

7 January Guesthouse. It's a dive, but at 5,000 riel that's what you get. It has a share bath and a seond-floor terrace.

Angkor Thom Guesthouse. Same as the 7 January, US$30 on a monthly basis.

Chann Chhaya Guesthouse. It's the same as the others at 5,000 riel.

Nava Guesthouse. In the middle of this pack of three others. There are small, clean rooms with a Western bath in each room at US$5 a night.

Monorom Guesthouse. Newly refurbished, they now have nice rooms with TV, fan, Western bath for US$5, adding a/c puts the cost at US$10. There is karaoke on the premises and the place always has working girls hanging around making this place fairly lively for Kampong Cham. It's located behind the Mekong Hotel.

Bopharik Guesthouse. It has a nice terrace overlooking the market. Simple fan rooms with Western bath for US$5, $10 for a/c.

Bopear Guesthouse. Located one block in from the river, it's a clean and well-run place. There is also a nice second floor terrace. Western bath and a big fan room go for US$4.

Sengly Guesthouse. This place has simple rooms with attached bath for US$4 w/fan or US$10 for a/c.

Hakly Guesthouse. Unfriendly staff make this place a bad choice even though the rooms are fairly decent.

Kimsrun Guesthouse. A simple place with a small restaurant on the premises. US$3 a night.

A Notch Up

Hotel Ponleurasmei. There's that name again. English-speaking staff with nice but mostly windowless rooms. There is a Western bath, TV, fridge, two twin beds and a fan for US$5 or US$10 for a/c.

Kampong Cham International Resort. Sounds impressive and it's right next to the river. It's a newer place and so far they don't have their act together. The bungalows have h/w shower, TV and Western bath, but at the moment it's being used as a sort of Karaoke World theme park. Being close to the Mekong Hotel and the pier it may be worth a look to see if they changed back to the original resort concept.

Mekong Hotel. Right next to the river and the bullet boat pier. It affords nice views and location, with one downside to that. At 6 am the line of boats starts the hyperactive blowing of air-horns non-stop for half an hour. They don't understand the concept that they have their schedule posted

and when departure time comes, you simply go.

Anyway, the rooms are nice and clean and come with a Western bath, TV, a/c and river view for US$15, or US$13 for the backside hotel rooms. There are also $6 fan rooms with no TV.

Hotel Mittapheap. Another new addition to the hotel scene. There is a terrace overlooking the boulevard and market area. The staff speak English and the place has nice rooms with twin beds, TV, a/c and Western bath for US$12 a night. It's a quiet alternative.

Phnom Prosh Hotel. Last but not least is this newer hotel with a nightclub and restaurant on the premises. The US$5 rooms with TV, fridge, Western bath and a fan, and a/c rooms at US$12 are good value. The nightclub hours are 8:30 pm to midnight.

COMING & GOING

Bullet Boats

This is a nice option for your travels along the Mekong. Phnom Penh to Kampong Cham takes two hours and costs 10,000 riel. The boats depart just north of the Japanese Bridge on the Phnom Penh side of the river.

Kampong Cham to Kratie is a three-hour boat ride and the cost is 15,000 riel.

The boats usually do not continue on to Stung Treng as the water level must be very high to enable the boats to clear all of the small islands and clumps in the river between Kratie and Stung Treng. The boats usually don't even go during the rainy season.

Bikers: The cost for taking a motorcycle with you by boat for a section of the trip is the same price as for a person. It's not recommended, though, as the porters who load and unload the boats are a hassle to deal with and if they happen to drop your motorcycle in the river (a real possibility), it's your loss and not theirs. If you have a motorcycle, ride it. It's not recommended to combine the two modes of transportation.

Bus

Hoh Wah Genting Bus Company has a/c buses to and from Kampong Cham on a regular schedule every day. Their main bus terminal is near the southwest corner of the Central Market (or New Market) in Phnom Penh. The trip is 5,000 riel. In Kampong Cham, bus arrivals and departures are at the Kampong Cham Market. Please see the Getting Around chapter towards the front of the book for all bus schedules.

Share Taxis

With the air-con buses making the trip from Phnom Penh to Kampong Cham and doing it more cheaply, there is not much of a reason to take a taxi.

A share taxi from Kampong Cham to Kampong Thom is 8,000 riel. The road is good.

The share taxis do not go all the way to Kratie at this time, only as far as Snoul, the small town that is the juncture point for the road to Kratie and to Sen Monorom town in Mondulkiri Province. In Snoul there are only sometimes share taxis plying the route to Kratie. If you don't have your own motorcycle as transportation, your surest bet is to take the bullet boat if you want to go to Kratie from Kampong Cham.

Motorcycle Touring Info

Phnom Penh to Kampong Cham

As mentioned earlier, the highway from Phnom Penh is an excellent condition. You take Highway 6 from Phnom Penh (crossing the Japanese Bridge) and go to Skon where you will find a traffic circle with a

statue of children holding a bird. Highway 6 continues on to the left, going to Kampong Thom and Siem Reap. For Kampong Cham, you veer to the right and follow Highway 7.

A scenic option to this is to follow the river road on the eastern side of the Mekong River. It takes a bit more time but if you have time it's worth it. Security is not a problem.

Until the new bridge over the Mekong River is finished, you still take the big ferry across if you want to explore the eastern side of the province or continue on to Kratie or Mondulkiri Provinces by motorcycle or vehicle. It's 200 riel per person and 400 riel for a motorcycle.

Kampong Cham to Snoul and Kratie or Sen Monorom

The motorcycle ride from Kampong Cham to Snoul is on a road that's not great but is doable. Just before you reach Snoul there is a junction in the road with a police box on the right side. Follow the road to the left and you are on the highway to Kratie. You go through the town of Snoul just ahead where there is food and fuel.

Back at the junction by the police box just before you get to Snoul, following the curve to the right takes you to Mondulkiri. About 7 km past that curve you come to a four-way junction. Turn left there and you are on the highway to Sen Monorom. Fuel and drinks are available at the four-way, so you can bypass Snoul if you like.

From Snoul to Sen Monorom the road is in good condition. It's only a dirt road but it's nice and level because it was put in for the logging trucks. The road does get a bit tricky during the rainy season, however, when the clay gets wet and it becomes similar to riding on ice. The scenery is beautiful.

KRATIE

Kratie is a sleepy Mekong River town situated on the east bank of the mighty river. It's very picturesque with sandbars and big islands out front and bends in the river. Unlike in many towns around Cambodia, the war years were fairly kind to the French architecture and the roads, at least in the town itself. There are some nice-looking homes of French and Khmer style scattered about, adding to the pleasant feel of the place.

The rare freshwater Irrawaddy dolphins make their home in the Mekong River, just north of Kratie. With only around fifteen to twenty remaining, they are worth a visit.

Whether you are just on a trip seeing the river towns along the Mekong or taking a full circuit trip around the east and northeast, Kratie is a nice place to spend a night or two.

WHAT'S UP

River Scene

Kratie has a beautiful river boulevard with dozens of snack and drink stands in the late afternoon and evening, making this a nice spot to chill out and watch the people parading by. There are also a few big concrete decks along the river road from which to admire the river scene. The river road is a great place for a stroll or jog.

Irrawaddy Dolphins

About fifteen to twenty of these rare freshwater dolphins make their home on a beautiful stretch of the Mekong River near a small set of rapids. They make upward arches, breaking the surface of the water as they swim about the area. They are not jumpers like their sea-faring relatives and are quite a bit shyer as well. They have good reason to be shy towards humans as they have been hunted and killed by fishermen in the past. The hope is that their numbers will slowly increase as more fishermen in the area are educated about them.

They are most active in the early morning hours (around 6 am) and the late afternoon and early evening hours. However, we went during the mid-afternoon heat of the day and had numerous sightings. A local family hire out their small rowboat and a son to take you out on the river for a closer look. The charge is 3,500 riel per person.

To get there, just follow the road north from the Globe traffic circle for 14 km. Turn left at the dolphin picture sign. The family and river are there.

Irrawaddy freshwater dolphins

Phnom Sambok Temples

By heading north from the Globe circle you also reach the hilltop temples of Sambok village. Following the stairway up, you will come to three different levels of shrines, temples and living quarters for the monks. The second level features a reclining Buddha, and the top level a beautiful view of the Mekong River area.

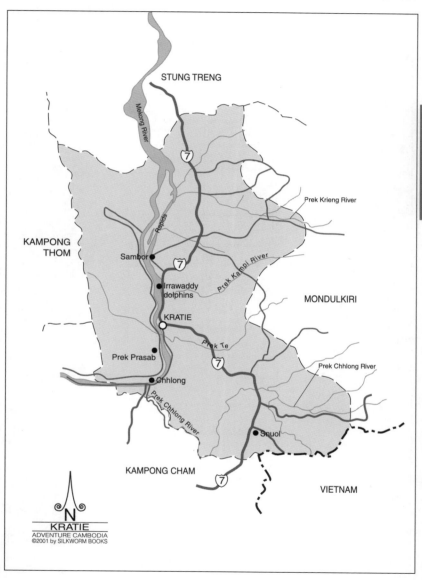

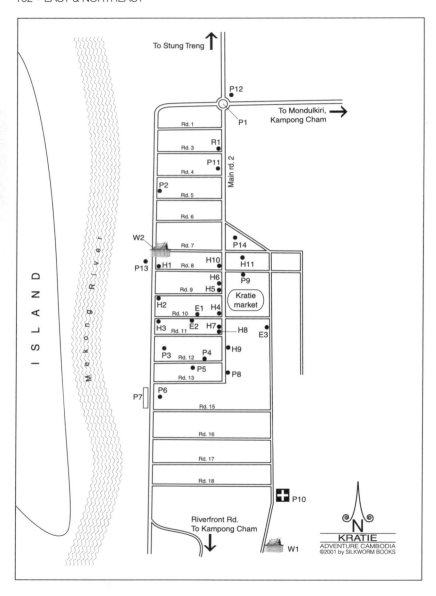

KRATIE

H=Hotels

H1	Santepheap Hotel
H2	30 December Hotel & Restaurant
H3	Heng Heng Hotel & Restaurant
H4	Star Guesthouse
H5	69 Guesthouse
H6	Hai Heng Guesthouse
H7	Phnom Meas Guesthouse
H8	Soksan Guesthouse
H9	Nyta Guesthouse
H10	Mean Tip Guesthouse
H11	Apsara Guesthouse

R=Restaurants

R1	Golden Star Restaurant

See hotel list for:
- 30 December Hotel & Restaurant
- Heng Heng Hotel & Restaurant

W=Wats

W1	Wat Preah Vihear
W2	Wat Stay Sahn-tah-rah-boh

P=Places

P1	World globe bird monument
P2	International English school
P3	Government office
P4	Post & Telecommunications
P5	Cobra monument foundation
P6	Government mansion
P7	View decks
P8	Water company
P9	Night market
P10	Kratie provincial hospital
P11	Motorcycle repair shop
P12	Gas station
P13	Boat taxi to Kampong Cham, Phnom Penh & Stung Treng
P14	Taxi stands for other towns

E=Entertainments

E1	Small karaoke place
E2	Small karaoke place
E3	Nightclub

Follow the road north of the circle 8.5 km and you will see the hill temple and dirt road leading to it on the right.

Wat Preah Vihear (Kratie)

Golden lions guard the gates that lead to peaceful and heavily shaded temple grounds. It bears the name of the internationally famous Preah Vihear Temple that straddles the Thai border in the Dangrek Mountains.

Sambor Town

For a nice ride through the countryside hugging the Mekong River, you can head north past Phnom Sambok and past the dolphin site. About 24 km from the Globe circle, you come to a fork in the road. The road to the right goes to Stung Treng, but you want to follow the road to the left. This is the better of the two roads and the one that hugs the river to Sambor town, another 11 km away. Stay left at the fork as you near the town and you wind your way to Wat Sambor, located near the river.

The front temple is fairly new, with a one-hundred-year-old temple just beyond the rear of that temple. The town is pleasant and food, drinks, and fuel are available.

As for the ruins shown on the official Cambodia map (south of Sambor), there is nothing left of them any more. Just one good-luck stone is all that the locals saved, putting it in a thatched temple hut a kilometer off the road.

Family times or ties at Kratie

Wat Sray Sahn-tah-rah-boh

It's a big name for a small temple on the river road.

MARKETS & SHOPPING

The Kratie market is right in the thick of things, just a block from the river. It's the usual all-purpose variety. There are two small night market areas. One is across the road from the northern side of the market. The other is on the street and just east of the Heng Heng Hotel. There are a couple of photo shops near the pack of guesthouses just west of the market.

GETTING AROUND

Moto-Taxi

The moto-taxi guys charge the standard 4,000 riel per hour to take you around. Add fuel cost if you head out of town.

Motorcycle Doctor

We found a very creative mechanic who is good at jerry-rigging needed repairs on big bikes, even though he has little to work with in the way of parts. His shop is located about 100 meters north of the share taxi stand, on the west side of Road 2.

CURRENCY EXCHANGE

As in many Cambodian towns, there is no bank in Kratie. The best place to change money is across the street from the western side of the market.

MEDICAL FACILITIES

The Kratie Provincial Hospital has Khmer and foreign doctors.

RESTAURANTS

Heng Heng Hotel & Restaurant. This place has some very good food and some Western dishes, with an English menu to boot. Some staff speak English.

Apsara Guesthouse & Restaurant. The food is okay and they can make a few Western dishes as well. The manager speaks English.

Golden Star Restaurant. It's a simple place with big ambitions. It features decent Khmer food and beer girls, with a small late-night dance venue thrown in as well.

Mekong Restaurant. Simple Khmer fare located just in from the 30 December Hotel.

30 December Guesthouse & Restaurant. They have an English menu and simple, cheap dishes.

NIGHT SCENE

The Golden Star Restaurant and the karaoke shops by the night market are about all.

ACCOMMODATIONS

Cheaper Places

Apsara Guesthouse & Restaurant. These rooms are small, with thin walls and a share bath. The place is kept fairly clean, however, and at 7,000 riel for one bed or 10,000 riel for two beds, it's okay. There is a restaurant on the premises.

Mean Guesthouse. Similar to the Apsara with rooms going for 5,000–7,000 riel per night.

Hai Heng Guesthouse. It's close to the Mean Guesthouse. With very low ceilings, a place for vertically challenged people. 10,000 riel per night.

Phnom Meas Guesthouse, Soksan Guesthouse, Nyta Guesthouse. These three places are near each other just south of the

market. They are all similar, clean, have a bathroom in the room and a fan. They are good value at US$3 a night.

Star Guesthouse. Nice clean rooms with a Western bath and fan for US$4. There is a second-floor terrace overlooking the market and part of the river down the street. The owner's sons speak English and are helpful sources of information on Kratie.

30 December Hotel & Restaurant. Simple large rooms with a share bath. Located across from the river. 10,000 riel.

A Notch Up

Heng Heng Hotel & Restaurant. Located just across from the river, this place has a nice second-floor terrace and rooms with a view. The staff are very friendly and some speak English. The rooms are nice enough and have a Western bath, TV and fan for US$7. The same room with a/c is US$12. There is also a good restaurant on the premises.

Santepheap Hotel. This is the new place just across the river road from the boat landing. It's the sister hotel of the Mekong Hotel in Kampong Cham town. It features rooms with a river view, a big Western bath, twin beds, TV and a/c for US$15 a night. The fan rooms are US$7, but have no TV.

COMING & GOING

Bullet Boat

There are several alternatives to get to Kratie, the easiest of which is by the bullet boats that ply the Mekong River. If you are coming from Kampong Cham and don't have a motorcycle, the boat is probably your only option. At the time of this writing, the share taxis were not making the full trip to Kratie; they were only going as far as Snuol.

The bullet boat from **Phnom Penh** departs from the bullet boat company docks located just north of the Japanese Bridge at 7 am. The trip takes just over five hours and costs 25,000 riel.

From **Kampong Cham** to Kratie, the bullet boat takes about three hours and costs 15,000 riel. The boat pier in Kampong Cham is directly in front of the Mekong Hotel.

The Kratie–**Stung Treng** bullet boat trip only runs during the rainy season when the water level in the Mekong is sufficient enough to allow the boats to get through the numerous stretches of shallow rapids and various other obstacles on this stretch of the river. As of May 2000 the rainy season was in full swing and the boats were running every other day at a fare of 20,000 riels. The trip upriver to Stung Treng takes around 6–7 hours, with the trip back down to Kratie, going with the current, taking about 4 hours.

EAST & NORTHEAST

> **CAUTION**
> From time to time there are reports from the share taxi drivers of robbery along the Kratie-Stung Treng Highway. We heard two such reports from the affected drivers while we were in Stung Treng. We encountered no such problems and only came across friendly people on the road, but we recommend that you try to get current reports of the road condition before making the trip, either in Kratie or Stung Treng.

Share Taxi

Kratie to Stung Treng:	20,000 riel
Kratie to Rattanakiri (Banlung town):	40,000 riel

Motorcycle Touring Info

Phnom Penh to Kratie

If you are going to Kratie from Phnom Penh, the road to Kampong Cham is excellent, the road from Kampong Cham to the

Snuol junction isn't that great, but it's definitely doable.

The last section taking you to Kratie from Snuol has some huge bomb craters that fill up and look like lakes during the rainy season, but it's also doable; you're just going to get wet.

Snuol to Mondulkiri

If you are heading to Sen Monorom from Kratie, proceed to Snuol and pass through the main town area. You will come to a fork in the road where you stay to the left. Follow this about 7 km and you will come to a four-way junction where you turn left. This newly-cut dirt highway takes you to Sen Monorom. The road is nice and level having been cut by logging companies for their trucks. Fuel and food are available in Snuol town and at the four-way junction. Security on these stretches is not a problem.

Kratie to Stung Treng

The road goes from asphalt to shredded tarmac to dirt. There are scattered bomb craters, but the road is not nearly as bad as some. The trip is 142 km and took four hours during the rainy season. For security, see the word of caution above.

Cargo freighter plying the Mekong

MONDULKIRI

This province is chock full of natural beauty, with thickly forested mountains, powerful waterfalls and the lush green rolling hills of the western side. Add to that the communities of hill tribe people who are not affected by mass-tourism, as they are in neighboring Thailand, and you have an area that is very attractive to the adventure traveler.

The town of Sen Monorom is the best base camp for travelers who want to explore the surrounding areas. A quiet but beautiful town nestled into the hills, it has a lot of potential to develop into a center for non-intrusive eco-tourism. At present, it's very undeveloped, which gives you a feeling of going somewhere off the beaten tourist trail.

Also interesting is the variety of languages being used: Khmer, hill tribe languages, Vietnamese and Laos.

WHAT'S UP

Sen Monorom

This is a pleasant little town to walk around and take in its natural beauty. The two small lakes in town are good spots for hanging out and watching the locals fish and swim. Jump in yourself if the heat of the day has slowed your pace.

The Market Life of Hill Tribe People

Mornings are the best time of the day to hit the town market and stroll about. This is when many people from the various area hill tribe communities come to the market to sell their wares and purchase supplies. It's a good environment in which to unobtrusively observe their attire and with their permission, possibly get snapshots of them going about their normal business at the market.

Old & New Wat

An old wooden temple on the hills at the south end of town is being revitalized with the construction of a brand new model next to it. This is where the monks of Sen Monorom teach.

Southwest Waterfalls

The waterfall about 5.5 km to the southwest of town is a nice and easily accessible sight. There is a fair-sized pool below the 7.5-meter waterfall that makes a good spot for a swim or picnic. To get there, just follow the map and don't turn off of that road, as it takes you to a parking circle near the top level of the waterfall. If you don't have a motorcycle already, hire a moto-taxi to take you out there for 4,000 riel per hour and a bit extra for fuel (1,000 riel).

Pahlung Village

It's possible to go on an elephant trek at this small village. It's a good idea to come out here the day before (possibly on your way to Bousra Waterfall) to organize it so they have the animal ready to go the next morning, instead of out working in the jungle.

You can take a half-or full-day trip in the surrounding area. It's good to wear long pants and bring some mosquito repellent, drinking water and food.

To get there, just head north from Sen Monorom. When you get to the fork in the road, go right. The village is about 8 km from town. People in the small houses on the right can fetch the elephant guy for you. If you go by moto-taxi, the driver can help

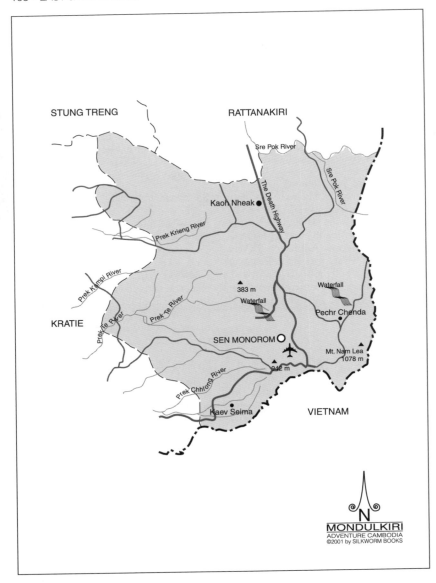

STUNG TRENG

RATTANAKIRI

Sre Pok River

The Death Highway

Sre Pok River

Kaoh Nheak ●

Prek Krieng River

Prek Kampi River

Prek Te River

Prek Te River

▲ 383 m
Waterfall

Waterfall

Pechr Chenda ●

KRATIE

SEN MONOROM ○

Mt. Nam Lea
1078 m ▲

▲ 942 m

Prek Chhlong River

Kaev Seima ●

VIETNAM

N
MONDULKIRI
ADVENTURE CAMBODIA
©2001 by SILKWORM BOOKS

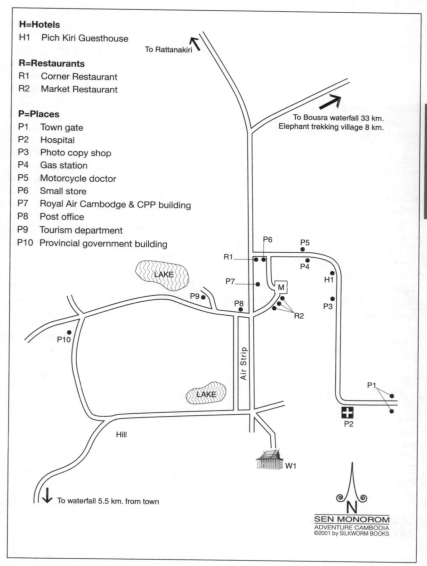

with the translation of arranging the tour. The guy at the town tourist office, if you can ever find him there and he's not sleeping, can also set the tour up for you, but he takes a cut. Figure around US$15 for a half-day or US$30 for a full-day tour.

Boo-sra Waterfall

This one is a bit further afield, but definitely worth the trip if the weather permits. The road actually goes across the top of the waterfall (about 10 meters back), so watch your step! It's a magnificent two-tiered waterfall with the river gorge cutting through the surrounding forest.

Getting there is part of the adventure. Continue on past Pahlung village (the elephant place) and follow this same road all the way. About 16 km from Sen Monorom you come to the first of two small rivers without bridges that you must cross. They are doable even during the rainy season. Just walk the bikes across and cool off in the water. The second river that you come to is a bit wider, but not very deep, even during a wet rainy season, as when we made the trip. Again, just walk across it.

Fishing

Although there is nothing organized as of yet, Mondulkiri's rivers and streams would probably make for some good fishing. Bring your own lightweight gear and give it a try.

Sen Monorom would be a great place for mountain biking. There are now no rentals there, so you would have to bring one along on the airplane.

COMMUNICATIONS & INFORMATION

Mr. Long Vibol (or simply Vibol) has a pharmacy in the first row of the marketplace. He speaks English and likes to discuss the attractions in the area. Just ask the vendors where his place is.

MARKET & CURRENCY EXCHANGE

Many of the goods in the market are from nearby Vietnam. It's an all-purpose market, but it doesn't have the feel of the typical Cambodian market, which is probably again due to the closeness of Vietnam and the hill tribe people who come here.

There are noodle, dessert and fruit stalls at the front end of the market and the money changers are in front as well. They change dollars, riel and the Vietnamese dong.

GETTING AROUND

Moto-Taxi

The moto-taxis charge a standard fare of 4,000 riel per hour or 500 riel for a one-way in-town destination.

Motorcycle Doctor

There is a motorcycle mechanic who knows a bit about big bikes. He's located on the road between the Pich Kiri Guesthouse and the airport, on the opposite side of the road from the gas station.

MEDICAL FACILITIES

There is a provincial hospital in town with a couple of foreign doctors.

RESTAURANTS

Because this is a small and little-developed tourist destination, the restaurants don't think about serving tourists. There just haven't been many coming to Sen Monorom. And with the locals usually eating at home, the restaurants don't stock much food. The procedure here is to go by the restaurant you want to eat at one hour or more beforehand and tell them what you want to eat. You can leave then, while they go to the market to buy the ingredients and return to the restaurant to prepare the dishes. An alternative would be to stop by in the morning and tell them what you want for a lunch or evening meal. It's certainly not the norm at destinations around Cambodia, but it seems to work out okay here.

Corner Restaurant. There isn't a name, but it's easy to find. It's a very simple place, but they do a good job with the food and they have drinks with ice. The prices are very reasonable.

Twin Restaurants. There are two restaurants near the entrance area to the market. They double as community entertainment centers; local residents gather outside to gaze at videos on the TV screens inside. They can also serve the necessary karaoke hall function.

NIGHT SCENE

Dream on—and enjoy nature.

ACCOMMODATIONS

There used to be two places in town until one of them burned down. Did the arson squad look at the competition?

Pich Kiri Guesthouse. This friendly place is really growing since it cornered the market. The Khmer husband-and-wife team that runs the place can speak some English and French. They serve complimentary French bread and espresso coffee in the morning. They have built a few different styles of simple rooms with share bath that range in price from US$3–$7. They also have rooms built around a garden courtyard area that have one large or two twin-sized beds. The rooms have a simple bathroom inside and cost US$8.

COMING & GOING

Air

Flying is by far the easiest way to get here. Royal Air Cambodge makes the flight twice a week at present and the flight lasts one hour and twenty minutes. Oddly enough, the office of Royal Air Cambodge is unmarked and inside the CPP (ruling party) headquarters. The airstrip is just across the way.

Motorcycle Touring Info

The ride passes by some beautiful and diverse countryside, regardless of which direction you are coming from. Security is not a problem these days.

Kratie to Mondulkiri

If you are coming on the bomb-cratered highway from Kratie, go straight when you get into Snuol town, and when you see the road curve to the right or left, go left. After about 7 km you come to a four-way junction, where you turn left to Mondulkiri. Snuol to Mondulkiri is about 130 km, and if you are coming from Kratie the entire trip is 215 km.

Kampong Cham to Mondulkiri

Kampong Cham to the Snuol turn off (to go to Mondulkiri) is a lousy but doable stretch of Highway 7. It's about 143 km to Snuol and 275 km for the entire trip.

Just before you reach Snuol town you will notice a police box on the right. The road curves to the right or left, and you go to the right to reach Mondulkiri. About 7 km down you will come to a four-way junction where you turn left for the ride to Mondulkiri.

The road from Snuol to Sen Monorom, Mondulkiri, is a decent, level dirt variety that you can make fairly good time on. This changes during the rainy season when rainfall will make the wet surface as slippery as ice.

Food and fuel can be had in Snuol town, with fuel and snacks available at the four-way junction 7 km from the Snuol turn-off.

Sen Monorom to Banlung, Rattanakiri

If you want to go by motorcycle from Sen Monorom to Banlung, Rattanakiri, and it is rainy season, read the section entitled "The Death Highway." Or follow this simple advice: don't do it.

Even in the dry season, it's a tough trail that will put your riding skills to the test. Make sure you have spare parts for your motorcycle (see Getting Around chapter for our Biker Checklist), and plenty of food and drinking water. The trip will take a couple of days during the dry season and Kaoh Nhek town (near halfway) is the only place that sells bottled water and some food. Fuel is available there as well.

Don't do it alone. It's best to have some help if you have a bike breakdown or a mishap. You are a long way from help in most stretches of this remote trail. It would also be best to bring along a Khmer speaker, as the trail sometimes intersects with other trails and you will want to clarify that you took the proper way when you do come across somebody.

It's definitely an adventure. If you try to tackle it, be fully prepared so you have an opportunity to enjoy it.

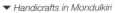
◀ *Working elephant*

▼ *Handicrafts in Mondulkiri*

Finally bridging the Mekong
River at Kampong Cham

Nokor Temple at Kampong
Cham

◀ Hilltop temple at Kampong Cham

The Buddha in Nokor Temple ▶

Bousra waterfalls

Crossing the hard way—the only way in Mondulkiri

Gone fishing in Sen Monorom, Mondulkiri

THE DEATH HIGHWAY

This is also known as the cow path from Mondulkiri to Rattanakiri. When we completed the journey during a very wet rainy season, our Khmer interpreter gave the trail this name. She jokingly (or was it?) compared it with the Buddhist way of thinking that if you do wrong and don't lead your life properly, this is where you end up, on a place like this trail, struggling endlessly each day among the bad conditions that you made of your life. I guess we had some penance to fulfill.

It's an arduous journey any time of the year, but the rainy season adds a whole new dimension. The trail goes through, and is often indistinguishable from, flooded rice paddies. There are numerous streams and rivers with no bridge that you must deal with. During the dry season the streams are barely flowing or dried up completely, but we were always faced with a challenge on our rainy season journey.

We were usually able to walk the bikes across the rivers, lifting them up when the water was deep to keep it from getting into the engine through the exhaust. A couple of times, in areas where the water was a bit deeper, we were able to enlist the help of villagers to lift the bikes onto four sets of shoulders and wade across the fast-moving water this way.

On one occasion, at a river that had become too deep to get across, we thought we were going to have to turn back and just scrap the trip. But after a moment of discussion we agreed that we had no desire to relive the stretch of trail that we had already passed over. So we put on our thinking caps, which were rain soaked at the time, and looked about for something to lay the bikes on and swim them across. Finally, a bit of

luck came our way. Someone had cut a few pieces of bamboo and left them near the far bank of the river. Swimming across, I retrieved them and swam them back to where the motorcycles were—no easy task with the river current trying to rip the bamboo from my hands and send it downstream.

My companion had, for whatever reason, brought along a section of rope that we cut up and used to lash the sections of bamboo together. Twice we put one bike onto the makeshift raft, laying it sideways with the exhaust pipe facing upwards, and swam it across. All that for about 25 meters. Easy crossings become major projects during the rainy season.

The inability to make much headway through the nasty trail conditions of the "Death Highway" meant that we had to seek shelter for the three nights that we spent on the passage. As the afternoons began to wane, we usually found ourselves crossing our fingers, hoping that we would come across a small village or at least a bamboo hut. We got lucky on all three nights, finding people who were more than a bit surprised and amused that we would make such a trip at that time of the year. We always gave them a donation for staying the night and for the community dish we would eat together. Families in this area usually only have food enough to get through until the next harvest, so they should be given some compensation.

The people who live along parts of this sparsely populated stretch of Cambodia are forgotten souls. They have been left by the central government to fend for themselves, without any thought given to basic needs, such as a useable road to travel on or simple health information and access to medicine.

You certainly don't trip over any NGO aid groups here to help, either.

Having seen few, if any, foreigners close up before, the families found us very interesting subjects to study. In each of the three homes we stayed along the way, the family sat down in front of us to study each of our little mannerisms, much as we might study the mannerisms of a monkey at the zoo.

When we wanted to change clothes and hinted that we wanted a bit of privacy, there they sat. There was no way they were going to give up their seats for that show. We ended up shielding each other with bath towels, one at a time, while we changed, which really brought down the house from an entertainment standpoint. Brushing teeth seemed to be thought of as an exercise in vanity and a complete waste of time, judging by the looks on the faces of our hosts as they watched us. When one of us took out his contact lens kit in the evening, the circle of the curious would move in to arm's length. It took a good bit of explaining to get them to understand this modern invention for the eye. Curiosity would really get the best of them any time one of us went through a gear bag. The entire family watched with bated breath to see exactly what item from the other world we might pull out of there.

Most of these people own nothing from the modern-day world and live in rough bamboo huts lighted in the evening by the bamboo torches they make for themselves. Very few living in these areas have mosquito nets to sleep under, even though it's a malarial region. When we mentioned that we wanted to get some drinking water, in most cases people would produce a bucket of dirty water from a nearby river. Since nobody has apparently ever come through these parts to tell them of the dangers associated with untreated drinking water,

they don't realize that many of the illnesses their families suffer from are due to this. Surprisingly enough, the simple procedures of boiling river water or catching and storing rainwater have never been introduced to most of them. When we told people that they should do these things to have clean drinking water, we were asked why anyone would go through that much trouble when the river is so close at hand.

One family we stayed a night with told us that they had lost two children to different illnesses. They said that because there was no doctor or even medicine available in the area they were unable to deal with what were probably very treatable problems. "Death Highway," indeed. Spending a few days on it is one thing; living an entire lifetime there is a scary thought. We lucky ones were able to move on, enduring the challenging trials of our adventure along the way, but moving on.

The jungle rivers are full of leeches during the rainy season. Khmers are deathly afraid of leeches, firmly believing that they suck all of the power from your spirit along with the blood that they take, leaving you just a shell of your former self if you are lucky enough to survive. One time, upon emerging from the water after another river crossing, I began pulling at a leech that had dug in around my ankle. A couple of rural folk who happened to be bathing in the river nearby, began to scream and looked terrified, grabbing their belongings and high-tailing it out of the water. They kept looking back at me over their shoulders, unable to fight the urge of one last glimpse of the poor soul before he succumbed.

When they later saw me in their small village, they approached cautiously, apparently trying to decide which world I was now a part of. They asked a couple of questions about how I was and if I felt exhausted. I told them that leeches are no problem and they laughed nervously, still observing me as they departed. Obviously, I was now a being that could not be trusted.

Another problem on the Death Highway during the rainy season is the surface of the trail (only in a few places can it be called a road). It consists of the same thick mud as in the nearby rice fields. Since the trail was never actually constructed as a real road, the surface was never built up and has no crown. Because of this the water can't drain away, which is why the trail becomes indistinguishable from the rice fields along many stretches. Dirt bikes are no match for a plowed and flooded rice field. Ox carts provide the only means of transportation for the rural folk who occasionally use the trail, and an ox cart going across this kind of ground produces a trail that is much the same as a plowed rice field. It's all one and the same.

The big bikes, nice knobby tires and all, sink right into the muck, making the mud-filled knobby tires about as useless as slicks. This results in endless fun and games as all become mud from head to toe, taking turns pushing each other through the mess. The mud is of just the right consistency to quickly cake on the wheels, brakes, and drive chain, causing the bike to seize up, unable to proceed. Throughout bad stretches, we had to take sticks and spend ten minutes scraping mud off a bike for every one minute of riding. Ten to fifteen km for a very long day was all that could be completed. As the Khmers say, *suhb-ai-rih-ree-ay*—what fun!

The Honda Dream would actually be a better bike on this surface than the 250-cc dirt bikes that we were riding. They are much lighter and so would not sink quite as much in the mud. Being much lighter, they are also easier to lift out of the muck and maneuver around. Dirt bikes are great for most off-road conditions, but not this one.

One stretch of the Death Highway saw my motorcycle finally succumb to the brutal conditions and refuse to go on. Old and brittle ignition wires that the rental company had probably never changed, became wet and practically disintegrated when I tried to dry them. The battery also died at the same time, and with road conditions as they were, a push start was not in the cards.

We were in the jungle by now, and not having seen anyone for some time, we thought we were in a real jam, when through the mist and out of nowhere appeared a Khmer guy driving an ox cart who looked like he came from the hills of Tennessee. We figured we were in luck after we talked the guy into letting us load the broken motorcycle aboard to take it to the Sre Pok River, where we might find a boat to take the bike downriver to Lumphat town and a bike shop with parts.

The only problem with this pleasant scenario is that old Earl (probable name for the ox cart driver) drove his oxen really slowly, as such a driver is supposed to, until he saw that the trail descended down a ravine to a stream. I really doubt Earl had ever seen a Wild West cowboy film, but when he saw that ravine he stood up and whipped the oxen, much as a stagecoach driver might have, causing the animal to go into his highest gear. Riding on the cart and holding my bike in place, I knew what was probably going to happen. (I'd seen several of these films as a kid.) Sure enough, the cart hit the hump on the top of the ravine and quickly spilled over sideways, sending the motorcycle and me airborne. Luckily, I've also always been a fan of stuntmen and instinctively pushed the in-flight bike away from me and went into a defensive roll. Amazingly, nothing was the worse for the mishap except the side of Earl's cart. We lashed it together as best we could, gave Earl a lesson on slowing down instead of speeding up when approaching a ravine and proceeded cautiously. Never a dull moment for this trip.

Believe it or not, the Sre Pok River is the river in the movie *Apocalypse Now*, where Colonel Kurtz (played by Marlon Brando) set up an army encampment, not with U.S. military personnel, but rather with his own handpicked army of Cambodians. He had gone mad in Vietnam and headed up a river and into Cambodia, figuring that he could rule his own country.

When we finally reached the Sre Pok River, we found a small village whose people obviously had access to a few things from the outside world, such as Lao Beer and a couple of long-tailed boats with motors. After a fast and furious haggling session, we settled on a price for loading the two bikes onto the two small, narrow boats and going downriver to Lumphat town. By the time we loaded the bikes—no easy task, having had to carry the bikes down a rain-slicked muddy river embankment—dark had settled in and we were heading down the river by the light of a beautiful full moon. The thick jungle crept to the river's edge on both sides and the scene intrigued and spooked us at the same time. Having already imbibed one of those Lao Beers, I found it easy to imagine that I was heading down this river in search of the elusive Colonel Kurtz.

Being on the Sre Pok River, with the jungle as the only living entity around us on that moonlit night, I realized that the writers of *Apocalypse Now* had done their homework. This jungle river could easily pass as the one that a Colonel Kurtz might have followed from Vietnam to set up his strange encampment in the middle of the Cambodian nowhere. The two men steering our boats, along with the other guys at the small river village we had departed from

were all ex-soldiers with very little money for their families to live on. They were an odd combination of former Lao, Cambodian, and ex-Khmer Rouge soldiers, disgruntled about hardly ever having been paid during their soldiering days. It was not at all a stretch of the imagination for the writers to envision Colonel Kurtz hiring guys like these to be his own private army in this part of Cambodia during the Vietnam War days. I also got the feeling, from seeing and talking to these guys, that if some nut came by today and offered them a monthly salary for a swath of land and their soldiering services, he could be the Colonel Kurtz of today. It was almost a shame that I was already tied up with this guidebook project.

By the light of a flashlight that we used to scan the shoreline, we finally found the landing spot by the trail that led to nearby Lumphat town. From the river we could see no lights that a town would have, so we protested that we were not near a town and they had better not try to dump us off in the middle of nowhere (as if we really had any bargaining power). We knew that it would have been easy for these guys to produce guns, take the money that we had negotiated for the trip, and leave us right there.

But they insisted that this was the spot and that the town was indeed very close. There was, of course, another steep and muddy river embankment that we had to haul the bikes up, so I told the guys that they would only be paid after they helped us get the bikes up the hill and into town. It was their turn to protest because, they told us, they had heard that foreigners always took advantage of Cambodians by hiring them for a job and then not paying. They suddenly had the feeling that I was a slick guy with that same intention. I felt like Colonel Kurtz when I told them that if they just did what I told them, they would be paid, and saw them then set about the task of unloading the motorcycles from the boats.

We did not see any lights from the nearby town because, as at it turned out, Lumphat had only one working generator that supplied light to one small restaurant. Lumphat used to be the home of the airport (airstrip, to be more precise) for Rattanakiri Province. When the airport was relocated to Banlung a number of years ago, however, the already small town sort of died. There were no bike shops and no hotel or guesthouse, but we were told that we were welcome to sleep at the local wat with a bunch of real shady-looking characters who told us that's where they slept. With no lights around the entire area, except in the small restaurant that we were all conversing outside of, our paranoid (or was it?) instincts told us that this was not the place to spend the rest of the night. We wanted to wake up with our wallets and lives intact.

Having already asked how many kilometers it was to Banlung town and if the road was doable by vehicle, I told them that we wanted to hire a truck or jeep to load the bikes onto and take us to Banlung as soon as possible. They protested that although the road was fairly decent, it passed over a mountain and because it was ten o'clock at night, it just wasn't possible. Besides, there was no such truck or jeep available. I then told the restaurant owner that there was US$25 in it if he could, by chance, produce such a vehicle and if we could, by chance, depart soon even though it was nighttime. He turned and ran off into the darkness and disappeared for about fifteen minutes. We then heard a loud, unnerving sound approaching from the distance that we soon saw was made by a very old and tattered Russian jeep. The driver, apparently a friend of the restaurant owner, smiled as

he got out of his rig and said that we could in fact make the trip immediately, if we could increase the fare to US$30. Impossible by night—but not for the right price. Will the wonders of Cambodia never cease?

We quickly loaded the bikes onto the back of the old jeep and tied them securely into place for the steep mountain road that we knew they had to endure. Then we set off in the loud and sputtering jeep, heading down the final stretch to Banlung, with the road quickly burying itself in the surrounding jungle. We soon came across a downed tree in the road and when the driver tried to detour into the bush around it, the wheels sank deeply into a muddy slew area. Another mud-slinging session ensued as we tried to rock and push the jeep out of the quagmire. Twenty minutes later, we were all muddied but on our way.

The bikes gave us a couple of thrills as they shifted around going over the mountain, but it was a surprisingly uneventful ride the rest of the way to Banlung. After finding a guesthouse and unloading the bikes, we happily paid the beaming driver, who was proud of getting us to our destination, and of the pay that he had negotiated. Our penance on the "Death Highway" had finally been fulfilled.

RATTANAKIRI

Rattanakiri is a bit of paradise for the naturalist. Remnants of an ancient volcano exist in the form of a crystal-clear lake that was formed after the active volcano went dormant. There are also a few ancient lava fields that testify to the fact that the area was quite lively at one time. Beautiful waterfalls, clear rivers winding through stretches of jungle, and rolling hills that meet mountains near the Vietnam and Laos borders provide a full agenda for nature lovers.

Rattanakiri is the home of Cambodia's version of the Golden Triangle. Unlike the other one of illicit drug fame, this triangle is gaining popularity for its natural beauty and self-sufficient hill tribe communities, untouched and not a part of the tourism industry as they are in neighboring Thailand. Non-structured, low-impact, custom trips to outlying villages and natural areas can be organized (strictly by yourself or with help from a guesthouse).

You will soon realize that this area has not seen a lot of tourists. If you do happen upon hill tribe people in the areas outside of Banlung, don't be surprised if they look at you in horror and turn to run away. They just haven't seen many, if any, foreigners.

Banlung town is the seat of the province. It has recently grown more visitor friendly, with more places to stay, some good food, and a decent market area. This is all made possible by the recent influx of Cambodians from other parts of the country who see the eco-tourism potential of the area and have moved here to set up some supporting businesses to try to catch the wave of this small boomtown. They see Banlung as a nice quiet area in which to raise their families and try their hand at being entrepreneurs.

WHAT'S UP

Yeak Laom Volcano Lake

This beautiful place is not far from town and is great for a swim, picnic, or hike around the crater rim of the old volcano. And it has a small informative local museum thrown in to boot.

In 1995 the governor of Rattanakiri officially set aside a 5,000-hectare (12,350-acre) protected area, of which the lake is a part, and in 1996 got help from the International Development and Research Center of Canada and the United Nations Development Program to develop an effective resource management program. This area represents Cambodia's finest attempt at preserving a site. Full-time rangers work to ensure the area is protected. They receive regular training and have put up signs throughout the area reminding people not to litter, wash clothes, bathe or toilet in the lake. Amazing for Cambodia.

The main swimming and picnic area features a nice wood deck that's great to use for a jump into the sparkling clean water. Nearby, park rangers erected a couple of examples of hilltribe construction in the form of non politically correct bride and groom homes, where the man gets the elevated home (his status in the relationship) and the woman has the one nearer to the ground.

A few hundred meters down is the Cultural and Environmental Center which has information about area history and displays of local hill tribe tools and handiwork. They also sell some of the handicrafts made by the hill tribes: musical instruments, beaded belts, shirts, and hats.

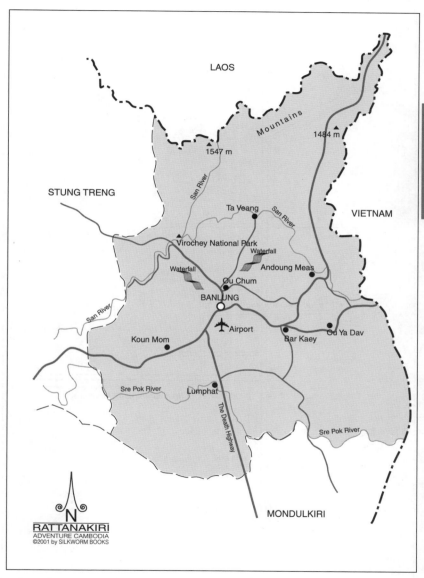

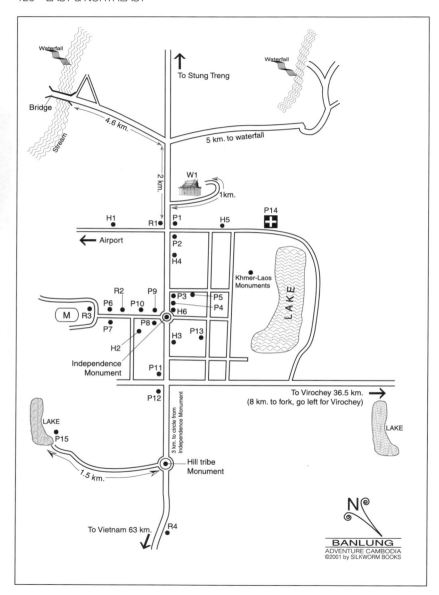

Waterfall

Waterfall

Bridge

Stream

↑ To Stung Treng

4.6 km.

5 km. to waterfall

W1

2 km.

1km.

H1

R1

P1

H5

P14

← Airport

P2

H4

Khmer-Laos
Monuments

L A K E

R2

P9

P3

P5

P6

P10

P4

M   R3

P8

H6

P7

P13

H2

H3

Independence
Monument

P11

P12

To Virochey 36.5 km.
(8 km. to fork, go left for Virochey)

3 km. to circle from
Independence Monument

LAKE

LAKE

P15

1.5 km.

Hill tribe
Monument

N

To Vietnam 63 km.

R4

BANLUNG
ADVENTURE CAMBODIA
©2001 by SILKWORM BOOKS

BANLUNG

H=Hotels

H1 Banlung Guesthouse & Restaurant
    (near airport)
H2 Banlung Guesthouse (near market)
H3 Rattanak Hotel
H4 Mountain Guesthouse 1
H5 Mountain Guesthouse 2
H6 Labiensak Hotel

R=Restaurants

R1 American Restaurant
R2 Dessert & drink stands
R3 Noodle & rice stands
R4 Gengliang's Place

See hotel list for:

• Banlung Restaurant (near airport)

P=Places

P1   Shell gas station
P2   Nightclub
P3   Big bike mechanic
P4   Fuel stand with super fuel
P5   Royal Air Cambodge
P6   President Air
P7   Share taxi stands
P8   Western food mini-market
P9   Pharmacy
P10 Konica
P11 Caltex fuel
P12 Post & Telecommunications
P13 Seattle space needle
P14 Hospital
P15 Yeak Laom volcano lake

W=Wats

W1 Wat Rah-tahn-ah-rahm & reclining
    Buddha

From the center you can take a nature trail around the entire crater rim. King Sihanouk had a chalet built on the shores of the lake and used it during the 1960s. It was destroyed in the 1970 war between the Lon Nol government and Khmer Rouge guerillas. You can still see the remnants of this and also—in different spots around the lake—trenches that held gun emplacements during the fighting.

The indigenous inhabitants of the area, the Khmer Leu hill tribe people, have always recognized the lake as a sacred place, home to the spirits of the land, water, and forest. Here those spirits interact with humans and, according to the local legend of Yeak Laom Lake, fabulous, spiritual aquatic beings reside here. The surrounding forests of the area are also said to be the home of spirits and therefore can't be cut. This helps to explain why the hill tribe people took so strongly to the idea of protecting the area.

It's very easy to get to—just go east from the Independence Monument circle 3 km to the Hill Tribe Monument circle and go right about 1.5 km to the entrance gate. The local hill tribe community connected to the lake get to collect an entrance fee, giving them a source of income and revenue for protecting their resource. It's only a few hundred riel per person and a few hundred for a motorcycle.

Wat Rah-tahn-ah-rahm (Reclining Buddha)

From the American Restaurant, follow the road toward Stung Treng just over half a kilometer and turn right on the dirt road that goes to a temple area. The main temple is on this level. If you continue on the road that goes upward behind the temple for just over another half a kilometer you come to the hilltop area. There is a reclining Buddha resting and enjoying the nice view of the countryside and the mountains off in the distance.

Waterfall Sites

The first part of the short journey to either waterfall is the same. Continuing on the road from the American Restaurant toward Stung Treng, you come to a dirt road intersection (2 km from the American Restaurant).

For the waterfall to the south, turn left and follow that road past the stands of rubber trees until you come near a small bridge. You can then either turn right about 100 meters before the bridge or just before the bridge, and go back about 100 meters to the stairway going down to the waterfall pool area. This is a nice place for either a swim or just to kick back and look at nature in the downstream jungle area.

Continuing on the road and over the bridge, you get into the heavy, cool shade of a large rubber tree plantation.

Back on the main road that you took from the American Restaurant, turn right (instead of the left you took to get to the last waterfall) and follow this road to the other waterfalls. You will eventually come upon three sets of forks in the road. Each time you approach one of these forks, you follow it to the left. At the last fork you can see the small stream off to the right. Since you forked to the left, you will see a small wooden house up ahead and a small footpath going off to the right. Take this and follow it back to the clearing where you can park your bike. A footpath going straight will bring you down to the bottom of the big waterfall—a beautiful jungle gorge area.

The footpath going to the right from the clearing would have taken you to a ledge of mini-waterfalls dropping into a pool area. It's a peaceful spot and if you follow the stream's flow, you arrive at the top of the big waterfall nearby. Watch your step.

Khmer-Laos Friendship Monuments

At the north end of town are a few Lao- and Cambodian-style monuments that attest to the fact that Laos is not too far away. Looking off to the north you can see the border mountains. With the lake in the foreground, it's a pleasant setting.

Virochey National Park, Tonle San River and Beyond

To get to the various sights in this area, head west from Banlung to a big fork in the road that has a large painted sign in English (the fork is 8 km from the Independence Monument). The sign says that the road to the right takes you to Taveng, 67 km away (that's from town, not from the sign). Following this road for a few kilometers brings you to a large clearing on both sides of the road. You soon notice that this is an ancient lava field where the flow followed the downward slope of the area and left the cooled volcanic rock in its wake. The forest surrounding the entire area is honeycombed with footpaths that the hill tribe people of the area use to gather their various bounties from the jungle. It's possible to hike off onto these trails and come upon individual hill tribe homes scattered about. Just keep track of your direction, as it's easy to get turned around and lost back there.

Continuing on toward Taveng, the road condition worsens and is not suitable for a rainy season journey. If it's the dry season and you are keen on an adventure through some pristine countryside, it's possible to go all the way to Taveng and cut back on the small river road to Virochey. You could take in the activities there and complete the triangle journey by heading back to Banlung on the other road from Virochey.

The road to Virochey (going left from that fork 8 km from Banlung) is definitely the better of the two roads and can be used during the rainy season as well. Virochey is just under 37 km northwest of Banlung. As you approach the town, you will see the Virochey National Park headquarters on the left. They sometimes have an English-speaking ranger there who can give you a bit of information about the area.

Continuing further along the road, you will come to the end of the line—the Tonle San River. There are cheap food and drink stands there and they also have fuel. Across the road is a local general store with clothing, fishing boat accessories and other gear. This is the place to inquire about renting a boat to take you northwest on the Tonle San River toward Laos. The river is very clean and the boat ride is scenic so it makes for a fun trip to follow the river for a swim and some photos. You will see and can stop at a temple on the south bank of the river. Fishermen working the river with nets from small boats, and the mountains ahead in the not too far distance complete the picturesque scene. There are several sandbars along the way if you want to stop for a swim. The cost of the motorized boat and driver is US$10.

The beach and boat landing area are just behind the food stands where you reached the town. It's a gorgeous and extremely wide white sand beach and also makes a good spot to cool off in the clean river. There is a small boat there that serves as a ferry, taking people across to the Chinese and Lao village on the other side. It's 200 riel per person and 1,000 riel for a Honda Dream (if you rented one in Virochey). It's an interesting village to hike or motorbike around.

From the food stand area, it's also possible to motorcycle down about 1.5 km to the riverside temple.

Fishing

Although nothing has been organized yet, the streams and rivers around Rattanakiri would be fine for fishing, one could bet. Bring your own lightweight gear and give it a whirl.

Hill tribe husband and wife houses

Gem Mines and the Road to the Vietnam Border

Gem mining has pretty much faded away compared to what it used to be. There are only a couple of small-scale operations still going on around the village of Bokeo. If you are in the mood for a ride through the countryside anyhow, head east from the Independence Monument and after 28 km you come upon a fork in the road where you go right. About 38 km into the trip you come to Bokeo village. After 38.5 km you come to a stand of huge trees on the left with a small dirt road that after 5 km arrives in the village of Dtih Jahk. Point to a ring or ring finger and the people will know that you want to see the gem mine area. Someone will direct you to where it's possible to buy uncut stones for a few dollars.

The Vietnam border and market are farther down the road about 63 km from the Independence Monument in Banlung. It would be nice to be able to stroll around the market on the Vietnamese side, but the Cambodian and Vietnamese immigration officials haven't gotten the go-ahead from their governments to permit this.

Only 5.5 km into this journey from the Independence Monument, you reach the bottom of a hill in a valley full of banana trees. There is a nice little outdoor restaurant with some good, simple Vietnamese dishes. See the Restaurant section.

Elephant Trekking and Guides for Hill Tribe Excursions

The best place to organize an elephant trek and find a guide if you aren't keen on independent journeys is the Banlung Guesthouse (by the airport). The only elephant had recently died before we went through Banlung and they were in the process of reorganizing things.

Banlung would also be a great place for mountain biking. There are at present no rentals available, so bring your own if you come by airplane and are so inclined.

MARKETS

The market is the standard "all under one roof" (and spilling out the sides) Khmer variety with a lot of merchandise coming from Vietnam and Laos. The fruit vendors are mostly outside on the west and south sides of the market.

The night market sets up south of the Independence Monument, along the road leading to the market.

Western Food. An enterprising Khmer lady came up with the idea of shipping some of the things that Westerners crave from Lucky Market in Phnom Penh. It's a bit pricey, but a welcome addition to Rattanakiri.

GETTING AROUND

Moto-Taxi

Moto-taxis will take you around for the standard fee of 4,000 riel per hour, plus extra for fuel, heading to the outlying sights.

Motorcycle Rental

The American Restaurant as well as many of the guesthouses rent out Honda Dream motorcycles for US$5 a day.

Motorcycle Doctor

There is a fairly creative motorcycle mechanic who can perform some minor surgery on your motorcycle if it is feeling the effects of the surrounding roads. Check the map near the Independence Monument.

CURRENCY EXCHANGE

As yet, there is no bank in Banlung. There are money changers with the telltale glass cases along the road leading to the market, as well as in the market area. Dollars, riel and the Vietnamese dong are traded.

MEDICAL FACILITIES

As in most places around Cambodia, it's not a good idea to get sick. If you do and need immediate attention, the Rattanakiri Provincial Hospital is in the northwest part of town. They occasionally have foreign doctors on staff with the Khmer doctors.

Pharmacy. There are many, but a good one run by a married couple who speak English is located next to the Konica photo shop near the Independence Monument.

RESTAURANTS

The American Restaurant. An unlikely name for a restaurant with the best food in town. It turns out that an American used to be the owner and cook of the place. He taught the staff to cook the Western dishes on the menu and also to be meticulous in the cleanliness of the place. They got the idea, as it's a simple but well taken care of restaurant. If you've been in the bush a while, they serve up a mean hamburger with all of the trimmings of a California Burger, and tasty fries on the side.

There are plenty of choices of Western and Khmer food and if you want something special made up for you, the friendly staff are happy to accommodate you. Open all day. The restaurant rents out Honda Dream motorcycles for US$5 a day.

Banlung Guesthouse Restaurant. Next to the airport. They serve Khmer, Western and Thai food throughout the day, starting with breakfast. It's a friendly place and the food is good.

Market Food Stands. Located near the market and share taxi area is a bunch of simple noodle and rice dish shops. Real cheap eats.

Gengliang's Place. Located 5.5 km from the Independence Monument on the road toward the Vietnamese border, is an outdoor restaurant set amid trees and a small stream in a valley. It's a nice, simple setting that serves up a very good Vietnamese noodle and curry cold dish. They have a few other treats, as well as fresh fruit and drinks. The name of the friendly Khmer owner of the place is Gengliang and she speaks French.

NIGHT SCENE

That this town is on the move is evident by the small night scene that has developed here. As mentioned, the section of road going toward the market is where a lot of the locals sit for a drink or snack during the evening.

Khmer Nightclub. This funky place is catty-cornered from the American Restaurant. It features a dance floor with a sickly techno-sound system playing all the pop music that you have grown so weary of in Phnom Penh. There is a small karaoke area, and a bunch of taxi girls work the place. There are even some beer girls on hand to tend to your thirst.

There is also a small nightclub on the road just west of the market, about a kilometer to the south, but the road is particularly dark and unappealing at night.

The moto-taxi guys are all too pleased to show you the brothel area just outside of town. This place must be growing.

ACCOMMODATIONS

Banlung Guesthouse. Near the market. Very clean rooms with a share bath go for US$3.

Banlung Guesthouse. Near the airport. This friendly place has fan rooms with a bathroom inside for US$5 and a/c rooms for US$10. They have a restaurant and can arrange guided trips to the local attractions and beyond. They also have guides who speak the various hill tribe dialects and can take you to some outlying villages.

They rent Honda Dreams for US$5 a day and also a pickup truck with a driver for US$50 a day, including the fuel. They are currently trying to reorganize their elephant trekking after the recent death of the elephant that was normally used.

Mountain Guesthouse. Fairly decent simple rooms are available at US$5 a night for a room with a fan and bathroom. The walls are paper-thin so watch the hanky-panky. They have a small restaurant that serves breakfast. They also have Honda Dreams for rent at US$5 a day.

Mountain Guesthouse 2. This is run by the sister of the owner of the similarly named place mentioned above.

They have Spartan accommodations that are not well cleaned for US$5. There is a funky share bath area. The upside is a nice second-floor terrace and they also serve a breakfast.

Labiensak Hotel. With no staff anywhere to be found on the three occasions when we stopped by, it is not recommended. Belongings can easily disappear if nobody is minding the store

Rattanak Hotel. It may be the top place in town, but that isn't saying much. They did some remodeling in the front outside area of the building, but the rooms are the same as before. Rooms in front have a terrace and window overlooking the street. They have an attached Western bath, double or twin beds with a/c for US$10 a night. It's a clean place, but when we went through, not overly friendly. Maybe it was just a bad-hair day.

COMING & GOING

Air

Flying is, of course, the easy way to go. Royal Air Cambodge makes the flight six days a week and the newer addition to the airline scene, President Airlines, flies to Banlung three times a week. Check the map for office locations if you took a taxi here but want to fly back.

Share Taxi

The share taxi pickup trucks only go from here to Stung Treng. Bring food, water, and mosquito repellent because if there is a breakdown on this bumpy backwoods road you may be caught in the jungle for the night. Share taxis usually go in groups in case of a breakdown, but with the other vehicles usually full as well, people do get stranded at times. The five-hour trip stretches to seven hours for share taxis during the rainy season.

The fare is 30,000 riel per person for an inside seat.

Motorcycle Touring Info

Banlung to Stung Treng

The 146-km journey from Banlung to Stung Treng took 5 ½ hours during the rainy season, so knock at least an hour off that in the dry season. The road is generally lousy, passing through areas of bomb craters that create deep lakes during the rainy season, but you can skirt around the perimeter of most of them. Where you can't, the road goes zigzagging through the jungle, and is slow and slippery in the wet months. However, there are a few decent stretches, and the last 19 km on Highway 7 are fairly easy ones. It's certainly not one of the better roads, but it's not the worst either. There is some nice scenery, but as with other bad highways around Cambodia, you are

usually too preoccupied with the road to enjoy it unless you stop.

The same suggestion we made in the share taxi section applies for riders on this road. Bring food, water and mosquito repellent. If you have a breakdown there may not be anyone else coming by, depending on the time of day. It's always best to get an early start to improve your chances if you do have a problem.

Banlung to Mondulkiri

If you came from Stung Treng and want to try the back trail to Mondulkiri (Sen Monorom) and it's the rainy season, read the Death Highway chapter. Or follow the simple advice we gave in the Mondulkiri section: don't do it.

In the dry season, it's a tough trail that will put your riding skills to the test. Make sure you have spare parts for your motor-cycle (see Biker Checklist in Getting Around chapter), and bring plenty of food and drinking water. The trip will take a couple of days during the dry season and Kaoh Nhek town (near halfway) is the only place that sells bottled water and some food. Fuel is available there as well.

Don't do it alone. It's best to have some help if you have a breakdown or a mishap. You are a long way from help in most stretches of this remote trail. It would also be best to bring along a Khmer speaker as the trail sometimes intersects with other trails and you will want to clarify that you took the proper way when you do come across somebody. It's definitely an adventure, so if you try to tackle it be fully prepared so you have an opportunity to enjoy it.

Security these days has not been a problem.

Going to market, Rattanakiri

EAST & NORTHEAST

STUNG TRENG

Stung Treng town is an important trade hub with a few hints of Lao influence scattered about, owing to the fact that the Lao border is about 50 km away.

It's a friendly, quiet country town situated near the confluence of the San River and the Mekong River. It actually sits on the banks of the San River, with the mighty Mekong coming into the picture on the northeastern outskirts of town.

The San River goes by three names, depending on which of the locals you speak to. Some call it the Kong River because the San and Kong Rivers merge together about 10 km northeast of Stung Treng town, confusing people about which name the river should bear. Others call it the Sekong River, which is the combined name of these two rivers.

Whatever name the river beside the town goes by, it's another one of Cambodia's beautiful picture-postcard river towns. It's a nice place to kick back and chill out if you are on a circuit tour of the Northeast.

WHAT'S UP

River Scene, from Here to Laos

The San River is fronted in Stung Treng by a nice stretch of paved road. It's the center of socializing (as in most Cambodian river towns) in the late afternoon and early evening hours as the locals ride up and down the stretch enjoying the view and each other. Drink and dessert stands spring up earlier to serve the daily merrymaking crowd. It's a nice spot for a walk or jog any time of the day as the river road turns into a pleasant rural road that leads to the airport 4 km north of town.

The river port area just in front of the small city park is fairly busy, handling trade between Cambodia and Lao.

The ferry across the San River to where Highway 7 continues north to the Lao border is also at this pier. The fare is 300 riel per head. We went for a ride on this stretch (2,000 riel for taking a big bike on the ferry), but there is not much to see along the way besides jungle and the remnants of a road that was a target of carpet bombing during the Vietnam War years. The road works its way eastward so it does not afford views of the Mekong River as one would hope. The few residents we saw along the way were truly amazed to see the likes of us, probably wondering why in the world we would want to be there.

Mekong River Trip to Laos

The Mekong River between Stung Treng and the Laos border is very light on population and heavy on beautiful scenery. Boulder outcroppings, numerous sets of rapids, swirling pothole currents, wide sweeping stretches of river and forested landscape along the banks all await the boat traveler. It makes for a great trip, either for the traveler that wants to continue on to Laos or for those wanting to enjoy a wild stretch of the Mekong in Cambodia.

The trip is difficult to downright impossible to make on this shallow stretch of the Mekong during the dry season, with countless sunken islands and a virtual forest of trees growing right in the middle of the river. The trip becomes an obstacle course for the boat drivers this time of the year, as they carefully try to choose the best way to guide their craft through the maze that nature has created without losing a propeller to the

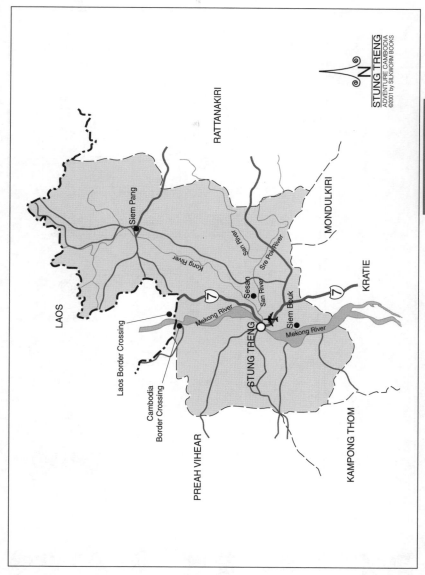

EAST & NORTHEAST

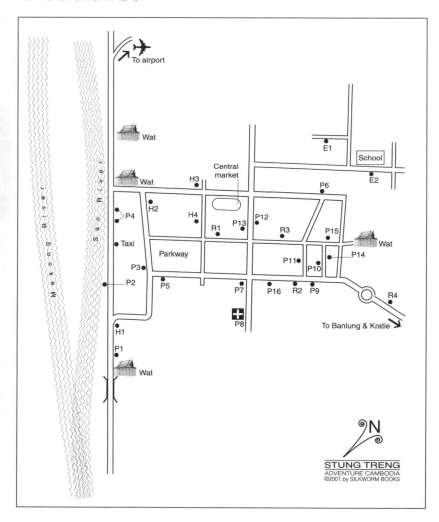

To airport

Wat

Wat

Central market

E1

School

E2

H3

H2

P4

Taxi

H4

R1

P13

P12

R3

P6

P15

Wat

P11

P10

P14

Parkway

P3

P2

P5

P7

P16

R2

P9

P8

R4

To Banlung & Kratie

H1

P1

Wat

Mekong River

San River

N

STUNG TRENG
ADVENTURE CAMBODIA
©2001 by SILKWORM BOOKS

STUNG TRENG

H=Hotels

H1   Sekong Hotel
H2   Amatak Guesthouse
H3   Sok-Sabat Hotel, Restaurant &
       Night Club
H4   Preap Sor Guesthouse

R=Restaurants

R1   Noodle & rice shops & stands
R2   Arunreas Restaurant
R3   "No Name" Restaurant
R4   Kolap Stung Treng Restaurant

See hotel list for:

- Sok-Sabat Hotel, Restaurant &
  Night Club

P=Places

P1   Cambodia People's Party building
P2   Boat docks, transportation to Kratie,
        Phnom Penh & Laos
P3   Fountain monument
P4   Two gas stations
P5   Royal Air Cambodge ticket office
P6   Main police station (for permission to
        cross to Laos)
P7   Film & photo shop
P8   Health clinic & hospital
P9   Post & Telecommunications
P10 Gas station
P11 Gas station
P12 President Airlines ticket office
P13 Night market
P14 Monument park
P15 School
P16 Motorcycle doctor

river. The best time of the year to take this trip is from May to November when sufficient upstream rains have raised the river to a level that allows the boats to pass through carefully.

There is not a whole lot to do once you get to the border area, but travelers can leave their passport with Cambodian immigration (at the small checkpoint on the west bank of the river) and cross to the Laos side to eat at a riverside restaurant and look at the tiny market in the Lao village of Geedahn. Cambodian immigration officers may ask you for a US$5 contribution to do this when you see them, but it is not a fee set by the central government so you don't have to pay it.

There is also a guesthouse to stay at near this village (on the Lao side of the river, but a couple of hundred meters south along the riverbank where it is still Cambodia), which was built here for border traders that lose the daylight hours and need a place to spend the night. It's a nice enough place, but overpriced, with a room that includes two big beds and a fan going for US$8 a night. Electricity is running between dusk and midnight.

To take the trip, head down to the riverbank area (near the small bullet boats just east of the pier) in Stung Treng town before 8:30 am and talk to one of the operators of the small freight boats. The fare is 15,000 riel (one way) and the trip to the border area takes about 5 ½ hours, but is cut down to just over three hours on the trip back south as the swift current on this stretch of the Mekong pushes the boats right along. If you want a faster journey, approach one of the small fiberglass boat operators, the ones that have the 40-hp outboard motors—they want US$20–$25 (one-way) to make the trip—but if you are looking for a quick trip or fast fun, the trip time going upriver is cut down to only 1 ½ hours.

The slow boats are fast enough coming back downstream so you could save money by grabbing one of those on the return trip.

For those wanting to cross into Laos using this route, you will need a Lao visa in your possession and you also need to stop at the main police station in Stung Treng town (see map) to get a letter of permission to cross the border at this point. This is shown to Cambodian immigration at the river checkpoint. Cambodian immigration will not let you stamp out of the country without this letter.

West River Wat

Heading west from the pier just under half a kilometer is a temple that faces the confluence of the Mekong and San Rivers. There are a couple of bucking broncos guarding the gate and wall murals on the outside of the temple. It's a nice setting.

East River Wats

Heading east from the pier and toward the airport is a seventy-year-old temple complex with a recently built wat.

Continuing east on the River Road and just across a small bridge is another temple complex facing the river. The wat is a strange-looking two-story affair with murals on the outside.

Wat Phnom, Stung Treng

Borrowing the name of the famous landmark temple in Phnom Penh, this one isn't high enough for a good view of the area, though you can see the mountains along the Lao border to the north. A new wat is currently under construction on the site.

MARKETS

The market is a bustling place, selling goods from Laos, Vietnam and, of course, Cambodia. There is also a small night market

that sets up on the southwest side of the market, and there are also small drink and food market shops near the Preap Son Guesthouse on the opposite side of the market.

GETTING AROUND

Moto-Taxi

The standard fare of 4,000 riel per hour for cruising around is in effect. Figure 500 riel for one-way trips.

Motorcycle Doctor

The motorcycle doctor (see map) gets an "E" for effort. This guy, a fan of big bikes, tries to make do with the little that he has in parts. Get that chain tightened and lubed.

CURRENCY EXCHANGE

There is no bank in Stung Treng. Money changers are in and around the outside of the market area.

MEDICAL FACILITIES

The Stung Treng Health Clinic and Hospital is your only choice for a medical problem that can't wait.

The pharmacies are around the perimeter of the market.

RESTAURANTS

Arunreas Restaurant. They make the most of their parkway location by having a small sidewalk eating area. It's a pleasant enough early evening spot as the locals ride by on their evening motorcycle pleasure cruise. They have good food (Western and Khmer), and an English menu to go along with English-speaking staff.

No Name Restaurant. Located across the parkway from the Arunreas, this place is easy to spot, as it always seems to have Coca-Cola and Player umbrellas set up. The food is tasty, but be prepared to try your hand at Khmer as they don't speak English and there isn't an English menu. The staff is very friendly, though.

Kolap Stung Treng Hotel & Restaurant. Good Khmer and Chinese food with an English menu and beer girls, to boot.

Hotel Sok-Sabat & Restaurant. At the time of our trip, the hotel was talking about expanding its restaurant. It was only serving a soup breakfast and catering to wedding parties at the time.

Noodle and Rice Shops. Along the parkway and near the market are some dirt cheap, simple Khmer food stands.

NIGHT SCENE

Kolap Stung Treng Hotel & Nightclub. The hotel has shut down but the restaurant and nightclub are alive and kickin'. It's a small-scale affair with a Khmer band, beer girls and the usual Khmer nightclub contingent of taxi girls.

Hotel Sok-Sabat & Nightclub. It's been open hit or miss, but when it's open they have a Khmer band and all the trimmings that the Kolap Nightclub has. They seem to convert to wedding parties only, during the spring and summer wedding season.

Sabay-Man Restaurant. The English sign says that it's a restaurant, but it's really a small nightclub with taxi girls.

Scattered about Stung Treng are a number of small karaoke joints with the typically friendly female staff.

ACCOMMODATIONS

Amatak Guesthouse. Very basic rooms with a floor fan, bed and mosquito net. It's clean and there is a share bath for US$5 a night.

Preap Sor Guesthouse. Clean and simple rooms with a Western bath for US$10 a night with a fan. It's double what the price should be. Adding a/c puts the price at US$15.

Sekong Hotel. This is a very pleasant place with its nice layout and location next to the San River. Big rooms with nice old wooden furniture and a Western bath are US$10 a night with a fan, or a whopping US$20 a night to flip on the a/c. They say the electricity is expensive in these parts. A better bargain are the simple rooms in the back of the complex. They have a fan and Western bath for US$5 a night. The friendly Khmer lady owner has her staff (family) head to the market for warm French bread in the mornings and serves it with espresso coffee.

Hotel Sok-Sabat. It's a fairly new place with nice rooms that go for US$10–20 a night. They also have a Chinese breakfast in the morning.

COMING & GOING

Air

The easiest way to get here is by air. Royal Air Cambodge makes the flight three times a week and President Airlines covers two other days of the week. This gives Stung Treng five days of service per week on the Phnom Penh route. Both airlines have offices near the parkway.

The airport is abandoned and left wide open, except when there is a plane coming or going. The locals use the nice asphalt runway as a cut-through to connect with the river road. It is a nice open straightaway, so join the crowd with your big bike and see if you can achieve airborne status. We tried, but the bikes were not quite up to it.

Bullet Boat to Kratie

Unfortunately, the bullet boats usually don't journey beyond Kratie. The stretch between Kratie and Stung Treng is loaded with small islands and clumps, with a fair number of dead trees thrown in for good measure. The journey is made only when the water is very high, which doesn't occur during a good portion of the rainy season.

When the boat is running it beats taking a share taxi as, unlike the road, the river affords a smooth ride. The trip downriver to Kratie takes around 4 ½ hours and six to seven hours coming upstream from Kratie. As of May 2000, the bullet boat was running every other day at a fare of 20,000 riel. If the boats are making the run, take it— it's a pretty stretch of the river.

Share Taxi

Share taxis ply two routes from Stung Treng: one to Banlung (Rattanakiri) and the other south to Kratie.

For the trip to Banlung, bring food, water and mosquito repellant because if there is a breakdown (not uncommon) on this bumpy backwoods road you may be caught in the jungle for the night. Share taxis usually go in groups in case of a breakdown, but as the other taxis are usually full as well, people do end up stranded and sleeping out in the elements at times. The five-hour trip stretches to seven hours during the rainy season.

The fare is 30,000 riel for an inside seat. From Stung Treng to Kratie, the fare is 20,000 riel.

Motorcycle Touring Info

Banlung to Stung Treng

The 146 km journey from Banlung to Stung Treng took 5 ½ hours during the rainy season, so knock at least an hour off of that in the dry season. The road is generally lousy,

passing through areas of bomb craters that create deep lakes during the rainy season, but you can skirt around the perimeter of most of them. Where you can't, the road goes zigzagging through the jungle, which is slow and slippery in the wet months.

Having said that, there are a few decent stretches and the last 19 km (after the road merges with Highway 7) are fairly easy ones.

The same suggestion we made in the share taxi part of this section applies for riders on this road. Bring food, water and mosquito repellent. If you have a breakdown, there may not be anyone else coming by, depending on the time of day. It's always best to get an early start to improve your chances if you do have a problem.

Stung Treng to Kratie

The road goes from asphalt to shredded tarmac to dirt. There are scattered bomb craters, but the road is not nearly as bad as some. The trip is 142 km and took four hours during the rainy season. As far as security, see the word of caution under Share Taxi, above.

WARNING

From time to time there are reports from the share taxi drivers of robbery along this stretch of National Highway 7. We heard two such reports from the affected drivers while we were in Stung Treng. We encountered no such problems and only came across friendly people on the road, but it's recommended that you try to get current reports of the road condition before making the trip, either in Kratie or Stung Treng.

SVAY RIENG & PREY VENG

Svay (pronounced Swai) Rieng and Prey Veng are a couple of sleepy Cambodian provinces that just happen to have one of the country's busiest highways running straight through them—National Highway 1, which links Phnom Penh and Ho Chi Minh City in Vietnam. Svay Rieng town sits just 58 km from the Moc Bai border crossing and is a fairly prosperous place as a result of the border trade traffic, business people and travelers passing through. The town is a very friendly place and makes for a pleasant overnight stop whether coming from or going to Vietnam. Highway 1 is asphalt and not an extreme challenge to travel on any time of the year (riddled with potholes in spots, but hey, it's Cambodia), so it's also a nice overnight trip from Phnom Penh. The pleasant ride takes you through Kandal, Prey Veng and Svay Rieng Provinces, which are chock full of rice paddies and sugar palm trees that dot the country-side as far as the eye can see. The trip also entails a boat ride on the Neak Loeung Ferry that connects Highway 1 on both sides of the Mekong River.

Svay Rieng town is situated near the Waiko River and its vast, scenic marshlands, the result of a wide stretch of the river drying up significantly over the years. It's a pleasant setting and one that can be enjoyed at several different spots along the river and marsh. A bridge over the Waiko, not far from the main part of town, bears a plaque that states the bridge was donated by Hun Sen, the all-powerful prime minister. This is definitely the ruling party's stomping-ground, and conversations with locals will attest to it. Although it's close to the border and has more than a little bit of Vietnamese influence noticeable around the town and province, locals still express deep gratitude to the ruling party for teaming up with Vietnam to finally purge the government of the Khmer Rouge regime in 1979. The powerful director of the National Police, Hok Lundy, is also from this province and owns the top hotel in town. Also by no small coincidence, the brother of Hun Sen is now the governor of Svay Rieng Province. The government likes to shore up its support here, as well as in other places, by taking credit for high profile projects like the bridge, which is something the people see and use everyday. I guess that's politics, in any country.

Greeting all upon arrival from Phnom Penh is a traffic circle with its statue of a nice rural farm couple holding hands and smiling. The hoe resting on the husband's right shoulder is a nice touch. However, as you continue around the circle you realize that the man also has an AK-47 rifle slung over his left shoulder and resting on his back. Does the surreal feel of Cambodia ever let up?

Neak Loeung Ferry Info

The Neak Loeung Ferry is located about 63 km from the traffic circle next to the Monivong Bridge in Phnom Penh. It crosses the Mekong River, connecting the east and west sections of Highway 1. It's another example of how far behind the times Cambodia is that the busiest highway in the country still has no bridge across the Mekong. Large transport trucks overflowing with goods from Vietnam, share taxis, and all the regular traffic, still must stop and wait in line for the ferry crossing.

At least the wait isn't a long one and there is plenty of entertainment on hand to keep

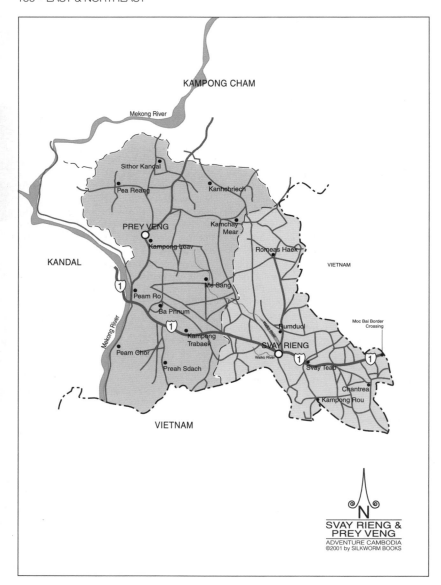

KAMPONG CHAM

Mekong River

Sithor Kandal

Pea Reang

Kanhehriech

PREY VENG

Kamchay Mear

Kampong Leav

KANDAL

Romeas Haek

VIETNAM

Me Sang

Peam Ro

Ba Phnum

Mekong River

Kampong Trabaek

Rumduol

Moc Bai Border Crossing

SVAY RIENG

Peam Chor

Waiko River

Svay Teab

Preah Sdach

Chantrea

Kampong Rou

VIETNAM

N

SVAY RIENG &
PREY VENG
ADVENTURE CAMBODIA
©2001 by SILKWORM BOOKS

you amused. As soon as you pull up near the ticket shack you are greeted by five cans of Coke, three bags of sugar cane and half a dozen packs of moist mini-towels being thrust into your face by the hordes of vendors. Yeah, it's possible to get refreshments here. There is also a small contingent of Khmer beggars on hand to throw you their highly polished and most sorrowful looks. I usually give them a quick swipe with a mini-towel so the looks are at least clean ones. There are also some never-traveling minstrels to serenade you during your waiting minutes. The fare is 200 riel per person and 300 riel for a motorcycle. It's a nice stretch of the Mekong but you are on the other side before you can say "South China Sea."

There are a couple of decent Khmer food restaurants on the left side just after you get off the ferry. They also have money changers there. Just beyond is a large monument greeting you in the middle of Highway 1 as you continue your journey. It features a big statue of Cambodian and Vietnamese soldiers marching forward in solidarity. Similar ones were put up around the country to try to make the masses feel good about the Vietnamese occupation of Cambodia following the defeat of the Khmer Rouge government. They are not favorites among the Khmers, who still harbor a strong dislike and distrust of their neighbor.

There are large markets loaded with goods from Vietnam near Highway 1 on both sides of the ferry crossing, with the one on the Phnom Penh side the larger of the two.

WHAT'S UP

Prey Veng

Just after you cross the Mekong River by way of the Neak Loeung Ferry there is an interesting site in Prey Veng Province.

Phnom Chi-gaht

The drive from Highway 1 takes you through a beautiful swath of countryside. You pass by a couple of rural temples surrounded by an area of lakes, rice fields and waterlily ponds. Arriving at the hilltop temple, you find a stairway that leads up to one of two peaks. At the top is a Buddhist shrine and an open gazebo that gives you a wonderful view of the lakes, rivers and rice fields spread across the province. There is also a hiking trail for crossing to the next peak and another nearby hill. To get there, go about 2 km from the ferry crossing to where a small market sits next to a road that comes into the highway from the left. This is where you turn left. The small market and village is called Kampong Sahng. Follow this road another 2 km to where the road gives you the option of going straight or turning to the right. There is a blue sign with arrows pointing to the two options. Turn right here. Follow this until you get to a village with a yellow school building on the right. Take a left on the dirt road there and follow this to the base of the temple stairs.

River Scene, Svay Rieng

Drink and snack stands spring up in the evening near the Hun Sen Bridge over the Waiko River. Locals use this area and the main drag as an evening social promenade on their motorcycles. A nice early evening stroll would be to start at the Monument Circle and cut down the river road past the bridge.

Boat Rides

Local fishermen use small wooden rowboats along the Waiko River and marshland. They can easily be talked into giving you a tour of the area by water for 4,000 riel an hour. Check around the Hun Sen Bridge.

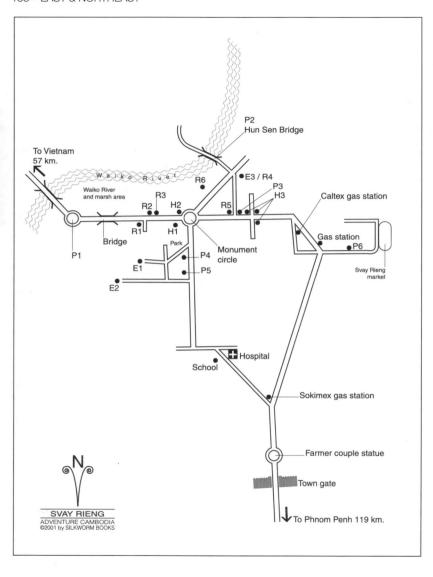

P2
Hun Sen Bridge

To Vietnam
57 km.

Waiko River

E3 / R4

Waiko River
and marsh area

R6

P3
H3

Caltex gas station

R3

R2   H2

R5

Gas station

R1

H1

P6

Bridge

Park

P1

Monument
circle

Svay Rieng
market

P4

E1

P5

E2

Hospital

School

Sokimex gas station

N

Farmer couple statue

Town gate

SVAY RIENG
ADVENTURE CAMBODIA
©2001 by SILKWORM BOOKS

To Phnom Penh 119 km.

SVAY RIENG

H=Hotels

H1   Vimean Monorom Hotel
H2   Waiko Hotel, Restaurant & Night Club

R=Restaurants

R1   Rasmey Nimol Restaurant
R2   Pich Restaurant
R3   Svay Rieng Restaurant
R4   Riverside Nightclub & Restaurant
R5   Corner Restaurant

See hotel list for:

• Waiko Hotel, Restaurant & Nightclub

P=Places

P1   Soldier monument
P2   Hun Sen Bridge
P3   Mini-mart & Western food
P4   Post & Telecommunications
P5   Government building
P6   Share taxi stands

Temple guardian

Back Deck of Serei Pheap Thmai Restaurant

Also not far from the Hun Sen Bridge is this restaurant with a deck in the back built out over the Waiko River. Svay Rieng is a place for kicking back and relaxing, and with a good view of the river and marshland and its wildlife stretching out before you from the deck, this is a great place to do it. Cold drinks are at hand. Yes, there are full modern facilities including a Western-style bathroom. But there is also an old-style outhouse off to the side of the deck for the purist-traditionalists who like to watch their makings plop down into the river below.

Monuments

Besides the statue of the cute farm couple mentioned earlier, the traffic circle in the east end of town has a statue of a soldier carrying a dead war victim. Svay Rieng is the first province that the Vietnamese and disaffected Khmer Rouge faction (the ruling party of today) rolled into on their way to Phnom Penh from Ho Chi Minh City (formerly Saigon). The province was among those heavily affected by the Vietnam War and its terrible spillover effects on Cambodia.

MARKETS

The market is a bustling Cambodian affair with loads of goods from nearby Vietnam. Fruits, snacks and supplies are plentiful here.

Mini-Mart with Western Foods. This doublewide mini-mart has a number of Western foods to satisfy your craving. The other side is filled with cases of all brands of beer available in Cambodia—enough to quench even the driest whistle.

GETTING AROUND

There are a couple of small bike shops along the perimeter road of the market for that chain adjustment and lube.

MEDICAL FACILITIES

For a problem requiring immediate attention, the Svay Rieng Provincial Hospital is your choice.

CURRENCY EXCHANGE

The Svay Rieng Market is the place to change money. There are plenty of the telltale glass cases of the money changers along the front, as well as inside the market area. They readily change dollars, riel and the Vietnamese dong.

RESTAURANTS

Serei Pheap Thmei Restaurant. This is the one with the deck overlooking the water mentioned earlier. They have good food and the staff can speak English.

The following three restaurants are just east of Monument Circle and quite close to each other. They are all open throughout the day, starting at the crack of dawn with Chinese noodle soup and omelets with French bread. All have signs and menus in English, and pleasant staff.

Svay Rieng Restaurant. It's a pleasant, small restaurant with Khmer and Chinese food.

Pich Restaurant. This doublewide restaurant is very popular with the locals. They have some Western food as well as the usual Khmer and Chinese fare.

Rasmey Nimol Restaurant. This corner restaurant catches a breeze better than the other two. They also serve up good food.

NIGHT SCENE

Waiko Hotel Nightclub. This is the top club in town, which still means it's a pretty mild place. They have a decent live band pumping out all the Khmer hits and a few Western ones to catch you off guard. The Beer and Taxi Girl Union has a fair representation here.

Tonle Waiko Nightclub. This one has an outdoor deck so you can sit outside by the river and away from the loud volume of the music that Cambodians seem to love so much. Usually just a handful of customers, if it's a good night.

Riverside Nightclub & Restaurant. This one is close to the Hun Sen Bridge and has a handful of its temptresses stationed by the nearby drink stands to entice those easily lead astray to cross the street.

ACCOMMODATIONS

The Three Guesthouses. All on different sides of the same corner, these guesthouses have more than the location in common. They all have fairly well-cleaned rooms and are US$4 a night without a fan, US$5 with.

Vimean Monorom. This is a fairly new place with rooms that feature two beds and a Western bath. The rooms are US$10 with a fan or US$15 with a/c.

Waiko Hotel. This place was shut down for a while for a complete renovation. Reopened in May of 1999, it has a restaurant and nightclub in the complex. The rooms are nice and have a flat rate of US$15. They feature a/c, TV and video, and in-room phone. Pretty fancy place for a small town.

COMING & GOING

Security is not a problem in this region. National Highway 1 is full of potholes and the only road construction going on is being performed by rural peasants along the way. They scoop dirt from nearby rice fields, fill in a pothole and hold out a basket as traffic passes by, hoping that a few riel will be dropped in for their efforts.

However, the road is asphalt and so is easily traversed all year round.

Share Taxi

The fare from Phnom Penh to Svay Rieng is 5,000 riel. Grab an extra space for a bit more comfort.

Motorcycle Touring Info

Phnom Penh to Svay Rieng

This trip is a fairly easy one for motorcycles, as you can easily skirt the potholes that slow down the cars. Keep those eyes open, though, as the share taxis that ply this stretch from Phnom Penh to the Vietnam border all seem to be trying for the Cambodian Land Highway Speed Award. They do fly and they don't let a little thing like a motorcycle hinder their flight.

Nice couple with Ak 47 at the ready, Svay Rieng

KAMPONG THOM

The pleasant country town of Kampong Thom has plenty of activities to keep a visitor busy and is easily accessible from Phnom Penh (just under 2 H hours or 162 km from the Japanese Bridge) via a good stretch of National Highway 6. The town has a nice layout and is situated on the banks of the Sen River, which is a long, winding body of water that originates in the Dangkrek Mountains of Preah Vihear Province (near the Thai border) and finally empties into the Great Lake, Tonle Sap.

The town is well situated as a crossroad to the important sights of Angkor (Siem Reap), Preah Vihear Temple (abutting Thailand), and the ancient capital of Sambor Prei Kok, only 29 km northeast of Kampong Thom town.

An unsecured area of Cambodia in the not-so-distant past, the town has become fairly lively with residents of Phnom Penh driving up to see the area's sights and have a weekend getaway, which testifies to the fact that security is no longer a problem. There are even a few sights to see along the way from Phnom Penh, making the short journey an interesting one.

WHAT'S UP

Sambor Prei Kok

This is the site of an ancient kingdom of Cambodia, Chenla. It predates the Angkor Empire, with many of the temple ruins nearly 1,400 years old. Southeast Asian travelers will find the brick monuments and temples similar to those in the ancient Siamese kingdoms of Sukhothai and Ayutthaya, or Pagan in Burma, though Chenla predated all of these. Along with construction similarities, the large number of struc-

tures in the area is also reminiscent of Pagan. There are 106 temple and monument structures in the area, varying significantly in the degree to which they stayed intact over the centuries. Looters have had a field day with the ruins—a persistent problem throughout Cambodia and Southeast Asia in general.

The surrounding forest had been working hard to overrun and reclaim the area through the years, but the good news these days is that the site has been given a growing amount of attention by the government and international preservation aid groups. Norway has sponsored a work-for-food program that has seen crews of Cambodians toiling each day, making fine progress at sprucing up the appearance of the area. It's a peaceful place with only the sounds of nature around you.

The site is surely worth a visit and the trip is quite easy these days with relatively quick access from Phnom Penh and Kampong Thom. The ruins of Angkor, with its magnificent architecture and artistry, overshadow all other ancient capitals and ruins in Cambodia. But put this site in another country in the region and tourists would be flocking to it.

To get there, take Highway 6 northwest toward Siem Reap for 5 km (using the Kampong Thom Market as the starting point) and go to the right as Highway 6 forks to the left. A big sign announces that this is the highway to TM Chey (T'beng Meanchey of Preah Vihear Province), Highway 12. After 9 km you come to another fork in the road where you again go right. Follow this for about 15 km more and you come to a small road and sign telling you to go north to the ruins.

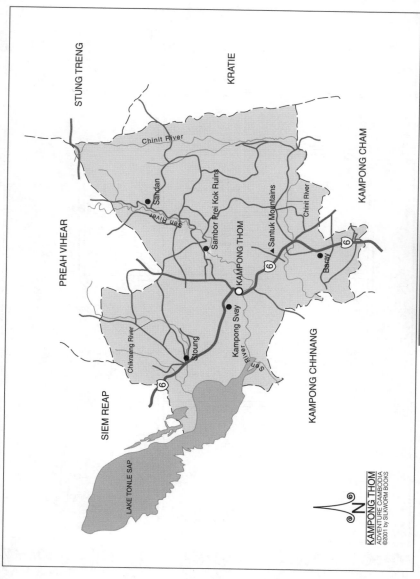

NORTH & NORTHWEST

KAMPONG THOM
ADVENTURE CAMBODIA
©2001 by SILKWORM BOOKS

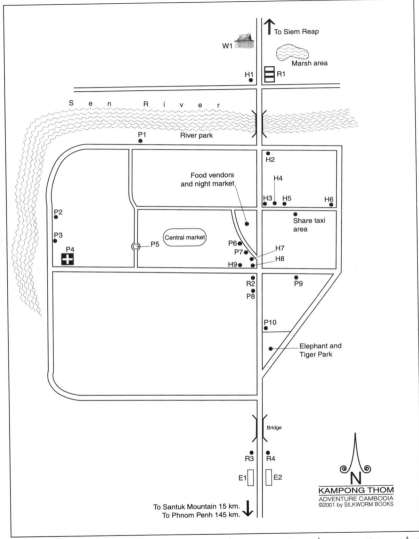

To Siem Reap

W1

Marsh area

H1

R1

S e n R i v e r

P1

River park

H2

H4

Food vendors
and night market

H3 H5

H6

P2

Share taxi
area

P3

Central market

P4

P5

P6

H7

P7

H8

H9

R2

P9

P8

P10

Elephant and
Tiger Park

Bridge

R3

R4

E1

E2

N

KAMPONG THOM
ADVENTURE CAMBODIA
©2001 by SILKWORM BOOKS

To Santuk Mountain 15 km.
To Phnom Penh 145 km.

KAMPONG THOM

H=Hotels

H1	New Hotel
H2	Stung Sen Royal Hotel
H3	Mohalleap Guesthouse
H4	Visalsok Guesthouse
H5	Suksan Guesthouse
H6	Penh Chet Guesthouse
H7	Aruneas Guesthouse & Restaurant
H8	Neak Meas Guesthouse & Restaurant
H9	Vimeansuor Guesthouse

R=Restaurants

R1	9 Makara Restaurant
R2	Outside patio noodle stands
R3	Reaksmay Restaurant
R4	Khemen Restaurant

See hotel list for:
- Super Soup Restaurant at the Stung Sen Royal Hotel
- Aruneas Guesthouse & Restaurant
- Neak Meas Guesthouse & Restaurant

P=Places

P1	River boat for hire
P2	Old two-story mansion
P3	Health clinic
P4	Kampong Thom Provincial Hospital
P5	Bayon monument
P6	Photo Fuji film & Konica
P7	Stationery store
P8	Post & Telecommunications
P9	Aquaduct culture center
P10	Youth sport building & area

E=Entertainment

E1	Outdoor bars & restaurant
E2	Outdoor bars & restaurant

The only problem with the directions is that the best road to take can vary at different times of the year, with the rainy season making it necessary to snake around alternative roads to get there. Your best bet is to grab a moto-taxi guy in front of the Aruneas Guesthouse (Soh-Kohm is the English-speaking guy we hired) and have him lead the way on his bike if you have your own wheels. If you use a moto-taxi outright for the round trip and and to go around the ruins, it's a reasonable 20,000 riel (under US$6).

Santuk Mountain

This heavily forested mountain site features a couple of levels of very interesting temples, caves and boulder-covered hillsides and beautiful views of the countryside, river and mountains. Good things usually don't come easy in Cambodia and this good thing means climbing up an 809-step stairway to the top. Fortunately it's not as tough as it sounds, with several resting spots and big shade trees lining the way. There are also a couple of drink stands at the bottom and top. There is a 1,000-riel fee to park your bike or moto.

The neatly constructed stairway features rails in the form of a continuous tug-of-war with figures holding up a serpent and pulling on it. Donation plaques next to each figure show the donor's name. The first level you reach has a Buddhist shrine and temple area set amidst huge boulder outcroppings that hang out over the hillside. Up on top the tug-of-war is continued with the figures surrounding temple spires and a Buddhist compound.

There are a few cave areas scattered about the top level—one featuring a reclining Buddha almost on top of a couple of sitting Buddhas. There are also a lot of weird figures and themes surrounding the neat temple areas, making this one of Cambo-

NORTH & NORTHWEST

dia's Buddhist theme parks. This place is a photographer's delight.

To get there, take Highway 6 back toward Phnom Penh and at around 16 km (from Kampong Thom Market) you will see the sign in English announcing "Santuk Mountain Site," where you take a left. The big hill is visible almost as soon as you leave Kampong Thom.

On the way there is another, smaller hill with a temple on top and a couple of other picturesque country temples.

River Scene

West of Highway 6 on River Road 1 is a nice stretch of parkway where locals hang out at in the early evening. Wooden rowboats are available to take you around the town area for 4,000 riel an hour during the day.

Wat Kampong Thom

Huge tiger and guardian figures greet you at the three gates to the town's namesake temple. There are three temple buildings, one being a strange-looking, three-story, multi-colored temple. Statues of temple characters abound. It's an ornate place.

Dam Site, Further Afield

There is a recreational site near a dam on the way to Kampong Thom from Phnom Penh. The highway is good approaching it from either direction.

A large picture sign written in English on Highway 6 says "Dam Site." The picture on the sign shows what people normally do there—swimming, tubing and picnicking. There are also vendors on weekends.

The sign and turn are 50 km from Kampong Thom or 113 km from the Japanese Bridge in Phnom Penh, so it's a nice stop when you are coming or going between the two cities. The dirt road going back to the dam site is okay all year around, except when it's had a particularly thorough soaking of rain. The distance is even marked on the picture sign.

Prey Proh Lake

A favorite with the locals for a weekend swim and picnic, it's a beautiful setting on a lake that stretches far out until it finally connects up with the Great Lake Tonle Sap. To get there, just head toward Siem Reap on Highway 6 for 17 km until you come to the lake. Take a left about 100 meters before the wooden bridge that crosses part of the lake and follow the dirt road back just under a kilometer to the resort area.

Prasat An Daet

This small temple ruin is from the Sambor Prei Kok era, built in the 6th or 7th century and made of the same brick construction as those ruins. There is only one temple and the place has been heavily looted. A few artifacts were saved by the locals, who have gathered them together and set them on top of the shrine inside the temple. There is a modern-era (1968) working temple next to the ruins. The inside walls and ceiling areas are covered with murals, a couple of them featuring scenes of King Norodom Sihanouk in his heyday, out among the masses, decked out in military attire—before everything started to go very wrong with Cambodia.

The temple grounds are extensive and it's a nice rural setting. Not necessarily worth a trip on its own, it is a nice stop en route to Siem Reap from Kampong Thom (or vice-versa). To get there from Kampong Thom, head out on Highway 6 toward Siem Reap. At about 28.5 km from the Kampong Thom Market, turn left (just past a small wooden bridge that crosses a canal. There are also landmine awareness signs for the public at this exact spot). Follow the canal road—it's dirt—for 2 km and turn right. Follow this just 300 meters to the temple grounds. Note that the canal is dry during the dry season.

MARKETS

The Kampong Thom market is the standard Cambodian all-purpose place and a night market springs up along the east side in the evening. Fruit, drink, and dessert stands line the street in front.

There is also a huge day fruit market that sets up along the boulevard on the west side of the market, stretching to the river road.

A stationery store just north of the Arunreas Guesthouse has the *Cambodia Daily* and *Phnom Penh Post* newspapers.

There are also a couple of film shops close to the Arunreas.

GETTING AROUND

Motorcycle Doctor

Phnom Penh is only a short ride away on decent roads, so that's the place to get a big bike worked on. There are a couple of small shops around the perimeter of the market for oiling and adjusting the chain.

CURRENCY EXCHANGE

There are no banks in town yet. Most money changers are on the east (front) and north ends of the market. Dollars and riel are readily changed.

MEDICAL FACILITIES

Kampong Thom Provincial Hospital. There are Khmer and foreign doctors here. It's the place to go if you have a problem that needs immediate attention.

RESTAURANTS

Aruneas Guesthouse & Restaurant. This is a very popular spot to eat in town. They serve good Western, Chinese and Khmer food at cheap prices, which of course is why they are popular. An English menu and staff that can speak the language are other nice features.

Neak Meas Hotel & Restaurant. This restaurant serves good Chinese and Khmer food in the morning and throughout the day until the nightclub kicks in around 8:30 pm.

9 Makara Restaurant, in row of three. Just north of the river bridge, on the east side of Highway 6 is a row of three restaurants, with the middle one being 9 Makara Restaurant and Nightclub. The restaurants are enclosed and serve Khmer and Chinese fare, with beer girls there to greet you in the evening.

"Restaurant Row" of Kampong Thom. About a kilometer toward Phnom Penh on Highway 6 is Kampong Thom's version of "Restaurant Row" outside of Phnom Penh. There are a number of Khmer and Chinese food restaurants on both sides of the highway that get rolling in the evening and have the Cambodian requirement of beer girls on hand.

Reaksmay Restaurant. One of the first restaurants you come across at "Restaurant Row" is this new and upscale place. It's fairly fancy for Kampong Thom. They serve up a bit of Western food to go along with the Khmer and Chinese fare and it's the home of the fancy-pants beer girls of Kampong Thom.

Super Soup Restaurant at the Stung Sen Royal Hotel. The Super Soup soup restaurant (try saying that quickly ten times) is everything that it's billed to be—a soup restaurant.

Cheap Food Stands. There are simple rice and noodle dish stands in front of the market, east side.

NIGHT SCENE

For a country town, Kampong Thom holds it's own in this department.

Neak Meas Hotel & Nightclub. This is where the top band in town struts its Khmer-medley and Western stuff from 8 to 11 pm nightly. Beer girls and a handful of taxi girls are ready to greet you.

9 Makara Restaurant & Nightclub. This restaurant has a small nightclub.

Reaksmay Restaurant. This new addition to "Restaurant Row" has been threatening to start a nightclub, but there's nothing yet.

ACCOMMODATIONS

Aruneas Guesthouse. A clean, well-run and friendly place, it has an attached Asian bath and is good value at US$3. The moto-taxi drivers who can take you to Sambor Prei Kok hang out in front and the restaurant here is a popular place to eat.

Vimeansuor Guesthouse. Business must be good, as they have been putting up an addition. It's a very clean place with nice rooms, attached Western bath and ceiling fan for US$6.

Mohalleap Guesthouse. It's another clean place with an Asian bath and fan room going for US$3.

Visalsok, Soksan and Penh Chet Guesthouses. These three are all similar with small rooms and share bath going from between US$1 and 10,000 riel. The cleaning leaves a lot to be desired.

Neak Meas Hotel. The roof of this five-story building represents the highest point in Kampong Thom and affords some nice views of the town, the countryside, and Santuk Mountain. There are also nice wrap-around terraces on each floor, and the rooms on the third floor, south side, have a good view, making it a decent spot to chill out with a cool drink. Clean rooms with a/c, TV, and double bed are US$10. For a room on the first floor with hot water, add US$5. The nightclub downstairs closes at 11 pm, so it's not much of a problem. If you like to turn in early, get a room at the back on the third floor. There is also a restaurant in the hotel.

Stung Sen Royal Hotel. It's named after the river that it's next to. This is the other top spot in town. All rooms have a/c, TV, fridge, Western bath and hot water shower. Depending on the room size, they go for US$20–25.

COMING & GOING

With the road to Kampong Thom in decent shape from Phnom Penh, it's just a matter of time before air-con buses ply the route. For the time being, it's the share taxi if you don't have your own transportation. Once you are in Kampong Thom and want to continue to Siem Reap or T'beng Meanchey (Preah Vihear Province), the roads are worse, but the share taxis ply the route all year round.

Share Taxi

Phnom Penh to Kampong Thom (same in reverse)	7,000 riel
Kampong Thom to Siem Reap (5–6 hours)	10,000 riel
Kampong Thom to T'beng Meanchey (5–6 hours)	20,000 riel

Motorcycle Touring Info

Security in all directions is no longer a problem. As mentioned earlier, the road is a breeze from Phnom Penh. Starting at the Japanese Bridge in Phnom Penh, head out Highway 6 to Skon where you go left at the traffic circle (it has a statue of kids holding a bird). This takes you the rest of the way.

Kampong Thom to Siem Reap

It's 145 km, with the road in nice shape for a while after you leave Kampong Thom town, then gets rougher, but much re-grading work has been done. It's not like it used to be; bomb crater holes used to be so deep that during the rainy season one could have a family picnic at a crater's shoreline.

The Kampong Thom–T'beng Meanchey

See warning below. To take the 137-km journey, you follow Highway 6 toward Siem Reap for 5 km to the fork in the road. A sign in English will point to the right side of the fork for T M Chey (T'beng Meanchey town, Preah Vihear Province) down Highway 12. The road here is much improved,

as there has been a lot of resurfacing done to accommodate the droves of logging trucks heading to and from Preah Vihear Province. The downside of the easier road is the dust that the trucks whip up as they chug along the road. It can be a real hazard as the thick dust clouds practically blind you from seeing possible oncoming traffic when you want to pass these slow moving vehicles.

The final 37-km stretch through the mountains and into T'beng Meanchey is still tough going. This is how the entire road used to be—bomb craters, erosion gulleys, and rocks are all here for your motorcycle fun. It can actually be an enjoyable stretch if you like this kind of riding, and the scenery is brilliant. This stretch can also be done during the rainy season, though the road may be slippery and dotted with small mud ponds after heavy rains. Enjoy.

NORTH & NORTHWEST

WARNING

The Kampong Thom–T'beng Meanchey road passes through many areas still riddled with minefields. You will see many of them marked (landmines not removed) but many are not marked at all. When you go through the rural countryside, DO NOT go walking off the road to relieve yourself. Just keep your feet on the road and do your deed. There is not much traffic on this road so it's not a big deal. Or wait until you pass a village with a drink stand and a safe toilet area.

PREAH VIHEAR & PREAH VIHEAR TEMPLE

Situated midway between east and west and far to the north, straddling the borders of Laos and Thailand, Preah Vihear is Cambodia's most remote province. With no decent air, land or water access, and with the government vs. Khmer Rouge king-of-the-hill battles for the mountain temple of Preah Vihear, the province was kept fairly well sealed off to outsiders.

While road access to the heart of Preah Vihear Province leaves a lot to be desired, it's not the worst road you will come across in Cambodia, and share taxis ply the route to T'beng Meanchey, the seat of the province, all year round. If you are an adventurous soul, there is some beautiful country and some interesting sights to be seen that will provide you with a bit of a challenge in reaching them. The trip does qualify as an adventure.

T'beng Meanchey town is a pleasant, laid-back place that at present doesn't have a lot going on, but gives the impression that it holds some promise. This is probably because the town is a junction point for the magnificent Preah Vihear Temple to the north and the ancient capital of Koh Ker (also known as Chok Gargyar) to the west. The town also sits near the banks of the Sen River, which originates not far to the northwest in the Dangkrek Mountains, and continues its long journey east and south going through Kampong Thom town, finally ending up in the Great Lake Tonle Sap. Because it's one winding snake of a river, it isn't used too much as a transportation link between Kampong Thom and T'beng Meanchey, but does hold the possibility of being used for ecotourism and adventure river trips.

WHAT'S UP

Preah Vihear Temple

The temple ruins of Preah Vihear (Khao Phra Viharn to the Thais just across the border) were again opened to visitors in 1998, thanks to an agreement between the Cambodian and Thai governments and the disbanding of the Khmer Rouge forces. The agreement was a necessity because Preah Vihear Temple is a Cambodian national landmark that is much easier to access from Thailand than from Cambodia. The Cambodian government opened the site to foreign visitors in a campaign to promote the country's tourist destinations and attract much-needed foreign currency.

Preah Vihear Temple

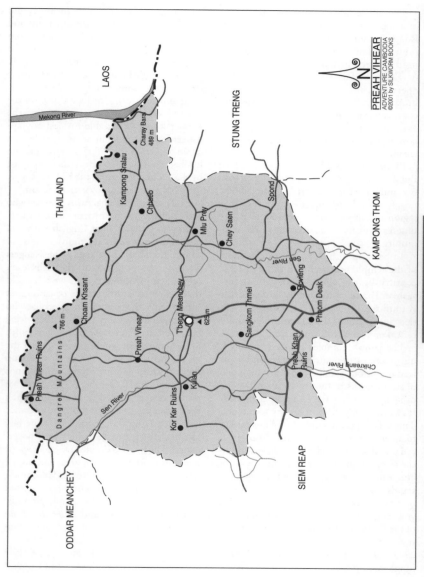

The entire area surrounding the ruins remained the last stronghold of the Khmer Rouge, including the town of Anlong Veng (only 250 km from the temple) which was, until his arrest on 6 March 1999, the home of Ta Mok, Pol Pot's chief of military operations. Ever since the death of Pot Pol in April 1998, the area has been awash in controversy as Khmer Rouge commanders and different factions of the Cambodian government fought to benefit from a power alliance.

By bringing Ta Mok (nicknamed "The Butcher" for his hand in murdering almost two million people) to trial, Prime Minister Hun Sen hopes to gain control of this region and also to gain international recognition and financial aid from the world community.

To back up in history, the construction of the temple was begun in the mid 10th century by the Khmer King Rajendravarman II and continued by Suryavarman II until the 1100s. It is interesting to note that Suryavarman II also built the temples of Ankor Wat near Siem Reap.

The temple complex has been restored, but many of the entrance ways and walls lean precariously and a two-story-high pile of stone blocks in the last courtyard, some ornately carved, have yet to be assembled. It's a fascinating piece of history to explore. The walkways and temple buildings extend to an area of over 800 meters. The original stairs and stone-lined pathways leading to the temple complex are in good condition and unfortunately lined with souvenir stands (but not on weekdays).

If you walk to the far end of the ruins, you will have a sweeping panoramic view of the Dangrek Mountains as they zigzag in saw-tooth fashion along the Cambodia-Thailand border and of the thickly forested jungles and plains that seem to stretch out forever into Cambodia. Standing on the temple grounds, one can see for miles into Cambodian territory. Small dirt roads and trails are visible well into the distance from this beautiful vantage point. Recent and ancient history blend together as you walk past the fortified bunkers built from temple stones by the Khmer Rouge. Two long-barreled anti-tank cannons look down on the flat valley below. It's easy to imagine the Khmer Rouge being able to blast any approaching Cambodian army vehicle that dared approach the hill. This strategic site has been at one time or another occupied by the Cambodian army, the Khmer Rouge, the Thai army and the Vietnamese army.

Black uniformed Thai Army Rangers who are friendly, well informed and quite willing to practice their English with you now mostly serve to aid tourists, most of whom are Thais these days. The Rangers warned us never to step off the paths, even on the temple grounds, and we were told that below us lay thousands of landmines still buried in the ground. The guerrillas who held the temple from 1993 to 1997 were never seriously in jeopardy, as any attempt to dislodge them would have required the government troops to mount an attack up the very steep and heavily-mined Cambodian side. On 10 October 1999, five Thai teenagers were injured by a landmine when they attempted to go around the entrance without paying the 50-baht fee. One boy lost his left leg and the others were hospitalized. The five had decided to ignore warning signs stating that some areas around the temple had yet to be cleared of landmines.

Beautiful Khmer women and girls sell old Cambodian notes on the temple grounds, along with cold soda and water. Most are the wives and children of the Cambodian soldiers protecting the ruins.

Because the site is still much more easily accessed from Thailand, we'll run through some directions on how to get to Preah Vihear Temple from there first.

From Thailand, the town of Si Saket is the best place to start your trip to the temple ruins. Si Saket's main street, Kukham Road, runs directly into Highway 221 and then it's an easy drive of about 101 km on well-paved blacktop roads.

From Si Saket, the easiest way to visit the ruins is to rent a car and driver, which can be arranged through your hotel.

On weekends, *songthaeos* (Thai passenger pickup truck with seats) go all the way to the temple from Si Saket. On weekdays the *songthaeos* travel only as far as the town of Kantharalak. From there you must take a motorbike taxi or hire a driver to take you the remaining 11 km.

For 245 baht you could also take an air-con bus from Bangkok's northern bus station to Si Saket. The buses leave at 9 am and 9:30 pm and the trip takes 8 ½ hours. A train from Bangkok's Hua Lampong Station takes ten hours.

If possible, don't go on the weekend, as bus tours from Bangkok arrive early in the morning and the grounds are filled with Thai tourists. The hotels in Si Saket are all a good value, as in most of Isan. The downturn in the economy has brought hotel prices down quite a bit. Air conditioned hotel rooms that were 1,000 baht are now going for almost half price.

As you near the temple, there is a Thai army checkpoint in the middle of the road where you must stop and show your passport. You do not need a Cambodian visa and your passport will not be stamped. One of the reasons for this is the agreement between the two countries and also the fact that it's not desirable for most tourists to travel beyond the temple on the cliff into Cambodia. You must leave your car in a free parking lot, lined with food vendors. We had a nice meal and there are many small

restaurants to choose from. Souvenir stands sell calculators, old army clothing, wristwatches, Buddha statues and temple photographs. There are plenty of straw hats and there are hand-knitted wool caps for sale, as the sun is quite strong. Among the best buys are Khmer scarves and hammered tin and silver alloy serving spoons and bowls.

Admission to the grounds is 100 baht for foreigners, 30 baht for Thais and free for Cambodians. For an additional 5 baht, a farm tractor pulling a row of ten carts will transport you the last thousand meters to where the asphalt ends. From there, it's a ten-minute walk up a dirt path to the temple complex where more souvenir stands and Khmer vendors await you.

Meanwhile, Back at the Ranch...

The Cambodian government has been heavily promoting the Preah Vihear Temple as another of Cambodia's unique and exciting cultural sites at various tourism conferences around the world. They are quick to say that now it is possible to reach Preah Vihear Temple by road, but have precious few little details on how to go about this task or even of the possible hazards to avoid in making the journey (see the warning box below). The journey takes you through some beautiful parts of Cambodia, but it's another case of good things don't come easy here.

Here's the Dope on Making the Trip—

First of all, forget the rainy season—the share taxis don't even make the trip then as the Sen River (just north of T'beng Meanchey town) has no bridge and is only served by small wooden boats shuttling people, goods and motorcycles across. But the bad part for riders is that just north of the river there is a vast lowland area that fills in with water during the rainy season, making the road disappear. Attempting to go around it all is quite dangerous due to

WARNING

Many of the roads in Preah Vihear Province (like the ones going to Preah Vihear Temple and the ancient capital of Koh Ker, along with the main road between Kampong Thom and T'beng Meanchey and from T'beng Meanchey to Choam Khsant), are still lined on the sides with landmines and many of the minefields are still unmarked. Stay on the road or on a well-worn pathway. Some of the roads that lead to the temples still have landmines buried in them and different routes have been cut around these stretches through the forest making it necessary to choose which route to follow. It is very important to keep alert where roads intersect and only go on the roads that have tire tracks or footprints on them. The roads that have no tire tracks on them—bicycle, car, or motorcycle—probably are mined and that's why the locals are going around that stretch. If in doubt, don't go on it. When you stop to relieve yourself along the way, keep you feet on the road or a well-worn pathway while doing your deed.

hidden landmines still lurking about from the days of the Khmer Rouge and government forces fighting for control of the temple. The road has a forest canopy shading it and as a result does not dry up to a passable condition until about a month into the dry season, which means that your current window of opportunity for attempting the journey (it will probably still be sometime before the road is upgraded) is best kept to late January until the start of the rainy season (usually around May in this part of the country).

Starting at T'beng Meanchey town (see Coming and Going and the map for T'beng Meanchey, both in this chapter), go to the Sen River just north of town. During the dry season, it is normally possible to ride across the river as the water level is down considerably then. Follow the main body of road where you see all the tire tracks (this is the road to Choam Khsant town, the gateway town to Preah Vihear Temple) and you will be on the right road. The first 22 km is real tough going with things a bit (but not too much) easier for the balance of the stretch. At 46 km from T'beng Meanchey you come to a clearing and you turn left here instead of continuing straight ahead. More info on Choam Khsant town follows in this chapter.

I came upon a couple of jungle hardened platoons on this desolate stretch of road (T'beng Meanchey to Choam Khsant) that were supposedly out patrolling for bandits who reportedly prey on locals and share taxis, although local officials that I spoke to said the situation has much improved since the patrols began. It's no wonder—the guys are fully equipped with automatic weapons and rocket launchers and are on foot weaving through the road and jungle areas. They are usually friendly souls, but it can make one a bit nervous happening upon a tough looking bunch like this all of a sudden. A smile or a wave usually leaves them breaking out into a grin, and they start hooting in amazement at seeing foreigners way out there.

At about 54 km from T'beng Meanchey, you arrive at Choam Khsant town.

Share taxis ply this stretch for 15,000 riel and the trip takes two to three hours, depending on the current road conditions and the craziness of the driver. See Coming and Going section and the map for Choam Khsant in this chapter for more details.

The rest of the journey, from Choam Khsant to the army encampment at the base of the mountain that Preah Vihear Temple sits on, is just over 46 km. There are a number of confusing turns to make enroute and it is best to try to find a moto-taxi guy in front of the Old Market in Choam Khsant to take as a guide. They will take their own vehicle and lead the way for you to the encampment, hike up to the temple with you (a 1 ½ to 2 hour hike) and lead you back to Choam Khsant for US$10, plus fuel for their moto-taxi—not bad as the entire journey will take all day, even with an early start. If you did not ride up to Choam Khsant on your own bike, you could of course jump on the back of his bike, but the quality of the road will leave you pretty sore from bouncing along on the back of a small moto-taxi. The moto-taxi guys don't speak any English (most speak Thai as well as Khmer), but if you simply say *prah-saht*, which means temple, they will know that you want to go to the mountain temple and from there you should be able to get through the transaction part (take out a US$10 bill and shake your head when they ask for more). It may be possible to get a pickup truck share taxi to take you to the base of the temple and back at the Old Market area in Choam Khsant town, but it will set you back at least US$50.

Along the way to the mountain temple, you will notice pieces of vehicles hanging up in the trees here and there from unfortunate souls that hit a landmine. It's an eerie reminder in this peaceful and uninhabited forest area of the deadly devices that are still lurking about this area in big numbers—see the warning box above.

The soldiers at the base camp are a friendly lot that will allow you to park your bike at their base camp while you hike up to the temple and you can figure that the bike will still be there when you return. It's not required but it's a real nice gesture to give these underpaid guys a few thousand riel to watch your bike—good insurance and you will make some friends.

It's a good idea to have the moto guy or a soldier lead the way on the winding upward climb to the temple. The mountain is riddled with landmines and while, if you follow the golden rule for Cambodia— always stay on worn pathways and roadways —you will be okay, there are intersecting pathways where it's difficult to figure out which way you should go. I did the hike alone but there was some question on which path to follow at a couple of spots. The hike takes you through a piece of the beautiful Dangrek Mountains, but never forget the hidden danger that is right nearby as you are walking—landmines. That aside, it is a scenic and peaceful walk through a former battle zone.

Before you can see the temple, you will be surprised to see a clearing off to the left that has a beautifully paved road in the distance heading your way. Yes, it is Thailand, the land of peace and prosperity, alongside the Kingdom of Cambodia, which not so long ago was falling apart—and not just at the seams. It's not much further beyond that that you come to the temple gateway and ancient stairway leading to the temple and the gorgeous view of where you just came from. You will see Thai and foreign tourists milling about that have no idea of what you had to go through to get there. It's a sweet taste at that point knowing that you did it the hard way and met one of Cambodia's adventure challenges.

Koh Ker (a.k.a. Chok Gargyar)

This early 10th-century capital of Cambodia was the direct result of a power struggle within the monarchy at Angkor. Jayavarman IV grabbed the throne in Angkor and decided to set up shop somewhere else and what resulted is the ancient city of Koh Ker. According to Cambodians from the area, the city had around fifty temples. Following the king's death, the monarchy was again moved and seated in

Angkor and was poised for a very significant period of the powerful empire's history.

The jungle definitely has the upper hand in reclaiming the ruins, which have been very difficult to reach due to very poor roads and landmines from the war years. Weathering, neglect and heavy looting have taken a toll on Koh Ker and it is still a long and arduous journey to get there (more on this in a bit), but it is possible these days. The struggle is worth it for the hardy as you will be in a part of Cambodia and among an ancient city that has seen very few visitors. This place and the Preah Khan temples, sort of conjure up a feeling of being in the Hollywood adventure movie "Indiana Jones and the Lost Temple of Doom." There wasn't a soul around when I was there—just the sounds of the forest coupled with these ancient ruins that were peeking out from the shadows here and there.

The first temple that you come to is Prahsaht Nee-ung K'mao (about 62 km and three to four hours from T'beng Meanchey town). It's of laterite block construction and in a dilapidated state, but it will give you a feeling of amazement when you come to this first site of Koh Ker, on the right side of the road. The areas around the temples have reportedly been cleared of mines, but stay on the worn pathways to be sure.

The next ruin you see, further along the road, is on the left. There is not much left of Elephant Temple—it definitely qualifies as a ruin. Further along and also on the left you come to Ahn-dong Prehng, an ancient well supplying Koh Ker. Handfuls of Cambodians walk there daily to draw water and have a bath, much as they did over a thousand years ago.

Continuing further along the road is the most impressive complex of Koh Ker, Prahsaht Groh-hohm, or Red Temple, so named because of the color of the stone used to construct it. The main structure of the complex that you see was the royal throne room and the middle part is where the throne stood. A rainbow design was carved above the entry door but, unfortunately, that fell victim to temple looters. Galleries and two man-made ponds for collecting water surround the temple, which locals also hike to for their water needs. Locals obviously don't see many foreigners as a couple of them started to run away as I approached, but then again, it could just be a natural reaction to seeing the likes of me.

Continuing just a bit further down the road, or following the surrounding wall of Prah-saaht Groh-hohm in the same direction, you come upon the stone block hill temple of Kohmpang. It is another of Cambodia's replicas of the mythical Mount Meru dedicated to the gods of Hinduism. The semi-pyramidal structure is said to be 65 meters high and the climb up the stone temple gives one a view of the surrounding forest, with its sounds of birds, monkeys and other wildlife. One can also see the modern (a real stretch of the term here) village of Koh Ker just beyond. There is no gasoline, cola or bottled water available here, so don't get your hopes up. That simply reinforces the fact that this ancient city is rarely visited and certainly sees close to zero tourists.

T'beng Meanchey town is the best place to begin your trip to Koh Ker. It's best to go to the front of the main market and try to find one of the few English speaking mototaxi guys that are familiar with the road out there. A couple of the roads enroute still have landmines and they will steer you clear of these. There are also a number of confusing turns to make. The trip is a full-day deal—you can figure about 10 hours to go, look about the sites a bit and get back to town—so start early. US$10, plus fuel for the mototaxi guy's bike is a fair price for the journey, either to have them lead the way while you follow on your bike or to just jump on the back of his bike (this will entail a bouncing, grueling ride). Another alternative is to hire a share taxi in front of the market or just around the corner in front of a building they are just constructing for the share taxi stand. This will run from US$40–50.

The road quality is very poor with heavy bomb craters and stretches of deep sand. On a motorcycle it's possible to go around many of the bad stretches by following the small alternative paths that line the roadway.

One warning—at 21 km from the circle in T'beng Meanchey (see map), go left instead of straight at the fork—going straight is supposedly a shortcut (but not too short) to Preah Vihear Temple, but it is still full of landmines. Just remember anywhere you go—stay off the roads or paths that don't have any tire prints (bicycle, car or motorcycle) or footprints on them.

Just under 33 km into the journey is the village of Kulen. This is the last spot enroute where you can get drinks, food and fuel so grab something here if you need it.

The police in T'beng Meanchey town can be a bit of a problem when it comes to going to Koh Ker. I got up and going one morning and headed towards Koh Ker, only to be told by police in Kulen town that I had to go back to T'beng Meanchey town to meet with police for approval. Needless to say, I was not very happy having already rode 33 km on a nasty road.

Upon returning, the police asked why I didn't tell them of my plan to go to Koh Ker, to which I replied I didn't know anyone cared and there is no sign anywhere asking visitors going to Koh Ker to check in with the police. Since they didn't know how to handle the idea of people wanting to go to Koh Ker (as few have gone), I told them to put up a sign in English, in front of the police compound, instructing visitors to check in there. They will write down your name and passport number here and will also want to collect a fee of 5,000 riel for going to Koh Ker—that is what it's all about. This is not the Cambodian government's idea and unfortunately the fee does not go toward road improvement or restoration work at Koh Ker. Check the T'beng Meanchey map for the location of the police.

Preah Khan (Bah Kahn)

Preah Khan means Sacred Sword, which usually refers to the sword of a king or god (kings were considered to be godlike). Preah Khan is a complex of ancient temples and structures of the supporting city that surrounded them. It was built in the 10th century for Hindu worship and later changed with the times to incorporate the Buddhist beliefs that evolved in ancient Cambodia.

Preah Khan is situated in the remote southwestern corner of Preah Vihear Province. It is a long and tough full-day journey to get there and then back again to a place for spending the night, but yes, it is worth it. It's another one of Cambodia's truly amazing ancient sites that has been frozen in a time warp and is nearly inaccessible to those wanting to visit. When you finally arrive at the first temple complex that greets you, with its four-sided tower and those Bayon-style faces smiling at nobody, and nothing around but forest, you would be hard pressed not to let out a WOW!

Here are a few directions on getting there, thrown in together with info on Preah Khan, but like going to Koh Ker, there are a number of turns to make that are unmarked so it's best to hire an English-speaking moto-taxi guy in front of the market in T'beng Meanchey to show you the way. The same fee as described in the previous two sites is fine for going here as well—$10 plus fuel for the moto-taxi, whether he simply leads or you jump on the back of his bike. As with Koh Ker, you could also try to grab a

NORTH & NORTHWEST

share taxi near the market in T'beng Meanchey for US$50, although going to Preah Khan is a bit more expensive because it's further away. Moto-taxi guys in Kampong Thom town are not familiar with the ruins, so don't think about using them instead.

Heading south from the circle in T'beng Meanchey (towards Kampong Thom town), you go 37 km to where you see a sign in English on the right side of the road announcing that it's 56 km to Preah Khan after you turn right. Coming up the same road from Kampong Thom town to this turn off is 93 km (from Kampong Thom Market), so you can see that to go to Preah Khan, the best place to begin is T'beng Meanchey town.

About 19 km from where you turned off from the main road (at the Preah Khan sign) is the village of Sahng-kohm T'mai. The small market lines the road and this is the last place that you can get food, drinks and fuel, so it's best to replenish here.

About 30 km past the village is Roh-ah-say village. There is a lake to the right, and next to the road on the left you can see a small semi-pyramid-style hill temple. This is Prahsaht Damrei, or Elephant Temple, not to be confused with the one at Koh Ker. It was built about the same time as Preah Khan—a few elephant statues, a partial gallery with a couple of apsara figures and part of a walkway are about all that remain.

WARNING

The pretty little lake looks very inviting on a hot day, but DON'T GO SWIMMING IN IT!! The locals say that it has a dangerous parasite that bores into the skin and into internal organs—this is indeed a problem in a number of lakes in Southeast Asia and the locals would be the ones to know. The parasite is very difficult to detect until it has done a lot of damage.

Continuing on past the village about 7 km is a sign welcoming you to Preah Khan. Continue on past the remains of a small temple and you arrive at Prahsaht Ta Phrom. This is the temple with the Bayon-style four-faced tower that was just mentioned. This temple, along with the Bayon in Angkor and Banteay Chmar Temple in Banteay Meanchey Province, are the only ancient temples in Cambodia with the four-sided tower of smiling faces.

Just sitting there surrounded by the forest, alone in time, Prahsaht Ta Phrom seems to have the ability to transfer you back in history as you explore the small complex. There are reportedly no landmine problems anywhere around Preah Khan (locals say that this was one ancient temple site spared by the Khmer Rouge), but it's always best to stay on the worn pathways to be safe.

Like the rest of Preah Khan, heavy looting in the past is apparent. One can find statues and artifacts intact, though, as you scout around. Preah Khan is of the same designs and construction as Angkor.

About 300 meters beyond Ta Phrom lies the wall and gateway of the main Preah Khan complex. After entering through the gateway, the first temple-like structure on the right was actually used as the prison for the town—must have been a pretty gruesome experience being holed up inside of there a thousand years ago.

Further into the interior of the walled complex—the middle, actually—is Prahsaht Neeung Boh S'ray S'aht, or the Temple of the Pretty Woman—some ancient Roy Orbison must have named this place. There are a number of small temple ruins to explore in this mid-size complex, but the problem is time—it's a full day starting early in the morning from T'beng Meanchey, getting there, exploring for a couple of hours and then heading back to T'beng Meanchey or Kampong Thom town. Figure a good ten hours and like all of these sites in Preah Vihear Province, you really don't want to be out on the roads in the dark of night because they are just not good roads—even by the light of day.

AHNSAI BORDER CROSSING

Twenty-three kilometers to the north of Choam Khsant town (see map in this chapter for info on this town) is the border market and crossing of Ahnsai. It takes about forty minutes to get there and it is a beautiful short trip in a very scenic part of the Dangkrek Mountains. There is also a fairly active cross-border trade market on the Cambodian side every Tuesday and Thursday. Thai immigration officials at the border say that foreigners can cross into Thailand here, but you have to go to the immigration office in Choam Khsant town to obtain a visa as they do not issue them at the border (see map). The Thais also say that you could cross with your motorcycle into Thailand from here as well, but the Cambodian immigration officials say that motorcycles can't enter into Cambodia here.

A share taxi in front of the Choam Khsant Old Market makes the run to the border Tuesdays and Thursdays for 8,000 riel.

T'BENG MEANCHEY TOWN

This is the gateway to the Koh Ker and Preah Khan ancient sites and also on the way to Choam Khsant town, the gateway to Preah Vihear Temple. The small town referred to by the locals as simply Kait (which means province or provincial seat in Khmer), should only become more active as more venture this way to see the ancient sites that have been so hard to access during the recent turbulent past of Cambodia.

Temple

There is a small temple on T'beng Meanchey town's main drag that is not much to write home about, but it's where the resident monks teach the faith.

Market

The T'beng Meanchey market is a good place to stock up on supplies or replenish your supply of tie-down bungy cords for your gear bags.

Getting Around

The moto-taxi guys hang out in front of the market. A couple of them speak English and are a good source of road information.

The town bike doctor is about half a kilometer north of the circle. He can help with minor problems and chain adjustments.

Currency Exchange

The market is where the money changers are set up, with dollars and riel readily changed.

Medical Facilities

There is a small provincial hospital with Khmer and sometimes, foreign doctors. It's on the main drag.

Restaurants

Ahartan Bakan T'mai. This very friendly place has the best food in town and is run very efficiently by a Khmer couple and their three lovely daughters. The food is a cut above the others and local NGOs like to eat here—prices are very reasonable.

Main Drag Restaurants. As you come in from Kampong Thom and just past the town temple there are a couple of restaurants. The first one you would come to has English speakers and surprisingly enough for out here in the boondocks, big screen TV with CNN. The food is good and cheap and

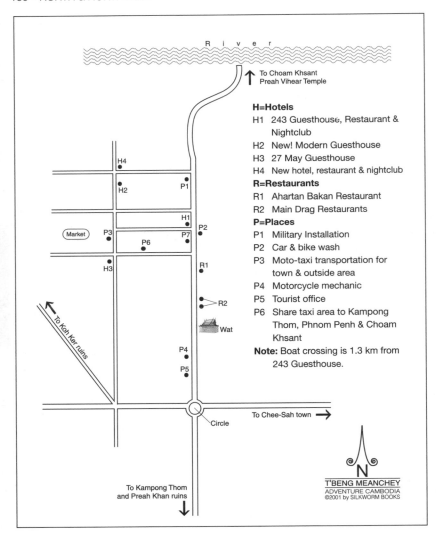

River

To Choam Khsant
Preah Vihear Temple

H=Hotels
H1 243 Guesthouse, Restaurant & Nightclub
H2 New! Modern Guesthouse
H3 27 May Guesthouse
H4 New hotel, restaurant & nightclub
R=Restaurants
R1 Ahartan Bakan Restaurant
R2 Main Drag Restaurants
P=Places
P1 Military Installation
P2 Car & bike wash
P3 Moto-taxi transportation for town & outside area
P4 Motorcycle mechanic
P5 Tourist office
P6 Share taxi area to Kampong Thom, Phnom Penh & Choam Khsant
Note: Boat crossing is 1.3 km from 243 Guesthouse.

H4

H2   P1

H1
Market   P3   P7   P2
        P6

H3   R1

          • R2

          Wat

P4

P5

Circle   To Chee-Sah town →

To Koh Ker ruins

To Kampong Thom
and Preah Khan ruins

N
T'BENG MEANCHEY
ADVENTURE CAMBODIA
©2001 by SILKWORM BOOKS

the drinks are cold—perfect after that long ride.

No Name Restaurant. This place is just down the street from the market and serves simple and cheap Khmer food—if the staff can figure out your order.

243 Guesthouse & Restaurant. The staff speak English and there is an English menu. They serve up Khmer, Chinese and a bit of Western food. They are open from breakfast until late (late for T'beng Meanchey, that is).

Night Scene

As you have probably guessed by the remote location of the town, it's pretty quiet here. There are a couple of karaoke spots around town with a few hostesses each. The 243 Guesthouse is the current "hot spot" of T'beng Meanchey. Check the map for the location of the new hotel—it should be completed by the time you get this book in your hands and will sport the only nightclub in T'beng Meanchey.

Accommodations

243 Guesthouse. A very friendly English-speaking Khmer couple run the place and hold court over the handful of staff that they employ for the guesthouse, restaurant and karaoke place in the nicely landscaped compound. Nice enough rooms with two beds, mosquito nets, fan (when the generator is turned on) and attached Western bath, go for 10,000–15,000 riel. They also are a source of information on the area.

27 May Guesthouse. This simple but clean place has single rooms with a share toilet for 5,000 riel, and 13,000 riel gets you a simple attached bathroom. Mosquito net and fan.

New! Modern Guesthouse (It's what the sign says anyway). Simple and clean rooms go for 8,000 riel and share bath. Mosquito net and fan.

New Hotel (name unclear—still under construction at the time of writing). Big things must be foreseen for the town as a real swank hotel (for this part of Cambodia) is in the making and should be done by the time you get there. An educated guess would put the rooms at US$10 for a/c, or US$5 for the same room with only the fan. Should have cable TV as well. A good restaurant and the town's only nightclub should also be up and running.

Coming & Going

Share Taxi

Share taxis ply the route between Kampong Thom and T'beng Meanchey year around with the trip taking three to five hours depending upon the season. The good news is that because of the heavy logging going on in Preah Vihear (which is not good news), most of this route has been leveled out smooth for the logging trucks so that only about 30 km of the 137-km stretch is still nasty bomb craters and a rocky mountain pass. The bad news is that with all of those logging trucks the dirt is kicked up so much that it becomes a real hazard trying to pass the slow moving vehicles—be very careful as the oncoming vehicles are driving like maniacs even though they can't see either. Share taxis charge 20,000 riel for the trip in the cab.

During the dry season, share taxis also make the run between T'beng Meanchey and Choam Khsant towns. The 54.5 km trip takes 2 H to three hours and alternates between bumpy and slow going on the sea of sand stretches. Keep your eyes open for the bits of vehicles hanging in the treetops from hitting a landmine. 15,000 riel is the fare.

NORTH & NORTHWEST

Motorcycle Touring Info

See warning box below.

Kampong Thom to T'beng Meanchey

From Kampong Thom to T'beng Meanchey you follow Highway 6 toward Siem Reap for 5 km to the fork in the road. A sign in English will point to the right side of the fork for T M Chey, which is T'beng Meanchey town and Preah Vihear Province. You are then following Highway 12 which is now much improved. The 137-km stretch is now a fairly decent dirt and gravel road, courtesy of the logging operations in Preah Vihear Province, until the last 30 km or so, when it turns into what the entire stretch used to be—deep bomb craters and a rocky mountain pass to go over. But it is doable year around although this last stretch gets pretty slippery during the rainy season. Use caution when trying to pass the logging trucks as visibility is poor from the dirt they kick up and share taxis coming from the other direction are thinking about anything but a set of wheels approaching head-on —they are maniacs, to put it kindly.

T'beng Meanchey to Choam Khsant

The 54.5 km stretch from T'beng Meanchey to Choam Khsant town is best saved for the dry season, starting about a month after the rainy season has ended (about the end of January up there). If the Sen River just north of T'beng Meanchey is low enough, you can ride across it—just look for tire tracks going into it on both sides. If it's still high, locals shuttle people, goods and moto-taxis across in small wooden boats. Figure 2,000 riel for you and your bike.

The road varies from bomb craters to seas of sand that are very difficult and slow to get through—it's a lot of work. Unless there is a well-worn path going around the bad spots, stay on the main body of road as there

are a lot of landmines still present. Landmine clearing organizations are busy working up here but there is a lot of ground to cover.

Anyway, after crossing the river stay on the main body of road and at 46 km from the river you come to a clearing. Turn left here instead of following the road straight— most of the tire tracks do go to the left and this goes to Choam Khsant.

WARNING

Many of the roads in Preah Vihear Province (like the ones going to Preah Vihear Temple and the ancient capital of Koh Ker, along with the main road between Kampong Thom and T'beng Meanchey and from T'beng Meanchey to Choam Khsant), are still lined on the sides with landmines and many of the minefields are still unmarked. Stay on the road or on a well-worn pathway. Some of the roads that lead to the temples still have landmines buried in them and different routes have been cut around these stretches through the forest making it necessary to choose which route to follow. It is very important to keep alert where roads intersect, and to choose only the roads that have tire tracks or footprints on them. The roads that have no tire tracks on them—bicycle, car or motorcycle—probably are still mined and that's why the locals are going around that stretch. If in doubt, don't go on it. When you stop to relieve yourself along the way, keep you feet on the road or a well-worn pathway while doing your deed.

CHOAM KHSANT TOWN

Choam Khsant town is a small but fairly prosperous town, by Cambodian standards, in Preah Vihear Province that is your best gateway to the Preah Vihear Temple on the Cambodian side of the Thai-Cambodia border and also the border market and crossing at Ahnsai.

It's fairly prosperous because of the border trade with Thailand and the resulting Thai goods that many of the townsfolk deal to people in Preah Vihear Province and beyond. It's also the home to Division 2 of the Cambodian military so there is some resulting extra activity including a small touch of nightlife to keep the soldiers happy.

The What's Up section in the front of this chapter has all the information on Preah Vihear Temple and the Ahnsai border area. The following is just a bit of info to go along with the map.

Markets

The markets are small all-purpose style where you can stock up on items that you may be low on up here in the boondocks.

Getting Around

Refer to the Getting Around section in T'beng Meanchey town just prior to this section for motorcycle touring information.

Currency Exchange

Either the Old or New Market is the place to change dollars into riel or baht and all three are readily accepted here. Most bills are made out for the amount in riel, however.

Restaurants

There are cheap rice and noodle stands lining the road in the morning and afternoon by the Old Market and also outside of the New Market, southwest side.

The **Sok San Guesthouse** has fairly good food and it's easy, as that's where you are staying.

Night Scene

The **Sok San Guesthouse** has a karaoke room and girls working there that will undoubtedly express their undying love for visitors. Yes, the karaoke chamber can hinder a good night's rest, but even worse is the…

Open Air Disco. Just down a few hundred meters from the guesthouse is an open area that has been converted into a night time social place, complete with refreshments and a big dance area. There are loads of dance girls that Cambodians pay 500 riel per ticket for the thrill of dancing with them. The music alternates between popular Cambodian music and all the techno Western hits and is played at absolute full volume (the only volume that Cambodians seem to think makes a club legitimate) until 1:00–1:30 am. Yes, you will hear it back at your room and yes, the repetition of their favorite hits will have you climbing the walls.

Accommodations

Sok San Guesthouse. The only game in town at this point. For 10,000 riel you get you a mosquito net, fan (for part of the night) and a small red light bulb that reminds you what this guesthouse is also used as. The food here is okay and the folks that run the place are friendly so be happy that your bike didn't break down enroute to Choam Khsant and that you aren't sleeping in a tree.

Coming & Going

Refer to the tail end of the Coming and Going section of T'beng Meanchey town, just prior to this section.

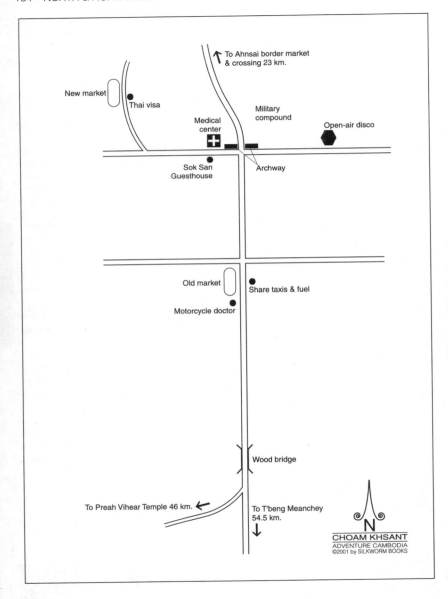

To Ahnsai border market
& crossing 23 km.

New market

Thai visa

Military
compound

Medical
center

Open-air disco

Sok San
Guesthouse

Archway

Old market

Share taxis & fuel

Motorcycle doctor

Wood bridge

To Preah Vihear Temple 46 km.

To T'beng Meanchey
54.5 km.

CHOAM KHSANT
ADVENTURE CAMBODIA
©2001 by SILKWORM BOOKS

▲ Preah Vihear Temple

▼ Money souvenir hawkers at Preah Vihear Temple

PREAH VIHEAR

Approach to Preah Vihear Temple

Illegal logging problems persist

▲ The monks at Preah Vihear Temple

▼ Khmer Rouge bunker at Preah Vihear Temple

*Rural people near Koh Ker
ruins, Preah Vihear Province*

Hard work for water

Leftovers from the long war

SIEM REAP

Siem Reap is a pleasant, laid back Cambodian town that just happens to have the country's number one tourist attraction, Angkor, almost within arms reach from it. To be sure, the magnificence and grandeur of these archaeological and architectural wonders form the basis for staying in Siem Reap and using the town as the gateway to Angkor.

However, the town itself is an appealing part of the visit, with it's genuinely friendly townspeople, colonial architecture and the small and placid Siem Reap River that gracefully glides through it. The pace of life is slow and almost rhythmic, much like the Khmer classical music that was played in the ancient royal courts nearby. There are also a number of other sights to see and things to do that might just make you want to spend an extra day or two in Siem Reap, to chill out and take it all in.

The history of Siem Reap Province reads much the same as that of Battambang and Banteay Meanchey Provinces, also in the northwest region of Cambodia. Since the downfall of the Angkor Empire and Khmer dominance over its neighbors, control over these three provinces has changed hands many times, between Cambodia and Siam (the ancient and not so ancient name of Thailand). The name of the province and town is very indicative of the struggles and battles that took place in the area. Siem Reap means Siam defeated, in Khmer.

There is still some Thai influence noticeable in Siem Reap, from the Thai products that dominate the big market on the eastern side of town, to the features of some local faces that appear to be a blend of Khmer and Thai. Eastern Thailand is much the same, but with many of the people looking more Khmer than Thai. The history and culture of these two countries is very interwoven, indeed.

And like the other provinces of the region, Siem Reap Province suffered long and hard through the years of struggle with the Khmer Rouge. On my first visit to Siem Reap, I was having an early breakfast at a sidewalk stand along Highway 6, thinking happy tourist thoughts, when a convoy of trucks carrying soldiers and tree-branch camouflaged big guns slowly rolled by en route to a battle front. The soldiers smiled and waved when they saw me, but I remember most of the smiles were nervous ones. Quite happily for the Khmers, those years

Banteay Srei Temple

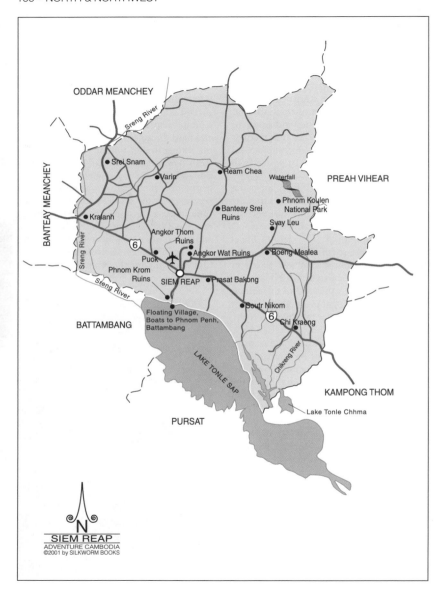

are over and Siem Reap is a safe, prosperous and friendly place.

WHAT'S UP

Angkor

See the next chapter.

Phnom Krom Hilltop Temple, Tonle Sap & Floating Fishing Village

Together these make a nice, half-day trip.

Phnom Krom Hilltop Temple. This is the big hill that you see near the landing if you head to Siem Reap by bullet boat. The hilltop area provides magnificent panoramic views of the Great Lake Tonle Sap, the surrounding countryside and Siem Reap town. The commanding view of the lake was used for a more practical, albeit more deadly, purpose in the fairly recent past as evidenced by a big gun mounted on the side of the hill and pointing toward the landing part of the Great Lake.

A modern-era active temple shares the hilltop with the temple ruins of Phnom Krom. There are seven crumbling towers among the ruins in two lines, with four towers east and three towers a bit higher up nearby and west. The 11th-century ruins are definitely in need of a facelift and it looks like they may get one at some point as a sign in front states that a project is underway. Unfortunately, the same sign has made the same announcement, with no results apparent, since a year ago when I last visited the site.

To get here, just follow Sivutha Street south out of Siem Reap. The road follows the river for much of the way and the road is in good shape for most of the short journey. You will arrive at the base of the hill after just fifteen minutes and there is an archway and stairway that you take up about halfway, which leads to the spot near the

big gun. From there you follow a small road to the temple area. You can actually ride all the way up by going past the stairway, beyond the house and tree area, where you will see a long out-building off on the right side. Follow the small road that runs alongside of the building and stay on this winding road to the temple area. There are drink and food stands at the base of the stairway to re-hydrate after the trip.

The Great Lake Tonle Sap & Floating Fishing Village. Continuing about ten minutes beyond the hilltop temple, on the same road that you took from Siem Reap, are a land-based fishing village and the bullet boat-landing site. Just hope for a good wind when you come as the combination of dead fish and raw sewage from the village can be a bit overwhelming. Just pass by this area to get to the water.

There are small motorboats for rent and a few locals that speak English will probably greet you when you approach the water. They will take you out for a tour of the floating fishing village area nearby (most structures are actually built on stilts), charging you US$5–6 for a one-hour tour. The village has its own "street" grid system and seems to have just about everything that a village should have. It's an interesting and scenic journey, with plenty of photo-ops on hand.

West Boray (Reservoir) & West Mebon Ruins & a Modern Temple

This is a great recreational spot with a couple of interesting sights thrown in to boot. It's not far from town and gives you the chance to see a bit of the countryside as you head out there.

West Boray. The West Boray is an Angkor era reservoir that was built during the reign of King Udayadityavarman II around the mid 11th century. It was a huge project and covers about 16 square km. The ruins of West Mebon sit on an island on the eastern end of the reservoir. As you approach the big body of water, you will be greeted by guys that want to know if you would like to boat out to the island, see the ruins and take in a swim while you are there. It's US$3 a head for the trip out and back, which includes their waiting time for you at the island.

Another boat trip that you might want to try is a slow trip around the entire perimeter of the lake, stopping off on the island as you pass by. They charge US$20, no matter how many people you fit into the boat. It makes a nice sunset cruise and you can pick up snacks and drinks from the vendors near the boats.

There is also a swimming and picnic area near the boat landing and it makes for a nice afternoon sitting on a shaded bamboo

Banteay Srei Temple

stand and having a drink or snack along with a swim. They also rent inner tubes for a float and *kramas* (Khmer scarves) if you don't have a swimsuit. The bamboo stand and inner tube costs 1,000 riel apiece and the *krama* is 500 riel to rent.

Wat Suai Ahniat. As you approach the reservoir from the road leading in, go to the right if you want to see a modern-day temple that sits on the far southeast bank of West Boray. It's a very scenic and quiet little spot and the temple is gorgeous, as the front of the temple faces to the west and gleams in the late afternoon sun. There is a huge wall mural on the outside with scenes that must portray hell, with all its nastiness thrown in for good measure. The ride along the south side of the reservoir to get here makes the trip worthwhile as well.

To get to West Boray, head west (actually northwest) out of Siem Reap on Highway 6 about 8 km. You pass the airport on the way. When you see a big Anchor Beer billboard and a small bridge crossing a canal, turn right (before the bridge and canal). Follow this canal road to the end where the canal meets the reservoir. You pass some nice rural scenery along the way—another bonus of the trip.

Phnom Koulen (or Koolen) National Park

Phnom Koulen sits on a southerly extension of the Dangrek Mountains. The hill, combined with those around it, served as quarry sites that supplied the massive amount of stone that was used in the construction of Angkor. It's a scenic and quiet area, with tree-covered hills stretching out into the distance and no development in sight. There is also a nice waterfall and picnic area near the top and some temple ruins just upstream from the top of the waterfall. There are also some ancient inscriptions (and some not so ancient) that were carved in the rock that the stream flows over, near the top of the waterfall. There are a couple of tiers to the waterfall area, with the main fall being about 11 meters high.

Unfortunately, someone has been given exclusive rights to privately develop this national resource and the guy apparently really wants to raise some revenue. Just where this revenue is going to go is another matter. He has set an entrance fee charge of US$20 (you read that correctly!) for a foreigner to ride up (your transportation) and see the waterfall, which is about 10 km from the ticket checkpoint area. If you wish to walk instead of ride a motorcycle, they drop the fee to US$10.

I have seen every mapped waterfall in the country and I can tell you that most are free to see (and many are much more spectacular), with the exception of Bokor Mountain National Park, where they charge a reasonable US$2 user fee. The guys that run the entry booth here are trained to say that the high fee is due to the road that was constructed. This site should not be visited until someone has a very big change of heart. Going there will only support the scam and may have some spillover effects in other parts of the country. Cambodians are also very upset as they are charged 5,000 riel per person and 20,000 riel for a car to go see one of *their* natural resources. The vast majority can't afford to go.

You take the road that goes past Banteay Srei for most of the way, so you could combine the two trips, which I did. To get to the two sites, just head out from the main ticket gate and turn right at the first T. Follow this road around the perimeter and when you see a small abandoned guard shack on your left, turn right—don't continue straight. You will then come upon two separate forks in the road and you go to the left at the first one and to the right at the

second one. Follow this same road (don't turn off it) about 9 km to the Phnom Koulen ticket booth, and it's about a twenty-five minute journey from there to the waterfalls. Not turning at the second fork would have landed you at Banteay Srei Temple, which is about 4 km from the fork.

Civil War Museum

The guy that runs this small and very new place was forced to join the Khmer Rouge as a boy and trained to make and lay landmines, something they were all too good at. The Vietnamese-installed government rescued him in 1985—so his story goes—and thereafter he helped the government in clearing areas where landmines have been laid.

His name is Akira and he is a friendly guy that speaks English and Japanese and is happy to visit with people that come by. He has a lot of the weaponry on hand that has been used over these past few decades, during Cambodia's civil war and the long struggle against the Khmer Rouge that followed. It's worth a look. Admission is free, but donations are appreciated. To get there, go past the Hotel Grande de Angkor (on the road to the Angkor ticket checkpoint) about 1 km to a small sign on the right for the Civil War Museum. Turn right, and follow this road to a four-way intersection and turn left. There is a sign for the place here. Go about 1 km and you will see it on the right.

Crocodile Farm

There is a crocodile farm on the south end of Siem Reap and they have about 300 crocodiles of various sizes and dispositions. They charge US$1 admission for foreigners and 1,000 riel for Cambodians. You can buy stuffed crocs on the premises. Just head south on Sivutha Street, cross the bridge and it's down another ½ km from there.

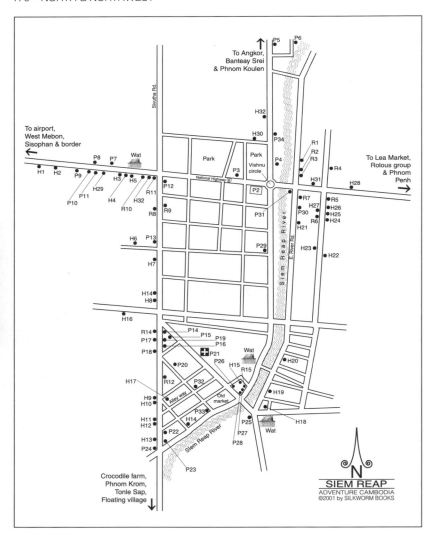

To Angkor,
Banteay Srei
& Phnom Koulen

To airport,
West Mebon,
Sisophan & border

To Lea Market,
Rolous group
& Phnom
Penh

Sivutha Rd.

Wat

Park

Park
Vishnu
circle

National Highway (6)

Siem Reap River

E. River Rd.

Wat

Old
market

Alley way

Wat

Siem Reap River

Crocodile farm,
Phnom Krom,
Tonle Sap,
Floating village

N

SIEM REAP
ADVENTURE CAMBODIA
©2001 by SILKWORM BOOKS

SIEM REAP

H=Hotels
H1   Nokor Kok Thlok Hotel
H2   Banteay Srey Hotel
H3   Aspara Angkor Guesthouse
H4   Ta Som Guesthouse
H5   Takeo Guesthouse
H6   Green Garden Guesthouse
H7   Eclipse Guesthouse
H8   005 Guesthouse
H9   Royal Hotel
H10   Vimean Thmei International House
H11   Reaksmey Chanreas Guesthouse
H12   Phkay Proeuk Hotel
H13   Bakong Guesthouse
H14   Ta Prohm Hotel
H15   Stung Siem Reap Hotel
H16   Naga Guesthouse
H18   Friendship Home
H19   Bayon Hotel
H20   Bopha Angkor Hotel
H21   Diamond Hotel
H22   Angkor Thom Hotel
H23   Siem Reap Guesthouse
H24   Mahogony Guesthouse
H25   Pailin Guesthouse
H26   Mom's Guesthouse
H27   Garden Guesthouse
H28   Sila Guesthouse
H29   Heritage Inn Cambodia Hotel
H30   Hotel Grande de Angkor
H31   Angkor Saphir Hotel
H32   Sofitel Hotel

R=Restaurants
R1   Seven-Up Restaurant
R2   Arun Restaurant
R3   Ranory Restaurant
R4   Sawadee Restaurant
R5   Bayon Restaurant
R6   Chivit Thai Restaurant
R7   Sampheap Restaurant
R8   Swiss Center Restaurant
R9   Koulen Restaurant
R10   Apsara Restaurant
R11   Chouk Rath Restaurant
R12   Monorom Restaurant
R14   Angkor Green Restaurant
R15   Continental Restaurant
See hotel list for:
- Banteay Srei Hotel & Restaurant
- Sila Guesthouse & Restaurant
- Bopha Angkor Hotel & Restaurant
- Hotel Grande de Angkor Restaurante

P=Places
P1   Vishnu circle
P2   King's villa
P3   Buddhist shrine & park
P4   Apsara dance performance
P5   Red Cross Millenium Park
P6   Civil War Museum
P7   Koulen Nightclub
P8   President Airlines
P9   Bangkok Airways
P10   Diethelm Travel
P11   Royal Air Cambodge
P12   Tourist Police
P13   Senge Plaza
P14   Sky Palace Nightclub
P15   Stationery store
P16   Pacific Commercial Bank
P17   Cambodian Commercial Bank
P18   Nasa Fuji film
P19   ABC Computer Rental
P20   Camintel Telecommunications
P21   Siem Reap Provincial Hospital
P22   Bakheng Nightclub
P23   Bullet boat tickets
P24   Night market
P25   Martini's Nightclub, Siem Reap
P26   Lotus Temple Market, Restaurant,
      Guesthouse & Only One Bar
P27   Liquid Pub & Restaurant
P28   Khemara Motorcycle Rental & Souvenirs
P29   Post & Telecommunications
P30   Fruit stands
P31   English newspapers
P32   Monument Books
P33   Ivy Bar & Guesthouse
P34   River Books

NORTH & NORTHWEST

River & Park Area

The Siem Reap River parkways and the big park in front of the Hotel Grande de Angkor are nice for a jog, stroll and people watching, especially in the early evening hours when the locals are out in numbers. The river area is pleasant and the park is nicely landscaped. There are plenty of drink and snack vendors around. The king's Siem Reap residence is just across from the park.

Khmer Classical Dancing

The Hotel Grande de Angkor has a restaurant and stage near the river that features nightly performances of the apsara-style dancers. The show and buffet dinner is US$22.

MARKETS

Bargain and be prepared to walk away when buying almost anything in Siem Reap. Vendors have seen many foreign tourists—at both markets—and they can get a bit ridiculous with the prices they ask compared to the rest of the country.

Old Market. This is the one near the river. There is a small, typically Khmer all-purpose market all under one roof, and loads of souvenir shops on the river side of the market.

Siem Reap Market. This is the big market in town and it's just a couple of kilometers east of the bridge going over the river, on Highway 6.

Fruit Market & Night Markets. There are a number of fruit stands that are set up along the East River Road, near Highway 6. This area also serves as a night market, with food and drink vendors setting up nearby.

There is also a small night market that sets up at the south end of Sivutha Street.

Senge Plaza & Workshop. This is where you, the tourist, are wanted. Loads of souvenirs and a small workshop.

Banteay Srei Stationery & Book Store. Not much in the way of books here, but they do have plenty of stationery supplies. The east side of the Old Market also has stationery and book shops.

GETTING AROUND

Moto-Taxi

Most trips in the Siem Reap town area will cost about 1,000 riel. To head out to check out Angkor and the outlying sights that were described in the Siem Reap What's Up section, expect to pay US$5–7 per day, plus fuel for sights far afield, such as Banteay Srei and Phnom Koulen.

Car & Motorcycle & Bicycle Rental

To rent a car, the best place to check on prices is the hotels and guesthouses, with the average rate being US$25 per day.

Khemara Souvenir Shop. This friendly place is located just across from the southeast corner of the Old Market. They rent Honda Dreams for US$7 per day, and have a few mountain bikes for rent (US$2 per day) as well as the souvenir shop that's in the name. Passport deposit required, and they supply a lock.

Angkor Thom Hotel. They rent Honda Dreams for US$6 per day and can arrange car rentals as well.

Service with smile

Big Dirt Bikes. A new outfit next to the Nasa Fuji Film shop rents dirt bikes for about $9 per day. Negotiate the price.

Motorcycle Doctor

Highway 6 is in real tough shape, no matter which direction you are coming from and you may just need a big bike mechanic when you get here. This guy can work on big bikes and also get that chain adjusted and lubed for you. His shop is about 50 meters before you get to the big market heading east on Highway 6, and on the opposite side of the road (off the map). His place is in the middle of a couple of parts shops and there is a small Total fuel sign out front.

COMMUNICATIONS & INFORMATION

Post Office

The local Post and Telecommunications Office is located on the West River Road.

Overseas Calls

Camintel. This small office features the cheapest overseas phone rates in Siem Reap and is located just off of the southern end of Sivutha Street. It's US$3.65/min. to telephone the USA.

Internet & E-mail

At a rate that figures out to be about US$55 per hour for using the Internet, it's wise to hold off on it. There are a few outfits where you can send/receive e-mail for US$1 a pop.

Abc Computer & E-mail. Located on Sivutha Street.

Computer Shop. Located two doors down from Banteay Srei Stationery & Book Store.

Lotus Temple. Just across from the Old Market.

Newspapers

There is a small newspaper stand on the corner of Highway 6 and East River Road that carries the *Cambodia Daily* and *Phnom Penh Post*, as does the Hotel Grande de Angkor.

Book Store

Monument Books. There is a branch in Siem Reap. See map.

Photo Shop

Nasa Fuji Film Shop. This place is by far the most reasonably priced place to buy fresh film and have film developed. The quality here is outstanding as well. They charge US$4 per roll of thirty-six, with a discount given for multiple rolls—US$3.50 if you have a bunch of them. They are near the south end of Sivutha Street.

CURRENCY EXCHANGE

The two markets are the best place to change money and they readily change dollars, Cambodian riel and Thai baht. Just look for the glass cases with wads of money stuffed inside. It's best to check a few of them as rates can vary.

There are now several banks in Siem Reap. Here are the most popular ones.

Cambodian Commercial Bank on Sivutha Street handles Visa cash advances for a 2% fee—there is no maximum limit.

Pacific Commercial Bank. Just across the street from the other bank.

MEDICAL FACILITIES

Siem Reap Provincial Hospital is the place to go if you have a problem that requires immediate attention. It's located just off of Sivutha Street. Fly to Phnom Penh, or better yet, go to Bangkok on

NORTH & NORTHWEST

Bangkok Airways if the problem is severe and you can still make the trip.

RESTAURANTS

There is no shortage of restaurants in Siem Reap—they have been opening steadily over the past couple of years.

Arun Restaurant. Very good Khmer, Thai and Vietnamese food is served in a nice outdoor courtyard. Reasonable prices.

Seven-Up Restaurant. Cheap Khmer fare in a very simple place.

Ranory Restaurant & Guesthouse. The place looks nice enough, but unfortunately the owner is a bit stuffy. Although most international travelers rely on English to communicate abroad, he will not add English to the French menu, on principle, I guess. Maybe English-language business is not wanted. Located just south of Arun Restaurant.

Chivit Thai Restaurant. Located in an old-style Khmer house, the place has a nice atmosphere and serves very good food at friendly prices. The service is quite good as well.

Bayon Restaurant. This popular place serves pretty good food in a red brick firehouse-like courtyard.

Sawadee Restaurant. Nice looking Thai-style place, but the food just isn't very tasty.

Sampheap Restaurant. Good Khmer and Chinese food in a friendly atmosphere on the river road.

Chouk Rath Restaurant. This corner establishment servers up very good Khmer and French food dishes in pleasant outdoor and indoor areas.

Swiss Center. It's an interesting looking and friendly place, but as of late they have cut back on some of the services that were offered. The food prices are quite high.

Angkor Green Restaurant. Very good Khmer and Western food served in a pleasant atmosphere.

Monorom Restaurant. Good, simple and cheap Khmer food is the order of the day at this friendly place. Nice second-floor terrace.

Continental Restaurant. Friendly laid-back restaurant on the river serving Western food. Small pool table on premises.

Bopha Angkor Restaurant. This is the riverside terrace restaurant that has tables next to the waterwheel on the Siem Reap River. It's a very pleasant setting and the food is good as well.

Apsara Restaurant. Basic Khmer fare at low prices.

Banteay Srei Hotel & Restaurant. Located west on Highway 6. This is a popular spot because of their good Chinese and Khmer food and good service.

Koulen Restaurant. This is a big, new, really decked out place that looks like it's ready to serve the masses that may one day arrive on convoys of tour buses. Don't let that turn you off though. The food is excellent and the service is outstanding—the help really hustles and are all very friendly. They have weekly Khmer dance performances and have fully outfitted private karaoke rooms available. Nice outdoor and indoor eating areas.

Grande Hotel de Angkor. Lavish and pricey buffets are offered at this colonial style landmark hotel.

NIGHT SCENE

Although Siem Reap is not overflowing with nightlife options, you will find that you can have a pretty good time out on the town, provided you aren't already exhausted from hiking about the temples and ruins. There are a few decent watering holes, a good handful of Khmer nightclubs and even a

Martini look alike. And those Cambodian brothels seem to be popping up all over town recently.

Koulen Nightclub. This Khmer club is doing quite well these days and has all of the normal features that one comes to expect—a live band, plenty of beer and taxi girls and lights that are turned out more than turned on.

Sky Palace Nightclub. This is an old standby in Siem Reap and still very popular with both locals and visitors from Phnom Penh. They seem to attract some pretty good singers from Phnom Penh and they get the weird looking circle-dancers looking pretty dizzy out on the floor.

Bakheng Hotel Nightclub. This nightclub changed formats recently, from a later night techno-dance place to another Khmer-style nightclub. The result? They are packed, same as the others. The other two Khmer nightclubs have a more festive atmosphere, though.

Martini's of Siem Reap. Hoping to catch the wave of popularity that Martini's of Phnom Penh has enjoyed over the years, this one is trying the same format. They have an outdoor sitting and drinking area where movies are shown and a dance place inside playing mostly techno-stuff. It hasn't really caught on much and the Khmer in-crowd and ladies still hang out at the Khmer nightclubs.

Liquid Pub & Restaurant. New on the scene, this is a restaurant with Western and Malaysian food and has a disco that starts up at 9 pm—the current hot spot, Western style, in Siem Reap.

Watering Holes

Elephant Bar—Hotel Grande de Angkor. This one is on the fancy-pants end of the scale, but they do have a pool table, sports channels on the tube and a whole bunch of friendly people working there.

Zanzybar. This is a low-key place that has a pool table and stays open late.

Only One Bar. Located across the street from the eastern side of the Old Market, this is a quiet place that hopefully gets more customers than the name might imply.

Ivy Bar. Friendly place, pool table, food and rooms for rent. See the map of Siem Reap.

ACCOMMODATIONS

There is no shortage of places to stay in Siem Reap, from the very cheap to the very expensive, and more places are going up all the time, in every price category. With so many places on offer, there is usually no need to make a reservation, unless you want a certain place or it's a holiday.

You will come across touts at the airport, boat landing and share taxi stand, offering "free" rides if you go look at their places, but of course there is no free lunch and you can sometimes get into a hassle with these guys if you don't stay at their place. It's generally better to have your own choices in mind or hire your own moto-taxi guy to show you a few. Just tell him to stay outside while you go in to check the place out, otherwise they hit the manager up for a commission, which you ultimately pay for. Also note that prices really fluctuate from low to high season. Always ask for a discount—you may just get one.

Guesthouses

Most of the guesthouses listed have cold water and shared bathrooms. All of the establishments can arrange for motorcycle taxis and tours of Angkor.

Naga Guesthouse. Double rooms are US$2 and singles are from US$1–4 in high season. The friendly staff speaks English and the rooms are clean and have fans.

Mom's Guesthouse. ☎ (012) 630-170 or (063) 964-037, fax (855)63 380-025.

Everyone knows where Mom's is and it's not a bad place to start when looking for a room in this catagory.

Rooms are US$5 with shared bath and US$10 with private bath. Business has been so good that Mom, yes there really is a Mom, has built a large new building in the rear where you may have a room with hot water and private bath for US$20. Rooms in the new building with TV and a/c are US$30. Mom serves breakfast for US$1.50. All of the rooms are clean.

Mahogany Guesthouse. Close to Mom's. Singles are US$4. Double beds US$5. Twin beds US$6. Attached bath is US$8 and includes two big beds. Very popular but the rooms are getting a little run down and are not as clean as they should be. The Mahogany can arrange a trip back to Phnom Penh by military helicopter for US$45 per person.

Garden Guesthouse. In the same area, Singles US$5, and doubles US$6. We found the staff to be strangely unfriendly. Some rooms have a private bath for US$8. This place is popular with French travelers, some of whom are not so friendly themselves so possibly they feel at home there.

Friendship Home. 0497 Collegue Angkor Road. ☎ (012) 866-465, 858-007. Singles US$5. Doubles US$6. Shared bathrooms. Clean rooms. Friendly and informative owner. Restaurant on premises, as are a number of crocodiles—this guy loves them and has a small pool in back with a few of the beasts lurking about.

Sila Guesthouse and Restaurant. National Road 6. ☎ (012) 878-189. Singles US$5. Doubles US$8. Some of the US$8 rooms have a terrace and private bath. There is a reasonable and excellent Thai and Chinese restaurant on the premises. All in all, a good value.

Eclipse Guesthouse. Sivatha Modol Street. ☎ (011) 630-195. Singles US$2–4.

Doubles US$6. A/c rooms with TV US$10. Reasonably priced restaurant on premise serving Khmer and Western food. This place has caught on with the backpacker scene and the staff is friendly.

Star Guesthouse. Rooms are US$5 with fan and shared bathroom. Clean and well kept. You can make overseas phone calls here for US$1 per minute.

005 Guesthouse. Singles US$8. Doubles US$10 with fan. A/c rooms US$15. All rooms with private bath and hot water. Community refrigerator. Clean rooms with large beds. A fair value.

Green Garden Guesthouse. ☎ (015) 631-364. Fan singles US$8; doubles US$10. A/c singles US$15; doubles US$20. A very pleasant garden setting at the end of a quiet street.

Pailin Guesthouse. All rooms US$4 with fan and mosquito net. Shared bathroom. Free morning tea or coffee.

Siem Reap Guesthouse. Singles US$6. Doubles US$8. A/c rooms US$15.

Angkor Thom Hotel. Nice rooms and a very friendly, helpful staff. Rooms priced from US$5–20. Includes TV, fridge—it's a good value. They also have motorcycles and cars (with driver) for rent.

Takeo Guesthouse. Singles US$2. Doubles US$4. Shared bathroom. Room with private bath is US$5. Not as clean as it could be.

Ta Som Guesthouse. Singles US$2. Doubles US$4. All with private baths. By far the best low-end value in town. Great location on Highway 6, just west of Sivutha.

Aspara Angkor Guesthouse. Singles US$3. Doubles US$5. Private bath US$7. Pretty good value here as well.

Upscale Guesthouses & Moderately Priced Hotels

All have hot water and a/c unless noted.

Phkay Proeuk Hotel. ☎ (015) 851-271 Singles US$5. Doubles US$10. A/c doubles for US$15. Clean and large rooms.

Heritage Inn Cambodia Hotel. Fan rooms US$7, a/c rooms US$15. All rooms have private bath, TV fridge. Clean and quite place. Beer garden on premises.

Bakong Guesthouse. ☎ (063) 380-126, fax (063) 963-419, e-mail <bakong@rep. forum.org.kh> Singles US$15. Doubles US$20. TV, fridge. This is a new and clean hotel with a restaurant and mini-mart.

Neak Angkor Villa. ☎ (063) 964-903. Fan rooms US$10. A/c rooms US$15. TV, fridge. Clean but not large rooms. A good value.

Royal Hotel. ☎ (015) 639-114. All rooms are US$15 and include TV, fridge. Plain rooms but a good value.

Stung Siem Reap Hotel. ☎ (015) 630-158, 634-058, fax (063) 380-139. Singles US$15. Doubles US$18. TV, fridge. A nice old colonial-style building with a friendly staff. It's on a peaceful corner with an old temple across the street.

Vimean Thmei International House. ☎ (063) 963-494. Fan rooms US$10, a/c rooms US$20. A/c rooms have large beds. All the rooms are very clean. The friendly staff speaks English and can give you advice on travel arrangements.

Golden Apsara Hotel. 220 Thvay Dangkum Mondol 1. **☎** (063) 963-533, fax (063) 963-533, e-mail <awt@pec.rep. forum.org.kh> Fan rooms US$10. A/c US$10. Doubles with a/c US$20. Pleasant staff. Nice open air spaces for socializing. Does not have TV and the place is a bit old but it is often busy.

Reaksmey Chanreas Guesthouse. 330 Sivatha Street. **☎** (063) 963-557 or (012) 849-967. Fan rooms US$10. A/c rooms US$15. A/c with bathtub and h/w, US$20. Simply furnished rooms.

A Notch Up

All have hot water and a/c unless noted.

Golden Angkor Hotel. 063 Mondell 11. **☎** (015) 838-041 or (012) 867-769, fax (063) 964-039. Singles US$15. Doubles US$20. TV, fridge, large beds. Clean large rooms are an excellent value. Car rentals, boat tickets and travel advice on premises.

Ankorian Villa. ☎ (015) 630-096. Fax (015) 630-096. Singles US$20. Doubles US$25. Reservations recommended, with only five rooms. TV, mini-bar. Free pickup from airport. Friendly place.

Freedom Hotel. ☎ (063) 963-473. Fax (063) 964-274. On Highway 6, heading east and before the market. Fan rooms with bathroom US$15. Rooms with TV and fridge US$30. Nice enough place, but they are well known for outrageously priced "surprise" laundry bills.

Bopha Angkor Hotel. Singles US$20. Doubles US$30. Local TV only. An old hotel with fairly plain rooms. Ask for the 10% discount. They do have a nice riverside café that is worth a sit-down.

Another Notch Up

These hotels are likely to add on a 10% government tax and a 10% service tax. All have a/c, hot water and TV.

Banteay Srey Hotel. On National Highway 6, on the way into town from the airport. **☎** (015) 913-839 or (063) 380-128, fax (063) 380-128. Singles US$35. Doubles US$40. Includes fridge. Very clean and well maintained. The hotel is one of the better values in this price range. Good restaurant downstairs.

Diamond Hotel. ☎ (015) 633-130, fax (063) 380-038. It's a fairly nice bungalow setting near the river. Singles US$35. Doubles US$45. Breakfast is included in the price. There is also a Thai restaurant on the premises. The owner says that you get a 10% discount when you show this book.

Bayon Hotel. ☎ (015) 631-769, fax (063) 963-993. Low season US$35, high season US$45, and prices include breakfast. A bit old, but clean, with a river view.

Angkor Saphir Hotel. 82 Highway 6. ☎/fax (063) 963-566. Singles US$30. Doubles US$60. The rooms are a bit small but attractive. A comfortable hotel with all the amenities including slot machines. Remember, they call these one-armed bandits for a reason.

Hotel Nokor Kok Thlok. Airport Road. ☎ (015) 537-301 or (063) 380-201, fax. (063) 380 022, e-mail. <nokorkokthiok@ worldmail. com.kh>

Singles US$85. Doubles US$95. Suites US$120. Includes breakfast. Pool on grounds. Visitors may use the pool for US$5. A beautiful new hotel but a bit overpriced. Owned by the person that charges outrageous entrance fees at Phnom Kulen National Park (check the What's Up section). Voice some displeasure if you stop by and maybe the practice will stop.

Ta Prohm Hotel. Next to the Siem Reap River. ☎ (063) 380-117, 963-528, fax (063) 380 116. Singles US$60. Doubles US$70. Suites US$120. Has all the amenities including in-room mini-bar and a restaurant terrace overlooking the river. One of the nicer hotels in this price range.

The Top Notch

Hotel Grande de Angkor. ☎ (063) 963-538, fax (023) 368-118. Singles US$226. Doubles US$271. Pool-view rooms, US$247–291. Suites from US$460 and US$510, up to US$1900 for a two-bedroom villa. Twenty-four-hour butler and room service. By far the nicest spot in town and they have the prices to prove it. Built in 1920 and completely renovated by the Raffles Group, along with its sister hotel, the Le Royal of Phnom Penh, in 1997. The place features 60,000 square meters of

beautiful manicured gardens in front of the hotel. There is a swimming pool, health spa and sauna. They also have bars and superior restaurants with prices to match. Those who expect the very best will not be disappointed. Travel agency on premises. Worth a visit just to see the wood-paneled walls, architecture and an open-shaft cage elevator, completely restored, in the lobby area. The bakery and deli here is pretty good and the Elephant Bar downstairs has a pool table and a very friendly staff.

COMING & GOING

There are a number of options available, so we'll start with the quickest and easiest. Check our map for locations of everything listed below, including airline offices.

Air

Royal Air Cambodge makes the flight to and from Phnom Penh at least two times each day for US$55 one way.

President Airlines makes the flight just once a week, on Sunday, for US$55 one way.

Bangkok Airways has three flights daily between Bangkok and Siem Reap.

The airport departure tax is friendlier in Siem Reap, costing US$4 when you fly to Phnom Penh (compared to US$10 when you fly from Phnom Penh). The tax is US$8 when you fly to Bangkok from Siem Reap (compared to US$20 when you fly from Phnom Penh).

Mahogany Guesthouse has a connection in the Cambodian military and the guy there can get you on one of the daily helicopter transport flights between Phnom Penh and Siem Reap for US$45 one way. I believe the two sides share in the rewards.

*Waterfall at Phnom Koulen,
Siem Reap*

*Keeping the faith on a hot day,
at Siem Reap*

Say Ahh! Crocodile Farm, Siem Reap ▲

◀ *Admiring the Great Lake, Battambang to Siem Reap*

Floating medical clinic, Battambang to Siem Reap
▼

Bullet Boat

The bullet boat to Phnom Penh departs at 7 am, down at the Great Lake (actually a small inlet to the lake). The cost is US$25.

For Battambang, if you don't like the idea of the taking the nasty road between the two towns, try the boat. The cost is US$15 and the trip is scenic.

Tickets for both trips are available at the ticket shack located on the far southern end of Sivutha Street, across from the night market.

Share Taxi

The roads are pretty nasty going either direction on Highway 6, but never fear, the government says they will repair and pave it in its entirety—don't hold your breath waiting on that one. Best to buy two seats for a little extra comfort along the way.

Siem Reap to Phnom Penh	15,000 riel
Siem Reap to Kampong Thom	10,000 riel
Siem Reap to Sisophan	15,000 riel
Sisophan to Poipet	5,000 riel

Motorcycle Touring Info

Phnom Penh to Siem Reap

Coming from Phnom Penh, the stretch to Kampong Thom and just beyond is quite easy and fortunately, the remaining stretch to Siem Reap has seen re-grading work so while it isn't great, it's nowhere near as bad as it used to be.

Phnom Penh to Kampong Thom is 162 km and Kampong Thom to Siem Reap is 145 km.

Siem Reap to Sisophan

Ditto the above, only another step or two worse. Some of the bomb craters on this stretch are so deep that during the rainy season the Cambodia Olympic Committee could construct a high-dive platform next to one of them and use it for diving practice. This stretch can get real mucky during the rainy season, but yes, it can be done. It's about 100 km between the two towns. Regrading is slowly being done.

Security is not a problem on either stretch these days.

NORTH & NORTHWEST

THE TEMPLES OF ANGKOR

Between the 9th and 14th centuries, Angkor was the capital of the mighty Khmer Empire, the largest and most powerful empire in Southeast Asia during that period. King Jayavarman II united this civilization in the year 802 and was worshiped as a god-king. Each successive ruler built his own temple in the area, along with canals to irrigate the rice fields which fed Angkor's nearly one million people. The temples and other parts of the ancient city and civilization that remain today testify to the magnificence of the Khmer kingdom. Architecturally and artistically, the grandeur of the structures that remain today is unrivaled by any other ancient monuments around the world.

Angkor came to the attention of the Western world in 1860 when French explorer Henri Mouhot brought back word of the fabulous temples in the jungle. Others soon arrived and one member of an 1874 trip took seventy statues back to France. The world's looting of Angkor had begun and continues to this day.

The Angkor district covers over 350 square km and has over seventy sites. The term Angkor Wat is often used to identify the entire area. The chief sites are Angkor Wat, the city of Angkor Thom (which includes the Bayon) and Ta Prohm. These are a few of the main tourist attractions, and many days can be spent viewing the other temples and structures.

Angkor Wat was built between 1113 and 1150 and was the funerary temple for King Suryavarman II. It symbolizes heaven on earth. It is estimated to contain the same cubic volume of stone blocks as Egypt's pyramid of Cheops and is the largest religious temple of any kind in the world and the best preserved in Angkor. As you enter the area, you walk down a long causeway that crosses a 190-meter-wide moat, which forms a large rectangle 1.5 by 1.3 km. There are five main towers in the main building. The tallest is 65 meters high. The ters e wall enclosing the central temple is covered with bas-relief carvings, which extend an incredible 800 m. The wall is about 3 meters high and depicts armies, battles, wars, heaven, hell and everyday life. The central temple complex is three stories high.

As one looks at the magnificent scenes of battles with various enemies on the walls of Angkor Wat, it's more than ironic to think that after so many centuries there have still been far too many battle scenes in Cambodia to witness, especially over the past thirty years. Only, in this recent period, it has mainly been the Cambodians fighting other Cambodians.

Angkor Thom means the great city. Jayavarman VII, who ruled from 1181 to 1201, built it. The massive 8-meter-high walls extend for 12 km and enclose 15.5 square km containing dozens of temples, including the Bayon temple. Built in 1200, it sits in the very middle of the complex. It has fifty-four lotus-shaped towers with four huge faces. The wall carvings depict early Cambodian history.

Ta Prohm, a Buddhist temple, is one of the areas that the archaeologists have purposely left much as it was first found, overgrown by jungle. You have probably seen the photographs of huge trees growing out of the monuments, their huge roots prying apart the stones. Many of the pas-

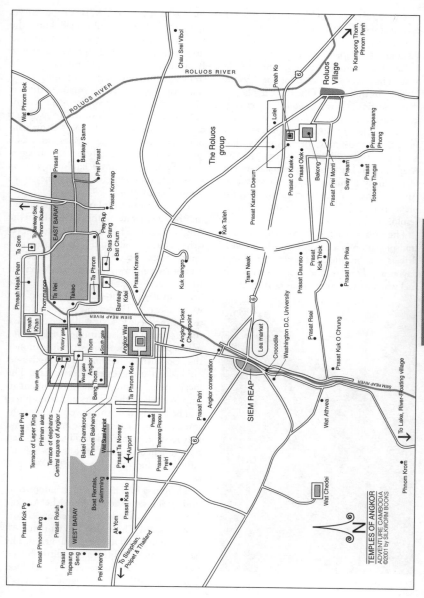

TEMPLES OF ANGKOR
ADVENTURE CAMBODIA
©2001 by SILKWORM BOOKS

sageways are clogged with jumbled piles of carved stone blocks and overgrowth.

Visiting the Temples

Passes are required to visit the temple areas. The prices are US$20 for one day and US$40 for three days. One certainly hopes that a portion of the fees collected actually goes towards upkeep and preservation efforts, not just the lining of pockets. As of June 2000, Sokimex, the company that manages and collects revenues for the Angkor sites, began a controversial system of requiring a photo from each visitor to Angkor. This is a security measure and also prevents tickets from being used and then resold.

The area is so spread out that all-day transportation is a must. Motorbikes with drivers can be hired for about US$5–7 a day at any hotel or guesthouse—more for fuel when you go to the areas farther afield,

Gate of Angkor Thom

such as Banteay Srei. Most of the drivers speak some English and usually know the best way to travel in the area. Cars and drivers are about US$25 a day. The trip to Banteay Seri will cost just a bit more. Seven o'clock in the morning is not too early to start your day. There are small children at most of the sites who will want to accompany you on your tour of the ruins. They are all kind of cute and expect a small tip but are not much in the way of guides. The government has recently banned beggars from the grounds, mostly landmine victims who eke out a living begging money from sympathetic tourists.

This year the Cambodian government may ban all private motor vehicles from the Angkor area. This includes moto-taxi drivers, automobiles and YOU (if you have rented a motorcycle so you can cruise the grounds at your own leisurely pace). In their wisdom and greed the powers that be are using open-air, eight-seat electric carts in a weird take on a Disneyland theme. Operators of the electric taxis will have exclusive rights to ferry tourists around Angkor. This will deprive the locals of what little money they can earn by renting out themselves as guides and using their bikes or cars. The locals are appealing to the government to stop. We believe the scenery and atmosphere will be damaged by this government-sponsored commercial enterprise and hope that they reconsider this action. The Cambodian government claims this to be an eco-friendly enterprise and indeed it may be. We shall see.

There is a line of four nice indoor/outdoor restaurants across from the Angkor Wat entrance causeway. The first ones in the line are good Khmer food restaurants. All speak English and have English menus. The last one along the line is a good little French restaurant, which features good French food and a selection of French wine. There is a menu in English. All of the restaurants are open throughout the day, starting with breakfast.

You will need a good two to three days to see most of the sites, but remember, you are not on a mission, you're on holiday. I've seen far too many harried-looking tourists being carted all over on the regular tour circuit, looking overdosed on temple ruins. It's best to slow down and take in the aura of just a few less sites. Along those same lines, the best time of day to get photos at Angkor Wat may not be late afternoon and early evening, as conventional wisdom and tour guides will tell you. There are just too many tourists (and beggars) cluttering the area, making it very difficult to get nice shots of Angkor Wat without people in them. If you go during midday, the hottest time of the day, there are no beggars lining the cause-way, as they are all hiding from the sun. And the tour operators have the masses where they have decided the most strategic spots for that time of the day are. I was there at 1 pm and with the place almost to myself, I got nice, uncluttered photo shots. There are plenty of cool and quiet places to avoid the sun once you are inside, so it's not a prob-lem. Here's a tip: break away from conven-tional wisdom that tells you only to go to certain sites only at certain times and you will be treated to much smaller crowds, fewer beggars, and better photo opportuni-ties.

Tour agencies in Bangkok and Phnom Penh have many of these package tours avail-able, but I am sure that you will be sorry to be rushed about this enchanting region. I urge you to have as much time available as you can spare when you visit here. You can see plenty of sites in two to three days and just may want to stay in Siem Reap for an extra day or two to enjoy the quiet local life during the day. At night parts of the town really come alive.

We will list here an itinerary for two-day visits and then for a longer visit, but go ahead and take a peek at the map and be creative if you like.

Angkor Wat is surrounded by a rectan-gular moat almost 200 meters wide and running 1.5 km on one side by over 1 km on the other side. The causeway or bridge approaching the wat from the west is almost 11 meters wide and 248 meters long. At the start of the causeway you will find yourself on a raised sandstone terrace in the shape of a cross guarded by giant stone lions. As you walk toward the wat, you will pass, on both sides, an entry tower, small buildings once used as libraries, basins filled with water and then nearer the wat, the Terrace of Honor, just in front of the entryway where the steps are guarded by stone lions on pedestals.

The central temple complex consists of three stories with elevated towers, chambers, covered galleries and courtyards all on dif-ferent levels. The height of the central tower is 212 meters, and five smaller towers sur-round it. Angkor Wat was built to repre-sent the universe. The central tower repre-sents the mythical Mount Meru that is at the center of the universe and it represents heaven, as it is at the center of the wat. The five towers represent smaller mountains. The lower courtyards are the continents and the moat is the ocean.

As you walk toward the wat imagine that it is truly the center of the universe and you are approaching the beginning of time. Imagine the people who lived and wor-shiped here ages ago and the grandeur of the moment and of the centuries.

West, the area of the entranceway, is the direction of death, and it is believed that Angkor Wat may have been built as a tomb or burial place. The wat is breathtaking when you first see it, but more incredible

NORTH & NORTHWEST

sights await you as you move closer. The outer wall of the central temple is called the **Gallery of Bas-Relief**. It stands 2 meters high and 800 meters long and is covered with thousands of detailed carvings depicting battle scenes and stories from history. Parts of the mural are polished and almost look like metal or brass. They were possibly once covered with lacquer or preservative. The polished appearance also comes from being touched by thousands of hands over the centuries. From the entranceway, walk to your right and proceed counterclockwise to follow the stories. On your left will be the murals and on your right will be a row of sixty columns. As you walk around the entire gallery, poke your head outside on occasion and you will be treated to some nice carvings on the outside wall and views of other parts of the complex.

From where you are standing at the start in the West Gallery, there is a battle scene. Attacking infantry are on the lowest level and above them, officers riding elephants. This furious war is from the Hindu Mahabarata epic and depicts the Kauravas advancing from your left and the Pabdavas attacking from your right.

Continue around the corner to the south wall to view a triumphant march of Suryavarman II's army. Riding on an elephant, he is wearing a royal headdress and holding a battle-axe. There are many scenes of fierce hand-to-hand combat. Trees and animals appear in the background. On an upper level you will see the king again holding a meeting on a mountain along with women, servants, musicians and jesters. As you move along the mural you will see a group of Thai mercenary soldiers in pleated skirts. The Khmer troops alongside of them are carrying spears and tridents and wear helmets and have square breastplates and shields decorated with monsters and animals.

As you continue along the eastern wall, the gallery depicts the rewards of heaven and the punishments of hell. The eighteen-armed figure is Yama, judge of the dead, seated on a bull. Below him are his assistants, Dharma and Sitagupta. The lower part is the road to hell with people being dragged by devils, and hell itself with people being tortured, cut in two and having their bones broken and nails driven into their heads. Above, heaven is a beautiful place with desirable apsara dancing girls entertaining the good folk in fabulous mansions.

The East Gallery contains the **Churning Oceans of Milk,** the most famous section of the reliefs, derived from an Indian story. The ocean is churned by gods and demons to recover the elixir of life, lost treasures, and the source of immortality. The scene is divided into three parts. The lower tier contains real and mythical animals. The center tier shows on the left, ninety-two devils or demons and on the right, eighty-eight gods churning up the sea to extract the elixir of immortality. The body of a snake acts as a huge wand to churn the sea. In the upper tier female spirits dance and sing.

Opposite the Ocean of Milk is a large doorway called **The Elephant Gate**, used by the king for mounting elephants directly from the gallery.

Continuing along the East Gallery you will see a mural of Vishnu fighting the Demon King. The demons are mounted on rhinoceroses and there is a furious battle. Vishnu rides a Garuda and comes to a burning wall which halts his advance on the city. The Garuda extinguishes the fire with water from the river Ganges. This scene continues around to the North Gallery.

The North Gallery depicts twenty-one mounted gods of the Brahmanic pantheon fighting various demons. Kubera, god of riches, is holding a bow and arrow and riding a supernatural being. Skanda, god of war, has many arms and heads and is mounted on a peacock. Yama, god of death and justice, holds a sword and shield and stands in a chariot pulled by oxen. Brahma the creator rides a sacred goose.

The West Gallery shows the **Battle of Lanka** (Sri Lanka) in the famous Ramayana story. Rama enlists monkey warriors to fight on his side against Ravana who is riding a chariot pulled by monsters and has an army of giants. In a fierce struggle, Rama defeats Ravana and rescues his wife Sita.

After finishing your tour of the bas-reliefs you can visit the inside of the complex which is on three levels and has many passageways and chambers to explore. Over 1,500 apsaras, or celestial dancers, line the interior walls of the second gallery. Only kings and high priests were allowed on the third or upper section (and now you, as well), which is the base of the five central towers. You can climb a steep stairway to the top of the central sanctuary which is equal to the height of the Cathedral of Notre Dame in Paris. From here you will have a nice view of the grounds of Angkor Wat and beyond. Check out the cloud formations that seem to have shapes that blend in very well with Angkor Wat at certain times of the year.

Continue northward for about 3 km to the walled city of Angkor Thom. **Angkor Thom** is square-shaped, each side almost 3 km long. A stone wall 8 meters high around the sides contains an area of over 100 ha. Angkor Thom was the last capital of the Khmer empire and contained the royal palace and the homes of the priests, palace officials, and the military. Entering the area from the south gate you will see the **Bayon**, which was built a hundred years after Angkor Wat. The Bayon's first two levels are square; the third level has a circular central sanctuary. The Bayon has a total of fifty-four towers with over two hundred huge stone heads smiling down at you. The Bayon is decorated inside and out with over 11,000 figures depicting everyday life, ancient stories, and battles. You can walk inside the Bayon through numerous galleries and passageways. Some say the stone faces have a menacing grin, but I find it to be warm and reassuring. I guess it depends on the mood and outlook of the beholder.

Just north of the Bayon is the **Baphupon Temple** built in 1060 and dedicated to Shiva. The temple is in disrepair but is being rebuilt. On the inside of the west wall you can see a large reclining Buddha built into the structure. Its legs and feet are missing.

Continue your trip northward to the **Royal Palace** where the kings and servants lived. It has lost much of its grandeur through the years. Next is **Phimeanaks Temple** in the middle of the royal enclosure. There is not much left of either site except two pools in which local children cool off.

On the eastern side of the royal enclosure is the **Terrace of Elephants**, running almost 300 meters. It has three platforms. The main part is covered with almost life-size carved elephants and hunting scenes.

Just to the north and next to it, is the **Terrace of the Leper King**. The statue of the Leper King is a copy, the original being in the Phnom Penh National Museum. There are many ideas as to who the leper king was. Some believe the figure represents Kubera, the god of wealth, who allegedly was a leper. Others believe that it may be the god of death or the god of judgment and that this was the location of the royal crematorium. The bas-reliefs on the terrace

NORTH & NORTHWEST

are of mythical beings, serpents, women and animals.

Ta Prohm is reached along the Victory road and was built in 1186 by King Jayavarman VII. At one time the monastery and temple held over 72 thousand people. It has been left mostly untouched by archaeologists. It's an other-worldly experience to visit the site and imagine that you are discovering it for the first time, overgrown with jungle and huge tree roots enmeshed with the stone. There is a surreal and serene air about the place, especially if you go early before other visitors arrive. The complex includes 260 statues, 39 towers and over 500 groups of buildings. The center of the temple can be reached by a series of towers connected by passageways, some of which are tumbled down or overgrown with vegetation, which adds to the mysteriousness of the place.

After you have seen the above main temples there are many other wonderful sights in Angkor.

Start with the temple of **Preah Khan** which is just north of Angkor Thom. Built by Jayavarman VII, it has a wall reaching almost 3 km, enclosing more than 50 ha. The temple itself is enclosed by an inner wall 700 by 800 meters. The eastern entryway has a large terrace on two levels leading to an entry tower with five doors. The temple is two stories high and has a courtyard in the shape of a cross with four smaller courtyards on each side. Notice the large columns and carvings of apsaras, female and male gods, Garudas and Buddha. Preah Khan means sacred sword and the temple may have held such an item which figures in Thai and Khmer history. The temple grounds can be entered from the western side where there is a visitors' reception center and some small food and drink stands.

Just east of Preah Khan is the temple of **Preah Neak Pean**. It's a delightful, peaceful site with one large square pool and four small pools on each side. The central pool is a replica of Lake Anavatapta in the Himalayas at the top of the universe. There is a small island in the middle of the central pool. The bodies of two serpents encircle the base of the island. The central sanctuary is on the island. There is a statue of a horse swimming toward the sanctuary with figures clinging to its sides. There are also four small buildings on the side of each of the smaller ponds. Unfortunately, looters have been busy here.

Ta Som, east of Neak Pean, is a small quiet temple which has not been fully restored. Ta Som has a single tower on one level and the outside walls have entry towers on the east and west with carved faces. You can walk through the first entry tower over a walkway bordered by serpents and large Garudas. The central room is also in the shape of a cross and has small libraries and courtyards on the sides.

The Eastern Baray and **The Eastern Mebon** are just to the south of Ta Som. The Eastern Baray was a huge reservoir built by Yasovarman in the 1st century. It is 2 by 7 km long and was once fed by the Siem Reap River. It was a source of water for the irrigation of rice fields in the area.

The Mebon is a temple with five towers on a three-tiered base in the middle of this former lake. The towers represent the mythical peaks of Mount Meru. The temple is surrounded by three outer walls, and a series of galleries and rooms run in between the walls. The inner courtyards have eight small brick towers with decorated lintels. The five towers are located in the central sanctuary. There are many finely carved lintels and false doors. Look for the mounted figure of Indera, a three-headed elephant, horsemen, and mythical beasts.

Pre Rup lies 500 meters south of the south end of the East Baray. Pre Rup is built in the same style as the Mebon, with five towers. *Pre rup* means to turn the body and refers to the cremation of a body and then drawing the outline in the ashes, first in one direction and then in the other direction. It's believed that cremations took place here. The temple has two walls with four entry towers each. Inside there are many galleries, courtyards and libraries. The central area has a stairway on each of the four sides. Pedestals near the stairways are decorated with seated lions. The five central towers on the top open to the east. They all have three false doors decorated with figures and vegetation. The tower in the southwest corner has murals of Sarasvati, wife of Brahma with four faces and arms. There is also a god with four arms and heads in the shape of a wild boar. In the corners of the towers are flying apsaras. The big elevated platforms of Pre Rup are nice spots for panoramic views.

Another interesting trip would be to the **Roluos group of monuments**, Lolei, Prea Ko and Bakong. Roluos was the capital of Indrayarman I (877 to 889) and is one of the earliest temples. Located about 12 km southeast of Siem Reap on National Route 6, the three temples extend over an area of about 3 km.

Lolei is a Hindu temple built in the memory of the king's father. It was originally on an island in the middle of a lake. It has interesting carvings and inscriptions. Lolei is built on two tiers with stone-enclosed walls. The central area has four brick towers. It is believed that at one time there were six towers. The corners on the east are decorated with guards holding tridents and on the west are female gods holding fly whisks. Notice the fine workmanship on the door lintels. You will see Indra on an elephant, water monsters with the body of a crocodile and the trunk of an elephant, and Visnu mounted on a Garuda holding a branch of serpents.

Prah Ko is a funerary temple just to the south, originally built for the king's parents. Four walls, the first two badly deteriorated, surround the temple. The central area contains six brick towers in two rows. These were once covered with stucco and each tower contained an image of a Hindu god with whom the deceased was united. You will notice sandstone pillars and columns carved with large rings almost as if they were turned on a huge wood lathe. The central area has three stairways, the landings decorated with human figures. Sandstone lions guard the temples. The stone lintels are nicely carved with Garudas and men riding serpents and horses.

Bakong is to the south of Prah Ko. It was the center of the ancient town of Hariharalaya. It was built as a model of Mount Meru and served as the city's main temple. Two walls enclose it. The outer one is 700 by 900 meters. There were at one time twenty-two towers inside the enclosure. The temple is built of five tiers, with libraries, galleries, storehouses and a crematorium. The central area has five tiers with a stairway on each of the four sides. Carved stone elephants stand at the corners of the lower tiers.

There is an active Buddhist monastery at the northeast corner of the complex that may be visited. To get there, head east on Highway 6 past the big market. About ten minutes down the road you will see a small sign in English announcing the temple and pointing the way.

Banteay Srei

The trip to Banteay Srei can be done in half a day. It is 27 km northeast of the Bayon and the local transportation guys like to try to charge you an additional US$20 for the round trip, but don't go for it. A few extra dollars beyond the daily rate (US$5–7) is plenty. If you have the time, the trip is well worth it. Banteay Srei is one of the best restored and most beautiful temples in the entire area. It was off limits for some years due to Khmer Rouge and bandit activity but is quite safe now. The temple has been looted over the past years, as the statues and carvings are quite valuable due to the intricate work and the use of the unusual pink sandstone. Banteay Srei means citadel of the women and is often referred to as a jewel box or a precious gem because of the intricate artwork and its small size. It is a good deal smaller than the other famous temples. Do not be disappointed by the small size on your arrival, as great treasures await you.

There is an entry tower and a long causeway leading to the inner wall and moat. There are six smaller buildings and libraries on the grounds. The central group of buildings has three towers. Each tower has four recessed stories. All the walls are highly decorated. The towers are guarded by mythical beings with human bodies and animal heads. Unfortunately, the guards have been unsuccessful in stopping the looters, so see the remaining beauty while you can.

Figures of male and female gods in the corners are finely carved and detailed. The guardians in the corners of the central tower are fine examples of Khmer sculpture. Their hair is up in a rounded chignon and they hold lotus buds in one hand and a spear in the other. Yes, the ride up to Banteay Srei is well worth the trip. It also gives one a chance to see a bit of the Cambodian countryside along the way. To get there from the main ticket checkpoint, follow the road, go right at the T, and keep following this perimeter road to where, at just under 10 km, there is an empty guard shack on the left. Turn to the right here instead of going straight. You will eventually come upon another fork in the road where you go to the left. At the next fork you come upon, go to the left again and follow this to the temple. There are a couple of workshop tourist stops along the way for those interested. There are also a couple of small Khmer food restaurants next to Banteay Srei Temple that have very good food at real reasonable prices. There are no longer any police or military checkpoints heading out to Banteay Srei—very good news, as visitors don't have their extra 'fees' tacked onto trip costs any more. The trip from the main ticket checkpoint and entrance to Banteay Srei is 29.5 km. Security is not a problem. Stay on the well-worn pathways around the outside of the temple and in the countryside along the way, as there could possibly still be landmines lurking about.

A Proposed Route

Head out to Banteay Srei in the morning. On your way back to the main part of the Angkor complex, when you reach that vacant guard shack, instead of turning left to go back to where you came from, turn right. This will allow you to see some of the less-visited areas of the Angkor complex where there are not so many tourists. You can follow this road all the way back to the main part of the Angkor complex.

Angkor Wat

Apsara carvings on Angkor Wat

Terrace of the Leper King, Angkor

ANGKOR

Battle scene, bas relief at Angkor

◀ The Bayon at Angkor

The friendly faces of Angkor ▶

◀ Apsara of Angkor

▶

Ancient & modern culture meets at Angkor

ODDAR MEANCHEY PROVINCE
ANLONG VENG, O'SMACH & SAMRAONG

Oddar Meanchey Province is a recent creation that was carved out of the northernmost part of Siem Reap Province and it straddles the Thai border on its northern edge, which is also covered by the Dangrek Mountains (or escarpment, as they are sometimes called). It is a very remote province that has also been a notorious place because this is where the nastiest of the nasty Khmer Rouge made their last stand. The diabolical Pol Pot and his seemingly blood-thirsty henchmen, Nuon Chea, Ta Mok, Son Sen and Khieu Samphan holed up here for the last years of the Khmer Rouge's existence (another of the henchmen, Ieng Sary, already worked out a surrender and defection deal with the government in 1996).

Pol Pot died mysteriously here, after a supposed power struggle within the power elite (he had Son Sen and his family murdered) and after a controversial show trial. The debate focused on whether it was real or just a sham staged for the outside world to try to legitimize remaining Khmer Rouge figures. The trial took place in the power center of the Khmer Rouge, the village of Anlong Veng. Pol Pot died mysteriously after he was sentenced to house arrest and the international community began real efforts (for the first time ever) to capture and put this butcher on trial. His henchmen had more than enough reason to want him dead at that point because a Pol Pot on trial, as the ringleader most responsible for the genocide wrought upon his fellow countrymen, would probably have tried to shift portions of the blame (rightfully so in the case of these guys) to the rest of the power elite.

The Khmer Rouge kept fragmenting after that and Nuon Chea and Khieu Samphan worked out a surrender-amnesty deal with the Cambodian government and Ta Mok (also called "The Butcher") was subsequently captured and is still awaiting a trial in Phnom Penh. As of March 2000, the United Nations and the Cambodian government finally seem set to come up with an agreement on putting the top surviving members of the Khmer Rouge regime on trial in Cambodia, with assistance from and in a partnership with the international community. Stay tuned though, as this has been a real political football with seemingly more concern for one-upsmanship and personal gain than justice for the dead and surviving victims of Khmer Rouge brutality.

Another spot in Oddar Meanchey that came under the international spotlight is a hill in the Dangrek Mountains, butting up directly next to the Thai border, near the tiny village of O'Smach. This is where the top military officers loyal to Prince Norodom Ranaridh fled after the factional fighting or coup ended the co-premiership government of the prince and Hun Sen in July of 1997. It was on this hill that they mustered the small remains of their loyal forces and fought off onslaught after onslaught launched by Hun Sen's government in an attempt to annihilate all potential challengers to his solidified rule.

The tenaciousness of the hill's defenders (who heavily mined the hill's approaches on the Cambodia side and had a few big guns to shoot down on approaching hostile troops), along with heavy pressure on Hun Sen from an international community wanting to see reconciliation in Cambodia, finally brought about an agreement to rein-

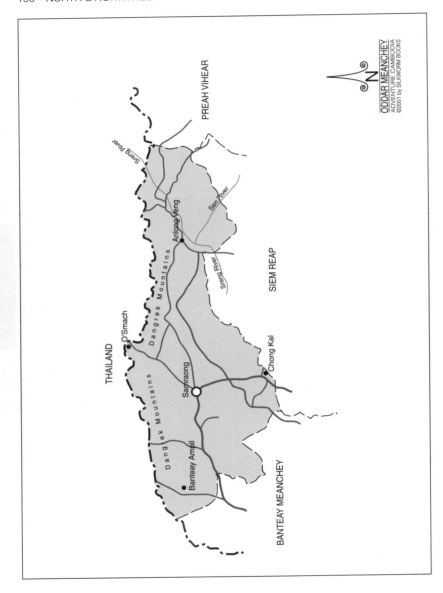

ODDAR MEANCHEY
ADVENTURE CAMBODIA
©2001 by SILKWORM BOOKS

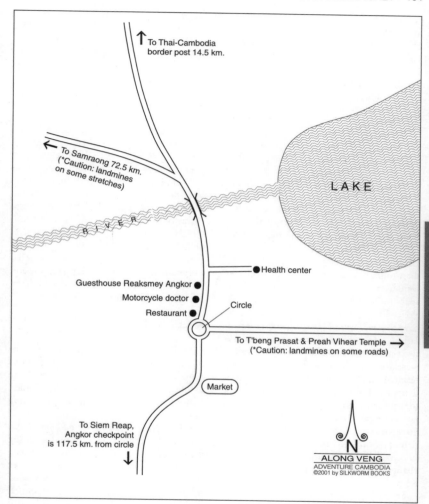

To Thai-Cambodia
border post 14.5 km.

To Samraong 72.5 km.
(*Caution: landmines
on some stretches)

LAKE

RIVER

● Health center

Guesthouse Reaksmey Angkor ●
Motorcycle doctor ●
Restaurant ●

Circle

To T'beng Prasat & Preah Vihear Temple →
(*Caution: landmines on some roads)

Market

To Siem Reap,
Angkor checkpoint
is 117.5 km. from circle

N
ALONG VENG
ADVENTURE CAMBODIA
©2001 by SILKWORM BOOKS

NORTH & NORTHWEST

tegrate the adversaries into the government and hold previously scheduled elections, about eight months after the fighting erupted in Phnom Penh.

In a recent development in O'Smach that hardly seems surprising or strange in Cambodia, a huge casino has been under construction on the cleared and bulldozed hill (where the fighting took place) in an attempt to lure gamble-happy Thais across the border from Surin Province. Of course it may end up being a welcome addition to the dirt-poor area if some local residents are among those finding employment at the casino or its supporting businesses. As of March 2000, however, the only thing that the new development has brought to many of the residents that moved back to the area after the fighting ceased is injustice. In a combined effort, casino developers and the Cambodian military drove residents off land they were living on so that they could claim the space for the new casino as theirs. They told the residents that they could have nearby land that was free of landmines as compensation. Sadly, the residents soon found out the claims that the land was free of mines were not true and some deaths and injuries resulted. Angry at the injustice, affected residents set off for Phnom Penh in an attempt to negotiate compensation for lost land and get some safe land for their families. The government supposedly agreed to the demands but when residents returned to O'Smach, they found that nothing had changed and few received any compensation.

Following another journey to Phnom Penh by the uncompensated residents in early 2000, another promise was made by the government to set things straight. In early March of the same year, making another trip to the area, I found that the practice of land grabbing by the military had become worse instead of changing for the

better. Along most of the route from the provincial seat of Samraong to the Thai border and O'Smach, there are reports that families have been pushed off their land alongside of the road—now freshly cleared of landmines—and back into the forest area that has not yet been cleared. The military then divided up the ill-gotten land and gave it to soldiers for their own families use. It's a sad situation that needs to be dealt with much more fairly, and human rights groups are trying to help deal with the problem, but they are probably fighting a losing battle.

There is not really a whole lot of sites to offer those making the journey to Oddar Meanchey Province, other than satisfying a curiosity to see these former areas of conflict. We are including some information on O'Smach, Anlong Veng and Samraong for curiosity seekers and also for those that simply are interested in seeing a remote and little-visited part of Cambodia and the Dangkrek Mountains.

ANLONG VENG

Completely sealed off from most of Cambodia by the hard-line Khmer Rouge, until quite recently a journey to Anlong Veng would have got you killed in short order, either by a landmine or the unwelcoming hosts.

It hasn't taken Anlong Veng long to catch up with the rest of rural Cambodia. Going from square one, the village now boasts a free-wheeling market (very un-Khmer Rouge), restaurants and a guesthouse among other things. And the place seems much friendlier than the town of Pailin did following the surrender of the Khmer Rouge based there in 1996.

What's Up

There is talk of making the homes of Pol Pot and Ta Mok some kind of tourist attractions—it's a thought that goes well beyond weird. Enough said.

Thai Border

The border is 14.5 km from the circle in Anlong Veng. There is no market there and it is not a legal crossing. There are plenty of tanks and tank shells to look at along the way and also a strange site in the form of a boulder that had Khmer Rouge soldiers carved out of the sides of it—they have all been decapitated since government forces took control of Anlong Veng. Anyway, it's an interesting little ride to a low-lying part of the Dangkrek Mountains. The road is in fairly good shape with the exception of the climb up a rocky hillside near the border.

Market

Check the map for the small market area that lines the road as you are coming into the town from Siem Reap. Locals are quite happy with their little market—a recent addition to Anlong Veng. The Khmer Rouge leadership thought that markets were far too Western oriented, so getting any little necessity for one's family involved a clandestine journey to the Thai border, then worrying about getting caught upon returning with the ultra-modern goods, such as cooking utensils and other basic needs!

Restaurants & Night Scene

A few noodle and drink stands surround the market area. The two simple but fairly decent restaurants are just north of the circle. See the map—one is at the guesthouse.

Karaoke has already come to Anlong Veng and if the village follows suit with the other former Khmer Rouge areas of Pailin and Poipet, it shouldn't be long before there are brothels and girls climbing out of the woodwork.

Guesthouse Reaksmey Angkor. There actually is a place to spend the night here, if

you are so inclined. There are twelve fairly clean, simple rooms with a fan, mosquito net and share bath for 10,000 riel (100 Thai baht).

Getting Around

See the map for a motorcycle doctor.

Medical Facilities

See the map.

Coming & Going

See warning box below. The best place to get to Anlong Veng from these days is Siem Reap. As of March 2000 most of the road has been either rebuilt or built up new. Only about 25 km of the route remained unfinished and at the rate that they were going it should be getting close to finished by the time you read this. Share taxi pickup trucks ply the four-hour route for 10,000 riel. Infrequent share taxi trucks also go between Anlong Veng and Samraong for 10,000 riel.

Motorcycle Touring Info

See warning box below and map for motorcycle doctor.

Siem Reap to Anlong Veng

Starting at the Angkor ticket checkpoint (you only need a ticket if you want to see Banteay Srei Temple on the way), take a right at the first T in the road in front of the moat. Go right at the monument marker (same as going to Banteay Srei), then at 9.2 km from the Angkor checkpoint go right instead of straight. At just over 11 km go left. At 26.5 km from the checkpoint there is a fork in the road—stay left. At 28.6 km you go by Banteay Srei Temple on the left.

Follow the main body of road the rest of the way, which has received a major upgrade in quality, as mentioned earlier. Keep an eye out for wildlife on this stretch, even deer.

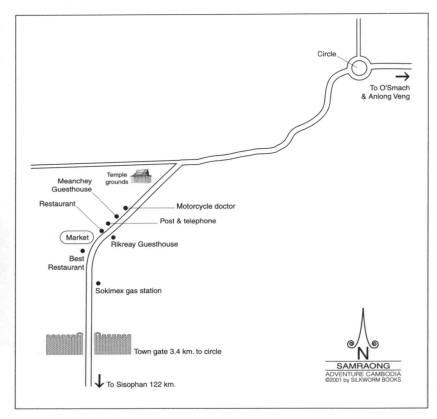

Meanchey
Guesthouse

Temple
grounds

Restaurant

Motorcycle doctor

Post & telephone

Market

Rikreay Guesthouse

Best
Restaurant

Sokimex gas station

Town gate 3.4 km. to circle

To Sisophan 122 km.

Circle

To O'Smach
& Anlong Veng

N
SAMRAONG
ADVENTURE CAMBODIA
©2001 by SILKWORM BOOKS

Anlong Veng to Samraong

This stretch is 72.5 km and the journey takes 3 to 3 ½ hours. The little-used road (a stretch of the word) varies between sand and dirt and can be confusing as there are a number of intersecting roads and nobody is around in this desolate area to ask directions, even if you did speak some Khmer. If you really want to go it anyway, follow the road at the intersecting spots that seem to have more, or at least some, tire tracks. Do yourself a favor and don't go during the rainy season. See warning box below.

SAMRAONG & O'SMACH

Samraong is one of those towns that went back and forth between government and Khmer Rouge control. It was used as a staging point for the struggle against the Khmer Rouge in Anlong Veng and more recently for the battle against the government resistance forces in O'Smach following the factional fighting in July of 1997.

The provincial seat of Oddar Meanchey Province is a quiet place, without much going on day or night. Having said that, the people are quite friendly and hopeful that some good luck will come to this poor and often troubled area.

What's Up

O'Smach

As mentioned a couple of times above, this is the recent battleground-turned-casino area. The casino is still under construction, but should be up and running as you read this. It's an impressive looking structure and the immediate area is also slated to include a hotel and bungalows, shophouses and a market here on the Cambodian side of the border. There is a shell of an armored personnel carrier sitting nearby, possibly to serve as a reminder of the recent fun and games on the hill. The nearby village of O'Smach is nothing to write home about, but you can get food, fuel and drinks there. The trip up from Samraong will also give you the chance to see landmine-clearing operations in progress. There are also plenty of photo-ops for those interested in getting pictures of tanks and big guns as you near the O'Smach area.

Thai Border Market at Kap Choeng

There is a fairly busy market that sets up on the Thai side of the border on Saturday, Sunday and Monday that sells various Thai and Khmer products and produce. It's worth a look if you go as far as the casino and the Cambodian and Thai immigration authorities seem willing to let you go have a look, but double check with the Cambodia authorities to be sure that they will let you re-enter on your current visa.

As for their part, the Thai authorities say that they can issue you a visa here if you want to go up to Surin town, 69 km north of the border. This info is as of March 2000.

To get to O'Smach, head out of Samraong from the circle at the northeast end of town (see map). Follow this road 35.5 km to the big dirt circle with the tree in the middle of it. Going to the right takes you into the village of O'Smach, going straight 2.5 km takes you to the casino and border. Although the road isn't very decent (a lot of weaving around bomb craters) it moves along and the 38-km trip to the border from Samraong takes just over one hour. On market days at Kap Choeng, there are share taxis running up to the border from Samraong for 5,000 riel. See warning box below.

Samraong Town Temple

The corner temple on the main drag (see map) is worth a look if you are wondering what to do with half an hour.

Market & Currency Exchange in Samraong

The Samraong Market is a very small affair where you can change dollars, baht and riel, as well as stocking up on any needed items.

Restaurants & Night Scene

Best Restaurant. The best restaurant in town is only open for breakfast and lunch. It's run by a friendly English- and French-speaking Cambodian gentleman and his family. They can make up most Thai-Khmer dishes that you may want and also serve a good breakfast of eggs, French bread and coffee.

The restaurants in front of and just northeast of the market offer the pre-cooked dishes in pots that you choose from. Unless the pots are still hot, it's a good idea to have them heat your servings up again so that you don't get more than you bargained for—like getting sick.

Accommodations

Rikreay Guesthouse. This is a simple but clean place with a bed, mosquito net, fan (for part of the night) and share bath going for 10,000 riel.

Meanchey Guesthouse. This place is similar to the Rikreay, only the power stays on for twenty-four hours, which means your fan should stay on all night. A room with a share bath, net and fan is US$4 and a double room with a simple bathroom inside of it is $10—expensive for what it is but you are paying extra for the power. The US$4 room is the better deal.

Getting Around & Communications

The motorcycle doctor and the Post and Telecommunications Office are located on opposite sides of the Meanchey Guesthouse.

Coming & Going

See warning box below. Share taxis ply the 122-km rough and tumble, bomb crater-filled route between Samraong and Sisophan town (Banteay Meanchey Province) for 100 baht. It takes four to five hours.

The Samraong to Anlong Veng route is the same 100 baht for the four-hour share taxi trip.

Motorcycle Touring info

See warning box below.

Samraong to Anlong Veng

This stretch is 72.5 km and the journey takes 3 to 3 ½ hours. The little-used road (a stretch of the word) varies between sand and dirt and can be confusing as there are a number of intersecting roads and nobody is around in this desolate area to ask directions, even if you did speak some Khmer language. If you really want to go it anyway, follow the road at the intersecting spots that seem to have more, or at least some, tire tracks. Do yourself a favor and don't go during the rainy season. See the warning box below.

Samraong to Sisophan

As mentioned above, this is a rough and tumble road filled with bomb craters. There are, however, some long breaks in that action where the dirt and gravel road is semi-smooth, allowing you to go at a more decent speed.

Leaving from the town gate on the southwest edge of Samraong town, go 73.5 km to the traffic circle where you go right (going left gets you to Siem Reap).

There is a guesthouse just off of this circle, in the direction of Sisophan, in case you get stuck for some reason here. Simple rooms go for 120 baht and there is also a restaurant here.

At about 99 km from the town gate in Samraong (or 25.5 km from the circle that you turned right at) you come to another circle in a small town. Just keep going straight through this one and onto the final 23 km to Sisophan town.

WARNING

Many of the roads in Oddar Meanchey Province, like the road going from Anlong Veng to Samraong, Samraong to O'Smach, Samraong to Sisophan, as well as parts of the Siem Reap to Anlong Veng route, are still lined on the sides with landmines and many of the minefields are still unmarked. Some of these roads have stretches that have been detoured around and are not marked as to why the detour, but landmines are many times the reason. Stay only on roads currently in use or on a well-worn pathway. It is very important to keep alert where roads intersect or there is an alternative road. Only go on the roads that have tire tracks or footprints on them. The roads that have no tire tracks on them—bicycle, car or motorcycle—probably are still mined and that's why the locals are going around that stretch. When you stop to relieve yourself along the way, keep you feet on the road or a well- worn pathway while doing your deed. If in doubt, don't go on it.

One of hundreds of remaining minefields littering the countryside, Oddar Meanchey Province near Samraong

Clearing landmines and taking an ice cream break at O'Smach, Oddar Meanchey Province

Clearing landmines in Oddar Meanchey Province

ODDAR MEANCHEY

▲ *Instant road median, Anlong Veng*

Cutting wood the old fashioned way, ▲
Oddar Meanchey Province

*Statues decapitated by
government, soldiers upon
takeover of Oddar Meanchey
Province*

*The mobile all-purpose store
en-route to Anlong Veng*

SISOPHAN TOWN & BANTEAY MEANCHEY PROVINCE

The town of Sisophan in Banteay Meanchey Province is today a charming, quiet place that only gives hints to its turbulent past upon closer examination. Like Siem Reap and Battambang Provinces, control of the province has changed hands many times —between the Thais and the Khmers in the more distant past, and the Khmer Rouge and central Phnom Penh government in recent decades. With the final demise of the Khmer Rouge (locals, however, firmly believe the present national reconciliation is only a Khmer Rouge trick), the province and town are striving to rebuild their culture and economy. It's a very friendly place with the locals genuinely happy to see foreign faces and the stability that it implies. Normally just a passing-through spot on the way to the border, or between Battambang and Siem Reap, the area has a few sights that warrant a visit, such as the Banteay Chmar temple ruins, the only other Khmer temple ruins besides the Bayon (Angkor) and Preah Khan (Preah Vihear Province) that features the famous four-faced monuments.

WHAT'S UP

Mountain Temple

Just a few kilometers outside of Sisophan town and on the way to Poipet, lies a surprisingly beautiful temple complex hugging the side and on top of what the locals call a mountain (large hill best describes it). It's hard to miss with a flag perched on top and a winding stairway going upwards visible from the highway.

The ground area features a simple wood frame temple with an ornate Foot of Buddha shrine. There is a flurry of activity about as different temple construction projects are going on around all levels of the mountain temple that you will notice as you hike up the long and winding stairway to the top. Once you finish your labors and reach the top, you will be treated with some dynamite views of the surrounding countryside, rural villages and the Ponlia River as it snakes its way around Sisophan.

Back on the ground you will see a large burial site and not far from that towards the road, a small building with the top of a well raised a meter off the ground. A Cambodian man brings a sixty-kilogram rock to the well everyday and in front of bedazzled locals, drops it into the well. The rock sinks of course, only to mysteriously rise to the surface in two to three minutes. Nobody

Mountain temple at Sisophan

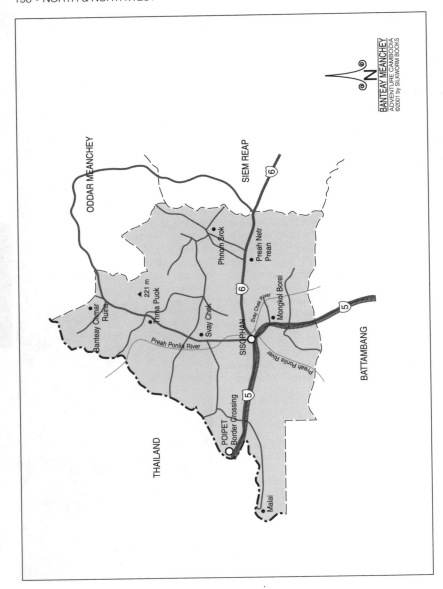

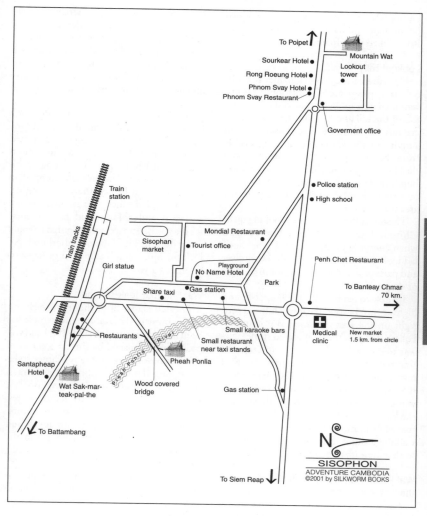

To Poipet

Mountain Wat

Sourkear Hotel

Lookout tower

Rong Roeung Hotel

Phnom Svay Hotel

Phnom Svay Restaurant

Goverment office

Police station

High school

Train station

Train tracks

Mondial Restaurant

Sisophan market

Tourist office

Penh Chet Restaurant

Girl statue

Playground

No Name Hotel

Park

To Banteay Chmar 70 km.

Share taxi

Gas station

Restaurants

Small karaoke bars

Medical clinic

New market 1.5 km. from circle

Small restaurant near taxi stands

Prean Ponlia River

Santapheap Hotel

Pheah Ponlia

Wat Sak-mar-teak-pal-the

Wood covered bridge

Gas station

To Battambang

N

SISOPHON

ADVENTURE CAMBODIA
©2001 by SILKWORM BOOKS

To Siem Reap

NORTH & NORTHWEST

knows why or how it happens. Buddhist phenomena perhaps, or is the "Mystery Rock" filled with foam?

Lookout Hill

Not sure of the Khmer name, but this one is appropriate. Government troops stationed here in the past used the tower on top of the hill as a lookout post to keep an eye out for Khmer Rouge movement and activity in the surrounding area. Visible from the main part of Sisophan town and the highway, it's a nice little hike to the tower building for another view of Sisophan and to reflect on the battles that raged in the area for so many years.

The tower itself is a strange-looking quasi Chinese-French structure. Use caution when climbing to the top level. The metal ladder is precariously attached to the tower and parts of the structure are not in the best of shape anymore.

It's easy to get to. Take the Poipet-bound highway just beyond the tower hill and turn right on the first dirt road you come to. Follow that past the dilapidated stone stairway to the back end of the hill and take the first right turn. Follow that past the small temple on the right, about 400 meters from the last right you made. You will see a path winding down from the top of the hill and the lookout tower. The locals say the hill is free of landmines and you will see them walking around different parts of the hill, so that appears to be the case.

Wat Preah Ponlia, Preah Ponlia River and the Covered Bridge

The wat is a simple temple with a sitting Buddha image and wall murals. The pretty river setting with the long covered bridge leading to it are the features that make this a pleasant short stop. The Preah Ponlia River is the one that you can see winding around Sisophan from the mountain temple (the map just shows a small stretch to orient you). There are small wooden boats close to the bridge that you can hire for an hour to take you around the nearby river area for around 3,000 riel. On hot days the river looks real inviting for a swim. We'll leave for you to decide on whether or not it's clean enough.

We stopped on the covered bridge for a bit of a break from the midday sun and my companion took out a yo-yo and started working the tricks that all nerds are famous for. An old Khmer guy came along on his horse-drawn wooden cart and stopped in his tracks when he saw the yo-yo routine. The old guy decided that he had to have that yo-yo and said he would trade his horse for the yo-yo. Apparently he figured it would make him the hit of the neighborhood. No luck for him though as a nerd never parts with his yo-yo.

Wat Sak-mar-teak-pal-the

Located across from the train tracks on the highway to Battambang, the temple has been under construction since 1989 and will probably be finished by the time you read this. It's beautiful with many Khmer styles incorporated into it—cobra head stairways, outside-wall mural carving, Angkor-style doorways, and multi-colored temple spires, to name a few. The outside sculpted mural is of the Buddha sleeping with angels and the masses watching and giving him the respectful *wai* (not the disrespectful high five).

This is one of the more beautiful modern temples that you will see in a small town.

And beyond:

Banteay Chmar Temple Ruins

These Angkor-era temple ruins beyond Sisophan town are the only ones in Cambodia, outside of the Bayon at Angkor

Thom and Preah Khan in Preah Vihear, that has the large four-faced monument that the Bayon is so famous for.

Unfortunately for Cambodia (and the rest of us, for that matter), antique looters have been on a rampage there and much of the beautiful stone artwork has been carted away to Thailand and Singapore markets for their illegal sale. Looting has been a big problem at most ancient Khmer ruins throughout the country, but Banteay Chmar is one of a few border area sites that has suffered even more because of its remote location close to the Thai border. It's been a cinch for Cambodian looters to do their dirty work by night and cart the bounty to the border where their Thai partners in crime are waiting to buy them.

It's a hard business to stop as the military and police that should be sworn to protect these cultural heritage sites are usually involved and profiting from it. The low salaries they receive make complicity hard to pass up. There was such rampant looting of Banteay Chmar that the looters caused major structural damage by cutting, digging and removing pieces near the base, which resulted in sections of the structures collapsing. It was a bit of karma when one group of looters had some of the structure collapse on them on one such occasion, killing seven. Apparently they were so entranced with the magnificent and priceless pieces they were cutting and digging out that they forgot to take care for the teetering structure they were creating. Possibly a little payback for the ancient gods?

The centuries of neglect and isolation have also allowed nature to take its toll on the ruins. It's tough getting around the temple areas with blocks strewn about the grounds and the jungle hard at work trying to reclaim all space. An army equipped with weed-wackers is needed to go in and clear some pathways. Good climbing or tennis shoes are in order as most areas do not have pathways and you will have to hop from block to block to get to some spots that you want to check out. Use caution and attention to the structure around you. Some doorways and walkways have blocks or a lintel above that look like they could come down with a hard sneeze. With all of the vegetation around one should also keep an eye out for snakes, although in our tour of the grounds we didn't spot any.

Having said all that, it's definitely worth the trip up here to have a look. There are still some sculpted walls depicting the everyday life of the people, the always ever-present in Khmer ruins mythical apsara dancers, other beautiful images as well as the four-faced, four-smile monument. It's an eerie feeling one gets standing there and looking at the structure with the vegetation

Banteay Chmar Temple

everywhere in the quietness of this remote location.

The entrance to the walled temple grounds is on the east side, the side that you arrived from. The area just outside the entryway has a picturesque freshwater pond where the few resident monks hang out. It's used by the locals for drinking water and throughout the day you can see locals coming and going, filling everything from pails to a water tank truck. There are signs in Khmer telling people not to bathe or wash their motorbikes in the two ponds in an effort to keep the water clean.

To get to Banteay Chmar from Sisophan (70 km), set your bearings by the map in this section and head out of town on the road that passes the New Market (the one that looks old).

About 7 km north of town you'll see a Red Cross processing and resettlement center that was used as a temporary housing and transit center for refugees that fled across the Thai border to escape the many conflicts in Cambodia. The UN, Red Cross and Cambodian government would work on resettling them around various provinces if the returning refugees felt unsafe going back to their home area.

About 54 kms north of Sisophan is a real gas station on your left if you forgot to get gas in Sisophan, but finding fuel is not a problem on this stretch of road—plenty of small Mom and Pop stands along the way. Just north of this area you will come to a four-way junction of dirt roads where there is gas, fruit and cold drinks for sale. If you back up about 20 meters on the west side of the road there's a good little Khmer restaurant that has omelets, bread and the usual Khmer rice dishes. The name is the Rihgree-yay Restaurant, which translated into English means fun. There is no sign so we told the owner to paint a smile on the road side of the wooden shack so potential for-

eign customers could spot it. Let us know if he did.

Back on the road to Banteay Chmar, just north of here, is a military compound on your right housing a couple of tanks and armored personnel carriers, which hopefully won't be used in this area again.

Continuing north you finally arrive at Banteay Chmar town. Just keep following the road as it curves to the left (past the market on your right side) and down about 200 meters on the left you will see a sign in Khmer accompanied by sign drawings of temple ruins. This is the entrance to the ruins. You will first come to a temple shrine building that has some sections standing but has been well stripped by looters. Continuing on you see the walls of Banteay Chmar Temple.

Gold Buddha Hill

On the highway to Battambang (10 km outside of Sisophan), there is a hard-to-miss hill next to the right side. A stairway from the roadside takes you all the way up to the huge sitting Buddha image at the top and—you guessed it—a nice view of the area.

MARKET

The Sisophan market in the central part of town is your best bet for anything you may need. It's the standard Cambodian "all under one roof" layout.

COMMUNICATIONS & INFORMATION

Overseas Calls

Located in front of the Phnom Svay Hotel, this is the place if you are looking for cheap phone rates to call overseas from Cambodia. It's 70 baht per minute to the USA, and if it's only Phnom Penh that you wish to reach it's 30 baht per/min.

CURRENCY EXCHANGE

Just look for the glass cases with money inside around and in the Sisophan market. Like the rest of the Northwest, Thai baht is preferred but the Cambodian riel is taken and they will give you a rate on the US dollar. If you want to change dollars, check a couple of different moneychangers, as they like to try pulling one over on you with the exchange rate. Forget about using traveler's checks in Sisophan.

MEDICAL FACILITIES

There is a decent medical clinic on the road (see map) to the New Market (it's really the old one). They can be of assistance for minor problems or worse. Phnom Penh trained doctors and nurses.

RESTAURANTS & NIGHT SCENE

Mondial Restaurant. This is the swank joint in town with good food and service, friendly staff and live Khmer music while you have your dinner (this is thankfully one place that keeps the volume down a bit). The staff is fair in their English.

Penh Chet Restaurant. A step down but it's a clean, basic place with good food and the usual friendly beer girls. There is also live music here in the evening. There isn't an English menu, but the beer girls will have a lot of fun trying to help you order.

See the map for the locations of the top two Khmer nightclubs in town.

The restaurant next to the Phnom Svay Hotel serves up the best food in Sisophan. It's a very simple place but the menu is varied and features many Western faves. Decent hamburgers, french fries, ice cream, among others are sure to satisfy your Cambodian road-weary appetite. The place draws a good crowd of foreign workers and locals alike.

There are restaurant stalls by the share taxi stand, along with loads of evening desert and fruit shake/drink stands all over town.

Sisophan has a rather rowdy (and seedy) brothel area built almost on the RR tracks near the train station. With the train tooting it's whistle and vibrating the shacks as it crawls by, it's surely Sisophan's version of the popular book, *Off the Rails in Phnom Penh.*

The ladies are out in full force in the late afternoon, beckoning you over, laughing and seemingly enjoying the festiveness of the area that time of the day. Drink and food stands dot the area, and with all the local males milling about it almost does seem like a carnival.

ACCOMMODATIONS

Rong Roeung Hotel. Fan rooms 200 baht, a/c rooms 300 baht. Western bath, sat. (satellite) TV, clean; and the owner speaks English.

Sourkear Hotel. Fan US$5, a/c US$10. The rooms have a large and small bed, Western bath and are clean.

No Name Hotel. The name was being changed when we stayed there—to what, they did not know. It's a nice place. The manager speaks English and the staff is very friendly. Western bath, sat. TV, wrap-around terrace overlooking a small park. Fan room 200 baht, a/c room 250 baht.

Santapheap Hotel. The name means peaceful and that it is. Located on the outskirts of town towards Battambang, the hotel is very clean with Western bath, single bed fan rooms for US$5, two beds for US$7 and a room with a/c and sat. TV goes for US$10. The owner speaks English.

The Top Notch

Phnom Svay Hotel (and restaurant). Nicely furnished clean rooms with a large bed, sat. TV and Western bath. Fan rooms are 200 baht, a/c rooms 300 baht. The restaurant is THE place for Western food in Sisophan.

COMING & GOING

Not a lot of choices—you either have your own motorcycle or you are taking a share taxi.

But wait, let's not forget the train. Or maybe we should. It's very slow—the railroad does not even want to quote you an arrival time because it's never the same.

The train from Battambang arrives in Sisophan sometime between 10:00–11:00 am (usually). The trip takes around 3 ½ hours, which is about double the time that the share taxi takes, but unlike most things in life, it's free! This won't last for long as the poor Khmers are paying while we are not. The government just hasn't organized the train service for tourists yet.

Sisophan to Battambang has a 2 pm departure and is free!

Share Taxi

Per seat inside:

Sisophan to Siem Reap	120 baht
Sisophan to Battambang	50 baht
Sisophan to Poipet	30 baht
Sisophan to Phnom Penh	250 baht
Sisophan to Samraong	100 baht

These rates should be the same in reverse.

Motorcycle Touring Info

As for your motorcycle tour, the Sisophan to **Siem Reap** road is a terrible bomb-cratered road that you will need to go slowly on, unless you are a moto-cross maniac. The Sisophan to **Battambang** road is fairly decent in certain stretches, not so nice in others, but definitely the better of the two roads. The Sisophan to **Poipet** stretch has some pretty fair stretches for a motorcycle, with other stretches having some humps in the road that are big enough to make any roller-coaster operator envious.

Alternative bridge next to damaged bridge on road to Sisophan

POIPET

Poipet in Banteay Meanchey Province is one of the handfuls of boomtowns around Cambodia that is attracting Cambodians eager to seek their fortune. A former Khmer Rouge stronghold until the number three man Ieng Sary worked out a sort of defection and semi-autonomy deal with the Phnom Penh government in 1996, the Poipet of today has Cambodians from all over the country, as well as former Khmer Rouge, calling it home.

An important supply lifeline for goods and arms coming from Thailand during the Khmer Rouge years, it is now a major entry point for Thai goods being shipped into the whole of Cambodia. One can't help but notice the long lines of tractor-trailer trucks hauling goods across the border. Unfortunately for Cambodia, it seems that all the trucks coming from Thailand are full while the ones going to Thailand are empty. The big neighbor is still having an easy time dominating the little-developed Cambodia.

Like the rest of Northwest Cambodia, the main artery coming into Poipet (National Highway 5) is a mess from years of bombing. The town itself is really just a dusty, dirty border town, but as mentioned, there is an air of optimism and speculation among the residents. A lot of building is going on for a town this size and there are other recent developments besides the border trade that has fueled it.

The two border casinos (one new in 1999) have attracted a fair number of Thai gamblers across the border that can't legally gamble back home. This has created some work as well as a bit of a trickle down for the local economy. Also, being a major entry and exit point for Cambodians and Thais crossing for work and business (the slow stream of tourists using this border crossing is gradually increasing) has had a positive influence on the economy.

All and all, Poipet as well as the other former Khmer Rouge areas, have seen a 180-degree change in lifestyle from when it was under strict KR leadership. Where there used to be complete control over most aspects of peoples lives and certainly no free-wheeling markets, nightclubs, casinos and brothels, it's certainly all here now.

As with other areas that are not far from Thailand, if you want to fall back on Thai language (if you happen to know some) you will usually be understood.

WHAT'S UP

Besides the casinos and the markets on both sides of the border, there is a fair amount of nightlife (see the map for locations). This is due to, again, the border location and the fact that there are a lot of truck drivers and businessmen crossing the border who are looking for evening entertainment. Fitting easily into Poipet's boomtown wild-west image are the scores of brothels along with a couple of fairly entertaining Khmer nightclubs. Step out to the street and talk to a motorcycle taxi (moto-dahp) driver about taking you somewhere and pretty soon you will be surrounded by a handful of them wanting to take you to see *s'ray sah-aht* (beautiful ladies). No doubt that there is a lot more of this form of "entertainment" going on here than across the border in the Thai town of Aranyaprathet (Aran for short).

The bigger and better markets are just across the border in Aran, with just about anything available that you might be look-

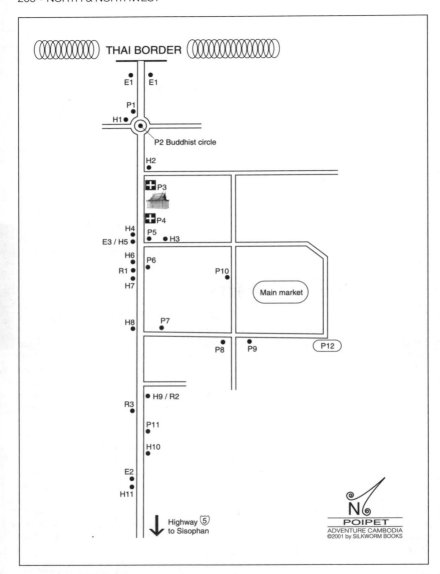

THAI BORDER

E1
E1

P1
H1

P2 Buddhist circle

H2

P3

P4

H4
P5
E3 / H5
H3

H6
P6
R1
H7

P10

Main market

H8
P7

P8
P9
P12

H9 / R2

R3

P11

H10

E2
H11

Highway ⑤
to Sisophan

N

POIPET
ADVENTURE CAMBODIA
©2001 by SILKWORM BOOKS

POIPET

H=Hotels
H1 Heng Ly Guesthouse
H2 Ly Hov Guesthouse
H3 Sin Ho Guesthouse
H4 Ochrov Hotel
H5 Neew Hotel, Night Club & Massage
H6 Neah Meas Hotel & Restaurant
H7 Khemarak Hotel
H8 Vimean Sok San Guesthouse
H9 Bayon Guesthouse & Restaurant
H10 Vihean Rasmei Preah Atith Hotel
H11 Poipet Hotel

R=Restaurants
R1 No Name Restaurant
R2 Hang Neak Restaurant in the Bayon
    Guesthouse
R3 Srah Trocheak Restaurant

P=Places
P1 Moto taxi
P2 Buddhist circle
P3 Sopheaktra Medical Clinic
P4 Chamroenphal Medical Clinic
P5 Bookstore
P6 School
P7 Share taxi & Food stands
P8 Karaoke area
P9 Karaoke area
P10 Karaoke area
P11 Caltex & gas station
P12 Market

E=Entertainment
E1 Casinos (2)
E2 Poipet Club
E3 New large Nightclub & Hotel

ing for, but bargain hard. The main market in Poipet is a pretty standard Cambodian town affair moved up a notch with more of a selection and—with bargaining—better prices.

There is also a single, small wat. (The Khmer Rouge was not known for their love of Buddhism). Apparently of Indian influence, it doesn't have much of interest to look at.

Besides that, there is very little sightseeing to be done in the Poipet area. It's not as blessed with natural beauty as other provinces close by.

MARKET

The main market is a pretty shabby looking affair, but you can get just about anything you want, from produce to electronics, at a good price, provided you do some negotiating.

CURRENCY EXCHANGE

As with the entire Northwest, Thai baht is a preferred currency. Cambodian riel is fine. US dollars are taken at some places, but not others. Money can be changed at the main market—just look for the small glass cases with currency wads inside. Forget about traveler's checks or credit cards.

MEDICAL FACILITIES

As with most of the Cambodia-Thailand border areas, malaria is present. For a serious illness or injury, it's best to get across the border into Thailand. For minor problems, you can seek help at one of these clinics. Forget the Public Health Center —it's downright nasty.

Sopheak Tra Clinic. Phnom Penh-trained doctor and pharmacy. They deal

NORTH & NORTHWEST

with local patients that have come down with malaria.

Chamroen Phal Clinic. Run by a Cambodian doctor, Mr. Vene Vuthy. Mr. Vuthy says that they are equipped to deal with sexually transmitted diseases (possibly a booming business in Poipet), as well as malaria.

RESTAURANTS

Look for the Angkor Beer signs for simple Khmer food and drinks.

Hang Neak Restaurant. Located in the Bayon Guest House, it's very popular with the locals in the morning. Features Khmer, Thai, Chinese and a bit of Western fare. Good food and friendly staff that speak some English.

Neak Meas Hotel Restaurant. A restaurant that is slated to open well before this book gets into your hands. It should be the top spot in town judging from the hotel and other parts of the establishment. Will feature Khmer, Chinese, Thai and some Western dishes.

Srah Trocheak Restaurant. Nice outdoor garden eating area in back. Moderate prices, English menu. Open late in the afternoon through the evening.

NIGHT SCENE

Best bet is sticking to the Neak Meas Hotel nightclub as the others are either too seedy or too far off the main drag.

The border casinos are ready to entertain you if you happen to think that losing money can be fun.

Also going on well into the night are the seemingly endless brothels, but use protection and use caution at night—these areas are dark and the locals hanging around them have copious amounts of booze on board.

ACCOMMODATIONS

Cheaper Places

Bayon Guesthouse. Best of this bunch. Clean well-kept rooms with windows, fan and Western bath. The friendly owner speaks English and also runs a popular restaurant on the ground floor. Good value at 200 baht.

Heng Ly Guesthouse. If you want to sleep right at the border, this would be the place. In spitting distance from immigration, it features drab, windowless, but clean rooms with an attached Asian-style bath. 100 baht for fan, 300 for a/c. The manager speaks English and is a friendly sort.

Ly Hov Guesthouse. Just off the main drag, it's a friendly place that is apparently doing a good business as they are putting up an addition that will double its size. A small fan room with attached bath but with no window in room goes for 100 baht. Larger room with two small beds goes for 150 baht. The addition should be complete by the time you read this.

Sin Ho Guesthouse. A step down from the Ly Hov, it has basic accommodation with a small Asian-style bath attached—bucket and bowl for showers. 100 baht.

Vimean Sok San Guesthouse. A real dive. Dirty place that runs short time relationships through it but doesn't bother to change the sheets, or rather, doesn't bother to put them on the filthy mattresses in the first place. 100 baht.

A Notch Up (not always)

Vihean Rasmei Preah Atith Hotel (a real mouthful). Small rooms that are windowless have satellite TV; small Western bath attached, but needs a bit more attention to cleaning. At 200 baht for a fan room, not bad value. To flip on the a/c, 400 baht.

Poipet Hotel. Not recommended because the rooms are not sheltered at all from the loud music in the restaurant-nightclub located on the premises. Fan room for 200 baht.

Khemarak Hotel. Clean rooms with a big bed, screened windows, Western bath for 200 baht. No English spoken here.

Ochrov Hotel. A fairly friendly place that always seems to be in the process of expansion, but does not pay too much attention to cleaning. Western bath, no TV and if you pay for a/c it doesn't get turned on till 7 pm and is shut down at the crack of dawn. At 250 baht for a fan or 300 baht a/c, there are better values in Poipet.

The Top Notch

Neak Meas Hotel. Definitely the top spot. Recently opened, it has clean, well-appointed rooms that have cable TV, large bed, and fridge, nicely done Western bath and windows with some type of a view. Good value at 500 baht. Also features the best nightclub in town (closes at midnight), massage parlor and karaoke.

COMING & GOING

Share Taxi

See the general Coming and Going section if you are coming from Thailand. Other than that, unless you are on your own motorcycle (or rental), you will have to rely on the share taxis. We were told that highway reconstruction was due to start within months covering the Poipet to Sisophan section, but we aren't holding our breath as we did this stretch after three months and saw no sign of construction.

Poipet to Sisophan (and the reverse)	50 baht
Poipet to Battambang	100 baht
Poipet to Phnom Penh	400 baht

Motorcycle Touring Info

As with much of Cambodia, half of the adventure is in getting there. The road is lousy, but it shouldn't take more than 1 ½ hours from Sisophan and less during the dry season, either by taxi or your motorcycle. Security is not a problem.

NORTH & NORTHWEST

The world's oldest profession

Beasts of burden at the border crossing, Poipet

BATTAMBANG

Cambodia's second largest city lies in the heart of the Northwest and until the war years was the leading rice-producing province of the country. Battambang did not give way to the Khmer Rouge movement until after the fall of Phnom Penh, but it's been in the center of the ongoing government–Khmer Rouge conflict ever since the Vietnamese invasion in 1979 pushed the genocidal regime out of Phnom Penh and to the Northwest. Until the surrender deal of Ieng Sary (Khmer Rouge number three man based in Pailin), Battambang was the government base for operations against the Khmer Rouge in the region.

Earlier history saw Battambang flip flopping back and forth between Thailand (called Siam before their 20th-century renaming) and Cambodia. It's been a part of Thailand most of the time since the 15th century, with Cambodia regaining control (more specifically, the French) in 1907. The Thais grabbed it again, with Japanese assistance, in 1941 and kept the region in their camp until after the World War II years in 1947. The Allied Forces helped persuade the Thais that the region was originally part of ancient Cambodia and the world community would not take kindly to the Thais holding onto it further.

Like the rest of the northwest, there is still a lot of Thai influence apparent. The main currency is still the Thai baht and many people are able to converse in Thai.

But the area is very Khmer, with ancient Khmer ruins scattered about and the ways of life much more similar to the rest of Cambodia than Thailand. Battambang is the main hub of the Northwest connecting the entire region with Phnom Penh and Thailand, and as such it's a vital link for Cambodia.

Battambang city is a peaceful and pleasant place these days. The main parts of the city are situated close to the Sangker River, a tranquil, small body of water that winds its way through Battambang Province. It is a nice, picturesque setting. As with much of Cambodia, the French architecture is an attractive bonus of the city.

WHAT'S UP

River Scene

The river roads are pleasant for a jog or walk by the river. Early evenings you will note that this is the area that locals like to cruise in their cars or motorcycles in order to be seen and socialize with others. There are loads of food and drink stands that set up for them on the west river road in a large area approaching the Lion's Bridge. Friendly people abound.

Inside the City

Wat Tahm-rai-saw

Situated between Roads 2 and 3, this ornate temple is worth a look, especially during the Khmer New Year festivities when it becomes the happening place in town for festivities. Entertainment, classical dancing and plenty of water and powder being thrown by the masses in search of fun and good luck for the coming year.

Wat Pee-pahd

Located between River Road 1 and Road 2, this temple is set amidst pleasant grounds and is an important spiritual center for Buddhism in Battambang.

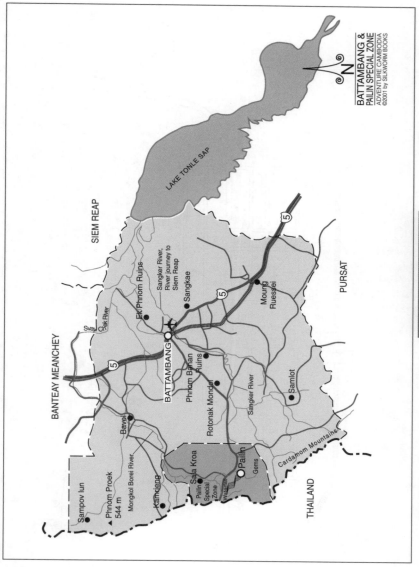

BATTAMBANG &
PAILIN SPECIAL ZONE
ADVENTURE CAMBODIA
©2001 by SILKWORM BOOKS

LAKE TONLE SAP

SIEM REAP

BANTEAY MEANCHEY

PURSAT

THAILAND

Sampov lun

▲ Phnom Proek
544 m

Mongkol Borei River

Kamdieng

Bavel

Svay Chek River

Ek Phnom Ruins

Sangker River,
River journey to
Siem Reap

Sangkae

BATTAMBANG

Phnom Banan Ruins

Rotonak Mondul

Sala Kroa

Pailin
Special
Zone

Pailin

Gems

Sangker River

Samlot

Moung
Ruessei

5

Cardamom Mountains

NORTH & NORTHWEST

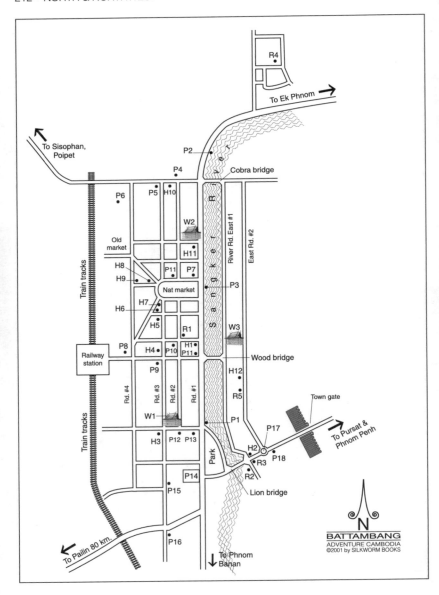

BATTAMBANG

H=Hotels
H1 Angkor Hotel
H2 Oda Hotel
H3 Teo Hotel
H4 Golden River Hotel
H5 Khemara Hotel
H6 Paris Hotel
H7 Chaiya Hotel
H8 Royal Hotel
H9 Golden Parrot Hotel
H10 7 Makara Hotel
H11 Monorom Guesthouse
H12 Heng Leng Hotel
See place list for: Pailin Nightclub & Hotel

R=Restaurants
R1 Good Khmer Restaurant
R2 Sub-i-na Restaurant
R3 Sopheak Mongkul Restaurant
R4 Wat Leap Restaurant
R5 T's Cold Nights Restaurant
See hotel list for: Teo Hotel Restaurant

P=Places
P1 Food & drink stands along the river
P2 River sightseeing boat rentals
P3 Neak Tip Disco
P4 Bopha Toep Nightclub
P5 Vietnam Embassy
P6 Share taxi stand to Sisophan & Phnom Penh
P7 Canadia Bank
P8 Cambodian Commercial Bank
P9 Pailin Nightclub & Hotel
P10 Paradise Nightclub
P11 Interphone center
P12 Boxing stadium
P13 Post office
P14 Governor's mansion
P15 Tourism building
P16 Share taxi stand to Pailin
P17 Statue circle
P18 Share taxi to Pursat & Phnom Penh

Wat Gahndahl

Located on the east bank of the Sangker River, the temple is a simple and run down place. There is an unusual wall mural on the outside of the temple that features a progressing story of a bad dude that apparently killed his own mother and finally had to board a boat bound for hell. Strange, indeed.

The interesting feature of this wat is the Angkor replica about 110 meters down a dirt path from the rear area of the temple. It was built in 1969 over a small concrete pool and is the pride of the monks staying there. They say spirits and relics of deceased monks are housed inside.

Battambang is not short on temples and you will see many more around town and on the way to the sights outside of town.

River Sightseeing & Boat Rentals

Just north of the Cobra Bridge, on the west bank, you will see a lot of boats hugging the riverbank. You can hire a non-motorized small wooden boat for around 4,000 riel, and a motorized boat (if available) for around US$5 an hour. It's a pleasant way to see the river life around Battambang town. There is also a boat you can take to Siem Reap for a smooth alternative to the lousy highway (see Coming and Going section).

Outside the City

Phnom Banan

This Angkor-era mountaintop temple is definitely worth a look. At the top are beautiful views of the winding Sangker River set amidst sugar palm trees, rice fields and small villages. To the south you will see a mountain range that features a crocodile-shaped mountain.

The temple itself is beautiful looking from the ground as well as the top. The structures are pretty much intact, but

NORTH & NORTHWEST

unfortunately like so many Khmer ruins, they have fallen victim to massive looting. Still, there are some interesting works to see. There are five temple structures, like Angkor, with the middle being the largest. (Use caution around the entrance to the center structure- there is a large hanging block—a headache-in-waiting for some poor soul).

As with Preah Vihear Temple (close to the Thai border in the province of the same name), there are a couple of big guns on the mountaintop next to the ruins. The guns are still pointing down at the surrounding area as they were during the more recent years of the government–Khmer Rouge skirmishes.

It's part of the sad irony of Cambodia that a place built for worship, harmony and tranquility was utilized as a place for making war.

Looking down the hillside to the southwest you can see more of the ruins. As always, if you go looking around, STAY ON THE WORN PATHWAYS AND TRAILS—there may still be undiscovered landmines.

Getting to Phnom Banan is easy—just head south on the River Road (Road 1) about 20 km, which at a moderate pace should take just over half an hour. You can't miss the big hill with the temple on top, visible on the right side of the road. Turn right at the dirt road that runs smack into the middle of the hill. There are drink and snack stands near the base of the stairway going up. There is also a dirt road going to the left by the stands that you could take up, but take the stairway as the Khmers did at the time the templewas in use. It's part of the fun.

A round-trip moto-taxi from Battambang is approximately 120 baht including their waiting time.

Ek Phnom

Situated about 10 km north of the Cobra Bridge are the ruins of Ek Phnom. It was built during the Bayon period and unfortunately is much worse for the wear than Phnom Banan. It's an interesting place, however, because there is a freshly constructed working temple right in front of the ruins. This temple, along with the temple ruins, is the center of holiday festivities for the people of the nearby village. They dress up in their Sunday best and have a celebration between the old and the new temples and climb all around the ruins with their families.

The ruins are on a very small hill so there is no workout involved in viewing them. Much of the temple is in shambles and was heavily looted. There are still some sitting Buddha images intact higher up on the walls. On the inside is a carving of a tug-of-war with participants tugging away on a serpent. The participants on the left have lost their heads to looters (they lost face), with the guys on the right still having their heads intact.

Ek Phnom is also easy to get to—just head north on the River Road (Road 1) a bit over 10 km (the road north of the Cobra Bridge snakes around a bit, but goes back to the river). As you are getting close to the temple, you will pass over a small concrete bridge. The road beyond will veer off to the right, but the modern temple is there to the left. Enter the new temple grounds and the ruins are located to the rear.

Again, a round-trip moto-taxi is about 120 baht from Battambang.

Phnom Sampeu (Sahm-bpoh)

Definitely worth a visit, it's about 15 km outside of Battambang city on the way to Pailin (Rt.10). Since it's closer to Battambang than Pailin, we'll include it in this section, as it's a trip that a lot of locals take from here. However, if you are going to Pailin just save it for a stop on the way. It's easy to do if you have your own motorcycle; if not you can negotiate a bit higher price and have the share taxi stop there—an extra 100 baht should do it, but don't pay until you get to Pailin.

Phnom Sampeu features an Angkor-era Baray-style pool, cave shrines with skulls and bones of Khmer Rouge victims and about seven hundred steps leading up to the main temple area, with its dynamite views. The mountaintop temple was built in 1964 and is a mix of old and new styles.

As you approach the top, take the dirt path that you will see forking off to the right. It leads to another hilltop temple area about 400 meters away. In the back of that, away from the view side, is a stairway leading down to a cave. Inside are some of the skulls and bones from this area's killing fields. Locals have brought them up here and set up a couple of shrines in caves for the spirits of the victims in the hope that they can finally rest in peace. It's another sobering place in Cambodia.

A bit further down is a cave with some small stalagmites and stalactites. Continuing the cave circuit, there is another cave area off from these areas that has a reclining Buddha and more skulls and bones nearby.

It's not a bad idea to bring a flashlight, although ladies working the temple have candles for a small donation.

The stairway and the areas on the top are packed with Cambodians on holidays as they make the pilgrimage with family and friends to see this mix of the old, new and a part of the tragedy of the Khmer Rouge era.

Also easy to get to (I don't mean to imply that the road is good), just head out of Battambang on the road to Pailin about 15 km. As you approach, you'll see the mountain and temple at the top and think that you are going to run right into it. The town

next to the mountain has the same name. As you get into town you go by a school and small stands until you see a sign in Khmer and English (amazing) on the left for Phnom Sampeu. Turn left here and as you go toward the stairs you will note some bits of ruins on the left.

Figure around 160 baht for the round-trip moto-taxi.

Gold Buddha Hill

This one is for your journey to Sisophan if you are heading that way (60 km or so from Battambang). It's easy to spot from the road. See the Sisophan section for more details.

MARKETS

Nat Market, next to the west river road, is a big, bustling affair that has just about anything you may need and also is the sight of a small night market on the riverside.

A large new market is slated for opening in late 1999. It's just off the highway heading towards Phnom Penh.

GETTING AROUND

Moto-Taxi and Car Rental

There is not a rental shop for motorcycles as of yet. Your best bet is talking to the moto-taxi guys about renting theirs. A good place to do this is at the Angkor Hotel and the Teo Hotel, where a couple of English-speaking drivers hang out. It's about the same price whether you have them drive you around or take it yourself, at US$5–7 a day and no need to leave your passport as in Phnom Penh. If you ride it yourself, they want the bike back before late evening as they worry about losing their rig to thieves.

Try the same hotels as above for car rental with a driver. It's US$30 a day, which can be negotiable.

NORTH & NORTHWEST

Motorcycle Doctor

There are a string of bike mechanics on Road 3 (east side), between the Teo Hotel and the Nat Market.

COMMUNICATIONS & INFORMATION

Post Office

The post office is catty-cornered from the night food stands off the west river road. The mail gets through sometimes.

Overseas Calls

Like Sisophan, Battambang is a much cheaper place to make your international calls than Phnom Penh. One minute to the US is US$1.60, whereas in Phnom Penh it's around US$5.50. There are a few other places around town, but the interphone centers on the river road just south of the Angkor Hotel are the easiest to find.

Internet

The Internet has arrived in Battambang! Abc Computer charges US$6 per hour for on-line use. They are located on the river road, about 35 meters north of the Angkor Hotel, on the same side of the street.

Vietnamese Embassy

Fueling Khmer fears of Vietnam still having intentions of swallowing up Cambodia is the Vietnamese embassy in Battambang. Not sure why one is needed up here, but it's located on the Parkway road, west of the Cobra Bridge at Road 3.

CURRENCY EXCHANGE

It's easy to change money, with baht, dollars and riel all being changed and accepted in and around the markets. Thai baht is still the more preferred.

Canadia Bank has a branch office on the north side of Nat Market for cashing traveler's checks.

Cambodian Commercial Bank has a branch office near the railway station where you can get cash from your Visa card for a 2% fee—you won't find a cheaper fee in Cambodia. Remember the rule for changing Thai baht and Cambodian riel: add two zeros to the baht and that's the amount in riel. Take two zeros away from the riel and that's the amount in baht.

MEDICAL FACILITIES

Nat Clinic. Located across the street from Nat Market on the north side. They have English speaking staff and doctors to help you with minor problems.

Battambang Provincial Hospital. Located on the west river road, just north of the Cobra Bridge. Like most of Cambodia, getting good care can be a bit of a crapshoot. But there are usually a couple of foreign doctors on staff so it's the place to go if you need immediate care.

RESTAURANTS

Good Khmer Restaurants. Across the street from the Angkor Hotel and near Road 2 are a few good Khmer restaurants. The doublewide one in the middle is usually packed and has the best food. The other restaurants aren't bad either. All have very reasonable prices.

Restaurants over the Lions Bridge. There are also a couple of good Khmer restaurants across the Lions Bridge near the statue circle on the right.

The first one you come to is the **Sub-i-na**. It's a simple place with good Khmer and Chinese food.

Better yet is the **Sopheak Mongkul** just beyond the Sub-i-na. The owner is a very friendly Khmer lady that speaks English and likes to chat while her staff is tending to you. Good food, and the owner will custom-make dishes for you if they're not on the menu.

Wat Leap Restaurant. On the winding river road heading north—the part that comes away from the river for a few blocks. It's close to the temple of the same name. Khmer and Chinese food with English-speaking staff that are very friendly and attentive. If you are dining alone the lady that manages the place figures that you are not happy so she has a waitress or two sit down to chat with you. The food is good. There are also karaoke rooms in the back end, but the noise does not seem to travel into the restaurant.

Teo Hotel. They have the top restaurant in town, featuring good Western, Khmer and Chinese fare at reasonable prices. If you are craving Western food, this is the spot for you.

Cold Night Restaurant (T's). This place has the best Western food in town and also good Asian food in a nice relaxed setting—it's popular with ex-pat workers living in Battambang.

It's located on East River Road 2 and is next to the hotel.

NIGHT SCENE

As Khmer nightclubs go, the clubs in Battambang are fairly low key. But the beer girls are the same everywhere and in Battambang they also close you into a circle until you blurt out which beer you like. Always a friendly lot.

Bopha Toep Nightclub. The busiest of the bunch, this one shares the name of two sister Khmer nightclubs that are popular in Phnom Penh. Watch out for the mad-capped Khmer circle dancers.

Pailin Nightclub. Located next to the hotel by the same name, this one doesn't usually get much of a crowd so is not as fun to sit and drink beer while people watching.

Paradise Nightclub. Draws a pretty fair crowd on the weekends. The taxi girls are more straightforward about lining up their after dance activities here.

Neak Tip Disco. This is the after-hours place that picks up when the other clubs close at midnight. Techy music and loads of Khmer teeny-boppers.

As for the required Cambodian town brothels, Battambang seems to take the Khmer-Vietnamese dislike to a new level by having the Khmer and Vietnamese brothels on the far opposite ends of town.

ACCOMMODATIONS

There is no need to have reservations in Battambang—the place is full of rooms, with more coming. Room prices are generally reasonable for what you get. Where TV is mentioned, it includes cable.

Cheaper Places

7 Makara Hotel. Pleasant grounds and your choice for the rock-bottom price in Battambang. For value, however, some of the other choices are better. An ugly, spartan room with nothing but a bed goes for US$1.80, US$4 for a room with a bath outside, US$5 for a room with Western bath and TV, add a/c for US$8.

Golden Parrot Guesthouse. A simple, clean place with a terrace for viewing the Nat Market. Western bath. US$4 for a fan room, US$5 with TV, US$10 with a/c.

Royal Hotel (formerly 23 Tola Hotel). New ownership, recently nicely renovated. Friendly English speaking Khmer lady is the owner. US$4 fan, US$5 with TV, US$10 with a/c, h/w shower.

Monorom Guesthouse. Right on the river. Western bath, TV, fan. Try to grab a room with a window. US$5 per night.

Chaiya Hotel. Good value, but no English spoken. Western bath, clean, terrace, TV. Fan US$5, add fridge and a/c for US$10.

Paris Hotel. Again, good value and clean, but no English. Western bath, terrace, fridge, TV. Fan US$5. A/c is a good deal here at US$8.

Khemara Hotel. Similar to the neighbors, the Chaiya and Paris Hotels. Clean rooms with fan US$5, with a/c US$10.

Golden River Hotel. Another of the many that have sprung up on this street. Western bath, TV, okay rooms. Fan US$5, a/c US$10.

Pailin Hotel. With so many choices close at hand, this one is too noisy with the Khmer nightclub to justify a stay.

A Notch Up

Oda Hotel. This is the place on the Phnom Penh side of the Lions Bridge. It's a '50s-style place, and has friendly, English-speaking staff. A clean, simple room with a large bed, TV, fridge, Western bath and a/c is a good value at US$8. A room with two beds is US$10. There are also massage girls working there.

Angkor Hotel. Located on the west river road, the hotel has a nice setting and is well situated for the evening recreation along the river. The very friendly staff is a helpful source of information on things to see around Battambang. The front rooms are especially nice with a wrap-around terrace on each floor for viewing the river and watching people. Also the best spot for renting a moto-taxi to self-tour. Cars, with driver, for rent as well.

A/c, cable TV, h/w shower, one large or two small beds. Clean place. Good value at US$10 a night.

Heng Leng Hotel. On East Road 2, heading for Highway 5 and Phnom Penh. Nice, clean place with Western bath, TV, a/c rooms for US$10.

The Top Notch

Teo Hotel. Definitely the big boy in town, it's where the higher up government and military types stay when they come calling in Battambang. There is a friendly, English-speaking staff in this well-cared-for hotel. Rooms that feature all the amenities and come with a large and small bed are US$15. There are some larger, more tricked-out rooms that go for US$20. A climb to the roof level will get you a room with all the amenities for US$10.

COMING & GOING

Air

Royal Air Cambodge has discontinued (at least temporarily) flights to Battambang. President Airlines and Phnom Penh Airways have taken up the slack, however. Check the Getting Around chapter in the front of the book for more details.

Boat to Siem Reap

During the rainy season, it's a good alternative to the share taxi. The road from Sisophan to Siem Reap is lousy and the water is as smooth as ...well, water. The dry season eventually makes this impassable as the river water level goes down.

Depart Battambang at 7 am, arrive Siem Reap at about 10:30 am.

Cost is in the US$10–15 per person range, depending on demand. Negotiable.

Share Taxi

Battambang to Phnom Penh	300 baht
Battambang to Sisophan	50 baht
Battambang to Pursat	100 baht

1-2-3 go! at Battambang

River life in Battambang

Funeral procession

Railway station of Battambang ▲

◀ The temple at Battambang

▲ Rural train station

Rural train station ▲

Vendors in Ek Phnom at Battambang ▲

◀ Phnom Banan, Battambang

Train

The old saying goes "there is no such thing as a free lunch," but in Cambodia, the old train is still free . . . for foreigners, that is. It will cost you in time, however. The Phnom Penh to Battambang journey usually takes thirteen to fourteen hours, if there are no breakdowns. The scenery is not nearly as stunning as parts of the Phnom Penh–Kampot–Sihanoukville routes, but you certainly will get a good sampling of rural agriculture scenery.

Phnom Penh to Battambang—departs between 6:20 & 7 am daily

Sisophan to Battambang—departs at around 2 pm daily

Battambang to Phnom Penh—departs between 6:30 & 7 am daily

Battambang to Sisophan—departs between 6:45 & 7:15 am daily

Motorcycle Touring Info

Riding by motorcycle is the best way to see the countryside and the sights along the way.

Battambang to Phnom Penh

It's a tough but doable road if you are on a motorcycle circuit tour. They are slowly (slower than an ant's pace) resurfacing sections between Battambang, Pursat and Kampong Chhnang, from which the road is then pretty fair to Phnom Penh.

On the Battambang–Phnom Penh highway, daytime security is not a problem, but at night scores of military checkpoints spring up with logs being put across the road so that vehicles stop. They just want a "toll fee," but it's not a fun time of the day to be dealing with the soldiers as they are pretty liquored up by then. Avoid possible problems and just ride or taxi during daylight hours.

Battambang to Sisophan

The trip is about 64 km and takes about 1 ½ hours. Battambang to Pursat is about 103 km and the trip takes about three hours. Battambang to Phnom Penh takes about six to eight hours, depending greatly on whether you are riding yourself or in a share taxi (which most always takes longer)

Battambang to Pailin

The road between Battambang and Pailin is a very rough road that has only a few decent stretches—it's a lot better than it was a few years back, but that knowledge won't mean much to your sore tail-side.

Security is not a problem.

Family affair on the train to Battambang

PAILIN

Like Poipet, this former capital of the Khmer Rouge is now a boomtown attracting Cambodians from around the country seeking to make their fortune, or at least a better salary than back home. Pailin was the major revenue producer for the Khmer Rouge guerillas, being a major gem producing area as well as a prime logging area. While gem production seems to have tapered off a bit, other business opportunities and the lifestyle have attracted prospectors to the town.

Up until the surrender deal of Khmer Rouge's number three man, Ieng Sary, in 1996, the townsfolk lived under the strict rules of the KR hierarchy, with little freedom of expression and most aspects of life being completely controlled by the paranoid regime. Today, Pailin bears little resemblance to the way things used to be. Brothels, casinos, dance clubs and a fairly open business environment abound here, another of Cambodia's Wild West towns. And like the gold-rush days of California, people seem to be everywhere in the hills sifting through mud puddles and scratching at the dirt, looking to strike it rich with the find of a nice gem.

Still, there is more control of some aspects of life than in other areas of Cambodia. Criminals are dealt with swiftly and harshly (locals say some petty crimes result in execution, although local authorities insist they only "reeducate" criminals). But this seems to have attracted people rather than kept them away. I talked to several people who had moved to Pailin from Phnom Penh and gave this as the main reason they made the move. They liked the idea that criminals did not enjoy the same im-

punity that they seem to enjoy in Phnom Penh.

The influx of residents from other parts of the country has produced a friendlier Pailin. When I first visited Pailin, it was just months after the Ieng Sary surrender and the place could hardly be described as friendly. There were a lot of hard stares and mean looks passed along by the former guerillas, who had always been taught to hate and destroy evil foreigners. Nowadays the mixed lot of Pailin residents seem happy to see foreigners coming in to holiday and check the place out, realizing that their presence means that normalcy and revenue are arriving in Pailin. Even the Vietnamese residents seem to have been accepted, which is truly amazing given the hatred the Khmer Rouge have generally shown them.

Pailin is worth checking out. The town is nestled in a beautiful valley with picturesque sunsets over the mountains that separate Cambodia and Thailand close by.

There are a few sights to see and some recreational opportunities in the area. You can have an enjoyable couple of days in the area as long as you keep in mind our word of caution for rural Cambodia—STAY ON THE WORN PATHWAYS and don't go

The pathways

walking into the bush because landmines may still be present. Being the former Khmer Rouge fortress, the surrounding hills were fortified with landmines to slow any government advance on the area. Unfortunately, it's going to be quite some time before the area is cleared of this deadly, sleeping beast.

WHAT'S UP

Wat Gohng-Kahng

This features the much-photographed landmark gate of Pailin town that you face as you arrive on the highway from Battambang. This wat is the center of holiday festivities these days in Pailin and was the scene of the official Pailin reintegration ceremony in 1996, after the Ieng Sary faction of the Khmer Rouge worked out a surrender and semi-autonomy deal with the Cambodian government.

Wat Phnom Yaht

This is the hilltop temple next to Wat Gohng-kahng. The temple is a good example of how things have changed in Pailin since the surrender deal. A number of months after the deal a friend and I had a conversation with the head monk of the temple and he said that he still felt very intimidated by the local authorities, all ex-Khmer Rouge. He was strongly discouraged from giving Buddhist instruction to the townspeople.

With the influx of Cambodians from other parts of the country and a change of heart for some of the ex-KR, the temple has seen a rebirth. There is a beautiful new decorative stairway leading to the hilltop temple area, where a new temple is under construction and the monks openly teach the faith. Obviously, respect for monks has risen, and temple projects are receiving a lot of donations.

Great views of the Pailin area and the dynamite sunsets over the border mountains can be had from the hilltop.

Border Crossing & Casino Area

The locals refer to this area as simply Pbrohm. This was a main lifeline of the Khmer Rouge during the years of fighting with the government. Food, supplies and weaponry were brought over from Thailand here. The action today is of the gaming type with the Flamingo Casino open for business and another under construction. The casino sees a lot more business than the one in town, as the Thai people that represent the vast majority of customers like the idea of staying within spitting distance of Thailand. So if you like tossing money away, you have several choices in Pailin.

There are also a few seedy looking karaoke bars with ladies working near the casinos and border.

As for using Pailin as a border crossing to and from Thailand:

The Thais have no problem with it and will issue you a Thai visa or stamp you out between 7 am and 5 pm. The problem is on the Cambodian side as the immigration police say that it's not an officially sanctioned crossing and there is no way that a foreigner can cross here. So for now it's best to stick with Poipet and Koh Kong for land crossings.

Getting to the border is the interesting part. About 5 km on the way from Pailin is a small wooden bridge going over the Oh-chah-rah River. The water coming down from the mountains is clean, so a swim here is an inviting prospect.

You also pass by the bombed shell of a tank, reminding you which side of the border you are on. Tank bodies just sit where they die in Cambodia and simply become another part of the landscape.

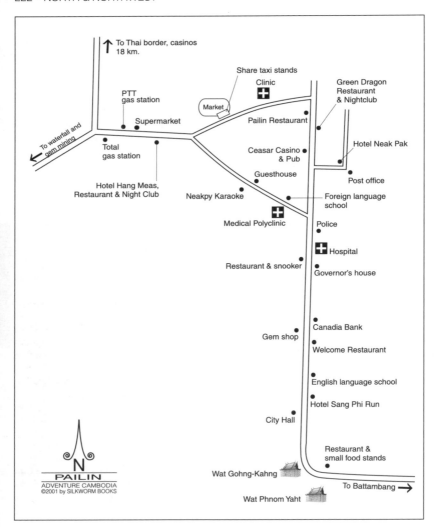

To Thai border, casinos 18 km.

Share taxi stands

Clinic

Market

PTT gas station

Supermarket

Pailin Restaurant

Green Dragon Restaurant & Nightclub

To waterfall and gem mining

Total gas station

Ceasar Casino & Pub

Hotel Neak Pak

Guesthouse

Post office

Hotel Hang Meas, Restaurant & Night Club

Neakpy Karaoke

Foreign language school

Medical Polyclinic

Police

Hospital

Restaurant & snooker

Governor's house

Gem shop

Canadia Bank

Welcome Restaurant

English language school

Hotel Sang Phi Run

City Hall

Restaurant & small food stands

N

PAILIN
ADVENTURE CAMBODIA
©2001 by SILKWORM BOOKS

Wat Gohng-Kahng

To Battambang →

Wat Phnom Yaht

The border is easy to get to—just the one turn on the map. It takes just under a half hour and is around 180 baht for a round-trip moto-taxi.

Waterfall

Like all waterfalls, the rainy season is the best time to go with the water flowing best then. But there are still pools of clean water to cool off in during the dry season and the heavily forested hills provide nice scenery. Locals and folks on holiday from Battambang come here on weekends and holidays and the well-worn pathways and picnic spots are safe for your use. Hiking to the upper level brings you to more pools.

Your best bet for getting out here is to take a moto-taxi or have one lead the way, as there are several turns on unmarked small roads. For the round trip, 120 baht should do it.

Bah Hoi Village

You will pass through an internal refugee camp enroute to the waterfall. These people come from different areas of the country that were formerly under Khmer Rouge control and are now in the hands of the government. The people feel more safe around their own kind (ex-Khmer Rouge) and with the Pailin faction of the Khmer Rouge still having effective control of the area, they don't worry about government soldiers hassling them. The people are quite friendly and don't mind a chat.

Goh-Ay Mountain

The destination here is a river that's great for a swim. Definitely for the dry season if you want to be a bit more adventurous and see more of the area. Your best bet is to talk to the guys at the English school next to the Hotel Sang Phi Run if you want to venture out this way, as they can help with directions or take you out there. Definitely stay

on the worn trails by the river area. There are landmines around.

Ceasar Casino

The casino and pub located in the same complex are open off and on these days. As mentioned earlier, the Thais prefer the Flamingo Casino with its border location. If they book a group of Thais to come to town they open the casino.

MARKETS

The market is a busy area with gem shops dealing the local harvest, karaoke joints cranking out tunes and food and drink shops all surrounding the market. The share taxi stand is located here as well. The market itself is full of produce and products from Thailand.

Going to the waterfalls

NORTH & NORTHWEST

Supermarket

Cambodia's second largest city (Battambang) doesn't have one, but boom-town Pailin does. It's similar to but smaller than the Lucky Market in Phnom Penh.

GETTING AROUND

Motorcycle Doctor

Pailin's motorcycle repair shops are mostly in front of the market—good idea to adjust and lube that chain after the Battambang to Pailin Roadway.

COMMUNICATIONS & INFORMATION

Overseas Calls

A few interphone centers are located along the main drag and next to "Guesthouse." They have reasonable rates that are comparable to Battambang.

Tours

The Foreign Language and Computer Center next to Hotel Sang Phi Run doubles as the first and only eco-tourism outfit in Pailin. Run by three Cambodians from Phnom Penh who are all fluent in English (Bonna, Ceta, Sata), they can line up a tour of anywhere that you want to go in the area. Not a bad idea in landmine loaded Pailin. They are friendly guys that are happy to just give out information if that's all you are seeking.

CURRENCY EXCHANGE

Pailin now has a branch office of Canadia Bank for travelers checks. The market area is the best place for exchanging currencies. The Thai baht is the preferred currency, but the dollar and the Cambodia riel have worked their way into the Pailin business community.

MEDICAL FACILITIES

Pailin is a high-risk malarial area so it's best to take precautions (see Health section).

The best bet for a minor problem is the clinic next to the market, or the medical polyclinic on the road that angles down to the market. There is also the Pailin Hospital.

Moto-taxis are 40 baht per hour and negotiable for round trips to the various sights outside of town.

RESTAURANTS

There are small soup and rice shops all along the main drag and next to the market. They offer decent, cheap food.

Welcome Restaurant. As the sign implies, this is a friendly place with an English menu and good food. They even have a Tiger Beer girl who is quick on the draw for those thirsty travelers.

Green Dragon Restaurant. Thatched-roof eating areas are next to the dusty parking area—it's best to eat inside if you go here.

Hang Meas Hotel & Restaurant. Chinese, Thai, Khmer and a bit of Western food are in this top spot of Pailin.

The beer girls do double duty between the restaurant and nightclub.

NIGHT SCENE

Green Dragon Restaurant & Nightclub. It's your choice if a funky place is what you are looking for. Featured is a not too good Khmer band, a few beer girls and some taxi girls that you would rather not meet.

Hang Meas Hotel & Nightclub. The top spot in town, which is not a difficult feat. This is the place if you are looking for a beer and loud Khmer music.

ACCOMMODATIONS

The change since early 1997 is dramatic. There was only one choice, a guesthouse run by a one-legged former rebel. It featured a wooden bed with no mattress, no mosquito net, no electricity and bathing facilities that you didn't want to use. There are a number of places now, four of which are worth mentioning.

Guesthouse. That's the only name on the sign. The rooms are small, but clean. The bathroom is to share. With fan, 150 baht.

Hotel Neak Pak. These are bungalows that have a large bed, Western bath, a/c, TV and fan. They are overpriced at 500 baht.

Hotel Sang Phi Run. There is a nice second-floor terrace with a view of the main drag and the mountains to the west. Most rooms are windowless, dark and stuffy places as the power is turned off in the middle of the night, which means you wake up sweating and bump your head on the way to the toilet. The cleaning leaves a lot to be desired. Mosquito net included, 300 baht.

Hotel Hang Meas. This is the new place in town and also by far the top digs. The rooms feature all the amenities (including satellite TV, h/w shower) and the hotel has twenty-four-hour power, a Pailin exclusive. US$11 gets you a nice room, with more tricked-out rooms going as high as US$50. Obviously, the owners are high on Pailin's prospects. The hotel also features a restaurant and nightclub.

COMING & GOING

An airport is in the works for Pailin, which will provide easy access to those wanting to get here but don't want to go on the lousy highways to do it. Not sure on the complete timetable, so check with Royal Air Cambodge.

The Cambodia-Thailand border crossing just west of Pailin town is reportedly opening for foreigners as of May 2000. It's supposed to be a full-service crossing issuing tourist and business visas. Unlike the Poipet and Koh Kong full service visa crossings however, this one is unconfirmed at the time of this writing.

Share Taxi

Pailin to Battambang	150 baht
(50 baht in the pickup truck bed)	

Motorcycle Touring Info

Pailin to Battambang

The Pailin-Battambang road is fairly lousy, but much better than it was a couple of years ago, with many new bridges. The scenery along the highway heading to Pailin from Battambang is nice and there are a couple of interesting sights. Security is not a problem.

Phnom Sampeu, the mountaintop temple, has memorials set up with skulls and bones of Khmer Rouge victims. It's located 15 km from Battambang on the Pailin road. See the Battambang chapter for details.

Pailin to Koh Kong

It is now possible to make a journey from Pailin to Koh Kong through the scenic Cardamom Mountains of Pursat and Koh Kong provinces. This route takes in areas that are considered to be the most pristine and untouched in all of Southeast Asia. The Coming and Going section of the Koh Kong chapter has all the details.

NORTH & NORTHWEST

PURSAT (POO-SAHT)

First impressions can be misleading. Pursat is not just the dusty, dirty stretch of road that is the only thing most people see on the way from Phnom Penh to Battambang.

Pursat has been given a bad rap for supposedly being an ugly town without much to offer, but those that venture off the main drag (National Hwy 5) find it to be a nice rural town, with the Pursat River adding beauty as it winds its way through town. The Cardamom Mountains to the southwest and the Great Lake Tonle Sap to the northeast add to the beauty of the province. There are also a number of interesting sights around and outside of town, giving the visitor a few things to do.

The road from Kampong Chhnang to Pursat has been slowly improved and the journey is much less arduous than it used to be. With the highway from Phnom Penh to Kampong Chhnang in pretty fair shape, the area is worth a visit if only to get out of Phnom Penh for a couple of days.

WHAT'S UP

River Scene

The river road north of the market turns into a boulevard where locals hang out and picnic in the early evenings. There is a park with gazebos and a small bridge going out to an island park area nearby. Continuing north, just beyond another bridge you come to a small dam/ spillway where locals swim, fish and hang out. On the east side of the river, about 100 meters north of the dam is a sandy beach area. The river originates in the mountains and is fairly clean. The area is beautiful and there is a restaurant just north of the dam (see restaurant section)

that's right on the river—a perfect spot to sip a beer and watch the show.

Wat Preh S'dai and Pursat River

This is the temple that you can see from National Hwy 5 looking south toward the river bend. There is a new wat under construction on the temple grounds as well. It's a nice setting with the river nearby. Just across the river road from the temple is a wooden bridge crossing the Pursat River. Just north of the bridge is a sandy beach.

O'Da Rapids

There is a river picnic area that the locals head out to on weekends to have a swim and kick back for a while about 52 km from town. There are Thais and Khmers working on building a logging road to extract timber from the area, which is why the river is now accessible for the locals on a fairly good gravel road for much of the way. The location is not really something to write home about, but the ride out gives you a chance to see life in the Pursat countryside.

To get there, turn left (if coming from Phnom Penh) at the small Caltex station (same as going to the hill temple). Down the road, 27 km from the turn, you come to the town of Leach; follow the curve to the right. At 0.7 km past that, turn left— you will then see a mountain ahead. At 52.5 km past the Caltex turn, you arrive at a gate with entry fees listed, although there was nobody there to collect when I visited. The fees are listed in Khmer script, from 500 riel to 5,000 riel, depending upon whether you had a motorcycle, car or just came with others. Go beyond the gate to find the river and picnic areas.

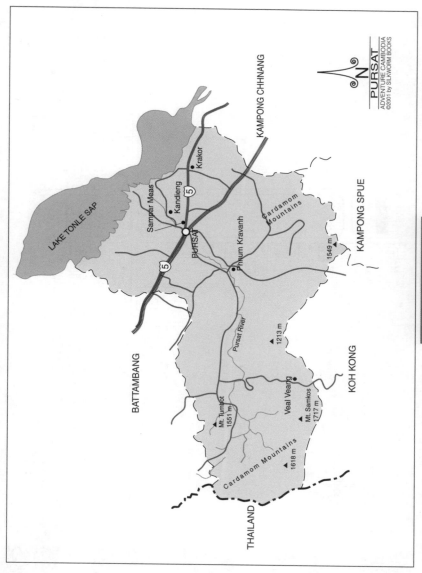

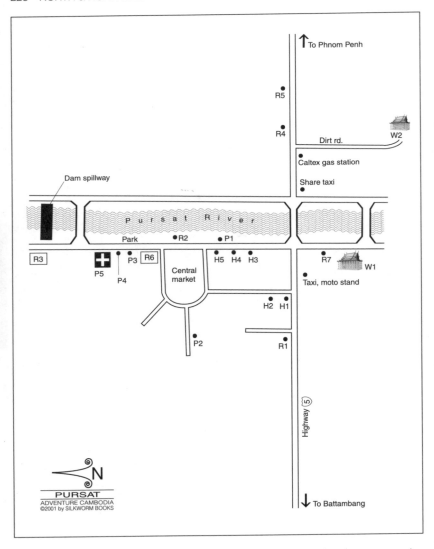

To Phnom Penh

R5

R4

Dirt rd.

W2

Caltex gas station

Share taxi

Dam spillway

P u r s a t   R i v e r

Park • R2 • P1

R3

P5 P3 R6

P4

H5 H4 H3

R7 W1

Taxi, moto stand

Central market

H2 H1

P2

R1

Highway 5

N

PURSAT
ADVENTURE CAMBODIA
©2001 by SILKWORM BOOKS

To Battambang

Scenic Drive to Wat Bpahk-Dtrow

A nice drive through rural farm country, followed by rolling forested hills, is what you get on the way to this hill temple area. With large boulders and trees lining the temple area, it's a favorite spot for the locals on Sundays and holidays. There are footpaths leading to the different temples and monuments throughout the area. There are food and drink stands near the parking area.

To get there just head east from the river bridge on National Hwy 5 (towards Phnom Penh) and turn right at the small Caltex gas station—you go under a brick and metal mesh gateway. Just follow this road for about twenty or twenty-five minutes (around 14 km) and you will see the hilltop temple in the distance on the left. Turn left at the blue-white pillars.

Leach Village

This village serves as a processing center for sandalwood oil, which in turn is used in perfume. The wood comes from the nearby forests of the Cardamom Mountains. Leach is around 27 km southwest of Pursat town.

Floating Village of Lake Tonle Sap

Heading east from Pursat town, about one-third of the way to Kampong Chhnang town is the town of Krakor. Just a few kilometers to the north are Lake Tonle Sap and the floating village of Kampong Loo-uhng. It's a complete village on the water populated mostly by Vietnamese fishermen. You can arrange for a small non-motorized boat to show you around for 4,000 riel per hour.

Cardamom Mountains

Check the Koh Kong chapter for information on the ride from Koh Kong to Pailin, which cuts through the Cardamom Mountains on the western edge of Pursat province. The Cardamom Mountains of Koh Kong and Pursat provinces are said to be the most pristine wilderness area remaining in Southeast Asia. This ride takes you through the area.

NORTH & NORTHWEST

PURSAT

H=Hotels
- H1   Hotel Orchidee
- H2   Hotel Than Sour
- H3   Hotel T'mei
- H4   Hotel Vimean Sourkey
- H5   Thmar Keo Guesthouse

R=Restaurants
- R1   Lam Siveeng Restaurant
- R2   Stung Pursat Restaurant & Nightclub
- R3   River Front Restaurant
- R4   Boray Thmei Restaurant
- R5   Pursat Restaurant & Nightclub
- R6   Food & drink stands
- R7   English menu restaurant

See hotel list for: Vimean Sourkey Restaurant

P=Places
- P1   Police
- P2   Photo shop
- P3   Post & Telecommunications
- P4   Rehab medical center
- P5   Hospital

W=Wats
- W1   Wat Preh S'dai
- W2   Wat Bpahk-Dtrow

E=Entertainment
See restaurant list for:
- Stung Pursat Restaurant & Nightclub
- Pursat Restaurant & Nightclub

MARKET

The main market is a standard Cambodian affair with supplies that you may need close at hand.

GETTING AROUND

Moto-Taxi

The fare is 4,000 riel or US$1 an hour. Add more for fuel when you head out of town.

CURRENCY EXCHANGE

Look for the glass cases with bank notes inside at the market.

MEDICAL FACILITIES

Head to Phnom Penh or Battambang.

RESTAURANTS & NIGHT SCENE

River Front Restaurant. Located about 20 meters north of the dam on the main river drag this is by far the most pleasant spot to have a meal. It's right next to the river, so there is plenty of entertainment on hand watching the locals swim, fish and socialize. The food is good and the beer girls are very friendly. Show off and practice your newly acquired Khmer language skills with them.

Stung Pursat Restaurant & Nightclub is the top nightclub in town, which isn't saying much. The food is fair to okay and the nightly Cambodian dance-a-thon, complete with band, starts at 8:30 pm. The beer girls will greet you at the door.

Boray Thmei Restaurant, Pursat Restaurant & Nightclub. Around 3 km heading down the road towards Phnom Penh are where you will see these two places. They feature the standard Khmer and Chinese fare.

Lam Siveeng Restaurant. Open for breakfast and throughout the day. It's a simple and friendly place with good food —the omelets, French bread and coffee are tasty and cheap. Some of the staff speak English.

Vimean Sourkey Restaurant. It's next to the hotel of the same name and has good Khmer and Chinese food.

There is also a good little restaurant about 50 meters before you reach the river temple (Wat Preh S'dai). There is a sign out front in English beckoning you in.

ACCOMMODATIONS

These next three places have similar good locations, close to the river and market:

Thmar Keo Guesthouse. There is a nice outdoor terrace here. The best bet is the fan room with a Western bath and single bed for US$5. An a/c room goes for US$10.

Hotel Vimean Sourkey. A little more room for the money here. Clean rooms with a partial Western bathroom, two beds, Khmer/Thai TV go for US$5/ fan room or US$10 if you use the a/c.

Hotel T'mei. Next to the Hotel Vimean Sourkey, this hotel was still under construction when we were in the area. Looks like it will be the best spot in town when it's finished. Who said Pursat wasn't booming?

These two places are near each other and just off National Hwy 5.

Hotel Orchidee. A very friendly place run by a mother-daughter team. There is a common living room, TV area on the second floor that has some nice Khmer artwork on display. Rooms with a Western bath, h/w shower and two beds go for US$7 with fan, and US$10 for turning on the a/c.

Hotel Than Sour. It's probably a step up from the Orchidee, and is a friendly place

Spillway at Pursat

Crossing the river at Pursat

New logging road being constructed in Pursat

PURSAT

Pursat town

Traditional ways linger in Pursat

The many weapons of destruction still littering Cambodia's countryside, public education billboard sponsored by Coke

as well. Nice rooms with TV, Western bath and fan go for US$5, a/c for US$10.

COMING & GOING

If you happen to be passing through from Battambang on your way to Phnom Penh and you're not to Pursat by around 5:30 pm, you should seriously consider spending the night here. The military checkpoints spring up after dark and are not always user friendly.

Share Taxi

Pursat to Battambang	100 baht / 10,000 riel
Pursat to Kampong-Chhnang	100 baht / 10,000 riel
Pursat to Phnom Penh	200 baht / 20,000 riel

The rates are for an inside seat and are the same going either direction, from the destinations mentioned. The share taxi stand is just east of the River Bridge on National Hwy 5, on the south side of the road.

Train

Pursat is on the Phnom Penh to Battambang route and the train makes a stop here, along with about 550 (or so it seems) other small towns on the trip. It's a very slow trip, but you certainly get a chance to see the countryside up close and personal.

Phnom Penh to Pursat (and Battambang—departs 6:20–7:00 am, arrives in Pursat 1:30-3:00 pm.

Pursat to Phnom Penh—departs 12:00 –2:30 pm.

That's about the best that can be given for a schedule. For now, it's still free!

Motorcycle Touring Info

As mentioned earlier and in previous sections, the road conditions on National Hwy 5 are slowly improving north and south of Pursat, with the Pursat to Kampong Chhnang section a bit better than the Pursat to Battambang section. It's all doable, but definitely easier during the dry season. Security is not a problem.

Phnom Penh to Pursat

The ride to Pursat from Phnom Penh is easy and then hard. Phnom Penh to Kampong Chhnang is an easy stretch of old but paved road, and the rest of the way into Pursat varies from a bit of pavement to long sections of bumpy and jarring dirt and gravel road. That stretch takes about 2 ½ hours.

Pursat to Battambang

The ride between Pursat and Battambang is not as bad as it used to be, but that is not saying much. For the most part, it's a bumpy and jarring 2 ½- to 3-hour ride. While the road is anything but good, both stretches can be done in the rainy season.

KAMPONG CHHNANG

Kampong Chhnang is an easygoing river port town that is worth a visit. It's easy to get to from Phnom Penh (a read good road) and the road goes by the old capital of O'Dong, as well as a nice sampling of Cambodian countryside along the way. It's only 91 km from Phnom Penh, so it's a quick jaunt up. Kampong Chhnang also gives you the option of taking an air-con bus to get there. There are also some sights to check out and the town has a fair selection of places to spend the night and a couple of decent spots to have a feed.

WHAT'S UP

River Scene

The bullet boats to and from Siem Reap and Phnom Penh make a port call here and there are also motorized boats to rent to explore the Tonle Sap River area around town. They are between US$5–8 per hour, or you can get one of the small non-motorized boats to take you on a more quiet tour for 4,000 riel per hour.

The new river walkway is the place for a stroll and is where the locals head to for the early evening social hour. It's the evening and weekend spot to be seen.

Wat Sahn-dtoot

This temple is on a hill full of rock formations. There are good views of the river and mountains from the top. To get there, just follow the road down from the Shell gas station, next to the Triangle Park. After about five minutes you will see boulders and the hilltop temple with the flags on top.

Wat Phnom Robath

There are a number of temples and hill temples along Highway 5 on the Phnom Penh side of Kampong Chhnang, but if you only stop to see one, this would be the choice. It's the highest hilltop temple in the area and affords a fantastic panoramic view of the surrounding area, including the Cardamom Mountains and the Tonle Sap River. There are a couple of different levels to the temple area and the main temple is only eleven years old. There are paths around the boulders at the top level so one can move about and take in the entire range of view.

To get there head out Highway 5 toward Phnom Penh around 10 km or fifteen minutes. You will see the smaller hilltop temple on the left (Phnom Chahm-bpoo) and the taller Phnom Robath beyond. There is a sign in English where you make your left turn "Attractive 750 meters" (they are correct, it is attractive) and also Phnom Robath. Coming from Phnom Penh, the turn (right turn from this way) is 76 km from the Japanese Bridge in Phnom Penh.

MARKET

The main market is a busy place, as one might expect in a port town.

CURRENCY EXCHANGE

There are money exchange spots around the market—just look for the glass cases with the dough inside. The one on the corner across the street from the market has a sign up giving the rate for the day.

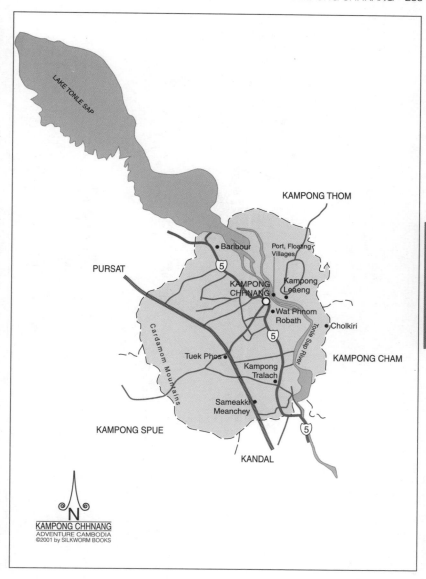

LAKE TONLE SAP

KAMPONG THOM

• Baribour

Port, Floating Villages

PURSAT

⑤

KAMPONG CHHNANG

○

• Kampong Leaeng

• Wat Phnom Robath

⑤

• Cholkiri

Cardamom Mountains

Tonle Sap River

• Tuek Phos

KAMPONG CHAM

Kampong Tralach

Sameakki Meanchey

KAMPONG SPUE

⑤

KANDAL

N

KAMPONG CHHNANG
ADVENTURE CAMBODIA
©2001 by SILKWORM BOOKS

NORTH & NORTHWEST

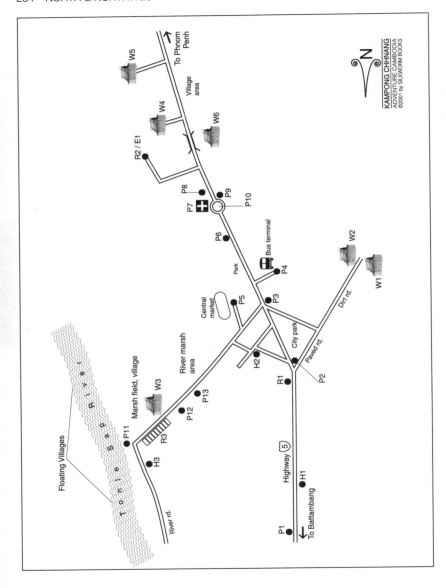

KAMPONG CHHNANG

H=Hotels
H1   Half Way House Hotel
H2   Krongday Meas Guesthouse
H3   Hotel Rithisen

R=Restaurants
R1   Mekong Restaurant
R2   Restaurant & Nightclub on the highway
R3   Rows of small restaurants

See hotel list for:
- Half Way House Restaurant

P=Places
P1   Non-commercial airstrip
P2   Shell gas station
P3   Telas gas
P4   Post office
P5   Money exchange
P6   Police station
P7   Hospital
P8   Red Cross
P9   Health office
P10 Big Khmer monument
P11 Police
P12 Market
P13 Water tower

W=Wats
W1   Small wat area
W2   Wat Sahn-dtoot
W3   River wat
W4   Phnom Chahm Bpoo
W5   Phnom Robath
W6   Large wat

E=Entertainment
E1   Restaurant & nightclub on the highway

MEDICAL FACILITIES

The hospital on Highway 5 has Khmer and foreign doctors.

RESTAURANTS & ACCOMMODATIONS

Mekong Restaurant. There is decent Khmer and Chinese food in this simple place.

You will also see several simple restaurants near the Khmer Monument Circle. The **Samaki Restaurant** is the best and has an English menu. Prices are quite reasonable.

Half Way House. Restaurant and pub, with bungalows for rent. This is a nice Western place run by the amiable Paul, a British-Kenyan that knows the area well. Paul has a Thai wife and lived in Thailand for a number of years.

The establishment sees most of it's business coming from the foreign de-miners and NGO community based in Kampong Chhnang Province. The place features good pub grub and ice cold drinks.

There are also eight, fully appointed bungalows for rent at US$15 per night. More accommodation may be in the works.

Hotel Rithisen. A good location on the River Parkway, the hotel also features a nice terrace on the third floor overlooking the river area and the rural scene beyond. The fan rooms are your best bet as the a/c doesn't get turned on until 6 pm and is shut off at 6 am. The rooms have a Western bath, two small beds, are clean and go for US$8 with fan, or US$12 for the partial a/c plan.

Krongday Meas Guesthouse. It's not too far off Highway 5 and not too clean either. Simple rooms with a Western bath and fan go for US$4 a night.

NORTH & NORTHWEST

NIGHT SCENE

If you really feel the need to go out in the evening, your only choice is the funky little disco off of Highway 5. There is usually a Khmer band with a few beer girls and a few taxi girls hanging about. Around a hundred meters on the Phnom Penh side of the Monument Circle you will see a large beer sign on the left. Turn left at the corner and follow the road down and to the right until you see the nightclub on the left-hand side. Your best bet is to remember you are near Phnom Penh and can get your night-life fix soon enough.

COMING & GOING

Bus

Your best bet if you don't have your own transportation is to take the Hoh Wah Genting bus. To and from Phnom Penh costs just 5,000 riel on the air-con bus.

Kampong Chhnang to Phnom Penh: departs 6:30 am, 7:30 am, 9:30 am, 11:00 am, 12:00 pm, 1:00 pm, 2:00 pm, 3:30 pm, 4:30 pm.

Phnom Penh to Kampong Chhnang: departs (from Central Market Terminal) 6:40 am, 8:00 am, 9:00 am, 10:00 am, 11:30 am, 1:00 pm, 2:00 pm, 3:30 pm, 4:30 pm.

If you like, you can get off at O'Dong and see the old ruins and newest addition (just grab a moto-taxi next to the entrance road), then go back out to the highway and grab the next bus heading your way.

Share Taxi

It's about a 1 ½-hour ride up from Phnom Penh. The share taxi costs 100 baht from Phnom Penh and the same for Pursat.

Motorcycle Touring Info

Highway 5 from Kampong Chhnang to Pursat is slowly getting some resurfacing work and while not good by any stretch of the imagination, it's not as bad as it used to be. As mentioned, the Kampong Chhnang to Phnom Penh stretch qualifies as a dream road in Cambodia. Security is not a problem.

TAKEO

Takeo town is an easygoing place that possesses a fair amount of natural and man-made beauty. The natural beauty is in the scenic river and lake area that faces a pleasant town parkway. The low-lying area seems to include much of the surrounding province area, which is probably why a kingdom that once had it's heart here was referred to as Water Chenla. There seems to be water everywhere in the surrounding countryside during the rainy season.

The man-made beauty mostly comes from a series of canals and waterways that were cut through the surrounding countryside, many a very long time ago, connecting towns, villages, rivers and Vietnam. Nearby Angkor Borei town (connected by water to Takeo town) may have been the heart of the Funan empire, which is called the "Cradle of Khmer Civilization" by Cambodians. Much older than Angkor, the Funan empire had its heyday between the 1st and 6th centuries and stretched across a vast area, from South Vietnam through Thailand, down through Malaysia and into Indonesia. Gold, silver and silks were traded in abundance in the kingdom, or, as some say, the series of fiefdoms.

Although Cambodians claim Funan was created by Khmers, neighboring Vietnam argues that they were the people of origin. Archeologists from the University of Hawaii of the USA, have made research trips to Angkor Borei in an attempt to piece together the history and story, as well as relics, of the Funan period.

In an odd recent twist, Reuters News Service reported in early November 1999 that locals saw the research team digging up ancient relics and figured the stuff must be valuable, so they started digging and looting objects from the area. Fortunately, the Cambodian government seems to be moving in on the problem quickly to try to save what they can of this important piece of Khmer heritage.

That was not the first time the locals have created problems in the piecing together of ancient history. Much of what did remain in the form of ancient ruins in Angkor Borei was destroyed not too long ago in the modern past. The official that runs the museum that's dedicated to the history of the Funan empire told me that much of what was still standing from this period (from parts of ancient walls to partial structures) was thought to be useless by locals and was bulldozed and razed to make way for more "useful" modern day structures! Talk about having a bad track record. Fortunately artifacts and history have been put together in the museum.

Takeo Province is full of other interesting sights as well and because of the short distance and good road from Phnom Penh, all are great day trips. Some sights can be combined in a day trip. If you have a bit more time, spend an evening in Takeo town and take in all the sights. There is a pleasant little place to stay overlooking the river and lake area.

WHAT'S UP

Phnom Da, Angkor Borei & the "Water Canal Highways"

Now that you are equipped with a bit of the history, here's the scoop on the trip. It's a lot of fun and highly recommended.

Follow our map of Takeo and head over to the canal waterfront, where the fast boats are located. There are a couple of different

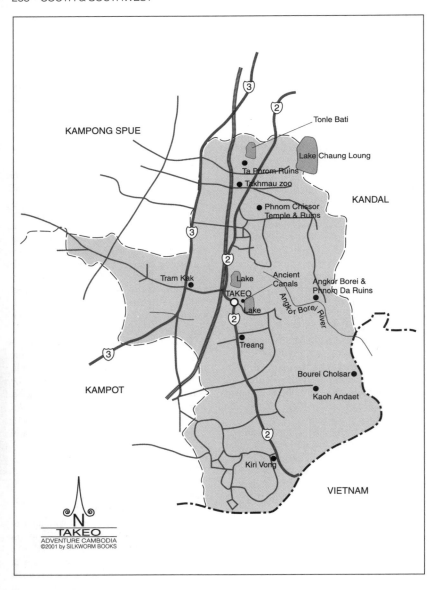

KAMPONG SPUE

Tonle Bati

Lake Chaung Loung

Ta Phrom Ruins

Takhmau zoo

KANDAL

Phnom Chissor
Temple & Ruins

Tram Kak

Lake

Ancient
Canals

Angkor Borei &
Phnom Da Ruins

TAKEO

Lake

Angkor Borei River

Treang

KAMPOT

Bourei Cholsar

Kaoh Andaet

Kiri Vong

VIETNAM

N

TAKEO

ADVENTURE CAMBODIA
©2001 by SILKWORM BOOKS

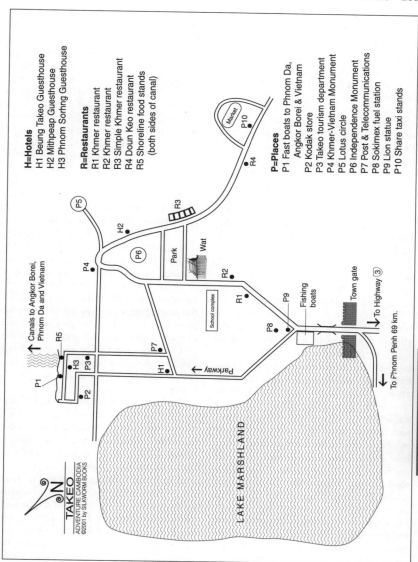

H=Hotels
H1 Beung Takeo Guesthouse
H2 Mithpeap Guesthouse
H3 Phnom Sorhng Guesthouse

R=Restaurants
R1 Khmer restaurant
R2 Khmer restaurant
R3 Simple Khmer restaurant
R4 Doun Keo restaurant
R5 Shoreline food stands
(both sides of canal)

P=Places
P1 Fast boats to Phnom Da,
Angkor Borei & Vietnam
P2 Kodak store
P3 Takeo tourism department
P4 Khmer-Vietnam Monument
P5 Lotus circle
P6 Independence Monument
P7 Post & Telecommunications
P8 Sokimex fuel station
P9 Lion statue
P10 Share taxi stands

ADVENTURE CAMBODIA
©2001 by SILKWORM BOOKS
N
TAKEO

Canals to Angkor Borei,
Phnom Da and Vietnam

LAKE MARSHLAND

Town gate

To Highway ③

To Phnom Penh 69 km.

sizes of outboard motors that the guys use, with most being either 25- or 40-hp outboards. The guy with the 40-hp rig must have sized me up as a speed freak (right on the money) and smiled when he said, "I think you want to go with me." I had talked to these guys the last time I went through Takeo, so I knew the price that I was quoted was fair. For the 40-hp boat the round trip that takes in Angkor Borei Museum and Phnom Da is US$20 (US$15 for the 25 hp), including the wait while you check out the sights along the way. The fee is the same no matter how many people you take and covers the expensive part for them—the fuel.

The main canal that heads out from Takeo town is like a super highway and the fast and slow boats that ply the canals are loaded with people and goods, coming and going to the Vietnamese border (among other places), which the canals also serve. One can hire a boat to go to the border, but it is not a legal crossing point.

Dozens of other canals crisscross the countryside, connecting scores of towns and villages. The smooth waterways are definitely one of the more efficient transportation networks in Cambodia. At each water-intersection that the boat comes upon the driver cuts the power back to slow down and check for crossing traffic—they follow traffic rules on these water-roadways better than they do on real roads around the country. They do seem like a roadway when the boat is flying down the narrow canal and the Khmer drivers even use the word for road (*bplow*) when they talk about the canals. The scenery is beautiful in its own right, with the canals cutting through marshland and rice fields. The other boats and people that you occasionally see are an extra entertainment bonus for your dollar.

Many of the canals are ancient in origin, having been dug out during the Funan period, with some serving defense needs and others being used for irrigation purposes. It's an amazing and little talked about area (and journey) in Cambodia.

The canal finally enters the Angkor Borei River and shortly thereafter you come to Angkor Borei town—it's a pretty, small town, with a modern temple built next to the river and a bridge spanning the river nearby. The museum is located next to the bridge and that's where the boat stops.

There is a fair number of ancient artifacts and displays in the small building, with information and history written out in English and French. Admission is US$1 for foreigners and 1,000 riel for Cambodians. The place is open from 8:30 am to 4:30 pm with a two-hour noontime break.

Continuing further along the river and turning off again on a couple of canals, Phnom Da temple is only about ten minutes from the museum. It's easy to spot the hilltop temple amongst the flat, surrounding countryside. Phnom Da is from the Angkor era, as its style attests. It's just a short hike from the canal and then up to the top, where there is a good view of the surrounding countryside and part of the canal network that you were just on. The temple itself is basically intact, though it is another victim of looting.

The boat ride takes a little under an hour one-way and the ride from Phnom Penh a bit over an hour, so the trip is easily doable from Phnom Penh year round, as a day trip if you don't want to spend the night in Takeo. If you ride a motorcycle down from Phnom Penh, just lock it up at the small drink stand next to the canal and fast boats in Takeo town. Buy a drink and maybe even give the drink stand lady a small tip (I gave her US$1) and the bike will probably be there when you return. If you take the air-con Hoh Wah Genting bus from Phnom Penh, just get off at the Independence

Monument and walk or take a moto-taxi to the canal.

The following sights are on the way from Phnom Penh and are easy day trips, even if you want to combine a couple of them. Distances for directions listed throughout this section are from the traffic circle near the Monivong Bridge at the south end of Phnom Penh. There are also highway mileage marker monuments along Highway 2. Complete directions are listed with each, and there is also some additional info at the end of this chapter in Coming and Going.

Tonle Bati & Ta Prohm

Tonle Bati is a popular lake and picnic area that has bamboo shacks built out over the water that people can rent out for eating and whiling away the day. It's generally a weekend get-away spot, which means it's nice and quiet during the week. Locals swim there, but the water does not look real inviting. There are all kinds of food and drink stands that sell everything you need for a picnic along the lake. Note that there are touts that follow you when you arrive on weekends and try to get you to go to their own place. It's best to pass right by them and find a spot on your own. Check prices beforehand on everything—they are famous for handing you an outrageously high bill when you depart.

Ta Prohm

King Jayavarman VII built this Angkor era temple. The ruins have a number of interesting features about them, including a couple of bas-relief scenes of some of the more unseemly sides of ancient life. The temple has suffered much from looting and the war through the years, but is worth a visit.

Just beyond Ta Prohm is a modern-day temple with some more ruins standing in front of it. It's an attractive combination on the shore of the lake.

The turnoff for Tonle Bati and Ta Prohm is just beyond the 33 km highway marker (or 28 km on your odometer from the Monivong traffic circle). Turn right at the picture billboard of a lake area. Follow this road 1.5 km and go right at the fork. There is a sign that says "Tonle Bati Tourism Area." There is a US$2 fee for entering the area, but it's free for Cambodians.

Ta Khmau Zoo & Phnom Tamao

Back on Highway 2 and continuing south towards Takeo is the Ta Khmau Zoo and Phnom Tahmao. Turn right just beyond the 39-km marker (34 km on your odometer from Monivong Circle). There is a picture sign with animals that says "Welcome to Ta Khmau Zoo" there. Follow this road all the way down toward the hilltop temple. You will come head-on to a sign that welcomes you to Takmao Zoological Gardens. At the left is a ticket booth where the fee is 1,000 riel for you and 500 riel for a motorcycle.

But going to the right, to begin with, brings you to a couple of hilltop temples and a picnic area. The first temple and stairway leading up to it is on the right nearby. Continuing further down this small road you come to a big spread out picnic area with food vendors and drink stands. They have bamboo stands with mats laid out for picnicking on. And just beyond this area is another hilltop temple that is built on a boulder strewn hill. Actually, there are large boulder hills spread out all around the area, making the landscape striking. Not bad for rock climbing either. Anyway, climbing up the stairway (the furthest temple back) leads you to the nifty little temple at the top and a great view of the distant countryside.

Meanwhile, Back at the Zoo...

Takhmau Zoo is a fairly new addition to Cambodia and was quite a project. The zoo is spread out over a huge area, blending in with the area's landscape (boulder hills abound here as well) very nicely. There are extensive wildlife exhibits that feature lions, tigers, crocodiles and monkeys, to name a few species. There is also a sun bear exhibit that has a natural setting on a hill and a fair-sized bird exhibit area nearby. The zoo area is huge and expanding all the time. You have the option of walking through the area or taking your wheels along.

Phnom Chissor

Continuing south along Highway 2 and towards Takeo, you come upon the hilltop temple of Phnom Chissor. You will see it from a long way off and you seem to be circling around it as you draw near the turn-off. Turn left just beyond the 52-km marker (about 47 km on your odometer from Monivong Circle), where you see a picture sign of the hilltop temple. Follow this dirt road 4.5 km to the foot of Phnom Chissor.

It's a long hike up the stairway to the top, but there are drink stands at the base and also the top. The spectacular views at the top of this huge hill make the hike up worthwhile, with the Damrei Mountains of Kampong Spue Province visible in the west, lakes dotting the entire area and rivers slicing through the glistening rice fields of the countryside.

The highest point of the big hill has a small Buddhist temple and shrine set up with an old monk giving blessings to Cambodians that make the pilgrimage to the top. Loads of Cambodians do so on weekends just to get blessed at this spot. He has holy water that he splashes on the faithful and they believe this spot and this guy are full of good luck, the kind that splashes in their faces.

The main temple area is the 11th-century Angkor era ruins on the other side of the hilltop area. It's an interesting structure that still has a few artwork carvings and inscriptions intact, although this temple has also suffered at the hands of looters. The east-side of the temple complex also offers more magnificent views of the area.

The Parkway

Back at Takeo town, this is a nice scenic area for a stroll about while taking in the easygoing pace of the town. Locals cruise and stroll about the parkway in the late afternoon and early evening hours—it's Takeo's place to see and be seen. Drink stands pop-up in the late afternoon hours.

MARKET

The "new" central market is of the all-purpose Cambodian variety and is chock full of goods from neighboring Vietnam, much of it coming in on those canals that you took a boat ride on.

GETTING AROUND

Moto-Taxi

For 500 riel you can get anywhere in town. The daily rate is US$5 plus fuel for distant sights.

Motorcycle Doctor

If your motorcycle has a medical problem, head back to Phnom Penh, as it's only an hour away. Call your rental outfit in Phnom Penh (always carry that rental agreement) and they will come down to perform motorcycle surgery or haul the bike back to Phnom Penh.

CURRENCY EXCHANGE

The "new" central market is your best bet for changing dollars, riel and Vietnam dong. Just look around the front area of the market for the glass cases crammed with dough.

MEDICAL FACILITIES

As for your motorcycle, if you have a medical problem, head back to Phnom Penh.

RESTAURANTS & NIGHT SCENE

There are a couple of decent Khmer food restaurants near the waterfront, at the canal that heads to Vietnam, Angkor Borei and Phnom Da.

Doun Keo Restaurant. This is another fairly simple place that has decent Khmer and Chinese food.

Khmer Restaurants. These two places are the first restaurants that you encounter as you enter Takeo from Phnom Penh. They are friendly enough places that feature rather decent Khmer and Chinese food.

And as for the night scene, there just isn't much going on in Takeo town—your best bet is to take it easy and remember that Phnom Penh is only an hour away.

ACCOMMODATIONS

Mithpeap Guesthouse. Located on the Independence Monument traffic circle, but not to worry, as there is not much traffic in Takeo. They have clean rooms with a fan and Western bath for US$5.

Beung Takeo Guesthouse. This is the top spot to stay because of the location, not because it's a fancy or swank place. Located on the parkway and overlooking the lake area, it's a nice place to kick back and chill out if you decide to spend a night in Takeo. They have clean rooms with a fan and Western bath for US$5, or US$10 if you use the a/c. A couple of the rooms overlook the lake area.

Phnom Sorhng Guesthouse. Located near the canal boat landing area, this is a simple place with fan rooms and Western bath for US$5.

COMING & GOING

Highway 2 is in great shape coming down from Phnom Penh. The trip takes just over an hour, tops. From the Monivong Bridge traffic circle to Takeo town it's 69 km.

The share taxi to Kampot is 5,000 riel.

Traditional medicine

Bus

The Hoh Wah Genting bus is an easy way to get to all the sights along the way from Phnom Penh, as well as Takeo town. The air-con buses charge 4,500 riel to Takeo, or between 3,000–4,000 riel to Tonle Bati and Ta Prohm, the Zoo and Phnom Tahmao and Phnom Chissor. Just follow the instructions in the What's Up section for where to get off the bus.

Motorcycle Touring Info

Phnom Penh to Takeo

Head south on Norodom or Monivong Boulevards to the traffic circle near the Monivong Bridge—this is where we set our odometer—if you want to use the odometer readings that we gave for directions. Follow the road due south from the traffic circle. At 4.5 km south you come to a fork in the road, where you veer to the right. Just 1.5 km further along is a traffic circle where you again veer to the right. This is Highway 2, the way to the sights listed above and Takeo town.

Takeo to Kampot

If you are on a circuit-tour of the south and are continuing on to Kampot from Takeo, it's no sweat. Just check our Takeo map and head out the road that you came into town on from Phnom Penh, but keep going straight instead of veering off to the right to Highway 2 and Phnom Penh. Highway 3 is just 12 km from Takeo and you go to the left when you get there.

This part of the journey to Kampot is just a bit rougher, but still easy riding year-round. It's just over 70 km to Kampot town. There are no security problems in Takeo or Kampot now.

Museum at Angkor Borei, Takeo Province

KAMPOT

Overshadowed by some of the more prominent destinations in Cambodia is the province of Kampot. Arguably the most beautiful province of Cambodia, Kampot offers the visitor ocean beaches and offshore islands, mountains, a national park, waterfalls, rivers and a picturesque setting in the main town of the same name.

There was good reason in the not too distant past for Kampot's failure to make the Top Hit Parade of spots visitors wanted to check out—it was the home of a particularly nasty faction of the Khmer Rouge. In 1994 they attacked a Sihanoukville-bound passenger train killing thirteen Cambodians and taking three foreigners hostage. World news focused on the ensuing negotiations for the release of the Briton, Frenchman and Australian who, unbeknown to negotiators at the time, were being very ill-treated and forced to perform grueling slave labor. Again demonstrating their stupidity and ruthlessness, the Khmer Rouge ultimately executed this young trio of tourists. Unfortunately, it was just another sad and tragic chapter of the decades-long struggle that gripped Cambodia. The government has finally bowed to international pressure and has begun the process of supposedly bringing those responsible to justice. There is a lot of uncertainty among observers that everyone responsible will be held accountable to the law. Politics driven impunity is a cancer in Cambodia that still must be resolved.

Thankfully things have settled down dramatically in Kampot over the last few years and the province is now a welcoming place for foreign visitors and Cambodians alike. The drive to Kampot town is just under three hours from Phnom Penh (138 km from Pochentong Airport) and although the road is still a bit rough on the southern stretch of the journey, it's easily done year round.

The town has a gorgeous setting with a trestle bridge going over the Tek Chou River, which runs through Kampot, with mountains serving as a backdrop to the scene. Located just a few kilometers upriver from the sea, the town is a pleasant, quiet place. The nice colonial architecture suffered during the war years, but much of it still remains intact and some new construction has been going on to add to it. Weekends see droves of Khmers coming down from Phnom Penh to enjoy the nearby beaches of Kep and it's only a matter of time before the natural beauty of the province begins to draw a lot more tourists here as well.

The back highway that connects Kampot with Highway 4 (a 54-km stretch) and ultimately Sihanoukville, takes you through a very scenic stretch of Cambodia. The road passes by colorful fishing villages, beautiful coastline and a forest-blanketed Bokor Mountain, which sits among the southern end of the Damrei Mountains. This presents a number of extra travel destinations and adventure options for travelers that want to make it to both of these beach resort areas of the Cambodian coast.

WHAT'S UP

Bokor Mountain

Bokor Mountain (elevation 1079 m) is now a national park that has much to offer the visitor, with magnificent coastline views, clear streams, waterfalls, thick forests and a former casino resort ghost town topping the lineup. Like Kampot, security is no longer

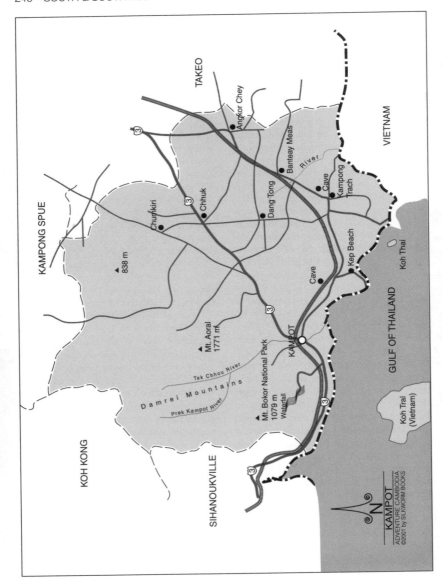

KAMPOT
ADVENTURE CAMBODIA
©2001 by SILKWORM BOOKS

a problem. Admission to Bokor National Park is just US$2 for foreigners. The entrance gate and ticket booth is 1 km from the main road turnoff. Starting at the entrance gate, here's an accounting of what's on tap.

Following the mountain switchback road as it winds through the mountain forests, you come to an area (10 km from the ticket booth) full of banana groves and pineapple fields. There is a small restaurant that's run by the park ranger and his wife that serves the fresh fruit from their fields and all kinds of drinks. Keep this place in mind for refreshments on your way back down the mountain.

At 21 km from the entrance gate you come to a plateau area that has the shells of gorgeous villas hugging the mountainside overlooking the coast, islands and the higher stretches of the mountain. The villa terraces offer fantastic views.

At 28 km from the entrance gate you arrive at a fork in the road that has a small

hand-painted sign. Going right takes you to hiking trails and a waterfall, going left takes you to the casino ghost town. About 3.5 km after going left at the fork you arrive at the former mountaintop resort of Bokor.

Like the villas passed on the way up, shells are all that remain of this once beautiful resort, all of which was destroyed during those mad Khmer Rouge years. There's a Christian church and casino-hotel building among the many structures that once served the resort town. The rainy season adds to the mystique and eeriness of the place as wave after wave of clouds blow across the mountaintop and make the buildings completely disappear and then reappear right before your very eyes. In the time it takes to pull out a camera to catch a photo of a building directly in front of you, it's gone without a trace.

There are stunning views of the coastline far below from the old casino terrace and front yard area. The large shell of the build-

River-ocean fishing village

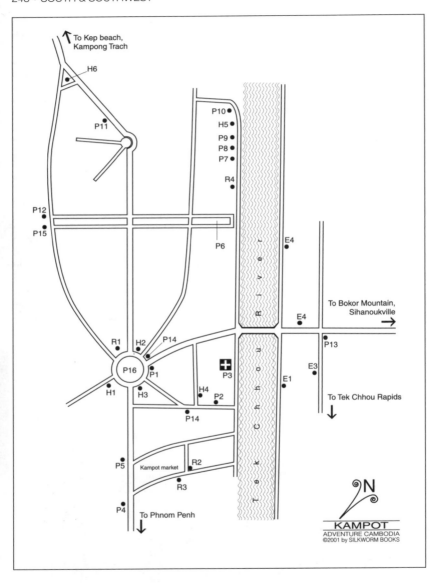

KAMPOT

H=Hotels

H1 Tekchhou Hotel
H2 Phnom Khoen Hotel
H3 Phnom Kamchay Hotel
H4 Borei Bokor Hotel & Restaurant
H5 Guesthouse National Bank
H6 Theng Guesthouse

R=Restaurant

R1 Monument Circle Restaurant
R2 International Restaurant
R3 Restaurant next to the International
R4 Marco Polo Restaurant

See hotel list for:
• Phnom Kamchay Hotel
• Borei Bolor Hotel & Restaurant

P=Places

P1 Soup gas station
P2 Outdoor basketball court
P3 Hospital
P4 International phone and fax
P5 24-hour international phone service
P6 Old market place
P7 Post & Telecommunications
P8 Red Cross
P9 Government office
P10 Government building
P11 Tourist office
P12 Total gas station
P13 Blue sign to Tek Chou River
P14 Night drink stands
P15 Share taxi stands
P16 Monument Circle

E=Entertainment

E1 River nightclub
E2 Bophar Kampot Dance Club
E3 Small karaoke place
E4 Karaoke places

ing, with its huge casino room and labyrinth hallways leading to guest rooms attest to the former grandeur of the place.

Going back the 3.5 km to the fork with the sign, head towards the waterfall area. The road ends at a clearing 3 km from the fork. There are a couple of signs up on trees in Khmer saying this is the spot to hike from. Follow the path through the trees and across a small hand-made log bridge built over a stream. The same path eventually (after 1.5 km) takes you to a tiny hand-painted sign and arrow for the waterfall. You have to cross the stream one more time and hike a short distance until you again come to the same winding stream and the top of the waterfall. Just follow the path upstream until it narrows and you can jump across the rocks to the other side. Following the path on the other side back downstream you come to a shell of a house. From here there is a path going down that you can follow for views of the two tiers of the waterfall, which are very impressive during the rainy season.

There are also hiking trails going off from the hand-painted waterfall sign, as well as other areas.

To get to Bokor from Kampot, just head out on the back highway towards Sihanoukville. From the Monument Circle in town, it's 8 km to the fork on the asphalt highway and the sign that announces that Bokor is 32 km to the right. As previously mentioned, the ticket booth is a kilometer from the fork. The road going up Bokor varies from chewed up asphalt to dirt and gravel. It is doable year round without much trouble. Make sure you have plenty of fuel in your tank.

There is a guesthouse of sorts just down from the casino shell at the top. The soldiers—park rangers that stay there—charge US$5 a night and you must bring your own food and water. The rangers say there is no

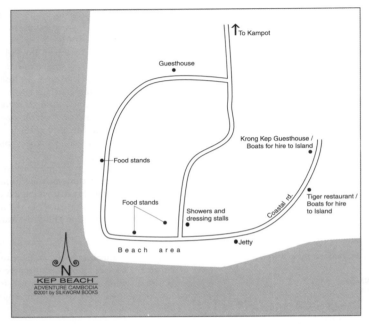

↑ To Kampot

Guesthouse

Krong Kep Guesthouse /
Boats for hire to Island

Food stands

Tiger restaurant /
Boats for hire
to Island

Food stands

Coastal rd.

Showers and
dressing stalls

Jetty

Beach   area

N

KEP BEACH
ADVENTURE CAMBODIA
©2001 by SILKWORM BOOKS

security problem with staying there, but the all-male soldier environment keeps me from recommending this place to females.

KEP

Upon arrival at Kep, one quickly realizes that this used to be a stunning beach resort area, before those "Masters of Disasters," the Khmer Rouge, destroyed it to the best of their abilities. Like Bokor, the hills overlooking the ocean, along with the rest of the small resort town, are dotted with the burned out shells of the once beautiful villas and other buildings. No matter how many times you've been to Kep, it still makes you pause and reflect on the waste and destruction of those troubled times.

Having said that, Kep is still the more beautiful of Cambodia's two beach resort towns. Sihanoukville is blessed with the nice white sand beaches, but the surrounding countryside and tree-covered oceanside hills of Kep are more attractive. The beach road is a joy to ride on as it skirts the coastline with the big hills next to it.

The main beach area is the place for swimming, tubing, picnicking and just soaking up some sun and relaxing. There are plenty of food stands and restaurants to keep the beach crowd fat and happy. Weekdays are pleasant and quiet, with the place filling up with Cambodians who make the easy drive down from Phnom Penh on weekends, when the fun of people watching really heats up.

A couple of places rent long-tail boats to take you out to one of the nearby islands. It's around US$10 to take you out, drop you off and come back to get you at a designated time. Don't pay them until after they come back to get you or they might just forget about you on that island. A small wooden restaurant (with a Tiger beer sign) on the beach road to Kep town is one place to rent a boat. The Krong Kep Guesthouse, near the municipality center, offers the boat trip as well.

Accommodations at Kep

Although Kampot town is more centrally located for other sights and not too far from the beaches at Kep, there are a couple of choices for those that want peace and quiet by the ocean.

Guesthouse. This one is just down from where you must turn right and follow the beach road. It's quiet and there is a great view of the ocean from here. As of now, they only have three rooms, which are big and have a connected Western bath. There is no fan or air, so they are a bit pricey at US$10 a night.

Krong Kep Guesthouse. This guesthouse is located near the old municipality. It's a friendly little operation, with rooms having a fan, mosquito net and attached Asian bath for US$5 a night. They also can arrange a boat trip to the island for you, which should cost about US$10 upon your return.

There are a few small restaurants and a store nearby for picking up drinks, snacks and small supplies.

There is also a semi-abandoned hotel on the beach side of the municipality that rents rooms. The people that run the place (possibly squatters) say that they can turn on the water for you and have electricity at 6 pm, but there is no maid to clean the room and security for your belongings looks dodgy. They want US$10 a night, which is real high for this place.

Motorcycle Touring Info to Kep

To get to Kep just head out from Kampot

town and at 15 km from Monument Circle, go right at the big triangle fork. Follow this road another 7 km to where a road sign directs you to turn right because the road going straight is a one-way coming at you. The beach road begins just a block down from the turn. The road is all asphalt and smooth sailing.

Phnom Roh-See-Ah Cave Temple

This is a convenient stop on the way to Kep beach and it's worth a visit as it combines a view of the area from the hilltop temple, a cave containing a sitting Buddha figure and shrine, and a bat cave!

Heading towards Kep from the monument traffic circle in Kampot, turn left on to a dirt road that passes underneath the temple's archway, 13.3 kilometers from the traffic circle. The working temple area is just under a kilometer from the turn and the stairway leading to the caves and hilltop temple is there.

After climbing the stairs, go left to get to the temple cave area or right to the bat cave and hilltop temple. The temple cave has a couple of small chambers with a stairway leading down to them—there is usually enough sunlight from a couple of openings to the outside, but a flashlight helps on the stairs.

The bat cave (sorry, no Batman) also has a couple of small chambers and a stairway

Temple cave in Kampot

leading down from the main opening. This cave is a bit darker so bring a flashlight.

The hilltop temple consists of a rather nicely painted up stupa and a working shrine area on the inside of it. A view of the rice fields leading to the nearby coast awaits you at the top.

The Caves of Kampong Trach

These are a series of caves that you may hear about while in Kampot. In reaction to government offenses, the Khmer Rouge and their families would at times retreat to and take up residence in the caves, where it was easier to hide and defend themselves. The area around most of the caves is still extremely dangerous to approach because of the high saturation of landmines. This was told to me by several ex-Khmer Rouge officers that I spoke with in the area—they don't even go near these areas anymore.

There is a cave and temple area nearby, however, that is safe to get to and it's quite nice. The cave-temple area is located within the big limestone hills that are visible from just about anywhere in the Kampong Trach area. When you arrive there, the first small temple and cave area that greets you is not that impressive, but if you walk around to the right you end up in the open area leading to the back part of the limestone hills and come upon a small outdoor temple. Following the path straight beyond this will take you to the opening of a larger cave where you actually walk straight through the hill and come upon an outside open area in the middle of the hills. There is a small temple here with a reclining Buddha and a couple of small cave shrines branching off from here. Back outside and going to the left (where you entered the cave walk-through area), there is a decrepit old stairway leading up one side of the hill that goes to yet another small shrine in a cave.

To get to the caves from Kampot, head out of town on the road to Kep beach to the Lion Triangle Park fork in the road —14.5 km from the town circle. Follow the left fork and go another 16 km where you will see a temple archway over a small dirt road leading to a hill temple. This isn't the spot, but the hill temple affords a nice view of the entire area.

Back out on the road at the archway leading to the hill temple, keep going away from Kampot and at 4.5 km from the archway, turn left—this is Kampong Trach town. Follow this small road down to where it forks and follow the right fork, which takes you around the big limestone hills and the first cave-shrine area already described.

Vietnam Border Area near Kampong Trach & Ha Tien, Vietnam

Leaving the hill-cave area and following the small road back to Kampong Trach, turn left (instead of right in the direction of Kampot) and go .4 km, then take a right turn at a small intersection. Here you have the option of making a side trip to the Vietnam border area (15 km from the turn) near Ha Tien, Vietnam.

This is a fairly active little cross-border trade area and the ride out to it is quite scenic. At this time, however, the Vietnamese authorities are not allowing foreigners to cross here, not even to visit the small market nearby.

Both of the rides to Kampong Trach and the Vietnam border area feature rough roads that get pretty sloppy, but are still passable, during the rainy season. Both areas combined can be done in a trip from Kampot and together would take just over half a day.

Tek Chhou River Rapids Area

A nice stretch of the Tek Chhou River has a fun little set of rapids that the locals use for tubing and swimming. They rent tubes there, and food and drink stands are set up near the rapids. It's a beautiful setting with large boulders near the rapids and the river slowly disappearing from view around a bend and into the mountains upstream. To enjoy the scenery and extend your ride time, hike up the small road next to the river. Or better yet, have a moto-taxi guy take you further upstream and tie a few sodas or beers to your tube, leaving them to keep cool dangling in the water, while you kick back for the long, scenic ride downstream. The rapids will amuse you before you exit the river. One can envision canoeing or kayaking here some day.

To get to the rapids, just head from the Monument Circle over the river bridge and turn right when you get to the sign that reads "Tek Chhou Resort 8 Km." Follow the road to the rapids, drink and food stands.

River Road
The river road in town offers a nice location for a jog or stroll.

MARKET

The Kampot market is the standard "all under one roof" affair with loads of goods coming from nearby Vietnam.

There is a night market spread out around Monument Circle and on a couple of the streets that angle off of it.

There is also a Konica film shop next to the circle.

GETTING AROUND

Moto-Taxi
For going around and seeing all the sights it's US$6 a day plus fuel. A short hop around Kampot town is 500 riel.

Motorcycle Doctor
For minor problems and chain adjustments and lube there are a couple of small motorcycle repair shops around the market area.

CURRENCY EXCHANGE

There are still no banks in Kampot. The market is the best place to change money (the usual glass cases near the front), with a couple of small markets next to the Monument Circle changing money as well.

MEDICAL FACILITIES

The Kampot Provincial Hospital is on the river road if you have a problem that requires immediate attention.

RESTAURANTS

Marco Polo Italian Restaurant. They have good Italian dishes, along with other Western foods to satisfy your cravings from breakfast and on through to dinner. It may be a bit pricey, but it's nice to be able to get this kind of food down here. They also can arrange guided tours of some of the spots around the area.

Borei Bokor Hotel Restaurant. This is a fairly popular restaurant with the locals and they serve up Khmer and Chinese food in the morning and throughout the day. They don't have an English menu, so your charade skills will be put to the test.

Hotel Kamchay Restaurant. This restaurant is fairly popular as well and serves up good Khmer and Chinese food and has an English menu.

Monument Circle Restaurant. No English name, so I gave it this one. It's a very popular place in the morning. They serve Chinese noodle soup, omelets and French bread with good expresso coffee. The food is good and cheap. They also cook up other Khmer and Chinese dishes throughout the day.

NIGHT SCENE

There is a bit of nightlife and the other extra-curricular activities that Cambodians love to have in their towns of all sizes, namely karaoke and brothels.

Bophar Kampot Dance Club. This is currently the only place in town that features a live Khmer band, beer and taxi girls, circle medley dancing and the dark dance hall that is the norm around the country. It sits on the banks of the Tek Chhou River.

ACCOMMODATIONS

Guesthouse National Bank. It has a weird name and a nice location. It sits next to the park area overlooking the Tek Chhou River and has a large courtyard. The rooms are clean, have a fan and Western bath and are US$6.

Theng Guesthouse. It's a simple place that could improve on its cleanliness. Fan rooms are US$5 a night.

Borei Bokor Hotel. Fairly new and recently expanded, this place seems to be doing a pretty good business. They have nice rooms with Western bath, a/c, TV, with a big bed going for US$10 a night, or a double room with two small beds for US$15. There is a big basketball court located right behind the place with late afternoon and early evening games going on for those of you who want to try a pick-up game in Cambodia. They also have a restaurant in the hotel.

These next three places surround Monument Circle:

Phnom Khoen Hotel. The rooms are a bit small, but clean. There is a Western bath,

fan and single bed for US$5, or US$10 for two beds.

Tekchhou Hotel. Also clean and well kept, rooms with a Western bath and fan go for US$6 with one bed and US$8 for 2 beds. The same arrangement with a/c is US$10 or US$12.

Phnom Kamchay Hotel. This is a fairly nice place and has several options, all with a/c, TV, and fridge. A room with one bed is US$10, two beds is US$15, three beds is US$20 and four beds in a large room goes for US$25 (you could sublet your own guesthouse out of that one). There is a restaurant on the premises.

COMING & GOING

Kampot is easy to get to with the drive from Phnom Penh taking just under three hours and covering 138 km from Pochentong Airport to Kampot town. As of now, share taxi is the only way to go unless you have your own wheels. Because the road is in relatively good shape most of the way, it's an easy taxi ride. The ride on the back highway to Sihanoukville has a stretch that will shake loose the cobwebs, but it's possible all year round.

Phnom Penh to Kampot	5,000 riel
Kampot to Sihanoukville	8,000 riel

Train

If you want to get up close and personal with Cambodia and its people, the train may be just the ticket you are looking for. The 2 ½- to 3-hour car or motorcycle ride to Kampot from Phnom Penh turns into a very slow eight to nine hour trip by train, but it can be fun if you have time and a lot of patience. The scenery is always interesting and gets pretty spectacular at times nearing Kampot and on the journey beyond to Sihanoukville. And yes, the train is still free

▲ Canal way in Phnom Da at
Takeo

▶

Harvesting near the ancient
water canal in Takeo

(top) View from Phnom
Chissor, Takeo Province

▲ Weathered but still working

No bridge? No problem ▲

▲ Trains to Kampot stop for track problems

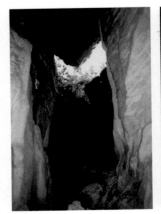

Temple cave in Kampot

Tek Chhou rapids at Kampot

River scene at Kampot

The old seaside resort of Kep at Kampot

▲ *Lifetime of experience*

Walking the rainy season tightrope ▲

▲ *Sausage short-takes*

Basket anyone? ▲

▲ *Banana lover's paradise at Kampot*

Snake or snake eggs, anyone?, at Kampot ▶

for foreigners in Cambodia. It's hard to complain about the pace at that price.

Phnom Penh to Kampot-Sihanoukville departs between 6:40 and 7:15 am daily and you could either stop off for a stay in Kampot or continue on to Sihanoukville.

Kampot to Phnom Penh departs between 10 am and 12 pm daily, depending upon when the morning train from Sihanoukville reaches Kampot (hey, this is Cambodia!).

Motorcycle Touring Info

Kampot to Phnom Penh

The highway from Phnom Penh is an easy ride and you have the option of coming directly down Highway 3 or taking Highway 2 down to Takeo and cutting over to Highway 3 from there. Highway 2 to Takeo has been resurfaced and is in better shape, but Highway 3 isn't too bad either. Highway 2 would also give you the option of seeing some of the sights that are near it on your way down. Those would be Ta Prohm Temple ruins and Tonle Bati, the Zoologi-

cal Gardens and Phnom Chissor, to name a few. Check the Phnom Penh Day Trip section for more details.

The Back Highway to Sihanoukville

As mentioned earlier, this stretch is gorgeous going along the coastline and the southern part of the Damrei Mountains. It's 54 km from the Monument Circle in Kampot to Highway 4, which takes you the rest of the way to Sihanoukville. The first 32 km from Kampot is asphalt and is in fairly good shape, with the final 22-km stretch to Highway 4 being dirt and gravel with some long stretches of bomb craters left over from when the Khmer Rouge controlled this countryside. Although it's far from nice, this stretch is doable year round, though it can be pretty mucky after continuous rains. Security is not a problem. The stretch from where you arrive at Highway 4 to Sihanoukville is another 39 km on what is the best highway in the country. The entire trip from Kampot can be done easily in about two hours.

River village in scenic Kampot

SIHANOUKVILLE/ KAMPONG SOM

Sihanoukville, also known as Kampong Som, was a sleepy port and beach town that has lately turned a few heads with its potential. The white sand beaches seem endless and are very attractive for those grown weary of the tourist-packed beaches of other countries, especially its next-door neighbor Thailand. It's easy to find a spot where you seemingly have your own private beach, or at least a long stretch of it, for the day. Weekends can see a couple of the beaches fill up with merrymakers from Phnom Penh coming down for a short holiday, but there are plenty of other beaches if you are not into crowds and people-watching, which also can be a lot of fun in Cambodia.

The water is nice and clear most of the year and has an easy, gradual increase in depth going out from the beaches. Sihanoukville is paradise for those who enjoy having a swim or just goofing around in the water. There is a nice, mellow feeling about the place, which is how a good beach resort is supposed to feel, but too few actually do. Sihanoukville is not chock full of the tourist traps, souvenir stands and pesky touts that are annoyingly ever-present in other places.

Things are still very simple and mostly undeveloped. It is possible to organize a dive and snorkeling trip, with the good news being that you are not going to be bumping into other dive boats when you get to a good spot. You can also organize a fishing trip to nearby waters that hardly see any recreational fishermen. Other opportunities for enjoying the coast are around as well.

More good news came a while back when Cambodia and Thailand finally agreed to open the border crossing at Koh Kong province, which has made it fairly easy for tourists in Thailand to cross by land and get a taste of Cambodia. Handfuls have been showing up in Sihanoukville on a daily basis to check out the beach town and possibly continue on to Phnom Penh (Check the Coming and Going chapter for details).

Sihanoukville town is a laid-back place that has a fairly prosperous look about it, mainly due to its being the only international deep-sea port in Cambodia, along with being a soft tourist destination. There is obviously more money floating around the local community than in most other towns around the country, causing word to spread and resulting in more Cambodians moving here to try their luck at getting in on the small boom. To visitors who have been coming here for a while, it's apparent that Sihanoukville is going to have more to offer as time goes on. For now, there is a nice choice of accommodations, some good restaurants and a bit of nightlife to be had. One can grow fond of this place.

Lion's circle at Sihanoukville

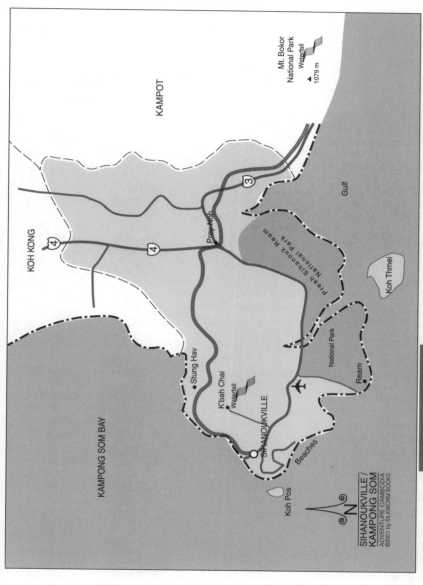

SOUTH & SOUTHWEST

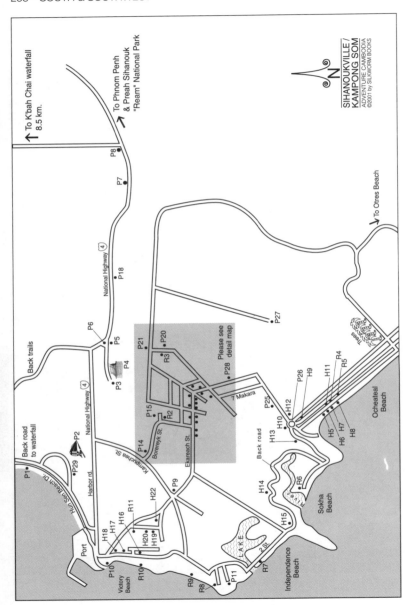

SIHANOUKVILLE/ KAMPONG SOM

H=Hotels
Ocheateal Beach
H5 Cobra Hotel
H6 Seaside Hotel
H7 Crystal Hotel
H8 Susaday Guesthouse

Near Ocheateal Beach
H9   Hotel Luon Heng
H10 Vimean Tao Meas Hotel
H11 Holiday Hotel
H12 CCS Hotel

Near Sokha Beach
H13 New Hong Kong Motel
H14 Chez Claude's

Independence Beach
H15 Sea Breeze Guesthouse

Victory Beach
H16 Holiday Palace Hotel & Casino
H17 Kam Sab Hotel
H18 So Nguon Hotel

Near Victory Beach
H19 Mealy Chenda Guesthouse
H20 Da-da Guesthouse
H22 The Melting Pot

R= Restaurants
Ocheateal Beach
R4 Maxi-Monica Restaurant &
    Guesthouse
R5 Les Feuilles Restaurant
See hotel list for:
• Susaday Hotel & Restaurant

Sokha Beach
R6 Sokha Restaurant

Near Sokha Beach
See hotel list for:
• Chez Claude's Restaurant &
  Guesthouse

Independence Beach
R7 Independence Restaurant

Victory Beach
R8   Koh Pos Restaurant
R9   Hawaii Seafood Restaurant
R10 Chner Molop Chray Restaurant
R11 Chhoukroth Restaurant

Near Victory Beach
See hotel list for:
• Mealy Chenda Restaurant &
  Guesthouse
• The Melting Pot Guesthouse &
  Restaurant

P=Places
P1   Bullet Boat to Koh Kong
P2   Railway station
P3   Samart Hill
P4   Wat Joh T'nian
P5   Angkor Brewery
P6   Triangle park
P7   Police check point & "Welcome to
     Sihanoukville" sign
P8   Military Sign, turn to waterfall
P9   Independence Monument
P10 Sihanoukville Port Park
P11 Independence Hotel viewpoint
P25 Nasa Nightclub
P26 Lions circle
P27 Go-cart race track
P29 Biba Discotheque

SOUTH & SOUTHWEST

Detail Map of Sihanoukville Town Center

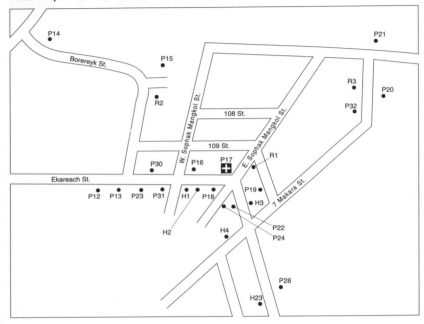

Sihanoukville Town Center

H=Hotels
H1   New Paris Hotel
H2   Hawaii Hotel & Restaurant
H3   Sem Sak Hotel
H4   Royal Hotel
H23   New York Hotel
See restaurant list for:
   • Sampov Meas Hotel

R= Restaurants
R1   Sampor Meas Hotel & Restaurant
R2   Sunday Restaurant
R3   Tee Lee Hong Restaurant
See hotel list for:
   • Hawaii Hotel & Restaurant
   • Sem Sak Hotel, Marlin Bar & Grill

P=Places
P12   Motorcycle doctor
P13   Cambodian Commercial Bank
P14   Galaxy Nightclub
P15   Angkor Beer Nightclub
P16   Angkor Arms bar
P17   Hospital
P18   Caltex & Star Mart (2 locations, same
      number used)
P19   Fuji photo shop
P20   Leu market
P21   Night market
P22   Night market
P23   Hoh Wah Genting bus station
P24   Red Snapper Bar
P28   Canadia Bank
P30   Good Luck motorcycle/car rental
P31   Big Boss Movies, KTV
P32   Share taxi stand

WHAT'S UP

The Beaches

Sokha, Ocheateal and Otres beaches are all accessible from the Lions Circle in town (Otres is a bit further afield). Sokha is a beautiful little beach that has always been the most popular weekend hangout for Phnom Penh residents. Drink and snack vendors line the beach, and the Sokha restaurant at the northwest end has just been demolished and completely rebuilt. Beach chairs, tables, and inner tubes are available for rent all along the beach (2,000 riel, 1,000 riel respectively, for the day). Sokha Restaurant also has a couple of windsurfing boards for rent. Big changes are slated for Sokha Beach as leveling work has begun for a new resort complex that looks like it will cover the entire beach. It will take some time, so we'll see how it affects the beach. The back road from Sokha takes you on a scenic stretch of road that overlooks the coastline and a small lake down below, before ending up at Independence Beach.

Ocheateal Beach

This is a long, gorgeous stretch of beach with open fields leading to rolling hills that serve as a backdrop. The far southeast end has a scenic little river that empties into the sea with large boulders surrounding it. There are long-tail boats for rent at the small fishing village here. They will take you out for a half-day outing for US$15 or a full day for US$30. Island hopping or fishing can be on the itinerary, though you would need to get fishing equipment somewhere else. Beach chairs and tables, inner tubes, and drink stands are mostly on the northwest end of the beach, although they seem to be spreading out. This beach is a fine one for a jog.

Warning: In the remote southeast end of the beach, as well as other remote beaches,

keep your belongings away from the tall grass and in sight on the beach when swimming away from chair rental areas. A few people have been known to crawl through the tall grass and steal belongings while the owners are in swimming and unable to see them. Aside from that, security is fine.

Otres Beach

Around the corner from Ocheateal Beach, Otres is as yet totally undeveloped and a nice place to ride to and hang out for awhile. The far southeast end, like Ocheateal, has a pretty little river that winds out from the inlands and empties into the sea. The south end of the beach road cuts inland past a small village and winds its way back to the north where you eventually come to a hill with a rocky trail leading up it and connecting to Highway 4 near the outer entry gate of Sihanoukville. The trail is fun for "rock climbing" with your dirt bike.

To get to Otres Beach from Ocheateal Beach, follow Beach Road 2 southeast about three-quarters of the way down. You come to an intersection and looking down to the left, you see a line of tall trees on the left side of the road. Turn left and follow that road. It turns first into a sand road, then a dirt road and winds around, crossing over a small bridge and finally leads to a small unmarked intersection. Going to the left would eventually take you to the back of Sihanouk-ville town. But you turn right and follow this until you come to the northwest end of Otres Beach.

Independence Beach

Here's another popular beach that you can get to either from the scenic back road from Sokha Beach or by paved road from town. It's a nice beach with drink stands, beach tables, and inner tubes for rent scattered down its length. There is also a small lake that you can see near the northwest end of

SOUTH & SOUTHWEST

the beach road, nestled in a small valley that meets the hills to the northeast. On the same end is a cheap but very good restaurant with great seafood and some Western food. A couple of beer signs mark the place.

Victory Beach

This long beach has a rocky point that juts out almost in its middle. There are drink stands, inner tubes, and chairs for rent on the south half, along with the popular Hawaii Seafood Restaurant. On the north end of this stretch is a small fishermen's area where some boats are kept. These guys will take you out to an island or just sightseeing for US$10. North of the rocky point is another stretch of beach leading to the port. It's a good area to kick back in and watch the port activities.

Other Beaches

There are plenty more beaches, with a couple of real nice ones within the Preah Sihanouk "Ream" National Park and a number of small beaches along Hun Sen Beach Road, north of the port and fishing village areas.

K'bah Chai Waterfalls

Seemingly unknown to everyone until fairly recently, this place offers a clear winding stream with several waterfalls descending from it in different, nearby sections, making it very attractive, as the waterfalls

Waterfall in Sihanoukville

surround the area. There are swimming, picnicking, and food and drink stalls on both sides of a series of handmade log bridges that cross the stream. The guys who made the bridges charge a user fee of 300 riel.

To get there, just head out Highway 4 toward Phnom Penh. Just under 1 km past the police checkpoint and "Welcome to Sihanoukville" sign, you turn left (there is a diagonal blue-red sign with Khmer script at the corner for a military installation just down the road). Just follow this all the way to the waterfall area—8.5 km.

Waterfall Circle Tour Route

Try this one to see a few more sights on your trip to the waterfalls. Head to the waterfalls as described above, then when ready to depart, walk your bike over the small log bridges to the other side of the stream (during the rainy season, when the river level is up). The guys who built the bridges get a real kick out of helping you negotiate your way across and will actually do it for you for 1,000 riel, which includes both you and the bike. During the dry season you could walk your bike across the shallow stream just upstream from the bridges more easily. From there you jump on the dirt road and follow it through the back countryside (and rural scenery) until you come out to the main, wide dirt roadway, which means you went about 8 km from the waterfalls. Turn left and follow this road just under 2 km, where you run directly into the north end of Hun Sen Beach Road. Following this back takes you the entire length of this scenic coastal road, passing by rolling hills, beaches, fishing villages, and the port.

Preah Sihanouk "Ream" National Park

This is a cool addition to the adventure scene in Sihanoukville and offers a number of possibilities, including hiking trails, remote island beaches and an outstanding river boat trip. The vast parkland boasts over one hundred species of wildlife. This place was developed with eco-tourism in mind and has recently become very user friendly. The staff of park rangers are a friendly and well-trained lot who provide a lot of information and assistance in accessing the different uses of the national park. They speak English and have an English information brochure, along with maps of the park area at the park headquarters building. The park rangers will go along as guides on the hiking trails. A US$2 donation fee is requested for this extra service. The park, like Sihanoukville, is free of landmines, so have some fun with it. There are also some Spartan accommodations for those who want to spend a night in the park, close to the beach. A US$5 donation is requested.

National Park Boat Trip

If you only go on one boat trip in Cambodia, make it this one. The itinerary is flexible, but a basic trip would be leaving the ranger station at Highway 4 and the Prek Toeuk Sap River and heading downriver 12 km to where it empties into the sea. You could then go around T'mai Island, just off the coast and stop for snorkeling and swimming on the way around. From the island you can jump back across the mouth of the river to a remote white sand beach for a swim and a bite to eat. The trip allows you to see almost the entire spectrum of gorgeous scenery in Cambodia: rivers cutting through the jungle, mountains, mangrove-filled marshes, flatland and the ocean coast and islands. You also pass by the occasional fishing boat with ladies busy working nets, wearing conical hats to protect them from the sun, to make sure you remember that you are in Indochina.

Cost for the trip, which starts at 8:30 am and finishes early evening (or half a day if you like), is US$20 for the smaller boat, US$30 for the mid-size boat, or US$40 for a large boat appropriate for a group. The small boat is generally good enough. The cost is split between however many you have along and includes a donation for the ranger who runs the boat and serves as a guide.

To get to the park headquarters, take Highway 4 toward Phnom Penh from the Angkor Brewery Park (in front of the

Ream National Park

brewery's main gate) for 14.5 km. You then see a sign that reads "National Park Headquarters" and you veer to the right as Highway 4 goes off to the left. Just under a kilometer from Highway 4 is the airport on the right and just beyond that, on the left, is the park headquarters. This is where you go for information, trail access, guides and the river trip.

Back Roads and Trails for Riding or Hiking

Sihanoukville is honeycombed with small roads and trails and it's great fun to explore on a dirt motorcycle. Back roads wind all over the countryside and usually lead to a reward in the form of a great view or one of the many beaches. Hiking is trouble free throughout the area, as the province has been declared free of landmines. Just take off and explore the roads that you come across and see where you end up. Sihanoukville is also a great place for mountain biking (as in bicycle), but as of yet, there's not a decent rental shop.

Wat Joh T'nian & Samart Hill

Following the road down from the front gate of Angkor Brewery takes you to this Buddhist temple. It's a pleasant place that has had some renovation work done lately, and there is even a friendly "Welcome" sign in English.

Just beyond the temple is the telephone tower for Samart Company. You can park here and walk down the path to the boulder area for a great view of the port, town and beaches. It's also a great spot to watch the sunset.

Independence Hotel Viewpoint

Located on the far northwest end of Independence Beach, this seven-story vacant hotel building is a great spot for close-up views of the coast and photos of the surrounding area. There are squatters living on the first couple of floors, but it's not a problem to walk up to the top for views. Better yet, once you get to the top of the stairs, go around to the left, where a back stairway takes you to the roof. This offers a panoramic view of the ocean, beaches, and

Port call at Sihanoukville

a lake that sits at the foot of nearby hills. An enterprising squatter lady has a drink stand set up by the front door of the old hotel and it's a nice place to quench your thirst after a hike to the top. You can even rent a room here for US$5 a night, but with so many nice, cheap spots available around Sihanoukville, it's not the best option.

Port of Sihanoukville

There is a park at the north end of Victory beach that is a good place to view the cargo loading area. Following Hun Sen Beach road also provides you with viewing spots. There is a colorful fishing port to see as you wind your way around from the port on this beach road.

Go-Cart Race Track

To the east of town there is a race track that offers speedway thrills. Ten-minute races are US$6, with two races going for US$10. They also have the place lit up for night races and sometimes on weekends nightclub merrymakers head over here after closing time for a race. To get there just head east on the main road behind the market until you see the Go-Cart sign, then turn right and follow the road about 1.5 km to the track.

Big Boss Movies & KTV

This new addition to the Sihanoukville entertainment scene features afternoon movies and is a first in town. It converts into a KTV karaoke hall in the evening hours.

Diving & Snorkeling, Fishing & Boat Trips

Sihanoukville offers plenty of opportunities for an adventure at sea in Cambodia —something not many tourists can say they have experienced. There are currently three outfits that can help you set up an outing.

Condor Marine Dive & Survey. Run by Steve, the amiable Australian who runs the Marlin Bar & Grill and the Sem Sak Hotel that the bar is located in. Fishing, diving and snorkeling trips and boat tours can be set up. Look him up at the Marlin, ☎ (034) 320-169, (015) 831-373, fax (034) 933-460, e-mail <condor-marlin@cambodia web.net>.

Chez Claude's. Claude is a long-time resident of Sihanoukville and knows the waters well. He can arrange diving and snorkeling trips, fishing trips, and boat tours. He is based at his new sea view restaurant on the back road of Sokha Beach. ☎ (015) 340-120, fax (034) 320-180.

Naga Dive. They run a dive course at the Olympic Stadium swimming pool in Phnom Penh. To organize a Sihanoukville excursion or a dive course, call: ☎ (023) 365-102, (012) 807-922.

Pool Tables

The Marlin Bar & Grill in town and Les Feuilles Restaurant near Ocheateal Beach have pool tables.

CURRENCY EXCHANGE

An up-and-coming place, Sihanoukville has four banks for you to choose from. Just check the map for locations. Hours are 8:30 am to 3:30 pm, Monday through Friday and half a day on Saturday, with the exception of Cambodia Commercial Bank.

Cambodia Commercial Bank is the place to go for a cash advance on your Visa card. They charge 2%, the same as their other branch offices around the country.

The other banks are:
Canadia Bank
Pacific Commercial Bank
First Overseas Bank Ltd.

The market is the best place to change money. There are money changers located throughout the front of the market. Just look for the telltale glass case with wads of money inside. The gold and jewelry sellers in front, toward the north end of the market, are the most concentrated location of them. The riel, dollar and baht are readily changed. Just check a couple of different vendors, as rates can vary.

MARKETS

Leu Market is the happening market of Sihanoukville. It's the standard all-purpose "everything under one roof" Cambodian affair. Everything is there, from produce to hardware and portable karaoke players, which of course nobody on the beach should be seen without.

Two small night markets set up in the late afternoon hours. Food, drinks, and produce are what's on tap. They usually stay open well past the bedtime of Sihanoukville. The main one sets up on the southeast corner of Ekareach and Sopheakmongkol streets. The other is just north of Leu Market where the road forms a T.

Caltex Stations-Star Mart Mini-Marts. If Western products and food are what you are looking for, these two stores are a welcome sight. Also a good source for the fine beach cuisine that everyone is so fond of —ice-cold beer, ice cream bars, and hot dogs with all the fixings.

Samudera Market. This store also has Western foods, but unfortunately, the staff are a bit rude and the store is quite an unfriendly place, at least every time I've been there. People used to put up with it because there were no options, but now there is Star Mart at Caltex. They actually smile and say thank you over there.

Fresh French Bread

Sihanoukville is blessed with legions of youngsters plying the streets with baskets of freshly baked bread. One can't help but notice the calling out of "Bahng-Bahng" as they walk around trying to sell the bread. Small loaves are 200 riel; larger ones cost 500 riel.

GETTING AROUND

Moto-Taxi

These guys are everywhere. The fare is 500–1,000 riel in town during the day, with about an extra 500 riel thrown in at night. Going out to a nearby beach is 1,500–2,000 riel or more, depending on where you are and how far away the beach is that you want to get to. Negotiate beforehand. The daily rate from morning until late afternoon is US$5–7, plus fuel cost if you want to head out to see the sights outside of town.

Car & Motorcycle Rental

For cars, talk to the guys at the taxi stand across the street from Leu Market. The usual price is US$20 per day with a driver.

Pech Arunn. Better known to locals as Mr. 10%. He rents out cars and small motorcycles alike. ☎ (012) 340-035.

Good Luck Motorcycle Rental. This new location with better bikes and service has brought to Sihanoukville a decent place to rent bikes. Bikes of 100 cc rent from US$3–4 per day with 250-cc dirt bikes going for US$7. They also have an open jeep to rent for US$15 a day if you want to drive yourself around. Located on the main drag in town. See map.

Motorcycle Doctor

Sihanoukville has a talented big bike mechanic located on Ekareach street, just west of the corner of Boray and Kamakor on the south side of the road.

COMMUNICATIONS & INFORMATION

Overseas Calls

Telephone rates are pricey in Sihanoukville, ranging from US$5–7 per minute for an international call. There are a few outfits with signs up along the main drag.

Internet

There are now a couple of Internet outlets in Sihanoukville and you can expect more to be popping up. Melting Pot Restaurant Internet is available at US$6 per hour, evening hours. Also check out Marlin Bar & Grill. See map.

Newspapers

There is a stationery and magazine stand outside and next to the northernmost entrance to Leu Market. They have the *Cambodia Daily* and *Phnom Penh Post.*

Photo Shop

The Fuji Film Shop is the best deal in town on prices for film and developing. They are on Street 108, not far from Sopheak-mongkol Rd.

MEDICAL FACILITIES

There is a new hotel-like medical center across from the Caltex in town. Actually, the place looks like a TV station with twenty-four small-screen TVs mounted on the outside wall. The locals like to hang out and stare at them in amazement. A new and clean place, this is your best bet for a problem that requires immediate attention.

RESTAURANTS

In Town

Sampor Meas Restaurant. This place has very good food and the prices are quite reasonable. Seafood, Western, Chinese and Khmer food. There is also a pleasant outdoor eating area, nice for evenings.

Apsara Restaurant. Located just across the street from Sampor Meas, the Apsara also has good Chinese, Khmer, Western and sea food.

Hawaii Hotel & Restaurant. Just a bit fancier than the previous two listings, this restaurant has good seafood, Chinese and Khmer food. They also have beer girls at your beck and call.

Marlin Bar & Grill. For those with a hankering for Western food, check out the menu at this place. It has a friendly, laidback atmosphere and there is a pool table at hand as well.

Sunday Restaurant. A new place that advertises Thai and Vietnamese food on a sign in English but has no English menu. I suggested to the owner that he might have better business if he made one up, so stop by and see if he did.

Tee Lee Hong. This place is near the market and has good food at reasonable prices. Chinese and Khmer dishes.

Mick & Craig's. This small bar and restaurant serves up Western and Khmer food at reasonable prices. Located across the street from the Angkor Arms Pub.

Khmer & Chinese Restaurants. Along the main drag and other well-trafficked roads you will see a number of small restaurants that serve pretty decent food at low prices. Just look for the telltale plastic chairs out front.

Sokha Beach Area

Sokha Beach Restaurant. Located on the far end of Sokha Beach, this place was recently demolished and built up new from scratch. Located right on the beach, it has always been a popular daytime spot for seafood.

Chez Claude's. Located on the back hill

SOUTH & SOUTHWEST

overlooking Sokha Beach, they feature Western and Vietnamese food and a great view.

Lions Circle

Monorom Restaurant. Just half a block toward town from the circle, they feature good Khmer and Chinese food at decent prices.

Khmer Restaurants. There are also some simple and cheap little Khmer restaurants dotting the south side of the circle.

Ocheateal Beach

Susaday Restaurant & Guesthouse. A new spot on the beach road that has Western, Chinese and Khmer food.

Maxi-Monica Restaurant & Guesthouse. Another new spot, this place on Beach Road 2 has Thai and German food.

Les Feuilles Restaurant. Good French (and other Western), Khmer, and Chinese food is served up throughout the day around a pleasant courtyard.

Sea Dragon Restaurant. Asian and Western food is on the menu here.

Independence Beach

Independence Restaurant (a.k.a. Heineken or San Miguel Restaurant). Beer signs front this restaurant are located right on the beach near the old high-rise hotel of the same name. They have excellent seafood and the prices are very reasonable. There are also beer girls here in the early evenings.

Victory Beach

Koh Pos Restaurant. Located near the corner point that separates Independence and Victory Beaches. It's a rustic-looking place located near a heavily wooded hill and right on the beach. There are monkeys foraging for food around the restaurant's garbage heap in back. The place has taken a step down in food preparation and cleanliness.

Hawaii Seafood Restaurant. This is a very popular late afternoon and evening spot. Nice views abound as the place is right on the beach with the port in sight. A bit pricey, but a nice splurge. Beer girls will keep your glass filled.

Chner Molop Chray Restaurant. This is located right on the north end of the beach. The restaurant dining area is on a deck that sits out over the water during high tide. The grounds of the restaurant are very well landscaped in a Buddhist theme park–like setting. The food is a bit pricey, but the views are hard to beat.

Up the Hill from Victory Beach

Chhoukroth Restaurant. A small, friendly place serving up good food at low prices throughout the day.

Mealy Chenda Restaurant & Guesthouse. The restaurant is a popular spot with its great view of the ocean to go along with a good and varied menu.

The Melting Pot. A small Indian food restaurant has sprung up in the area. It has a native cook.

There are also other spots popping up in this neighborhood all the time. Check it out.

NIGHT SCENE

There is a fair amount of nightlife in Sihanoukville, so if you didn't deplete your energy supply at the beach or on an adventure tour, have at it.

Galaxy Nightclub. This is the newest and the top spot in town for Khmer dancing, with a live band that plays all the Cambodian favorites and some Western hits thrown in for good measure. Beer and taxi girls abound. It also features plush, private karaoke rooms upstairs where a bunch of friends can crank out their favorite English tunes, smile at the hostess girls and drink beer out of bottomless glasses. It's not a bad time and it's cheap at US$5 an hour.

Angkor Arms. This is a friendly old standby in Sihanoukville and a good place for a quiet drink among friends. They have pub-grub, darts and an outside sitting area to boot.

Marlin Bar & Grill. This is a friendly and laid-back place featuring a pool table and a full Western menu.

Red Snapper. A fairly new addition to the scene, this is where the late-night owls hoot away the evening.

Angkor Beer Club. This is a rather funky nightclub that has not become real popular yet. It draws in some people after the Khmer nightclubs close.

Nasa Nightclub. It's the same venue as the Galaxy, but not nearly as friendly or fun.

Being a port area (and a Cambodian town), Sihanoukville has its fair share of brothels. They close from time to time, depending on which way the winds are blowing in Phnom Penh.

ACCOMMODATIONS

There is certainly no shortage of accommodations in Sihanoukville. You should have no problem finding a good choice of places to stay, in all price ranges, without a prior reservation. If you want a particular hotel and are checking in on the weekend, however, it may be best to call ahead just to make sure.

In Town

R K Resay Guesthouse. Downtown next to the Hawaii Hotel. Room with fan and shared bath US$5. Barber and massage on premises.

AngKor Inn Guesthouse. W. Sophak Mangkol Street, corner of Street 109. ☎ (034) 933-615. Rooms are US$4 with a fan and shared bath. Very clean and neat rooms.

Guesthouse One. Near the Leu Market. Nine rooms. ☎ (034) 933-579, fax 855 (034) 933-597. A/c, Western bath. Singles US$8, a/c doubles US$10.

Royal Hotel. 7 Makara Street, off Ekareach St. ☎ (012) 340-050. A/c, TV, h/w, fridge. Singles US$10, doubles US$15. Very clean rooms with Western bath. Good value.

New York Hotel. Ekareach Street. ☎ (034) 933-595. A/c, fridge, h/w, TV, western bath. Singles US$10, doubles US$15. Karaoke and massage on premises.

Sem Sak Hotel. Ekareach Street, ☎ (034) 320-169, fax (034) 320-027. A/c, TV, h/w, fridge, Western bath. Singles US$10. Doubles US$15. The Marlin Bar & Grill Restaurant are on the premises. Western and Khmer food. Opens at 7am.

New Paris Hotel. Ekareach Street, opposite Angkor Arms Pub. ☎ (034) 933-750, fax (034) 933-759. A/c, TV, h/w, Western bath. A new and popular place. Singles US$15. Doubles US$20.

Koh Rong Hotel. Corner of W. Sophak Mangkol and Street 109. ☎ (034) 933-456. A/c, TV, fridge, Western bath. Singles US$10. Doubles US$15. A good value.

Sompor Meas Hotel. E. Sophak Mangkol Street and 108 Street. ☎ (034) 933-700. A/c, TV, fridge, h/w, Western bath. Singles US$10. Doubles US$15. You can try to ask for a discount here on your room. Clean and reasonably-priced restaurant on premises.

Hawaii Hotel. Ekareach Street. ☎ (034) 933-750. A/c, TV, h/w, Western bath. Singles US$15. Doubles US$20. Triples US$25. Restaurant on premises. A popular spot.

Ocheateal Beach

Ocheateal Guesthouse. The first guesthouse on the beach. A/c, h/w,

Western bath. Singles US$10. Doubles US$15. Outdoor bar and restaurant.

Cobra Hotel. Nine bungalows. ☎ 320-048. A/c, TV, hot water. Singles US$15. Doubles US$20. A lively karaoke bar with taxi girls on premises. Best to stay somewhere more quiet and just visit.

Crystal Hotel. ☎ (034) 933-523. A/c, TV, h/w, fridge, Western bath. It's a nice and friendly place. Singles US$25. Doubles US$35.

Susaday Guesthouse. Brand spanking new on the beach road. Small rooms with Western bath, desk, closet go for US$8 per night. Stays of one week or longer, US$6 per night. Restaurant on premises with reasonable prices and good food. Great view of the beach.

Seaside Hotel. ☎ (034) 933-641. Luxury style hotel with a/c, TV, h/w, Western bath, and large rooms with terrace and ocean view. Singles US$25–50. Doubles US$- 30–50.

Near Ocheateal Beach

Hotel Luon Heng. Close to the beach, about 50 meters from the Golden Lion traffic circle. A/c, TV, h/w, fridge and Western bath. All rooms US$15.

Vimean Tao Meas Hotel, on the Golden Lion traffic circle two blocks from the beach. ☎ (015) 345-381. A/c, TV, h/w, fridge, Western bath. All rooms have patios. US$15 per room. Restaurant, karaoke and disco are on the premises, so beware of late-night crooners.

Orchidee Guesthouse. 23 Tola Street, one block from beach. A/c, TV, h/w, fridge, mini-bar, Western bath. Singles US$15. Doubles US$20.

Holiday Hotel. 23 Tola Street. One block from beach. ☎ (034) 933-658, fax (034) 320-113. A/c, TV, fridge, h/w, Western bath. Singles US$15. Doubles US$20 to US$30. Sauna and weight room on premises.

CCS Hotel. Ekareach Street, near the Golden Lion traffic circle. A/c, TV, fridge, h/w, Western bath, mini-bar. Singles US$20. Doubles US$30. Two-bedroom and two-bathroom bungalows with a car port go for US$40.

Colap One Hotel. This is located between the traffic circle and town. ☎ (034) 320-175. A/c, TV, hot water, fridge, Western bath. All rooms US$15. This place is looking a bit the worse for wear.

Sokha Beach Area

New Hong Kong Motel. Just off the Lions Circle, toward the beach. ☎ (012) 842-089. A/c, TV, h/w, fridge, Western bath. These are private bungalows with car ports and are nice for some privacy. US$20–25, depending upon the size of the unit.

Chez Claude's. Located on the back road to Independence Beach, the hill this place sits on gives a nice view of Sokha Beach. They were in the process of building some bungalows to go along with the restaurant, so they should be up and running by the time you read this.

Independence Beach

Sea Breeze Guesthouse. This place sits on the south end of the beach, near the back road heading over to Sokha Beach. ☎ (034) 320-217. A/c, TV, fridge, h/w, Western bath. An easy walk to the beach at about 40 m. Rooms are US$15–35, depending on size and extra amenities.

Independence Hotel. A large abandoned hotel that has been taken over by squatters who charge US$5 for a room. There is not much security and we do not recommend staying here. There are enough other choices in Sihanoukville. But if you like staying in a ghost-town-like atmosphere, this would be the place.

Victory Beach

Holiday Palace Hotel & Casino. Krong Street. ☎ (034) 933-737. This place is brand spanking new and definitely the top digs around for luxury. Fully appointed, nice rooms, with VIP rooms having some real elegance built into them. Each floor features a wrap-around terrace with an ocean view. There is a small casino on the premises and hotel tennis courts across the street. The hotel restaurant is across the street on the waterfront. Rooms have a/c, TV, h/w, fridge and Western bath and go for US$20–$60.

Kam Sab Hotel. ☎ (034) 933-742. A new three-story hotel on the port side of the beach. It's a friendly enough place, but they are not so used to foreigners staying there yet. A/c, Khmer TV, Western bath. Clean rooms are a good value for US$10.

So Nguon Hotel. ☎ (034) 320-289. A new three-story hotel with terrace views of the port. A/c, TV, h/w, fridge, Western bath. Singles US$13. Doubles US$15.

Near the Beach

Da-da Guesthouse. Next to The Mealy Chenda Guest House. ☎ (034) 933-583. Ocean-view rooms with a fan and Western bath are a good value at US$5 for a single room or US$7 for a double. The place is brand new and very clean and well run. Best value on this stretch.

Victory Guesthouse. ☎ (012) 852 868. Rooms with fan, US$4, US$5, US$6.

Mealy Chenda Guesthouse. ☎ (034) 933-472. This is the old standby of the area and the staff here are helpful and friendly. Singles with fan US$5. Doubles US$7. Large restaurant with ocean view. A good value. A recent facelift involved putting up a new building and taking down the old room areas. New rooms with a share bath go for US$2, while rooms with a Western bath and fan go for US$5.

COMING & GOING

As mentioned before, Highway 4 coming down from Phnom Penh is a dream come true highway in Cambodia, but you have a few alternatives for the three-hour trip.

Bullet Boat to Koh Kong

The boat leaves the Sihanoukville bullet boat pier (on Hun Sen Beach Road) daily at 12 pm. The trip takes about 3 ½ hours. The ride to the pier on a moto-taxi is 2,000 riel from town. The boat ride can be pretty rough during the rainy season. Check the Koh Kong chapter for all the details.

Bus

Hoh Wah Genting plies the route daily.

Phnom Penh to Sihanoukville—departs 7:30 am, 8:45 am, 12:15 pm, 1:30 pm. The cost varies from 8,000 to 10,000 riel, depending on the time of day.

Sihanoukville to Phnom Penh—departs 7 am, 8 am, 12:15 pm, 2 pm. The cost is 8,000 riel.

Share Taxi

The share taxi stand is located across the street from Leu Market.

Phnom Penh to Sihanoukville (and the reverse) is 10,000 riel.

The back highway to Kampot is a gorgeous stretch of road, passing by rice fields, mountains and the coastline. Share taxis ply the rough and tumble road all year round. Only 22 km of the 93-km stretch is really bad.

The fare for the share taxi to Kampot is 8,000 riel.

Train

Sure, it only takes a few hours to get to Sihanoukville by motorcycle, bus or share taxi, but what fun is that when you can see and actually become a part of the Cambodian scenery enroute to Sihanoukville by train? The scenery is spectacular at times and generally interesting.

The train travels at a snails pace and gets to Sihanoukville some 11 to 13 ½ hours after departing from Phnom Penh, so it's a real marathon. But if it is a real close look at the country and people that you want and you have plenty of time and patience, this may be the ticket you are looking for. And that train ticket is free, for the time being, anyway.

Phnom Penh to Kampot/Sihanoukville — departs 6:40–7:15 am

Sihanoukville to Phnom Penh—departs 6:45–7:15 am

Motorcycle Touring Info

Phnom Penh to Sihanoukville

Not much to talk about on the Highway 4, Phnom Penh to Sihanoukville stretch. It's easily done in three hours and the road is a breeze with some nice scenery along the way. Just keep your eyes peeled as various Khmers, who were also amazed at the quality of the road, built their houses next to it and sometimes use the highway as their living room.

Check out the Day Trips from Phnom Penh chapter for information on Kirirom National Park, which is on the way and about 80 km south of Phnom Penh in the Damrei Mountains.

The Back Highway to Kampot

As mentioned earlier, this stretch is beautiful, with parts of it passing by the southern part of the Damrei Mountains, as well as the rugged coastline and its fishing villages. From Sihanoukville head toward Phnom Penh on Highway 4. Using the Triangle Park in front of the Angkor Beer Brewery as a starting point, go 39 km and turn right on the highway that heads toward those mountains that you saw along the way. There is a Sokimex gas station on the left just before the turnoff (use this as a landmark), and it's in a small town. The next 22 km is the rough and tumble part, heading through a "Khmer Rouge Special" part of the road that is laced with bomb craters for riding up and down and around. It gets a bit sloppy and muddy during the rainy season, but it's doable year round. The final 32 km to Kampot is a fairly nice stretch of asphalt roadway.

Security is not a problem on either route.

▲ "Buddies"

▲ Fresh bread on the beach

▲ Happy vendor, unhappy coral

▲ *Quiet day on Sokha beach of Sihanoukville*

▲ *Aerial view from abandoned Independence Hotel, beach of Sihanoukville*
▼ *Patching the holes, Sihanoukville*

▲ Finding the "right" shooting angle

▼ Fishermen at Preah Sihanouk "Ream" National Park

KOH KONG & THE CARDAMOM MOUNTAINS

Located in the far southwest corner of Cambodia, Koh Kong is another of the country's more remote provinces. With the Cardamom Mountains in the north, the Damrei Mountains in the south and remote beaches dotting a rugged coastline that runs along the entire western edge of the province, Koh Kong is strikingly beautiful. Throughout the province, scenic rivers snake through lush, green hills and mountains. Although there has been a fair amount of illegal logging in the province by Thais and Cambodians alike, extremely limited road access around Koh Kong has left most of the region still blanketed with virgin forest.

Koh Kong was another stronghold of the Khmer Rouge and like other areas of the country under their control, was effectively sealed off from government-controlled parts of the country for quite some time. Roads connecting Koh Kong town with National Highway 4 to the southeast (a chunk of Hwy 4 actually runs through the southeast corner of the province) and Pursat, Pailin and Battambang to the north, were laced with landmines and to this day have yet to be completely cleared. However, getting to Koh Kong by land is now possible—check the Coming and Going chapter. As with other problem roadways around Cambodia, there has been a lot of talk about finally clearing and renovating these stretches of roadway to give easier access to the province. But since the entire country is basically one big road construction project still in the planning stage, when it will get done is another matter.

Not to worry, bullet boats that ply the coastline connect Koh Kong with Sihanoukville, as well as Highway 4, by way of Sre Amble town (northeast corner of Kampong Som Bay), making journeys to and from Phnom Penh possible either way. There is also an overland connection between Koh Kong and Thailand, which has seen increasingly larger numbers of tourists making the crossing since it was opened to foreigners a while back (see the Coming and Going chapter for details). This opened up a number of travel options for visitors to both countries who want to see what the country next door has to offer.

During a period of factional fighting about two years ago, a couple of landmines were laid on the dirt runway, resulting in damage to an Royal Air Cambodge airplane coming in from Phnom Penh. (There were no injuries.) The airport is now reopened and security for visiting the province is no longer a problem. As in other areas of former Khmer Rouge control, Koh Kong authorities deal harshly with criminals, which keeps the crime rate low, according to the locals. Koh Kong town is certainly not as pretty and idyllic as a number of other Cambodian towns, but it's not the worst place to spend a night or two and it serves as a good jump-off point for a number of interesting sights.

WHAT'S UP

Koh Kong Island

This huge island is the one near the mainland that you pass by while riding the bullet boat and is about a half an hour from Koh Kong town. You can hire one of those small boats with a 40 hp motor to take you to the island, hit a few of its beaches and finally take you back to Koh Kong town for about 700 baht. Only the occasional fish-

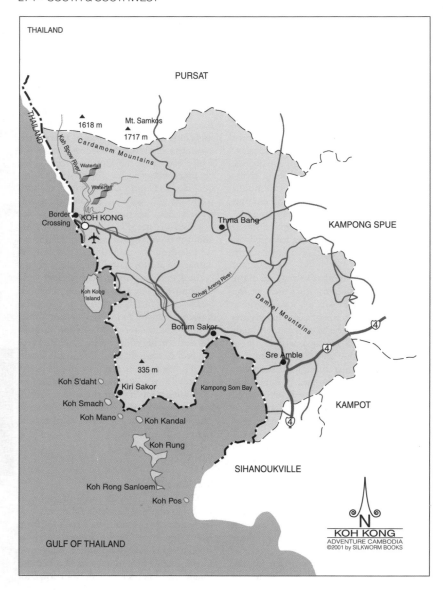

erman and a few military types on the mainland side of the island, who are, of course, still doing some logging, inhabit the island. The island is gorgeous and there seem to be endless beaches that follow the ocean side of the island. The water is nice and clear during the dry season.

"The Wilds of Cambodia River Trip"

A combination of a temple, Khmer Rouge Atrocity Theme Park, river gorge, and waterfalls.

Until fairly recently, the security situation on the river upstream from town was such that the boat-taxi guys refused to head that way more than a few kilometers. Khmer Rouge bandits posed a real threat to anyone venturing up this gorgeous river, which originates in the Cardamom Mountains of Koh Kong and Pursat Provinces. The river is considered secured now and we took a trip upriver about 27 km to a huge, thundering set of rapids and a long ledge of a waterfall. Let's start back in Koh Kong town and give some highlights of a possible combined site trip.

Start at the boat dock not far from Pacific Commercial Bank and hire one of the small boat taxis with a 25-hp or better yet, 40-hp outboard motor (350–400 baht is about right for the entire trip).

Heading just five minutes upriver and crossing to the far side, you can see a hilltop temple and as the boat pulls around the corner you will see a small cove set among boulders, where the boat can be tied up. As you approach the area from the river, the gruesome torture scenes depicted on the boulders certainly demand attention as they come clearly into view. Figures of ruthless tormentors engaged in wild scenes of bloody torture are scattered about this otherwise peaceful spot on the river. It's a strange combination of Khmer Rouge atrocities mixed with some scenes from what is presumably

hell. The nearby stairway takes you to the more pleasant temple that overlooks the Kah-bpow River. There are some nice wall and ceiling murals inside.

Back in the boat and continuing upriver, the scenery is stunning with tree-lined rivers branching off the wide body of water and the Cardamom Mountains creating the fast-approaching backdrop. This is beautiful, remote country where one only comes across the occasional fishing boat or the odd shack at the river's edge. The boat-taxi making a rare trip upriver reminds one of the bush planes that serve the remote wilderness of Alaska, when the residents of these shacks come running down to the river, arms waving, trying to catch a ride downriver for supplies. Not many people live along the river and the rare ones who do are obviously very poor.

About thirty-five minutes upriver from the theme park is a small, remote military outpost where the boat driver stops to hand a soldier a few riel as a token of appreciation for the secured river. Or it could just be a fee demanded by the soldiers, as is often the case. Anyway, no problems, as everyone seems happy. About ten minutes upstream from the checkpoint, the river becomes a wide gorge with rocky cliffs and boulders lining its heavily forested sides. As the thundering rapids and water-ledge come into sight, have the boat driver pull over and tie into one of the little boulder coves. From there one can hike along the rocks to look at this awesome stretch of river. The waterfall, or very wide ledge, is only about twelve feet high, but the width of it is impressive, and a tremendous amount of water streams over it during the rainy season, and probably a good volume even during the dry season.

The trip upriver is a lot of fun in the fast-moving small boats and I'm sure this would make a pretty cool trip by kayak or canoe.

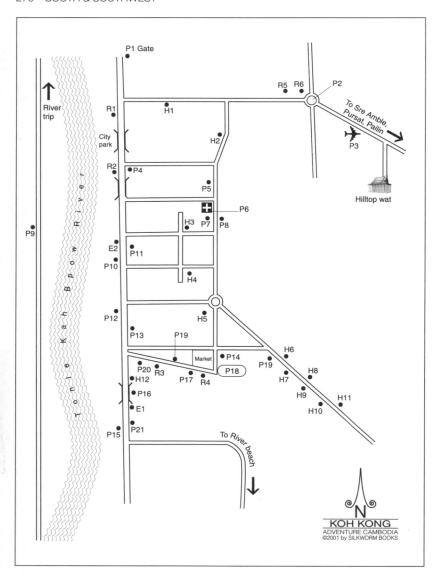

As the water comes down from the remote Cardamom Mountains, it's clean and would be great for a swim. I would also be willing to bet that the fishing in these little-used waters is pretty good. Bring your own light-weight gear and give it a try.

There is an additional set of rapids (although the Khmers call it a waterfall) to add to this river trip. As you head up river and toward the mountains, take the big fork in the river to the left and head up river about forty-five minutes to the rapids area. The rapids are much more dramatic in the rainy season, but the dry season is much more fun there. The water level is down significantly and very picturesque swimming areas are formed through the river gorge area, complete with boulder islands and plenty of ledges and cliffs on the sides to hike around. It's very peaceful and isolated back there and the water is crystal clear making it an ideal spot for a swim, hike and picnic.

From there the boat driver would go back downstream just a bit and then cut across the mangrove forest areas through the

KOH KONG

H=Hotels

H1 Koh Pich Hotel, Restaurant & Night Club
H2 Monorom Guesthouse
H3 Bopha Koh Kong Hotel
H4 Motel Hangneak
H5 Penh Cheth Guesthouse
H6 Preas Chann Penh Vong Guesthouse
H7 Rasmay Buntham Guesthouse
H8 Ly Ly Guesthouse
H9 Morocot Motel
H10 Juliana Guesthouse
H11 Raksmey Makara Hotel
H12 Koh Kong Hotel

R=Restaurants

R1 Food & drink stands
R2 Food & drink stands
R3 Simple restaurant
R4 Restaurant near the market
R5 Thai food restaurant
R6 Food stands near Thai restaurant
See hotel list for:

• Bopha Koh Kong Restaurant

P=Places

P1 Military base
P2 Independence monument
P3 Airport
P4 School
P5 Post & Telecommunications
P6 Hospital
P7 School
P8 Police office
P9 Boat dock & taxi stands to casino
P10 Boat ticket office to Sihanoukville
P11 Tourism office
P12 Boats to casino & up river
P13 P.C. Bank
P14 Koh Kong book store
P15 PTT gas station
P16 Fishing village
P17 International telephone company
P18 Mini market
P19 Motorcycle doctor
P20 Phnom Penh Airways
P21 President Air

E=Entertainment

E1 Night Club
E2 Moha Sakor Nightclub
See hotel list for:

• Koh Pich Hotel & Nightclub
• Raksmey Makara Nightclub

streams that connect the two main forks of the river and to the big water ledge and river gorge area that was described above.

During the dry season the huge waterfall ledge is dry and stands tall over the placid dry season version of the fast-moving river that this becomes in the rainy season. Great hiking is to be had out along this huge ledge and on both sides of the river at this time of year. And like the other fork of the river that you just came from, nice swimming holes abound at this time of the year and the water is nice and clear.

Including both forks of the river and their rapids-waterfall areas, along with the Khmer Rouge theme park described previously, the boat trip costs 800 baht. The number of people does not change the cost.

Border and Casino Resort, Koh Kong International Resort

The border area has a small market area on the Thai side (Ban Had Lek), that's actually not a town where people live, just a military outpost and immigration checkpoint where a cross-border market sprang up. On the Cambodian side of the border the huge and still growing Koh Kong International Resort is a sprawling complex with gaming facilities, shopping complex, restaurants and a hotel and bungalow area that surrounds a swimming pool, next to and overlooking the Gulf of Thailand. It's an impressive set-up and was built with Thai clientele in mind. As gambling is illegal in Thailand, a few casinos have been set up along the Cambodian side of the border to lure the gambling fanatics from Bangkok and other areas. They don't have many other foreigners using the facilities, but the Thai-speaking staff (this may be Cambodia, but who needs to know the language?) are friendly and will readily accept your money. Hotel rates have recently come down and are very reasonable for the quality that you

get. Rates range from 500 baht to 2,900 baht, with 800 baht getting you a real swank bungalow on the beach with all the goodies to make you real comfy.

The Cambodian immigration authorities at the border in Koh Kong are now issuing visas, both tourist and business, the same as their counterparts at the Poipet border crossing. It's US$20 for a tourist visa and US$25 for a business visa. See the Coming and Going chapter for more details.

Getting to the border area is easy—just head down to the boat-taxi dock by Pacific Commercial Bank and jump on a taxi to the other side of the river. The fare is 20 baht per person. The car-taxi stand is next to the landing where the boat lets you off and is on a wooden dock that sits over the river. The drivers start screaming at you while you are still out on the river, wanting to know if you are heading to Thailand. The fare for the ten to fifteen minute ride to the border area is 50 baht per person for a taxi, or 30 baht for a moto-taxi. Bring your passport, as the Cambodian immigration officials near the border may ask to see it. Don't worry, they don't hit you up for money here.

Beaches

Boat taxis can be hired to take you downstream to the mouth of the river and beyond to one of the many beaches along the coast and on the fairly distant islands. There is a decent beach just around the corner from the mouth of the river, to the right. The fee is highly negotiable, but 150 baht is about right for taking you there and waiting on you for the return trip to town.

"New Beach Area"

Koh Kong residents are fairly excited about a recently opened beach area along the Kah-bpow River. They have jet-skis for rent at 125 baht for half an hour and also rent inner tubes for wallowing around in the river. There are loads of food and drink stands here, especially on weekends when the locals come en masse for an outing. The beach isn't that great as it's near the estuary. Take care on the jet-skis. They are the propeller type and don't have a dead-man's safety switch to kill the machine if you fall off. That might be entertaining for observers, but not so much fun for the downed rider.

Picnic Area at S'nai River Rapids

This is another local weekend favorite that doesn't have many weekday visitors and allows you to see a bit of the countryside on the way there. It's a small river with a few unimpressive sets of rapids, but you may enjoy the ride out. There are food and drink vendors on weekends. To get there, head south from town and cross the small bridge on the outskirts of town. Turn left 3 km past the bridge; a post and bamboo fence marks the spot. Follow this road about 4.5 km and angle to the right where some roads meet this one. Don't make a full right turn onto the one road, just angle to the right on the other. Follow this to the beach. It's about 9 km from the bridge in town.

Independence Monument & Hilltop Temple

Another of Cambodia's independence monuments is located at the northeast corner of town. Angling off to the southeast from the monument brings you to the closed airport and a hilltop temple just beyond. It's a scrubby-looking temple in need of attention, but it offers a fair view. There are some interesting murals on the inside.

River Scene in Koh Kong Town

The river road offers a good place for a jog or stroll. The area is a popular early evening spot for the locals and some drink stands and BBQ chicken and sticky rice stands spring up in the afternoon on the north end of the river road.

MARKETS

The Koh Kong market is a fairly busy place that sells a lot of goods from nearby Thailand. There are a couple of clothing shops across the street from the eastern side of the market selling clothes from Thailand as well. Koh Kong Bookstore is nearby.

There is also a small night market that sets up in the evening along the road on the southern side of the market. Fruit stands are the main items featured.

GETTING AROUND

Moto-Taxi

To get around town the fare is 5 baht or 500 riel. For trips outside of town the fare is the usual 4,000 riel or 40 baht per hour, plus fuel.

Motorcycle Rental

The moto-taxi guys will rent a motorcycle to you for 150–200 baht per day, if you would rather move about independently. They usually want their bikes back by around 10 pm because they want to make sure the bike is secure. They will come to your hotel to pick it up.

Motorcycle Doctor

There is a very good mechanic in town if you try the old abandoned road between Sre Amble and Koh Kong or the recently doable stretch from Koh Kong to Pailin. See the map.

SOUTH & SOUTHWEST

COMMUNICATIONS & INFORMATION

Overseas Calls

International calls are very reasonable from Koh Kong town, with a call to the USA costing 60 baht per minute—much cheaper than in Phnom Penh. A good interphone shop is located along the road on the south side of the market.

CURRENCY EXCHANGE

Pacific Commercial Bank (PC Bank) has an office on the river road. They can change traveler's checks.

The market is the best place to change money. Thai baht is still the preferred currency in Koh Kong, but these days the dollar and riel are readily accepted as well. Money changers are located in the market area and are most prevalent outside, on the eastern side of the market area. It's best to shop around for the best rate quote. They can vary quite a bit in Koh Kong, as the changers here seem to try to rip people off more than in other provinces. To repeat info from other baht-accepting areas of the country: the conversion formula from baht to riel is an easy one. Just add two zeros to the baht to give you its amount in riel. Taking away two zeros from the riel gives you its amount in baht.

MEDICAL FACILITIES

If you have a problem, it's best to jump across the Thai border and head for Trat town. Thai immigration issues on-the-spot visas at the crossing. For a problem that needs immediate attention, the Koh Kong Provincial Hospital is located on the back road. Koh Kong is another malarial area, so take the usual precautions.

RESTAURANTS

For some odd reason, Koh Kong doesn't have much seafood. It must all get marched off to the better paying markets of Thailand, Sihanoukville, and Phnom Penh.

Thai Food Restaurant. Located next to Independence Monument, this place features an English menu with fairly good Thai, western, and Khmer food. The guy who runs the place has some fishing gear that he occasionally rents out.

A food stand next to the restaurant has some simple dishes, desserts, and drinks.

Koh Kong International Resort. Check the info in the What's Up section, but there are a few good Thai food restaurants in the hotel complex and the Jiriphon Thai Food Restaurant is just across the street from the hotel.

"Simple Restaurant". Simple and good Khmer and Thai food dishes are available here at a budget price.

Bopha Koh Kong Hotel & Restaurant. This hotel has a fair restaurant with Khmer and Chinese food.

Koh Pich Hotel. The food quality has taken a nosedive here and unfortunately the management seems to go out of their way to be rude to customers. It's a bad combination if they are trying to get some good word-of-mouth recommendations. They won't come from us.

NIGHT SCENE

Koh Kong is chock full of karaoke shops and brothels. Like Poipet and Pailin, it's another former Khmer Rouge area that used to be under their strict rules, but went 180 degrees the other way when the movement's influence began to wane.

Koh Pich Hotel & Nightclub. This place features the probable Cambodian Elvis lookalike, at least it did when we were there.

There is a live band, beer and taxi girls and that wild and crazy form of circle dancing here.

Moha Sakor Nightclub. This one is about the same as the hotel club, but a step more toward tacky.

There is one more small nightclub just beyond the river bridge that has a band along with the same things the others offer, and takes yet one more step toward tacky.

ACCOMMODATIONS

Cheaper Places

Monorom Guesthouse. This fairly new place has clean rooms with a fan for 100 baht. The bath is shared.

Koh Kong Hotel. This hotel is just across from the river, near the bridge. It has rooms with shared baths and fan for 100 and 150 baht, rooms with an Asian bath for 200 baht and a room with two beds, Western bath and a/c for 250 baht. The hotel is fairly clean.

Motel Hangneak. Basic rooms are 100 baht.

Penh Cheth Guesthouse. This family-run place is very clean and very friendly. Rooms with an attached bath and fan are 150 baht.

Rasmay Buntham Guesthouse. The rooms are 100 or 200 baht, depending upon whether you use the fan or a/c. It's clean and has an Asian bath.

Preas Chann Penh Vong Guesthouse. Can't they fit just one more word in the name? Simple fan rooms with a shared bath go for 100 baht.

Ly Ly Guesthouse. Simple rooms with a fan and shared bath are 100 baht.

Juliana Guesthouse. Fairly nice rooms with a fan and Asian bath are 100 baht. With a/c 150 baht.

A Notch Up

Morocot Motel. This is a pleasant little place that has clean rooms, Western bath, a/c and TV for 300 baht.

Bopha Koh Kong Hotel. This place has decent rooms with TV, a/c and Western bath for 300 baht. There is a restaurant on the premises.

Raksmey Makara Hotel. This one is at the end of the line. There is a back terrace with a view, snooker room, karaoke with hostesses, TV, a/c, Western bath, and clean rooms for 300 baht. Extra-tricked-out VIP rooms go for 500 baht.

Koh Pich Hotel. This is the newest hotel in town. Clean rooms with a TV, a/c, and Western bath go for 300 baht.

The Top Notch

Koh Kong International Resort. Check the What's Up section for details on this border resort. For reservations, fax 66 (039) 588-195.

COMING & GOING

Air

Phnom Penh Airways and President Air are now making regularly scheduled flights, although Phnom Penh Airways seems to be the most regular of the two at this point.

Phnom Penh Airways makes the round-trip flight from Phnom on Thursday and Saturday at 10 am. The return flights to Phnom Penh are on the same days at 12 pm. The plane makes one stop in Sihanoukville en route. **President Air** makes the round trip from Phnom Penh on Sunday. The fares are the same—US$45 one way, US$85 round trip.

Land

As mentioned earlier, the roads connecting Koh Kong town with other parts of Cambodia are not open as yet, so there is no share taxi or motorcycle touring info. For information on getting to or coming from Thailand, see the Coming and Going chapter.

Sre Amble to Koh Kong

March of 2000 brought reports of new logging roads that made it possible to get to Koh Kong by land via Sre Amble town, on the far north end of Kampong Som Bay (or Sihanoukville Bay if you prefer) and then from Koh Kong to Pailin. This information required checking as the old road from Sre Amble to Koh Kong has been abandoned for a couple of decades, and going from Koh Kong to Pailin has also been impossible because of the very remote section of the Cardamom Mountains that separates them.

Upon going down and checking on the Sre Amble to Koh Kong route, we were told by logging company officials that no, there certainly are not yet new roads that will take vehicles to Koh Kong. There is only about 47 km of new logging roads but even this short stretch was recently closed by the company due to heavy rains washing out newly built bridges. They say that possibly some time in the next year they will again start work on a road to connect with Koh Kong, but don't count on it, they told us.

So, we decided to try the old abandoned road to see if it could be done. At first, we got the same reports as we did 2 ½ years ago when we heard from Cambodians in Sre Amble and Sihanoukville that the trip was impossible to make because the jungle had grown over the road and there were landmines everywhere. Upon further scouting around in Sre Amble, however, we started to get reports that there were no landmines anywhere on this stretch and that it was in fact doable. The problem was that nobody that we talked to had ever done it themselves.

This time we decided to give it a go and try to get new reports from the locals along the way. We always got reports that there were no landmines on each stretch that we went on, although at each stretch we also mostly got surprised looks when people heard that we were going to actually try making it to Koh Kong by road—it just wasn't possible, or was it? We also got some pretty confident reports that, yes, they had heard that it was doable and no, they had never done it themselves. But these same people were always quick to tell us how many kilometers it was to Koh Kong and how many more hours it would take us to get there—they were always completely wrong as we were to find out.

This old route to Koh Kong just doesn't see foreigners and you can imagine the looks we got as we came riding into a small village out of this nowhere part of Koh Kong Province. Upon hearing where we had come from and where we were trying to get to, very surprised people would ask us the simple question, why don't you just take the boat? Because the road is there (well, sort of) and it just needs to be done, we tried to tell them. They usually just started talking amongst themselves at that point, about how we must be too poor to afford the boat, or just plain crazy.

We encountered terrible road conditions halfway through the journey, from stretches of road that were completely covered over by the jungle to endless stretches of difficult rock climbing with the motorcycles, up and down huge boulder and rock strewn hills in the beautiful Cardamom Mountains. We also had a number of bike problems to contend with, but as we talked over the reality that we probably should have been turning back, it became increasingly apparent that we just couldn't do it—it was now an all-out battle between us and that road.

The road won a lot of the battles, but in the end we won the war.

It was like we had just climbed Mount Everest as we finally road into Koh Kong town at the end of two long days on what is left of that old road. Wet as rats from a particularly hard rainfall, caked with mud from the stretches of road that didn't involve rock climbing, probably wearing goofy and dazed looks on our faces, we rode into Koh Kong town with faces that said it all…what rock did these motley looking guys crawl out from under?

There is beautiful scenery to be seen along this route, to be sure. From the lush, thickly forested mountains to the little-used and wide rivers that slice through them, there is a lot of beauty to take in en route. The problem is that usually when you are moving, it's over such a nasty section of old road that you don't dare to look at anything but the road. There are chances to enjoy the scenery to be sure, especially when you are crossing one of the four rivers that you have to boat across to continue on the road. The small boats that you have to lift or roll the bikes into are fairly stable, however, as long as you sit on top of it and keep one foot pressed against each side of the boat for balance.

Given the river crossings with only small boats, massively eroded, crevice laden roads through the mountains and flimsy wooden bridges along the first half of the route (which by the way is a pretty easy stretch), cars and trucks are not able to make the journey. But, as we can now attest, Sre Amble to Koh Kong along the old abandoned road is doable by dirt bikes. Because of all the rock climbing involved in getting the bike and rider through the mountains however, it's my opinion that only very experienced off-road riders should attempt this ride. Also, make sure you have what you need to repair your bike (see the Getting Around chapter for suggestions).

The map in this chapter for Sre Amble town will help get you to the start of the road and the following are the rest of the specifics of the 151-km journey from Sre Amble to Koh Kong.

Starting at the first river crossing in Chawng K'nahl village (8 km from Sre Amble town—zero your odometer here at the river for the distances described the rest of the way), take a small ferry across the river for 3,000 riel for you and your motorcycle.

At 13 km from the river crossing there is a small village with fuel—you can top off the fuel tank here if you didn't before.

At 36 km you come to the second river crossing and the village of Luhng Tuhk. There is food, fuel and drinks here, so top off the tank. It's 4,000 riel to get you and your bike across this river.

At 70 km along you come to the village of Bang Room and at 77.5 km you must cross another river (zero your odometer here again for the directions on the second half of the journey). There is again food, fuel and drinks here—take advantage of these things here, because things will turn ugly soon after you cross this third river crossing. It's 5,000 riel to get you and the bike across. After you cross the river, go about 200 meters and follow the road to the right at the fork.

Stay on this main body of road (you won't really be able to call it that later) all the way through the narrow stretches when the jungle wraps itself completely around the road and also when you go through the rocky gulches and hills that the road works its way through. Don't turn off onto the logging roads that intersect this old road.

At about 29.5 km (from that last river crossing) you come upon a big logging road. Going to the right takes you to Pursat, going left takes you to Koh Kong where you are heading. Don't get your hopes up too high on this nice logging road, things will go to hell again in a hurry.

At 34.5 km you come to a fork in the road—go straight, don't follow the road you have been on to the left. There are two shacks in the middle of the two sides of the fork.

At 40.5 km is the village of Poom Kath Tai. At 41 km you can get food, fuel and drinks near the fourth and final river crossing. An old Vietnamese guy (I estimated him to be 196 years old) and his rickety little rowboat, that I think he got as a gift when he was ten years old, handled this crossing. The water just kept creeping through the wide wooden slats and into the bottom of the boat as we each made the shaky and slow trip across the river. This is a particularly beautiful stretch of river, but it's not a good idea to go for that camera as you are balancing the bike in that fine little water craft. I did and almost ended up with my bike at the bottom of that beautiful stretch of river.

It's 24 km to Koh Kong town from the other side of that river, but there are some particularly nasty stretches of rock climbing standing between you and a better road in this next 14 km of the journey. The road also becomes a very narrow jungle trail through much of this stretch and passes through a couple of areas of downed trees and thick branches covering the road, for good measure.

Finally and happily the road connects up with a new logging road at about 55 km (from that second time you zeroed the odometer). Going to the right is the road to Pailin (through northwestern Koh Kong Province, western Pursat Province and Battambang Province). You want to go left here to Koh Kong town and victory lane for you. At about 64 km you turn right and follow this the last 3 km to the monument circle in Koh Kong town. The entire riding time of the journey is about ten hours (hard riding), so you could do it in a day with an early start, if you are lucky enough not to encounter problems en route.

Koh Kong to Pailin, through the Cardamom Mountains

This is a very welcome addition for the previously landlocked residents of Koh Kong town. How welcome it is is not clear as very few seem to be going that way and most don't even know that there is a road going to Pailin and still think it can't be done.

It can and it is a real treat to do it. This route passes through vast sections of the Cardamom Mountains, said to be the most pristine and untouched wilderness area left in Southeast Asia, which is of course due to all the turmoil in Cambodia these past few decades and the extremely remote location of the area. According to wildlife experts that have been through parts of the area, there are still elephant, tiger and even the extremely rare Siam crocodile that call this area home.

The route also passes through some of the tallest mountains in Cambodia so the scenery gets quite spectacular at times. And the real treat is that, for the most part, the road is in good shape which allows you to look up from it and take in that surrounding scenery (real nice for a change).

The new logging roads go for a good share of the journey and then connect up with the old roads that eventually lead to Pailin and other places. These old roads are not very difficult to travel on (by Cambodian standards) and if you make the journey during the dry season, which is the best time to do it) the old roads are not slippery and easily traveled on. Here are the specifics.

Head out of Koh Kong town from the Monument Circle (zero your odometer at the monument) and go past the airport. At

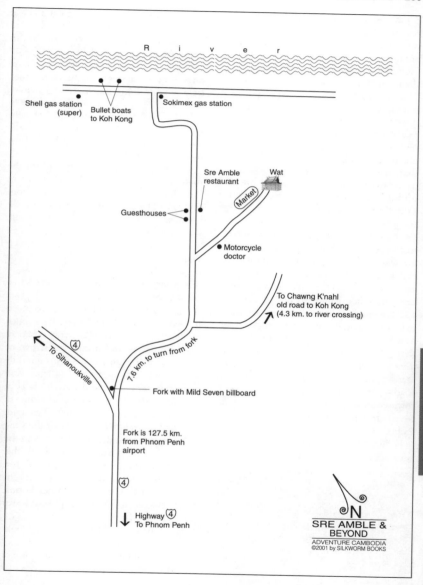

River

Shell gas station
(super)

Bullet boats
to Koh Kong

Sokimex gas station

Sre Amble
restaurant

Wat

Market

Guesthouses

Motorcycle
doctor

To Chawng K'nahl
old road to Koh Kong
(4.3 km. to river crossing)

To Sihanoukville

④

7.6 km. to turn from fork

Fork with Mild Seven billboard

Fork is 127.5 km.
from Phnom Penh
airport

④

Highway ④
To Phnom Penh

N

SRE AMBLE &
BEYOND

ADVENTURE CAMBODIA
©2001 by SILKWORM BOOKS

SOUTH & SOUTHWEST

3 km past the monument, turn left onto the big logging road. At 12 km past the monument, there is a fork in the road—going right is the old abandoned road to Sre Amble, so you want to stay left here, on the main body of road.

At about 30 km you will start passing sections of a very beautiful mountain river and it seems that wherever it is visible from the road the river is a stretch of rapids. The last remaining section of river to cross that does not have a bridge had a team of workers that were set to start working on it as we passed by. It should be done well before you read this and even if it's not, we were able to walk the bikes across at the start of the rainy season.

At 88 km you come to a fork in the road—go left for Pailin and Pursat. At 120 km from Koh Kong town (getting low on fuel?) you come to a village with fuel, food and drinks. Fill up the tank and relax, from here on in there are plenty of fuel stops. At 121 km and in the same village, turn right to go to Samlot, Pailin and Pursat. At about 128 km there is a small fuel stop and less than a kilometer after that you go through a very small stream (water in the rainy season) and then come upon a T in the road—turning right takes you to Pursat town eventually and turning left takes you to where you want to go—Samlot and Pailin.

Follow the main body of road and the tire tracks now and don't go off on the small offshoot roads. At 195 km, go straight at the fork. At 196.5 km, go right at the T in the road. This is a good logging road at this point. At 205 km, turn right. At 210.5 km, you come to Samlot town and no, there are no guesthouses at this point but there is fuel, food and drink. Go straight through Samlot town and at 225.5 km turn left to get to Pailin. This is the main road between Battambang city and Pailin and going to the right would take you to Battambang. Turn right at 228 km.

At 242.5 km, go left at the fork in the road. There are drink and food stands in the middle of the fork. Pailin is 35 km from this fork. The entire journey took us 11 ½ hours at a fairly good speed so make sure you start very early in the morning.

Water

Koh Kong to & from Sihanoukville and Sre Amble

There is now a faster bullet boat connecting Koh Kong and Sre Amble. It's a much smaller boat with two big Mercury outboard motors in back and it cuts the trip time down to just 1 ½ to 2 hours. This not only means that you can get to and from Koh Kong quicker by the land-water route, but it also speeds up your border crossings if you are coming from or going to Thailand. It's also cheaper at 300 baht. The Koh Kong to Sre Amble boat departs at 7 am and the return trip to Koh Kong departs Sre Amble at 10 to 10:30 am. Seating is limited on this boat so get there a bit early. This boat is non-stop to Koh Kong—another bonus. The Koh Kong to Sihanoukville boat leaves Koh Kong at 8 am.

The Sihanoukville to Koh Kong boat leaves Sihanoukville at 12 pm.

The Sre Amble to Koh Kong boat leaves Sre Amble at 11:30 pm.

> **WARNING**
>
> The rest of this journey takes you through areas still heavily infested with landmines. Stay on the well-worn roads and pathways in this area and when stopping along the road to relieve yourself, keep you feet on the road or a well-worn pathway. It's a beautiful area, but there is danger lurking for the unobservant.

The Koh Kong to Sre Amble boat leaves Koh Kong between 7:15 and 7:30 am.

Both options entail a boat ride of about 3 ½ hours (depending upon weather conditions). The boats continue to make the trip during the rainy season when the waves and swells on the ocean can get to be of fairly good size. The boats then become "The Barf Boat Express," as it seems that a fair share of the passengers get motion sickness and barf into plastic bags for the duration of the trip. Attendants hand out the plastic bags at the beginning of the journey.

The scenery along the journey is very nice as the boat goes by deserted islands with sandy beaches, the rugged, remote coastline of the mainland, and thickly tree-covered hills in Koh Kong Province. Riding outside during the dry season is the best way to enjoy the trip.

I usually ride outside even during the rainy season, as a couple of these boats have sunk in rainy season weather and the sealed windows in the cabin area probably mean that most inside would be trapped. Consider the weather and waves before you decide on making the trip during poor rainy-season weather.

Sihanoukville/Sre Amble to Phnom Penh

The Sihanoukville boat gives you the option of including this resort area in your travel plans. There are also a/c buses that ply the route between Phnom Penh and Sihanoukville which are more pleasant than the share taxis. Check the Coming and Going section in Sihanoukville or Phnom Penh for details.

Sre Amble is a bit shorter in distance to Phnom Penh, so the ride is also a bit shorter. Share taxis waiting by the boat dock cost 7,000 riel to get you to Phnom Penh. In Phnom Penh the share taxi stand for Sre Amble is in front of the Dusit Hotel near Monivong Road.

SOUTH & SOUTHWEST

Travel Notes

Rapids and water ledge at Koh Kong

▲ *Tricky river crossing at Koh Kong*

The abandoned road to Koh Kong ▲

▲ *Pristine river trip at Koh Kong*

Vendor taking it easy in Koh Kong ▲

ABOUT THE AUTHORS

Matt Jacobson

Matt is from the United States and had an active career there as a fire captain with an urban city fire department. Ever the adventure and thrill seeker, he is fresh off a series of motorcycle trips to the far reaches of Cambodia. During the past decade he has spent significant periods of time traveling and living in Southeast Asia. The last five years have seen Cambodia on the top of his list for intrigue and fascination. Matt set up residence in Phnom Penh three years ago.

Frank Visakay

Frank has traveled around the world and extensively in Southeast Asia. He has had numerous short stories published in the *Phuket Gazette*. Also from the United States, Frank was a long time resident of New York City. He now lives in Thailand and takes frequent trips to Cambodia. He is currently working on a novel.

We'd like to hear from you. Send your comments to the authors at <adventure_cambodia@hotmail.com>